THE SERPENT AND
THE DOVE

THE SERPENT AND THE DOVE

Celibacy in Literature and Life

A. W. Richard Sipe

Psychology, Religion, and Spirituality
J. Harold Ellens, Series Editor

Westport, Connecticut
London

Dedicated to Marianne, My Bridge over Troubled Water

Library of Congress Cataloging-in-Publication Data

Sipe, A. W. Richard, 1932–
    The serpent and the dove : celibacy in literature and life / A.W. Richard Sipe.
        p. cm. — (Psychology, religion, and spirituality, ISSN 1546–8070)
    Includes bibliographical references and index.
    ISBN 978–0–313–34725–2 (alk. paper)
    1. Celibacy—Christianity.   2. Chastity in literature.   I. Title.
    BV4390.S467   2007
    253'.252—dc22   2007026995

British Library Cataloguing in Publication Data is available.

Library of Congress Catalog Card Number: 2007026995
ISBN-13: 978–0–313–34725–2
ISSN: 1546–8070

First published in 2007

Praeger Publishers, 88 Post Road West, Westport, CT 06881
An imprint of Greenwood Publishing Group, Inc.
www.praeger.com

Printed in the United States of America

The paper used in this book complies with the
Permanent Paper Standard issued by the National
Information Standards Organization (Z39.48–1984).

10 9 8 7 6 5 4 3 2 1

CONTENTS

PART II FICTION, CELIBACY, AND THE SEARCH FOR TRUTH

Series Foreword

The interface between psychology, religion, and spirituality has been of great interest to scholars for a century. In the last three decades a broad popular appetite has developed for books which make practical sense out of the sophisticated research on these three subjects. Freud expressed an essentially deconstructive perspective on this matter and indicated that he saw the relationship between human psychology and religion to be a destructive interaction. Jung, on the other hand, was quite sure that these three aspects of the human spirit, psychology, religion, and spirituality, were constructively and inextricably linked.

Anton Boisen and Seward Hiltner derived much insight from both Freud and Jung, as well as from Adler and Reik, while pressing the matter forward with ingenious skill and illumination. Boisen and Hiltner fashioned a framework within which the quest for a sound and sensible definition of the interface between psychology, religion, and spirituality might best be described or expressed.[1] We are in their debt.

This series of General Interest Books, so wisely urged by Greenwood Press, and particularly by its editors, Deborah Carvalko and Suzanne I. Staszak-Silva, intends to define the terms and explore the interface of psychology, religion, and spirituality at the operational level of daily human experience. Each volume of the series identifies, analyzes, describes, and evaluates the full range of issues, of both popular and professional interest, that deal with the psychological factors at play (1) in the way religion takes shape and is expressed, (2) in the way spirituality functions within human persons and shapes both religious formation and expression, and (3) in the ways that spirituality is shaped and expressed by religion. The interest is psycho-spiritual. In terms of the rubrics of the disciplines and the science of psychology and spirituality this series of volumes investigates the *operational dynamics* of religion and spirituality.

The verbs "shape" and "express" in the above paragraph refer to the forces which prompt and form religion in persons and communities, as well as to the manifestations of religious behavior (1) in personal forms of spirituality, (2) in acts of spiritually motivated care for society, and (3) in ritual behaviors such as liturgies of worship. In these various aspects of human function the psychological and/or spiritual drivers are identified, isolated, and described in terms of the way in which they unconsciously and consciously operate in religion, thought, and behavior.

The books in this series are written for the general reader, the local library, and the undergraduate university student. They are also of significant interest to the informed professional, particularly in fields corollary to his or her primary interest. The volumes in this series have great value for clinical settings and treatment models, as well.

This series editor has spent an entire professional lifetime focused specifically upon research into the interface of psychology in religion and spirituality. These matters are of the highest urgency in human affairs today when religious motivation seems to be playing an increasing role, constructively and destructively, in the arena of social ethics, national politics, and world affairs. It is imperative that we find out immediately what the psychopathological factors are which shape a religion that can launch deadly assaults upon the World Trade Center in New York and murder 3,500 people, or a religion that motivates suicide bombers to kill themselves and murder dozens of their neighbors weekly, and a religion which prompts such unjust national policies as pre-emptive defense; all of which are wreaking havoc upon the social fabric, the democratic processes, the domestic tranquility, the economic stability and productivity, and the legitimate right to freedom from fear, in every nation in the world today.

This present volume, *The Serpent and the Dove: Celibacy in Literature and Life*, is an urgently needed and timely work, the motivation for which is surely endorsed enthusiastically by the entire Christian world today, as the international community searches for strategies that will afford us better and deeper religious self-understanding as individuals and communities. This project addresses the deep psychosocial, psychospiritual, and biological sources of human nature that shape and drive our psychology and spirituality. Careful strategies of empirical, heuristic, and phenomenological research have been employed to give this work a solid scientific foundation and formation. Never before has such wise analysis been brought to bear upon the dynamic linkage between human physiology, psychology, and spirituality in the life and calling of celibacy.

For fifty years such organizations as the Christian Association for Psycho-logical Studies and such Graduate Departments of Psychology as those at Boston University, Fuller, Rosemead, Harvard, George Fox, Princeton, and the like, have been publishing important building blocks of research on issues dealing with religious behavior and psycho-spirituality. In this present proj-ect the insights generated by such patient and careful research is synthesized and integrated into a holistic psycho-spiritual worldview, which takes seri-ously this special aspect of religious tradition called celibacy. This volume employs an objective and experience-based approach to discerning whether celibacy is a constructive or destructive calling, whether those who profess being called to the vocation of celibacy really follow that vow in real life, and whether following such a calling is a wholesome and responsible course for a human life and person.

Some of the influences of religion upon persons and society, now and throughout history, have been negative. However, most of the impact of the great religions upon human life and culture has been profoundly redemp-tive and generative of great good. It is urgent, therefore, that we discover and understand better what the psychological and spiritual forces are which empower people of faith and genuine spirituality to give themselves to all the creative and constructive enterprises that, throughout the centuries, have made of human life the humane, ordered, prosperous, and aesthetic experi-ence it can be at its best. Surely the forces for good in both psychology and spirituality far exceed the powers and proclivities toward the evil that we see so prominently perpetrated in the name of religion in our world today, par-ticularly in the destructive abuse of children by religious leaders who profess to live by the vocation of celibacy.

This series of Greenwood Press volumes is dedicated to the greater un-derstanding of *Psychology, Religion, and Spirituality,* and thus to the profound understanding and empowerment of those psycho-spiritual drivers which can help us (1) transcend the malignancy of our earthly pilgrimage, (2) en-hance the humaneness and majesty of the human spirit, and (3) empower the potential for magnificence in human life.

J. Harold Ellens, Series Editor

PREFACE

Celibacy is one mode of coming to terms with one's sexuality. It is hard, however, to get the real life story of a person who claims complete and perpetual celibacy. Autobiographical communications about celibacy are rare and perhaps not completely possible. The potential advantage of a first-hand view of celibacy would be having the celibate person's vision of that relatively rare lifestyle. Whether the personal witness to celibacy is spoken or written, it is likely to be affected by the inclination to distance the image and ideal of celibacy from the personal self.

An authentic autobiography of celibacy must fulfill certain criteria that likely include the following: First, any such narrative should record one's developmental relationship patterns, many of which precede any celibate intention. Nevertheless, early experiences vitally influence a person's eventual sexual/celibate pattern of adjustment. Family background, education, ethnic and cultural fixes, character traits, sexual preferences, unique talents, and loves and hates all come into play. Self-knowledge is fundamental to any successful celibate pursuit.

Second, celibacy is dynamic; it is a *process* of internalization and actualization of the celibate ideal from intention to achievement. Celibacy does not ordinarily begin with practice, but with the formation of an image of celibacy, often personified in one person believed to be a practicing celibate.

That step involves the achievement of a degree of self-knowledge—measuring one's own capacity to live with the sexual discipline and deprivation necessary to be celibate. Having some degree of self-awareness readies a person to proceed further in seeking knowledge about the process of celibacy and what it involves in realistic terms.

Because celibacy is neither abstract nor extraneous to the individual striving for it, these inevitable steps precede the experimentation and practice of celibacy. If, in time, celibacy takes personal root, it is often capped by a more or less formal vow. It is from a stable internal base that celibacy can be said to reach achievement once its integration is woven into the fiber of one's person. That is when celibacy becomes an integral part of one's sexual self. Such self-revelation is never simple.

Finally, celibate achievement is accountable and, to a degree, measurable. "By their fruits you shall know them." Although celibacy is capable of many faces, it is also capable of wearing many masks. In all of its variations, permutations, individualizations, frustrations, failures, or perversions, certain qualities measure its authenticity: service, complete self-honesty, awareness of the oneness of the human condition, and the capacity to love.

I have written books on theoretical and practical aspects of religious celibacy. The previous few paragraphs summarize my vision of the essence and process of celibacy through the lenses of my experience, research, teaching, and counseling. The goal of the following chapters is to elucidate further the principles of religious celibacy, first, through the eyes of those who have lived it and given their autobiographical testimony and, second, through the visualization of fiction writers.

The essence, process, practice, and achievement of celibacy are best recorded in two of my books, *A Secret World* (1990) or *Celibacy in Crisis* (2003).

All of the chapters are written against the framework of my understanding of the process of a celibate vocation and are predicated on the following definition of religious celibacy:

Celibacy is a freely chosen, dynamic state, usually vowed, that involves an honest and sustained attempt to live without direct sexual gratification, in order to serve others, productively, for a spiritual motive.[1]

Introduction

A. W. Richard Sipe, B. C. Lamb, and Harris Gruman

We do not apply the scientific method to faith nor faith to science, but both science and faith are part of the same dimension.

Pope John Paul II

In his short story "The Minister's Black Veil,"[1] Nathaniel Hawthorne writes of a clergyman in a small New England town who covers his face with a black veil after his fiancée dies. It is unclear whether his action is a lesson, a perverse joke, or a symptom of madness, but what is apparent is that by not removing the veil as days turn into weeks and years, his celibate vocation takes on a strange power and mystery. By shouldering the most profound personal solitude, he becomes the most public figure in his community. His ministry has a quality of marvel, and his service becomes the focus of his parishioners' greatest hopes and fears.

Through the allegory of the black veil, Hawthorne reveals what is at stake in the true spiritual vocation: the individual who becomes a witness to the transcendent. Such a person must go beyond the external institutional structures of religion and step into a sphere outside social norms, a sphere in which sexuality, power, and human potential take on new meanings, where the dangers of aloneness and the daunting struggle between one's own hopes and fears are ever present. It is a sphere open to misunderstanding, demanding necessary sacrifice, service, and suffering for a cause in which the individual can also be ridiculed or abused.

The betrayal of vocation, however, has as much to do with institutional and social forces as it does with individual weakness or evil. Whether it ultimately succeeds or fails in bearing witness to the human capacity for the spiritual, every vocation is constructed from a unique compromise between collective and personal experiences.

In these chapters, I explore the secret world behind the black veil through literature. As an adjunct professor teaching part time in a major Roman Catholic seminary from 1972 to 1984, I struggled to develop a course—"The Person of the Priest"—aimed at helping seminarians develop a pastoral identity. I wanted to go beyond the standard ascetic works, which were well known but frequently abstract, ethereal, and easily undigested because they proved personally impractical and unconnected to the daily realities of a minister and his own sexuality.

I turned first to autobiographies of religious celibates who wrote at least a chapter on celibacy as a personal testimony. This genre is rare, but the few writers who attempted it are worthy of attention.

While reading Edwin O'Connor's *The Edge of Sadness*[2] and the works of J. F. Powers, I was struck by the accessibility and realness of these fictional representations of priests. I recalled the profound influence Victor Hugo[3] and the French revivalists, Leon Bloy,[4] Georges Bernanos,[5] François Mauriac,[6] and Paul Claudel[7] played in my own growth and development. Their novels helped me reflect on my vocation and identity during my own preparation for the Catholic priesthood in the 1940s and 1950s, and they have remained wellsprings for meditation to me. Fundamentally, I wanted to make celibacy and the priestly vocation and its mystery more practical and intimate for my students instead of explaining them *only* as a theologically defined charism.

The work of priest-novelist Andrew Greeley formed a bridge for me between autobiography and fiction and had the additional advantage of recognition and accessibility to the seminarians I was teaching at the time. He spoke for many Catholics in the second half of the twentieth century. The expertise of B. C. Lamb has given substance to my understanding and reading of Greeley's work, 23 novels and more than 33 volumes in all.

Using fiction to explore psychic reality and human behavior is not a new idea. Sigmund Freud recommended that one who wants to fathom the workings of the human mind should not turn to psychological treatises but to literature. And, of course, he practiced what he preached, exploring literature from Oedipus to Hamlet and Faust. Robert Coles taught popular courses in the undergraduate, medical, and law schools at Harvard that made moral understanding vibrant through novels.

My experience has been that the institution of the church obfuscates and diminishes the radical reality of lived (or failed) celibacy behind the unexplored (and from its stance, an inexplicable) idea of charism. It bypasses the *real* mystery by positing "mystery," which in practical terms amounts to magic.

THE MEANING OF MYSTERY

In my work, I have deliberately shifted the terms of debate from the organizational forms (mandated celibacy) to spiritual content without abandoning a rational mode of communication or epistemology. The church demands sexual abstinence from anyone professing a vocation to the priesthood,[8] but it does not take celibacy seriously enough to teach it.

I have used a secular body of psychological and social theory to explain the reality of charism as a phenomenon grounded in psychobiological sublimation in a way that is not at all hostile to the quest for celibacy, as can be demonstrated in the novels I have chosen to explore.

I disagree with William James, who asserted that psychosexual theories of religious behavior are inevitably hostile to spiritual experience.[9] In my effort to understand rationally the *irrational* truth of celibacy as a spiritual experience, I have, in fact, taken a new tack on James's course of using that very process of rationalization in science and social life as a means of preserving mystery and eschewing magic. I am unapologetic about my call for inquiry and education for celibacy and for a shift from celibacy as a discipline of traditional authority back to celibacy as a charism of spiritual experience. I realize that this approach may have the uncanny status of a rational defense of the irrational.

VOCATION

The quest for vocation by the minister—the man of God, the man of *mystery*—is a narrative of existential and social struggle made accessible through the sensitive and insightful work of authors of fiction. Where nonfiction narratives of vocation and celibacy fail because of the public exigencies of institutional religion, or remain unwritten as a result of the personal humility of achieved spirituality, the author of fiction can provide us with a glimpse behind the veil, one that serves neither institutional nor personal demands but rather a disinterested desire to understand and broaden the limits of the human condition.

I knew that sex was, and still is, an area of human reality that has not been fully incorporated into Christian understanding and theology, thus often leaving celibacy an empty moniker. I also knew that sex and power, both spiritual and political, are vitally intertwined with the question of religious vocation. The hundreds of ongoing stories of clerical struggle, failure, and triumph amassing in my ethnographic study compelled me to do what I could to aid young men in their struggle for ministerial integrity, self-awareness, and reverence for the dimensions of sex and the use of power inherent in their vocation.

The 2002 blast of public exposure of priest sexual abuse was still 25 years in the future when I began this quest for understanding.[10] Somehow even then,

I needed to find a pedagogical approach adequate to the commitment my students were making and the questions they were asking: What is the essence of the power and mystery that surround the religious minister? In short, what is actually contained in the reality of the charism of celibacy? Does it emanate from some interior, psychological/spiritual space, or does the community of faithful who want to believe that God can be among men in visible, tangible form confer it? Or does the institution, backed up by legal and political force of immeasurable proportions, confer it? Is it only grace? Answers are necessary. Celibate practice needs more than clichés—even pious ones.

What is the place of women in a realm that severely restricts or positively excludes them from power? How is it that access to the power and mystery is reserved for one gender? What does sexual activity, grounded in the most corporeal realities of the evolution of human biology, have to do with the spiritual and the mystery of the Unseen? Is sex incompatible with ritual purity and spiritual power? What does sexual orientation have to do with ministry? Are men of homosexual orientation or limited sexual drive better or less suited to enter the mystery than other men?

How are we to bridge limited popular perceptions that the minister is the so-called ideal man or, contrarily, that all ministers are charlatans? How do we find our way through the maze of claims and counterclaims that there is a *man of God* worthy of that title and the trust it implies? It is a house of mirrors constructed by perceptions and wishes, failures and aspirations. But which is the real reflection, and what is the reality being mirrored?

How does a minister—or any man or woman—maintain idealism, direction, and spiritual balance, keeping one eye on the Unseen and the other on the practical necessities of existence? How does one shoulder the burden of helping others do the same?

In other words, how does one form a pastoral identity? How does one become a minister of God, engaging all of the inevitable dragons, internal and external, real and mythical, known and unimagined, while maintaining one's integrity as a sexual being as one enters the realms of power and taps resources beyond self and institution?

The challenges to integrity are protean, and the dangers of corruption are as many and as daunting as any faced by the protagonists of our greatest novels. That thought—that the intuition that writers of fiction and works of fiction could help people who want to understand the reality of ministry and pastoral care—led me to base my course on works of literature. I had already experienced the power of fiction in my own life.

THE TRUTH OF THE NOVEL

The novel has a so-called truth standard that is as rigorous as it is mysterious. Quantification of data and repeatability of sequence are of no value to its intuitive appeal, yet the success of a narrative does depend on its meeting real criteria.

Through its unfolding in a particular stream of carefully chosen words, images, and allusions, narrative bridges the unique and the universal at the moment it accomplishes communication between a writer and a reader. To be a worthy protagonist of fictional narrative, a character can be neither a statistic nor an aberration.

The statistical person already has a home in the studies of sociologists, anthropologists, and historians. The aberration is comfortable in tabloids, psychiatric journals, and *Ripley's Believe It or Not.* Both of these types declare their truth in the very fact that they exist. But the protagonist of fiction declares his truth in the fact that he need not exist in order to be believed. He must be recognized as true against that most demanding judge: the intuition of a reader.

The relevance of such an epistemology to these chapters resides in a shared valuation in the literary and the spirituality of uncertainty and ambiguity, a mutual need for a third term between reality and perception. Let's call it narrative irony, or the Unseen.

I chose to present chapters on a sample of novels that would comport well in their time and topic with my previous study. These are all novels of the twentieth century, allowing me to focus on an important yet delineated period in the history of spiritual vocation. This also makes the novels roughly coextensive with the lifetimes and life experiences of the priests in my ethnographic study.[11]

The novels are also what I would like to call *serious popular novels: serious* because, unlike most commercial novels, they are motivated by the ethical quest to understand the human condition; *popular* because their authors sought and obtained a wide readership.

They are classic realist novels whose authors decided against pioneering new ground in poetic language in order to write works that would be accessible—after a century-long flowering of realist fiction—to all literate people, challenging them existentially rather than linguistically. In other words, their form is user-friendly, whatever the demands made by their content. Furthermore, all of these novels, regardless of their authors' nationalities, were written to transcend particularities of national culture—that is, with an eye to translation—and all of them found a wide readership in the United States.

I have incorporated lengthy quotations from the novels in my reflections on them. This does not absolve the reader from the enjoyment of reading the whole of the original texts, which will provide a real understanding of my arguments.

Although the novels I chose for consideration in these chapters have Roman Catholic priests as protagonists, in the course of my research I have reviewed texts about Protestant ministers, by Hawthorne,[12] Sinclair Lewis, W. Somerset Maugham,[13] and others. They also offer particularly relevant and compelling case studies. I hope to remind readers that the significance of the questions presented not only extends beyond the Catholic priesthood; it touches on all human experience with sex, power, and the quest for the transcendent.

The search for vocation is always a highly charged struggle with sex, power, and witness, but the quality of that struggle changes dramatically with the degree to which it is a social or existential one.

ORGANIZATION OF THE CHAPTERS

The first chapters in this book look at crises in the institutions of vocation. One cannot speak about clerical vocation and celibacy at the beginning of the twenty-first century in any realistic terms without taking into account the sexual abuse crisis that festers within ministry, especially prominent among Roman Catholic priests and bishops. Public awareness raises fundamental questions. Do religious institutions harbor and encourage the manipulation of sex and power? Do they promote the degradation of women and charlatanism? Do institutional doctrines and rules inhibit or destroy the vocations of those who fail to abide by them? Is personal witness to the achievement of vocation, both spiritual and celibate, impossible within the institutional sphere?

Through careful readings of three autobiographical accounts of celibate practice by Mohandas Gandhi, Fulton Sheen, and Andrew Greeley and a biographical account of Charles Coughlin, I explore the severe limits placed on ministry and sainthood. Each of the purported celibates supports his celibacy through subtle appeals to its moral superiority over other sexual practices—an intolerance I have found incompatible with a fully integrated and *achieved* celibate vocation. The hypothesis that emerges is this: that public nonfiction witness to celibacy is, to a degree, antithetical to its practice and that the self-exposure is revelatory of the limitation and perhaps impossibility of celibacy. Fictional narratives thus become the most fruitful vehicle for expressing and testing its truth.

The Irish Catholic culture that has infused the U.S. church is the link that unites our famous priests and provides a transition from biography to the fiction of J. T. Farrell and James Joyce as well as that of the Irish-born Ethel Voynich and the Englishman Graham Greene. Through their portrayals, I explore the broader social and historical significance of the quest for vocation: power through resistance or conformism, the social meaning of a life and death guided by spirituality, and the failure and potential to overcome the misogyny of a patriarchal society through sexual/celibate life in the service of vocation.

The chapters on J. T. Farrell and James Joyce speak for themselves. Priests are real, worthy, and flawed human beings, and sexual abuse by some clergy has been a long-known if deliberately hidden reality.

Two novels, written from the apparently opposed viewpoints of anticlericalism (Ethel Voynich)[14] and devout Catholicism (Graham Greene),[15] treat, with surprisingly similar sensitivity and sympathy, the case of a priest whose love for his natural offspring impinges on the demands of his ministry. In the conflict between being a father and being a Father, the *meaning* of celibacy is perhaps most accurately comprehended as the sublimation of personal affections for communal ones, thus allowing a more significant exploration of vocation and its limits than do novels of sexual temptation and lapse. Whereas the latter can be assimilated and integrated into a process of achievement, a child remains present as both a symbol of the potential for meaningful vocation and an impediment to its practice.

THE SPIRITUAL VOCATION IN A SECULAR WORLD

The core of my thesis on celibacy in life and literature is defined by a consideration of the celibate vocation and the social challenge through a close reading of two major social novels of the spiritual vocation, Ignazio Silone's *Bread and Wine* and J. F. Powers's *Morte D'Urban*.

These two novels comprehend the sweep of twentieth-century Western society, in which, at one moment, resistance and a meaningful life and death appear still possible (Silone) and, at another, only conformity or failure seem to be options (Powers). In both cases, however, spiritual vocation functions as a litmus test of the possible, and the actual practice of celibacy is one of its most telling signs.

J. F. POWERS: THE COMEDY OF THE GOSPEL

Morte D'Urban holds deep personal ties for me. I first became aware of J. F. Powers not through his novels or short stories but because of George G. Garrelts, the assistant pastor of my home parish in Robbinsdale, Minnesota, in 1945. Garrelts, who had been friends with Powers since their grade school days, was an intriguing young priest and remained fascinating as a married man, father, and college professor until his death in 2005. As a newly ordained priest, he was a walking advertisement for vocations: tall, athletic, inspiring, with a keen sense of humor, piety, and accessibility.

Father Garrelts, at the time, was a Catholic radical, and Powers remained so. The Catholic Christian radical of 1945 was very different from the 2006 brand of the Christian right-wing radical or Opus Dei member. He was a pacifist in the strict sense. Powers spent four years in prison during World

War II because of his principles. He believed in voluntary poverty in the mold of the Catholic Worker (one step away from Communism), and the corporal works of mercy formed the framework of his spirituality.

I have been marked indelibly with this ideal of Christianity even if I am a rather poor example of its lived reality.

If Garrelts left any echo in the priests of *Morte D'Urban*, I have never divined where. On the other hand, Powers dedicated his last novel, *Wheat That Springeth Green*,[16] to G.G.G., and I think I see some shadow of Garrelts in those pages and an occasional glimpse of him in some of the short stories.

In 1993, Powers read a version of the chapter in this collection and wrote the following:

> I've read the MS and made a few comments. I enjoyed most of it. Some of it is done in a manner that is just too educated for me to follow closely and may or may not be true, for all I know. I don't consider myself an intellectual, but the times are such that I am often mistaken for one. What I am good at, though, is guessing and that is how I get by. I hope the book does well.

It is, of course, Powers's guessing that makes his intuition about the priesthood so valuable and accurate.

Between 1996 and 1998, I traveled to Collegeville, Minnesota, six times each year trying to help St. John's Abbey there deal with a sexual abuse crisis that had emerged from the shadows into the public sunshine during the 1990s. Powers was living in a small workman's cottage near the university. During each visit, he would invite me to a supper he had prepared. He always refused my invitation to dine at an area restaurant. I told him that I had to "confess that he served the best meal in Collegeville." I was the grateful object of a corporal work of mercy. His last note to me in 1998 was a simple word of encouragement for my discouraging work, capped with a wisp of humor and signed, "Jim."

Powers's life was transparent. He lived what he believed and was the Christian radical to the end. He reviewed a draft of the Silone chapter for this book, also. His comments and suggestions were invariably sensitive; that chapter itself is a better piece for his input, and I have included it there. He was like Silone's Don Paolo Spada: a *priest* beyond the boundaries of any institution.

In *Morte D'Urban*, J. F. Powers took on the difficult project of narrating the struggle for meaning in the inhospitable climate of the world of commerce in the United States of the 1950s. That he chose as his protagonist a Catholic priest by no means mitigates this aim of grappling with what Max Weber called "the disenchantment of the world" in such a calculating society. In fact, the "man of mystery" in a disenchanted world becomes Powers's ideal vehicle for testing that society's apparently infinite power, its necessity as the medium of human interaction. Four prominent themes present themselves for consideration: (1) the road to "eternal habitations" is paved . . . ; (2) vocation after disenchantment; (3) urbane celibacy: good cars and evil women; and (4) death of a spiritual salesman.

IGNAZIO SILONE: THE ESSENCE OF THE PRIESTHOOD

My youthful radicalism also introduced me to Silone. Inspired by Garrelts, I spent a summer at a Catholic Worker farm in Upton, Massachusetts, in the bosom of a community practicing voluntary poverty, farming, and stained glass art. I had met Dorothy Day previously, but it was there and then that I learned that she read *Bread and Wine* once every year, a practice that she continued until the end of her life. It was only years later that I fully understood its significance.

Silone, like Dorothy Day, was a Communist during his twenties. He left the party disillusioned, but he never lost his sense of the dynamic struggle between the promises of social redemption and spiritual transcendence. His creation, Don Paolo, captures the essence of a priest: outside the institution but true to it nevertheless.

The significance of Silone's contribution to the questions about the celibate vocation comes to fruition through a comparative reading of the two versions of his novel (1937 and 1956). Although his ideal of the spiritual vocation as resistance to society remained constant, his understanding of the roles of sexuality, gender, and celibacy underwent a striking process of reevaluation and development. That process has direct relevance to current debates on church reform and encompasses (1) Silone's ideal of the spiritual vocation; (2) spiritual vocation as a narrative of struggle; (3) sexuality, women, and the established church and Silone's first draft of celibacy; and (4) hopeful revisions: Silone's second draft of celibacy.

Timothy Radcliffe, former master general of the Dominican Order, expressed succinctly the same lessons of the novels: "Learning to live our chastity well is not primarily a question of the will, bottling up our wildest passions, but a way of life that sustains us in the truth of what and who we are."[17]

Harris Gruman deserves credit and my gratitude for applying my theory of celibacy to these two novels. His sensitivity to the radical nature of celibacy and his familiarity with Judaism and Communism infused a fresh view of Silone and Powers and educated me to a new depth of understanding of the celibate process.

This project, which began in 1975, has been through many versions, revisions, and attempts to organize the material in a useful way. This material has not been published previously. This effort remains for me like Freud's process: terminable and interminable. I will continue exploring the meaning and mystery of religious celibacy unto death. It is my vocation.

The title of this book, *The Serpent and the Dove*, is obvious in its allusion to symbols for sexuality and purity. Since the time of Freud, no one has to apologize for the immediate association of a serpent with a phallic symbol. The dove of purity is not without its sexual association in Christian iconography as the bearer of the impregnation of the Virgin through her ear—the Word made flesh through its instrumentality. Saint Bernard of Clairvaux wrote in his *Sermons on the Song of Songs*, "Only through the body does the way, the ascent to the life of blessedness, lie open to us." Celibacy cannot be seriously explored without coming to grips with sexuality in a realistic and practical manner. Without both elements, celibacy is deprived of reality and mystery and is reduced to myth and magic.

I have not included in this collection other essays prepared on the same subject, for instance, Sinclair Lewis's *Elmer Gantry*.[18] That novel presents a vocation without a protagonist. In Lewis's satire of evangelism, vocation becomes the vehicle for corruption in a corrupt world. The parallel plot of Frank Shallard, and its horrifying conclusion, however, acts as a guide rail to Lewis's narrative, reminding us that all vocations do not produce charlatans, but also that Everyman may not be fit for a religious vocation. These broad parameters of tragedy and satire construct the space explored more subtly in the social novels of vocation included in this volume.

Willa Cather's *Death Comes for the Archbishop*[19] and Graham Greene's *Monsignor Quixote*[20] explore in narrative form the importance of intimate male friendship to the strengthening of spiritual vocation and, especially, the celibate vocation. This is an important area for investigation because the question of homosexual orientation as a consideration for ordination has become a hot topic in recent days. Cather, who had personal experience of same-sex friendships, treats the more traditional bonds among fellow clerics and the tension between their personal loyalty, affection, and the demands of their ministry with a delicacy and insightfulness that is hard to match in literature of vocation. In *Monsignor Quixote*, Greene explores institutional limits through the story of friendship between a parish priest and a Communist mayor in which the personal bond liberates them from the ethical compromises of their previous commitments, and Cervantean irony is overcome through Quixotic hope.

PROCESS OF THIS STUDY

For two years after I published *A Secret World* in 1990, I engaged two research assistants, B. C. Lamb and Harris Gruman, who joined my quest to understand celibacy through literature. Neither of them came from a Roman Catholic background. I considered this a distinct advantage for the kind of objective reading of texts and intellectual dialogue I desired. They have been indispensable in this effort. They explored my theories of celibate process, and I learned from them some things about literary criticism.

They were the prototypical "struggling graduate students" at the time, and they were grateful for the employment my wife and I offered them to explore new areas for study. They have not been involved in this project for more than twelve years, and both said they would be satisfied with any acknowledgment at all for our work together. They bear no responsibility for any inadequacies in this final version, but I want to give them full credit of coauthorship with the hope that it will encourage others to carry on a vision of a lifetime: to divine the origins, meanings, and process of religious celibacy wherever they may be found.

B. C. Lamb, PhD, JD, Baltimore, Maryland, has his degree in comparative literature from the University of Maryland and his law degree from the University of Baltimore. He is currently a criminal defense attorney in Baltimore. He continues his studies in the relation between language and society; he possesses a more complete understanding and profound analysis of Father Andrew Greeley's body of work than any other scholar that I am aware of. He is a longtime mainstay of Saint John's United Methodist Church, an inclusive inner-city congregation. He is a remarkable man with wide literary and civic interests that he continues to develop in service to his community.

Harris Gruman is a graduate of Johns Hopkins University with a PhD in comparative literature from the University of Maryland. Together we attended the International Conference on Celibacy at the Vatican in 1993. His wife is from Italy and has her doctorate in Italian; she lectures at Harvard. They have two children. Currently, Harris is director of Massachusetts Neighbor to Neighbor, which builds political organizations in low-income communities across the commonwealth. He began his organizing career with 14 years of experience in Baltimore, working on affordable housing and health care. He also worked in Colorado as statewide health care organizer and in Hungary and Poland as a coalition organizer for the Institute for Transportation and Development Policy. At Neighbor to Neighbor, he has led organizing campaigns to increase child-care funding, the minimum wage, and universal health insurance.

I am honored to have this book included J. Harold Ellens' series— Psychology, Religion and Spirituality. I feel at home in the tradition he preserves and enhances: that of Seward Hiltner who was a mentor to me when I studied at the Menninger Foundation in the 1960s. I am a fortunate writer to have had the same editor and index specialist on every book I have published. Marge Nelson has edited for Johns Hopkins University Press among many other publishing firms. She knows my thinking and has helped me develop whatever exists of my style: clarity above all. The pleasure of getting this book to press has been increased by the attention of Debora Carvalco of the Greenwood Publishing. Along with these are other masters of the language I need to thank: Denys Horgan for his reading of the chapters on Coughlin and Joyce, and Eugene C. Kennedy who was encouraging in reading a very early version of the manuscript and the final version of the chapter on Farrell. Andrew Chan and Kourteny Murray continue to solve my current technical and research questions. They deserve credit for the degree to which I have reached my goal of communicating clearly and providing "easy reading." The rest, including all criticisms, belong to me.

These colleagues are examples of people who understand vocation. Each follows his or her path and continues to forge new trails, but all are people who have remained loyal to the ideals of their youth. Their integrity is a continuing inspiration to me. Their friendship remains a consolation beyond time and words.

PART I

Biography, Celibacy, and the Search for Fact

CHAPTER 1

FOUNDATIONS OF
A CELIBACY CRISIS

> The idea that defect, shadow, or other misfortune could ever cause
> the church to stand in need of restoration or renewal is hereby
> condemned as obviously absurd.
>
> Pope Gregory XVI, 1832

Contrary to what past and present popes say, the Roman Catholic Church
is in a profound crisis whose name is Sex. Its symptom is sexual abuse of
minors by clergy, but the misunderstanding of sex and celibacy burns at
its core.

Some Catholic Church apologists complain that the media are stirring up
anti-Catholic, antipriest, antireligion propaganda via the sexual-abuse crisis.
History speaks otherwise. Sexual abuse of minors by religious authorities has
been a continuing problem throughout the centuries of organized Christianity.[1] Sex, magic, and heresy consistently have been enmeshed throughout the
centuries.[2] Sex and celibacy concerns have been particularly entangled since
the time of the Protestant Reformation. Faust is but one example of the literary perpetuation of child abuse generating the power of literary and artistic
expression; notable examples are Johann Wolfgang von Goethe's *Faust*, Charles
Gounod's opera of the same title, and Hector Berlioz's *La damnation de Faust*.

The historical Faust (Johann Georg Faust, 1480–1540) was a professor of
alchemy and magic at various universities in Germany, including Erfurt. It
was here that he was purported to declare before a Franciscan friar, "I have
gone further than you think and have pledged myself to the devil with my
own blood, to be his in eternity, body and soul."

Rainer Nagele says that Faust "probably was a priest";[3] at the very least he was a minor cleric. He took a doctorate in divinity from the University of Wittenberg, and he was the product of Catholic pedagogy. Some scholars speculate that he was a victim of abuse, presumably by a cleric.

Complaints of pedophilia followed Faust from one place to another. (University students were much younger during the Renaissance.) Soon after Faust would begin teaching at each new place, one of the professors would inevitably complain to the local bishop, and the church's invariable response was to move Faust along to another place—the pattern so well documented in the U.S. crisis. Faust was a contemporary of Protestant reformers Martin Luther and Philipp Melanchthon, who feared and hated him; the latter pictured him with a rabid dog. He stood in some quarters as the embodiment of all that was Catholic. His story became legend, with his biography published first in German and translated into English (1587). Christopher Marlowe published *The Tragedy of Dr. Faustus* in 1616.

Understanding the dimensions of the present catastrophe in one of the world's great religions is not simple. The church is conditioned to resist investigation by centuries of tradition. Every conflict is elegantly bound up in an elaborate structure of secrecy and power. The honesty of the Desert Fathers places their accounts of monastic and clerical vice and virtue in a category all by themselves. But a fund of literature from Boccaccio[4] and Chaucer onward records the sexual misadventures of Catholic clergy. Explicit literary critiques and satires like those of Erasmus's *The Praise of Folly* and François Rabelais's *Gargantua* are not common among modern works. This finding is not really surprising because the breakup of medieval cultural unity on the one hand and the growth of secular society on the other have somewhat marginalized the institutional church. When the church was the intellectual and cultural universe, controlling all science and philosophy, liberal arts, law and ethics, broad-based satires like those of Erasmus, Rabelais, and Chaucer had force and interest. After the wars of religion and the Enlightenment, adherence to the Catholic universe was seen as a matter of personal choice (except in Spain and Ireland), and works such as *The Praise of Folly* were not possible. Implicit criticisms, however, abound, and so do affirmations, as in G. K. Chesterton, Flannery O'Connor, Anthony Burgess, and Georges Bernanos. Implicit criticisms can be found in James Joyce, J. T. Farrell, and Graham Greene. The contributions of each to the portrait of celibacy in this age will get careful attention here as well as notice of current films such as *Priest* (United Kingdom), *Mala Educación* (Spain), *El Crimen del Padre Amaro* (Mexico), and *The Magdalens* (Ireland).[5] Literary and artistic expressions of reality have tremendous durability, and they cannot be dismissed easily as scurrilous, biased, or blasphemous because they become more compelling as inevitable historical documentation renders them undeniable.

Thousands of Roman Catholic priests in the United States alone—five thousand named since 1950—have sexually abused minors.[6] Outrage over the sexual abuse of minors by clergy in the beginning of the third millennium, especially in the English-speaking world, has not been limited to liberal or conservative elements either in the church or in the general public. Literature about priests cannot be read in exactly the same way now as it was understood before the year 2000. To understand the scope and structure of the sexual abuse and its relationship to sex and celibacy, we have to turn to medical and psychological literature.

Questions about clergy integrity are not limited to the offending clerics or to the single problem of child abuse, but rather they involve the whole panoply of clerical sexual activity plus the church hierarchy and its participation in covering up abuse by priests. Questions remain of just how high and how broad the conspiracy to conceal crimes goes.

Why is this corruption in the Catholic Church such a dangerous symptom, even threatening to destabilize the foundations of the universal church? The hierarchy has blamed the written word—the press, the media—for distorting the problem and causing the crisis.

But how did wide-ranging public indignation spring up—seemingly so fully matured after January 2002—in response to the *Boston Globe* investigative reports of abuse? Many people date the crisis of the Catholic Church to that date and publication.

Excellent and powerful as the media reporting indeed was, in itself it would not be sufficient to destabilize an unconditioned populous. But the secular media form only another source of understanding sex and celibacy in life whether or not it is considered literature.

My basic thesis is that the *world* knew about this type of violation and other clerical sexual activity previously buried in the Catholic unconscious. I knew this was so from work as a therapist, from allusions, innuendoes, mimesis, and narratives in novels. The problem has existed so long and has involved so many victims and their families around the world that when the documents could be printed in a secular newspaper and talked about openly, many of the public were ready to say, "Yes, I know, it happened to me, and now I know it happened to others. I know it is the truth."

The world, victims' families, and the victims themselves could then hear once-silenced voices. Inexplicable pain and suffering, family tragedies, immoral and criminal activity, educational and economic failures that formerly made no sense to people and their families come into focus when sex with a priest is factored into the equation. The men they trusted had betrayed them. They were sexual victims of men who said they were dedicated to religion and celibacy, so they had to be sexually safe.

I expect that the reality of publicly exposed clergy sex will generate a great many literary portrayals beyond journalistic accounts.

It is abhorrent to many unbiased people to think that priests and bishops who are extolled as moral leaders could be the source of moral corruption. And yet it has been so and not only recently.[7]

THE VICTIMS OF CELIBATE VIOLATION

Certainly the crisis of sexual abuse of minors is an extreme of clergy behavior, but it opens a door to the sexual/celibate life of priests and bishops. The consequences of being abused are deep and long lasting. A victim cannot just put behind him or her this kind of abuse. The scars of abuse and betrayal by the trusted last forever. The mass of people abused by clergy has kept growing to a point at which a majority of Catholics who have not been abused know someone who has. The scope of the crisis requires us to look into scientific literature as a background to come to terms with the autobiographical and fictional representations of sex and celibacy in the clergy.[8]

Sexual Footprints

The consequences of sexual activity with clergy advertised as celibate are both psychological and physical. The vehicle of the damage and trauma is sexual.[9] Abuse of a minor, even more so, forms the basis for sexual dysfunction of some kind in the victim.

Some priests portrayed in literature manifest confusion about their sexual identity. This confusion is one of the first and most painful penalties a male victim pays in the aftermath of sexual abuse by a priest. Sexual functioning, even if it does not get mired in paraphilias, is often impaired and crippled for normal functioning. The confusion of sex with violence can result in sadomasochistic behaviors and rape, which are among the dire social consequences of abuse beyond personal tragedy.[10]

Freud originally taught that premature sexual exposure and abuse were the genesis of all neuroses. He later modified his theory to state that actual abuse was not necessary but that even infantile fantasies of sex with the forbidden could cause the same psychic result and trauma. One of the reasons for Freud's change of heart was the sheer number of the accounts of early abuse he heard. It was not popular in the nineteenth century to believe children when they contradicted or countered elders. This attitude plagues assault victims even today. Also, the social status of the family members who were the alleged abusers made Freud's conclusion impolitic and "doubtful." Nonetheless, Freud's original observations and conclusions, in spite of him, have withstood the test of time.[11] Even now, many people find it difficult to believe the enormous psychic consequences from what they would consider a minor sexual infraction or a minimal event of sexual touch. As early as 1893,

Freud wrote: "For we very often find that the content and determinants of hysterical phenomena [read emotional reaction] are events which are in themselves quite trivial, but which have acquired high significance from the fact that they occurred at specially important moments when the patient's predisposition was pathologically increased."[12]

Legacy of Anxiety

Overwhelming anxiety is the inheritance left to the victim of clergy abuse. A host of addictive behaviors involving alcohol, drugs, sex or other acting out, and out-of-control behaviors are endemic among many men and women who have suffered abuse. These behaviors are among the means victims use to mollify their confusion, the pain of trauma, and their unconscious.

If childhood sexual abuse is not promptly and effectively treated, long-term symptoms can continue into adulthood. A whole range of emotional and behavioral problems can be traced to early abuse, the most common being anxiety or post-traumatic stress disorder (PTSD), the sexual anxieties and disorders mentioned previously, low self-esteem, poor body image, depression, and thoughts of suicide.

These anxieties can lead specifically to phobias, generalized anxiety, panic episodes, obsessions, compulsions, and irrational anger perpetuated by the inability of their young personalities to absorb and master what has happened to them.

Seminarians traditionally learn about scrupulosity when they are studying to hear confessions. People with scruples are tortured by unwanted thoughts (or impulse-driven repetitive actions). These people often turn to a priest to counsel or absolve them of the thoughts, images, or desires that they find troublesome or abhorrent. Frequently, the ideation has to do with forbidden and intolerable sexual images or ideas.

Today, this condition would be diagnosed psychiatrically as obsessive-compulsive disorder,[13] and its etiology is often tied up with early sexual abuse because abuse impairs a child's sense of self-control and opens a person to addictive patterns of tension reduction.

Sexual abuse by an adult, no matter how kindly cloaked, is an assault.[14] Inevitably, most victims will experience sex with an adult as a genuine trauma because the occurrence does not fit into the psychic or social reality of the minor. The discordance of the relationship and exchange cannot be absorbed. Some victims of clergy abuse have distressing reactions at the sight of a Roman collar, a church, rosary, or anything that may trigger a memory of abusive events. Diagnostically, PTSD is a well-defined psychiatric condition that plagues countless victims of childhood abuse; in fact, studies indicate that between one-third and one-half of childhood victims of abuse develop symptoms of PTSD.

We have all learned a great deal about PTSD from treating war veterans who, after coming through battle conditions, life threats, death or injury to companions (often seemingly unscathed), have recurrent, distressing recollections, dreams, and emotional reactions. Unpredictable sights, sounds, or thoughts can reignite the trauma.

A Lifetime of Depression

Depression is a common affliction in the modern world. Some studies say that there is a 50 percent chance of one lifetime incidence of major depression among the U.S. population. But propelling the abused toward depression are distinct and added burdens that tend to be recurrent and sustained. In the abused, the loss of innocence, the loss of confidence, the loss of faith, the loss of self-esteem, and the loss of their youth lay down deep roots to inevitable periods or long-term states of depression.[15]

Trust Betrayed

Betrayal so deep and so fundamental is the experience of a minor violated by the trusted that the incident(s) becomes a life-altering condition long after the real threat of abuse has passed. Certainly, this severe result prevails when the abuser is a parent who represents the whole world of security for a child; when the abuser is a parental figure who also represents God, the spiritual world, and the eternal, the betrayal leaves the victim nowhere to turn. All supposedly secure and trustworthy persons and institutions become suspect.[16]

A minor who is a victim experiences fundamental abandonment and aloneness. How can persons revive trust when they have been wounded so vitally at a stage in their life when they were intrinsically able to give themselves without reservation to trust an elder only to be unspeakably violated? Many cannot ever recover confidence and trust in a world that betrayed their existence. They needed trust—as we all do—for a sense of survival. When the abusing elder is a parent or, even more spectacularly, a representative of God, the loss of trust is nearly irretrievable.[17]

Beyond loss of trust in the outside world, abuse betrayal attacks self-trust in a fundamental way: the loss of trust in one's memory and mind. A disruption of cognition and memory can occur during and after childhood abuse. Cognitive and neurological mechanisms that may underlie the forgetting of abuse have been scientifically identified.[18]

Relationships in Tatters

The person who has been abused in childhood is unable to weave his or her relationships out of whole cloth. The fibers of their personalities have been torn. The ability of the abused to establish solid relationships remains in tatters. Most times, victims do not understand why they cannot connect with other people in meaningful ways. They beat themselves up by repeatedly involving themselves in destructive liaisons. They become abusive in some way to the friend with whom they wish to be close. Or they cling to a burdensome dependence, constructed but unresolved in their childhood. No one can meet their needs because their needs are the deficits of a childhood lost. They are the phantom, wounded children in the skin of adequate-appearing adults. They constantly disappoint and mystify themselves and everyone else who could have meaning to them. Divorce, separations, alienation, antipathies, and hollowness mark the world they inhabit with family, friends, and coworkers.

None So Isolated

The survivors of abuse have a lonely core that isolates them from themselves and everyone else. That core is unassailable because it is entrapped in an unspoken and unimaginable secrecy. They cannot share it because the secret is often hidden even from them. Even if they have memory traces, they cannot put them together in any coherent way that will make sense to anyone. And even if the memories are clear, indelibly burned into their mind and heart, many men and women have no way to scale the wall of guilt and shame that surrounds their childhood secrets.

Victims, in their isolation, think that they must be the *only* victim. Sealed in their secrets, they are isolated from anyone they could hope might understand what they have been through. They do not understand themselves. How can they believe what happened to them in secret when their experience of their whole world—family, school, friends, church—appears so unaware and oblivious of their darkness and trauma?

Survivors guard their secret even if it makes them ill. Unto death some victims hug their secret because they promised to keep it. Some children defend their abuser because the abuse is bound up with the promise of security and the feeling of being loved and special in spite of evidence to the contrary.[19]

It takes victims of childhood sexual abuse years to straighten out their trauma experience. The mixed feelings of premature excitement, guilt transferred from the aggressor, and the challenges of separating fantasies from reality are tasks far beyond the ego capacity of most minors. It takes the average victims of abuse 25 to 30 years to come to the realization that it was not their fault. The guilt they feel is not rightfully theirs but the property of the abuser. The anger they experience is justified. It takes time to learn that they have rights and power even in the face of opposition from men and institutions they once considered invincible and infallible.

Personalities Derailed

Perverted may seem to be a strong word to describe the effect on the personality development of young persons who have been sexually abused. But the word is precise. Abuse twists the normal progression of personality growth and development.

Over and above the distortions of perceptions and reactions that anxiety and depression impose on the developing child, the behavior of a priest who acts in ways that are socially abhorrent and morally wrong challenges the child's conscience and judgment beyond reconcilable bounds. The clergyman presents himself and is accepted as a public moral arbiter. Yet this civic and religious leader draws the youngster into acts that are socially and morally unacceptable and must remain hidden. The bond of secrecy forms a noose that chokes maturing expression.

The association is essentially conflicted and confusing. The child is seduced into a seemingly loving, secure relationship that actually separates him or her from peers and family. The seducer grooms the child into a position of specialness that makes age-appropriate friends and normal activities less attractive and inaccessible.

What is real? What is pretense? Attention that seemed to be love and care turns out to be selfishness and exploitation.[20] One who appeared to be giving and generous was actually self-seeking and hateful. The abusive bond of childhood can become the model for adult interactions predisposing one to a schizoidlike personality pattern of interaction.

One of the most complex personality distortions is what is now termed the *borderline personality*. These people have a pervasive pattern of unstable interpersonal relationships. They fluctuate between idealizing and denigrating others, often to the extreme. They are saddled with an unstable self-image. They can mutilate themselves and threaten harm or suicide. They find themselves in the middle of outrageous angry outbursts. They feel hollow; at the same time, and perhaps because of their emptiness, they create havoc all around them.

These people have been psychically injured during the earliest years of their development. Their early basic insecurity makes them particularly vulnerable to multiple kinds of psychic and physical injuries as they grow up. A child's conscience is formed not simply by education but by adult example, experience, and relationships with others that have been meaningful to him or her.

Self-Destruction

Suicide is the ultimate act of self-destruction, and there are untold numbers of men and women, violated as minors, who resort to this ultimate act of desperation. But there are other behaviors of self-torture and slow death that are the result of being sexually attacked and abused by a priest. Here are some examples of the disastrous effects inflicted on the abused:

- Some persons cannot continue their studies because the injury to self-esteem is so fundamental that they simply are unable to muster the energy or confidence necessary to master tasks that are easily within their natural potential. Interference with education also limits earning potential.

- Persons can plunge into the world of crime because the abuse makes them feel that that is where they belong.

- Unconscious guilt over their sexual involvement (abuse by a priest or bishop) makes some victims feel that they are the ones who deserve punishment, so they unwittingly devise ways to defeat and humiliate themselves. They think they do not deserve success.

- Some persons get caught in addictive self-medication to the degree that they run afoul of family, work, and the law, and they impair their health and life.

- Some persons overdose, end up in fatal car accidents, contract incurable diseases such as HIV/AIDS, get themselves murdered without a suicide note; their fate was sealed by their betrayal. They are completing what the abusive priest or bishop began: the death of their sense of self-preservation.

PERSONALITY OF THE PRIEST PREDATOR

A man with any type of personality, certainly including psychotic, can sexually abuse a minor. Many abusers, even if they are clergymen, can be sociopaths and are deficient in their quality of conscience. We used to call these people *sociopaths*. It is still a good descriptive word, and it goes to the heart of the priest with such a personality. (Now if a diagnostic term is used, that person is identified an *antisocial personality*.)

People are usually loath to judge their minister antisocial because clergy do so many good and helpful things in the ordinary services they provide. Despite that seemingly mitigating circumstance, I prefer to understand many priests and bishops by the word *sociopath*, a term that could be applied appropriately to a number of fictional clergymen; Elmer Gantry is an example. It defines a person who fails to conform to lawful behaviors; he is a man who is often impulsive, lacks remorse, lacks empathy because he is adept at conning others for his own pleasure or profit; he feels entitled, above the law; and he can have a reckless disregard for the safety and welfare of others.[21]

Priest sexual abusers are con artists. They are pretenders. They often offend in financial ways also. The priesthood provides them with a mask of moral rectitude and sanity. This personality type represents itself in every rank of the priesthood and propagates itself in many ways, including through violating young boys and girls who learn their lessons too well. The progeny of these sociopath priests can express themselves in going on to abuse another generation of children or lie, steal, or cheat their way into prison or assume their own respectable masks to hide their real self, like their mentors.

Clergy pedophiles and abusers of minors prey on the vulnerable. Vulnerable families (the poor and dysfunctional), vulnerable circumstances (death or illness), or the overly pious and dependent can provide opportunities for clergy entré into the homes and lives of the trusting needy, making them targets for abuse.

No one has yet proposed that there exists one set type of person or priest who turns out to be an abuser of minors, and there is no test for predicting who will become a sexual abuser of a minor. We have now, however, enough experience with clergy abusers that clinicians are able to outline a sketch of the priest who has abused.

He tends to be *narcissistic;* that is, he tends to have a sense of self-importance and entitlement. He sees himself as special and tends to exploit others for his own gratification. Because his needs and pleasure come first, he lacks empathy for the feelings of others.

The priest predator is an *angry* man, often with the face of a calm and gentle pastor.

Outward grace, superficial interaction, and social charm frequently cover the *isolation* and friendlessness that an abuser feels. Of necessity (except when predators ban together to share their sexual predilection), a child sexual abuser has to hide his activity and his real self.

Sometimes the abusing priest may have been abused himself, and not rarely by a priest. The hidden life of the priest abuser requires that he split his life into two parts: The acceptable and even exemplary public life has to be separated from (and reconciled with) the socially reprehensible and morally defective secret life he pursues.

A priest frequently is a man torn. He struggles to make himself feel comfortable. Priests who profess celibacy publicly and are sexually active privately know what they are doing. No matter how constrained or compelled, they make a choice. They are *doubling.*[22] Their priesthood, their way of life, and all of the benefits and security of their profession hang on their promise to be celibate. If they publicly renounce celibacy, they lose everything. These men try to adapt a celibate requirement with their irreconcilable sexual urges. They pose good motives while participating in evil behavior.

Clerical rationalizations for being sexually active, even with minors, are legion. Here are some justifications I have heard, recited by men with a straight face and a conviction that they really were celibate: "I work hard and I deserve it." "Sex is natural." "It doesn't hurt anybody." "I'm showing God's love." "This child needs love." "I loved him/her." "I am giving good instructions in sex." "Priests are only human." "I'm only giving them what they were asking for." "She/he seduced me."

Because the darkness of the doubling cannot withstand the light of examination, the split priest often has to struggle with paranoid fears that he will be found out. He has to isolate himself ever more carefully from adult scrutiny and discovery.

Many bishops and priests, abusers or not, tend to minimize the effects of sexual involvement with a clergyman. "What's the big deal?" "It was only a touch." "It happened just once." "They had sex with others." "They knew what they were doing." "Why can't they get over it?" "They should just forget it." "It was at least partially their fault." "Christ stands for forgiveness." "Why can't they forgive?" I have heard every one of these justifications and more.

Sexual betrayal by a priest is rightfully called *soul murder*. Many bishops and priests still miss the full significance of this reality. They have cooperated in the process of abuse and selected and trained the perpetrators and protected them precisely because they minimized the effects. By neglect and inaction, church authorities justify priests betraying the trust of their people.

The church does not take celibacy or its violation seriously in action, only in documents and words. In 1051, when Saint Peter Damian addressed Pope Leo IX about the sexual violations by priests, he held superiors responsible for the behavior and the harm done. He spoke a truth that prevails today.

There is no doubt that for decades bishops and religious superiors have known about the sexual lives of bishops and priests and have covered up for them and intimidated victims when they could. Volumes of court documents indicate that cardinals and bishops lied and conspired to keep immoral and criminal activity secret from the public to avoid scandal at all costs.

The irony of the scandal of sexual abuse by priests and bishops is that secrecy was meant to save the church from scandal. Now people know the scandal, and they can say it: Sexual abuse of minors by bishops and priests—men bound by a vocational requirement of perfect and perpetual chastity and presented to the public as sexually safe—is a major social and religious problem. It is criminal.

WAYS OF UNDERSTANDING SEX, CELIBACY, AND PRIESTS

The chapters in this book attempt to study celibacy, priests, and sexuality through literature; we provide a few autobiographies, but we mostly search for the help of fiction: novels. Of course, this is not the ordinary way to study these realities, but I claim that it provides a rich field for understanding. The current crisis provides additional avenues for validation of creative observations.

We have already indicated that the crisis has forced us to turn to medical and psychological literature to deal with the conundrums about sex and

celibacy that face us. Journalistic accounts that record the voices of victims
and the church's responses to celibate violations form a modern historical
reserve that undoubtedly will be tapped for literary expression for years
to come. Grand jury reports and the reports commissioned by the United
States Conference of Catholic Bishops have already changed the general perception of sex and celibacy in the Catholic priesthood. A new history is being
written.

Three notable dramas that record this new perception have been produced
since 2002. Michael Murphy produced a play about the Boston crisis—*Sin
(A Cardinal Deposed)*—that drew upon the testimony of Cardinal Law. Play-
wright, actor, director Dakin Matthews produced *The Prince of LA;* although
it is billed as fiction, it echoes elements of the crisis from the California
church, and in the process it sketches an accurate and masterful portrayal of
the real working of the sexual power structure of the church. *Doubt,* a New
York production written by John Patrick Shanley, struggles with the perception of a nun that a boy is being abused and the denial of a priest that anything is awry. The play has been a commercial success, and it was awarded a
Pulitzer Prize for Drama and a Tony Award in 2005.

When I began to study celibacy, I asked questions: What is it? How is it
practiced? How does a man develop a sexual identity without experience,
and how does he form a celibate identity with sexual experience? What is the
process of celibacy? And finally, what does achieved celibacy look like? With
the encouragement of Margaret Meade, I embarked on a voyage of ethnographic research.[23] I have found that the quest provided a sturdy vessel, and it
resulted in a productive journey. Ethnography was compatible with the thera-
peutic model and the psychoanalytic theory I was familiar with at the time.

Sociological surveys that identify aspects of priests' lives and celibate
practice have been conducted, and they do teach us something about the
clerical structure of celibacy.[24] Sex remains a notoriously difficult area of
human behavior to research. Celibacy that is a life adjustment and by definition excludes any sexual activity poses daunting, if not insurmountable,
obstacles to standard means of investigation. For instance, random-sample
scientific surveys about priests' happiness have been conducted, and they
produced the conclusion that "priests are the happiest" men in the country.
Of course, this says noting about how they are practicing celibacy. Without
the family obligations associated with marriage and with sexual activity of
choice available to a priest, the social and economic security and rewards
concomitant with being a priest can produce contentment, if not happiness,
for such men.[25]

Cinema has been a powerful element that prepared the U.S. public to think
the (Catholic) unthinkable: that priests can be sexually active. Mixed with
the stories of strong priests—who fight sin and evil, stand up to oppressors,
protect the poor, and sacrifice themselves for their flock, celibate all—were

vignettes of less ideal clergy. Movies touched, however deftly, on problems of clerical immaturity, masturbation, homosexuality, sexual abuse of women, or conflicted loving relationships, abuse of minors, and abortion.

The movies—that particular U.S. medium that creates and reflects image—at first featured priests idealistically under the strict eye of Catholic censors. More recent portrayals, however, have intimated at a spectrum beyond the heroic.

Moviegoers witnessed the evolution of the Catholic priest's public image from immigrant protector and leader of small ethnic communities, predominantly Irish or Italian, to superstars and idols for millions to less honorable and more pedestrian souls.

Midcentury movies portrayed priests as strong, masculine champions of the poor, with no hint of sexual feelings or awareness. The roster of actors portraying priests contributed to an image of power and sensual appeal without sexuality: Spencer Tracy as Father Tim in *San Francisco* (1936), Pat O'Brien as Father Jerry in *Angels with Dirty Faces* (1938), Karl Malden as Father Barry in *On the Waterfront* (1954), Anthony Quinn as the saintly Pope-to-be Kiril Lakota in *Shoes of the Fisherman* (1968), Robert De Niro as Father Des Spellacy in *True Confessions* (1981).

Bing Crosby as Father O'Malley in *Going My Way* (1944) and Frank Sinatra as the poor, frail pastor in *Miracle of the Bells* (1948) neutered and sentimentalized the image of the priest, and in the words of Garry Wills, "celebrated all the Church's faults as if they were virtues."

Movies in the last three decades of the twentieth century hinted at individual priests grappling with sexual problems of conscience, including abortion (*The Cardinal*, 1963). Minor clergy characters began to appear as well-meaning but ineffectual pastors (*M*A*S*H*, 1970) or a childish masturbator (*The End*, 1978). A starkly negative view of a priest emerged as a manipulator and frankly sexual sinner a few years later (*Monsignor*, 1982).

The issue of sexual abuse and clergy was hinted at in two movies released in 1995: *Sleepers* shows the struggle of a priest who had himself been sexually abused as a boy, and *Primal Fear* peeks at an archbishop who is an abuser of young boys and girls.

The Priest, a 1994 English made-for-TV movie that made it to big-screen theaters in the United States, sympathetically portrayed two priests, one heterosexual and one homosexual, both sexually active.

An 1875 novel, *El Crimen del Padre Amaro*, which portrays a young priest who impregnates a young girl and arranges an abortion that leads to her death, is retold in a 2003 Mexican movie of the same name. Two other priests and the local bishop are interesting examples for the place of sex and celibacy in their lives.

Pedro Almodóvar released the Spanish movie *Bad Education (La Mala Educación)* in 2004. It was an outstanding portrayal of priest-teacher-abuser who broke up the relationship of two young boys in order to have one of them as his own sexual partner. Only a long review could begin to capture the artistry and impact of this film, which stands as an example of the future possibilities of the narratives to be told about celibacy and its crisis.

Documentary films recording the crisis have proliferated. Many of them sported the title *Sins of the Fathers*. Amy Berg's movie *Deliver Us From Evil*, the account of how a future cardinal (Roger Mahony) protected an abusive priest (Oliver O'Grady), was nominated for a Academy Award in 2007. The degree of knowledge and awareness of priest and bishop abuse of minors is so prominent that late-night comedians frequently allude to it, situation comedies are built around it, and editorial cartoons are commonplace and often scathing.

DOES THE CATHOLIC CHURCH NEED A REFORMATION?

Beyond the numbers, the atrocities of clergy sexual abuse against minors are the tip of an iceberg. Sexual abuse defines the symptom of an institution rocked to its very foundations, gasping for air, and trying desperately to keep its head above water. Or less kindly, in the words of one bishop, "the institution to which I belong is rotten to its core."

A fair question is why the impetus for an as yet ill-defined reformation has surfaced now and primarily in the United States. After all, sex is universal. The sexual offenses of clerics and religious controversies are not new.

One reason for the current upheaval is that the critical mass of men and women abused by priests has grown to a point at which the numbers of responsible priests ministering can no longer balance the number of offending priests. The John Jay study of the crisis in the U.S. (2004) records that between 9 and 11 percent of priests abused minors in the years 1960 to 1985. Of the priests serving in 1983 who have been credibly accused of abusive behavior, 11.5 percent of them were serving in the archdiocese of Los Angeles. The best estimates state that each abusive priest has between ten and fifty victims. In addition, during the twentieth century, Catholic priests became familiar and prominent on the U.S. horizon. They no longer operated under the radar of public scrutiny. In fact, the church sought an ever-higher public profile to match its growing influence. These factors conditioned the U.S. public to consider priests through bifurcated lenses. First, priests were accorded greater respect and even reverence, more so than ever before even in so-called Protestant America. But also, priests were judged in an ever more realistic light against U.S. democratic principles.

U.S. legislation defending the rights of children proliferated from the 1960s onward. This element prepared the U.S. public to face the problem of sexual abuse of minors more directly than it had in the past. Reporting laws required health professionals, teachers, and others to report suspected child abuse to state social services. Federal legislation put the full weight of its pocketbook behind the movement in 1974 when it refused funds to states that lacked reporting laws. Since the crisis exploded, more states include priests and ministers as mandated reporters.

In 1994, when he was asked why Rome had not helped the U.S. bishops in the sex abuse crisis, a long-time staff member of one of the congregations of the Vatican stated: "The Vatican cannot understand why the American Bishops can't control the courts and the media better." The U.S. hierarchy, indeed, has desperately tried to control the courts and the media, and it still does to a degree. Coordinated efforts from the central offices of bishops in Washington, DC, aimed a counterattack in the 1990s on any news story about priests who were abusing minors. They dismissed all reports as "a smear campaign, anti-Catholic, anti-church, anti-priest, or biased reporting." Even Vatican spokesmen supported the thesis that there was, in fact, no crisis, simply a media-driven attempt to exploit and sensationalize isolated misbehavior by a "few bad apples."

These church efforts will ultimately fail because documentation and an informed public have tipped the balance. Many who were reluctant to believe the worst were roused to anger, outraged at the deception by their leaders who knew of abuse and conspired to conceal it. Lay people, along with the civil authorities, demanded an accounting.

Lawyers representing the church fight furiously to exonerate abusing priests and to justify the involvement of bishops and dioceses in the crisis. Statutes of limitation have saved thousands of priests—but not all—from serving jail time. Civil suits have proliferated beyond count.

The United States has a highly refined tort system that has made civil litigation more possible than in European countries. High-profile, high-stakes jury awards and cash settlements in favor of victims sobered church officials: $32.5 million payout ($119.6 million jury award) for 11 victims in Dallas, Texas (1997); $7.5 million payout ($32 million jury award) for 2 victims in Stockton, California (1998); $5 million plus payment to 1 victim in Los Angeles/Orange County, California (2001). All of these settlements were awarded before January 2002. Since then, several dioceses have made group settlements: Orange County, California, $100 million; Boston, $85 million; Louisville, Kentucky, $25.7 million; $660 million in Los Angeles (2007). Five dioceses filed for bankruptcy protection by 2007.

Awareness of the depth of the crisis has evolved slowly. But even the highest church authorities now relinquish some measure of denial because cardinals and bishops are no longer immune from depositions and court appearances. Previously unheard of in U.S. history until this time, cardinals and bishops have now suffered the indignity of becoming targets of grand jury investigations.

The crisis is not simply abuse of minors. It involves three distinct elements of concern: sex, money, and loss of credibility in moral authority. These storm clouds on the clerical horizon were harbingers of the massive forces that combine like a Midwest tornado to threaten the very foundations of the church's sexual assumptions. Reformation is inevitable.

Beyond the symptom of sexual abuse by clergy is the threat to the problematic equation on which all of the church's reasoning about sexual behavior rests: that priest equals celibacy. When that myth dissipates, the whole sexual structure of Catholic teaching about sex falls like a house of cards.

THE EXPOSURE OF A PROBLEMATIC EQUATION

Two questions must be addressed: What factors laid the foundations for the climate of reformation? And what does religious celibacy, which affects only clerics, have to do with the disruption of the faith and confidence of millions of faithful who practice their religion for the most part within marriage? Central to my understanding of the present crisis is the disintegration of the myth that priest and celibacy are an identical and inseparable reality.

Three superstar U.S. priests of the twentieth century sold the priest-celibate image to millions of Americans at the same time that they conditioned the Catholic faithful for reformation.

Father Charles E. Coughlin, his celibacy unquestioned in the public mind, championed the links between religion, social justice, and democracy. Despite his obnoxious anti-Semitism, which was an authentic echo of the traditional Catholic teaching of the time, he gave the average Catholic a voice, the courage to speak up, and an expectation to be heard.

Bishop Fulton J. Sheen charmed a nation with his radio and television presentations. Doctrinally orthodox, especially in sexual matters such as birth control, he, nonetheless, encouraged Catholics to think for themselves.

Father Andrew M. Greeley has been the single most powerful clerical force preparing for a reformation by forming a bridge from mythical clerical stereotypes to penetrating analysis of hierarchical figures. No U.S. priest has been more influential than Greeley in encouraging Catholics to confront sexuality and the church hierarchy.

Never shy about addressing church problems or problematic churchmen, Greeley has been a consistent critic of bishops. He has called them to account for their inadequacies, intellectual and spiritual limitations, and failures. Since 1985, he has attacked the problem of sexual abuse by priests, and he has chided the bishops for dragging their feet as well as for their cover-up of the problem.

Greeley is himself a champion of clerical celibacy, but at the same time he introduced a generation of Catholics to fictional churchmen, including cardinals and Vatican officials, who were believable and sexually active. Although other writers have dealt with the same subjects, Greeley's stature as a priest and sociologist added a dimension of authenticity.

The practice of clerical celibacy remains largely ill defined and unexamined in practical terms. It has long been the sacred cow of the Catholic Church. Supposedly irrefutable, it remains unquestionable and unexamined by church standards. Only idealistic reflections or arcane reaffirming and defensive treatises are tolerated and considered authentic.

Despite the monolithic defense of the law of clerical celibacy by the Catholic Church, the very word has lacked sufficient definition and distinction to make meaningful dialogue possible. Is celibacy a religious ideal, or is it an image? Is it a vow or a promise? Is it a regulation necessary for ordination to the clerical office? Is it a state of nonmarriage or singleness whether one is sexually abstinent? Is it simply a situation of sexual abstinence in or outside of marriage for an indeterminate amount of time? Is celibacy a life adjustment? Is a celibate person one who has made a promise of sexual abstinence regardless of his sexual activity? Does a man qualify as a celibate merely by his acceptance into a group that demands a claim of celibacy but not necessarily a practice for inclusion in its ranks?

The deficiency of an adequate vocabulary of celibacy has rendered a great disservice to the practice, process, and achievement of an important human resource because it has relegated it to the realm of magic (mystery) and incomprehension rather than reality.

And what of the culture of celibacy? For instance, if every lawyer in the United States, in order to practice his profession and receive its benefits and status, were required to be male and unmarried, committed to perpetual and perfect chastity, would it change the legal profession? Would it change the culture of law?

That last question is a no-brainer when applied to the legal profession. But the reality of the social significance is mostly ignored when one considers the Roman Catholic priesthood. Clerical celibacy does constitute a culture, a fraternity, with social standing, an ethos, and ethical expectations and a mode of operation inherently wedded to secrecy. It is a culture with practical worldwide repercussions.

More critically, celibacy is a system. This system, with its sexual/celibate agenda, is the true vortex of the current monumental and epic crisis of the Catholic Church. Clergy sexual abuse of minors, the topic in 2002 that riveted the attention of a nation and shook the foundation of a centuries-old religion, is merely the symptom of a far deeper and wide-ranging problem in the system: its teaching and practice.

The sexual/celibate agenda of the Roman Catholic Church includes the questions of masturbation, premarital sexual activity, sexual activity after the death of a spouse or after divorce, contraception, homosexuality, abortion, the requirement of nonmarriage, perfect and perpetual chastity for ordination to the priesthood, a married priesthood, ordination of women, and the appointment of bishops. Those who claim that these issues are completely settled and require no dialogue only intensify the crisis of confidence in the authority of the church and expose it to ever-greater disdain for its hypocrisy.

All of the elements of the celibacy crisis have been presented in literature for centuries, even if in less dramatic doses than the current climate sustains. It is precisely the public glimpse into the hypocrisy of the secret, sexually active, celibate system revealed in the priest sexual-abuse crisis that has inspired an unprecedented degree of rage against the hierarchy of the church and mobilized historic demands for accountability, transparency, and reform.

CHAPTER 2

GANDHI AND FRIENDS:
THE SEXUAL/CELIBATE
TWAIN MEET

I hold that a life of perfect continence in thought, speech, and action is necessary for reaching spiritual perfection. And a nation that does not possess such men is poorer for the want. Purity of life is the highest and truest art.

Mohandas K. Gandhi

Sexual self-revelation is rare. Three popular twentieth-century male religious figures—Mohandas K. Gandhi,[1] Fulton J. Sheen,[2] and Andrew M. Greeley[3]—have written autobiographical accounts of their celibacy.

These three witnesses to their celibate calling share a significant commonality: They were all highly visible public figures. Gandhi's testimony, however, is unique among the rare confessions of celibacy in literature, and Gandhi reveals the process of his celibate discovery and development more clearly than any other religious writer, including Saint Augustine.

Each of our three protagonists has been widely read; each testimony comes from an openly avowed practitioner of celibacy. Each man generates fascination by the tale of his life story and the celibacy he extols.

Autobiography makes special demands on any method of inquiry, especially when the spotlight is focused on celibacy and its necessary links to the sexuality and personality of the writer. Of the three testimonies to the celibate vocation, Greeley's is the most likely—and the most calculated—to engage contemporary U.S. readers through its likable eccentricity. He employs a matter-of-factness, and he flatters his intended reader. He enjoys certain advantages in the freeness with which he can fashion his rhetoric because he is not an official spokesperson for an institutional status quo.

Fulton Sheen, Greeley's fellow Catholic, was constrained by his social position to employ the prophetic voice to express a predictable coda.

Gandhi has the disadvantage—or the mystique—of being from another culture and time. He was born a quarter-century before Sheen (and Coughlin), and he had a uniquely popular reception horizon. He remains intriguing for his unapologetically unconventional thinking. Gandhi can, in turn, be infuriating, unpredictable, and—most powerfully—unromantically honest. Each of these three figures teaches us something idiosyncratic, and yet all expose some common underpinnings of celibate life.

Not surprisingly, Gandhi's *Experiments with Truth*, as he termed the course of his life, expresses the most clearly of the three authors the developmental process of achieving celibacy. The reader can discern the stages and vicissitudes of the general practice precisely because Gandhi gave a personal, rather than public, account of his experience. He took advantage of the complete honesty afforded him by his independence from having to pander to the prejudices of an expected readership. He was also free from the need to uphold the authority of any mundane institution.

Gandhi's freedom from the normal social constraints on the public writer emerges from his position at the boundary of two radically different cultures. He revered both the British and Hindu traditions that had nurtured him. This reverence was crucial in making him such an unlikely yet powerful leader of the anticolonial movement.

The awareness of conflicting influences also gave Gandhi the ability to admit to profoundly differing stages in his own development and to document them with such accuracy of detail. In this autobiographical clarity, Gandhi expresses his freedom from the kind of institutional dogma imposed by Catholic sexual theory and teaching that accepts no subtlety or shading in its ideal of celibate practice: no developmental process, only knife-edge-sharp obedience.

Many priests report that the example of some celibate man was a powerful element in the formation of their would-be celibate intention. Gandhi credited the influence of Raychandbhai[4] as the predominant factor in his decision to observe brahmacharya (celibacy). Raychandbhai was a prominent poet who, although married, was evidently practicing celibacy.

It is noteworthy that Gandhi's initial inspiration to become celibate was accompanied by a discussion of the relative value of a wife's devotion versus that of a servant. Gandhi felt that the devotion of a servant was a thousand times more praiseworthy than the devotion of a wife to her husband because an indissoluble bond demanded the wife's devotion to her husband. Therefore, he considered a wife's devotion as perfectly natural and expected, whereas equal devotion between master and servant required a special effort to cultivate.

There is more to Gandhi's discourse than at first meets the eye. Arguably, both forms of devotion are the result of a social cultivation stemming from class and gender oppression.[5] There was, however, a two-pronged psychological significance in the distinction: Gandhi needed strength to break with both his wife and his idealization of marriage in order to take up the celibate life. Certainly, his enthusiasm—a thousand times more praiseworthy—reflects an attitude required to offset the sense of loss and grief, reminiscent of Saint Augustine's, that accompanied the double separation from wife and the sexual self required by the formation of the celibate intention.

The reader must be open, without prejudice, to consider the question to which Gandhi's—and to some extent Sheen's and Greeley's—celibate decision gives rise: Does male celibate intention require the demotion or denigration of women to support its own resolve?

The second prong of Gandhi's argument is also significant. Gandhi appeared indifferent to the Indian class distinction between master and servant, describing it with the same enthusiasm reserved for friendship between unconstrained individuals. This position contradicts that element in Gandhi's Hindu culture that anthropologist Louis Dumont calls, *Homo hierarchicus*.[6]

Still, it must be kept in mind that Gandhi was also the product of England and its culture, one in which the importance of the master-servant relationship was a prominent sentimental motif of British literature. This master-servant motif is linked to a world of male-male bonding in literature in which antisex and antifemale biases persist.[7] Consider, for instance, the sexless, misogynist, and avuncular world of the Hobbits in J.R.R. Tolkien's *Lord of the Rings* trilogy.[8] Tolkien's Middle Earth is dominated by the sentimental master-servant relationship of Frodo and Sam.

In his essay "The Knight Sets Forth,"[9] Erich Auerbach observed the significance of the connection between male-male bonding, master-servant fidelity, and avuncular kinship in adventure genre, on the one hand, and, on the other, male celibacy in the Grail quest genre of romantic literature and real spiritual vocation.

Again, without bias, the reader must carefully consider the relationship of celibacy to male-male bonding. It would be superficial to dismiss the question simply as a homosexual concern. Understanding the connections in these literary expressions has implications for understanding the celibate ideal, resistance to democratization, and women's rights in both Western culture and the Catholic Church. What is culturally determined and what is inherent in the nature of the bonding?

From the time that Gandhi determined the personal importance of celibacy, he records his progress toward the celibate achievement that follows an authentic pattern of celibate development: awareness of capacity and knowledge of the process, practice, and commitment. Both before and after his formulation of intention, Gandhi's awareness of his capacity for celibacy—that is, his capacity to live a life of service capable of balancing the deprivations of personal celibacy—expressed itself in a longing for some humanitarian work of a permanent nature.

After his meeting with Raychandbhai, Gandhi decisively shifted his humanitarian work from his family cares toward community, serving as a nurse and ambulance corpsman. Gandhi vowed his celibacy five years after he began practicing it; the vow was crucial in establishing his commitment to the celibate life.

Gandhi's greatest significance as a witness to celibacy is the frankness with which he treats the growing knowledge and experience of achieving celibate practice. He does not shy away from including accounts of his sexual lapses as he recounts his experiments with fasting and physical renunciation and their limits. He tells the tale of his changing, growing appreciation of what it means to achieve celibacy.

Some observers, such as George Orwell[10] and some of Gandhi's Hindu contemporaries interviewed by Erik Erikson,[11] had reservations about the level of Gandhi's achievement and integration of celibacy, even though Gandhi's service of humanity speaks eloquently to his internal achievement. These critics believed that there was a bit of showmanship and dissimulation in his physical closeness in his old age to young virgins to prove his self-control. Orwell, like Dorothy Day, held that the label *saint*, so often applied to Gandhi, was a facile dismissal of a person's message and a thing human beings must avoid.

A series of significant characteristics—along with service and the acceptance of all humanity—marks the achievement and integration of celibacy. Among these are a routine of prayer, vital intellectual interests, and a profound and living relationship with the transcendent, all of which Gandhi definitely had. He certainly demonstrated good humor, tolerance, and a subtle wisdom in social and political matters. Apparently, Gandhi also achieved the humility so common to the integrated celibate; even a critic as severe as Orwell is loath to accuse him of lacking it.

Gandhi's autobiography, however, confronts the reader with rigidity in the intimate character of the man, a failing easily overlooked before the inestimable accomplishment of his life of service. That inflexibility appears limited. But his area of greatest rigidity concerns exactly that arena in which the discipline and charism of celibacy is realized: the dynamics of human sexuality. His most dogmatic views dictate the proper sexual life of both the celibate and the noncelibate, and the puritanical interpretation of each reinforced that of the other. Some combination of his cultural heritage, which included the English Puritanism of his associate, the Reverend Mr. Hill, and his personal psychobiological constitution, locked Gandhi into a sexual rigidity from which he seems never to have been able to free himself.

Even before his vocation, Gandhi was committed to an archaic model of human sexuality, one similar to that threatening to undermine the credibility of the sexual teachings of the contemporary Catholic Church. Gandhi, who had engaged prostitutes from the time he was 13, felt that a married couple should never have sex out of lust[12] but rather only to conceive progeny. He had contempt for the idea that sex was a necessary act like sleeping or eating, and he felt that lust should be controlled at any cost.

To be sure, an archaic view of sexuality is at least as culturally and historically influenced as it is psychologically generated. Nevertheless, Gandhi was aware of alternatives. He had read about contraceptives and, considering the Reverend Mr. Hill's opposition, simply chose to reject them in favor of self-control. The necessity of using abstinence as the only form of birth control led Gandhi to his years of unsuccessful strivings. He rectified the process only by shifting to a commitment to a spiritual vocation and the vow of celibacy.

Gandhi spoke with heat and intensity about his struggle for sexual control: "There is no limit to the possibilities of renunciation." He pursued celibacy with an uncompromising regimen of sensual renunciation and extreme fasting. The importance of fasting as a means of achieving celibacy has been well documented in the lives of early Christian hermits. The focus, however, is not merely the subjection of the senses but rather the life system and productivity that reinforce the celibacy.

Celibates like Saint Paul or John Cassian,[13] who achieved an ascetic integration, do not demonstrate an imposition of their life solution on others, a situation one often observes in the fanatic or youthful enthusiast. There is a quiet discipline about the lives of integrated celibates and a consistently observed accompanying tolerance of others and their needs.

Significantly, the passion of Gandhi's asceticism was matched by his intolerance, even contempt, for the noncelibate, an attitude precisely inimical to what can be expected from the integrated ascetic. Worse still, Gandhi employed a rhetorical strategy similar to that of Fulton Sheen, by which the glory of the celibate ideal is established through a condescending comparison with the generic noncelibate, which is frankly absurd. Gandhi taught that there was a profound dividing line between the celibate and the noncelibate that was clearly apparent and that any resemblance between the two was an illusion. Although both had eyes and ears, the celibate used his to see and hear the glory and praises of God, whereas the noncelibate used his for frivolity and ribaldry. The celibate stayed up late to pray, whereas the noncelibate frittered his time in useless amusement. Naturally, Gandhi extended his diatribe to a comparison with eating: The celibate did so to maintain the temple of the spirit, the other to gorge himself and to make the sacred vessel a stinking gutter. Gandhi maintained that the situation only worsens with time.

In his Elmer Gantry-like diatribe, Gandhi swept aside precisely the ground upon which celibate and noncelibate can come to understand and support each other: the ground of mutual respect. Gandhi created a credibility gap with his rigidity on matters of sexuality. He exacerbated negative reactions and rejection of celibacy by his rhetorical dogmatism and intolerance. Many young people reject the spiritual values of the Catholic Church in much the same dynamic as Orwell rejected Gandhi.

Finding the form in which Gandhi declared celibate achievement to be one that excluded and denigrated Orwell's own choices of marriage and human service, Orwell devised an oppositional pattern through which he in turn excluded celibacy *and* religion from his own moral universe as well as from the realm of Eros, both intimate and communal. Orwell felt that love and living, whether sexual or nonsexual, were tasks that demanded hard work and caused pain. He judged that nonattachment was an escape, and he refused to argue the relative value of spiritual versus humanistic ideals. He concluded that they were incompatible. The choice between God and man was settled. Orwell chose man.[14]

This chain of argument, leading from the perception of intolerance and unreality in the religious position on sexuality to hostility toward religion altogether, is much the same as that found in the contemporary reactions of many young people. For them, there is no realistic framework offered by a teaching that labels as sin any sexual activity outside marriage for the developing—or even mature—single person. In their dilemma, many young people reject all religion. Beyond that, they fail to see any connection between rejecting sex and serving humanity, an ideal that is still vibrant for many young people.

It is precisely this link between celibacy and, by extension, spirituality, on the one hand, and an archaic anthropology with its Puritanism and misogyny, on the other, that threatens the continuing relevance of the Catholic Church and religion today. Hope relies on reconciling the Orwells of this world—those who follow their ethical and humanitarian vocation according to noncelibate or secular models—with the Gandhis—those who define their vocation in spiritual and celibate terms. Both can be enhanced by the achievement of the other as each seeks to penetrate and master the common reality that generated and continually nurtures them both: human sexuality.[15]

Only through a shared perception and understanding of that sexuality can the two value-judgmental stances, which share so many humanitarian ideals, reach a position of mutual respect and even communion.

CHAPTER 3

IRISH AMERICAN PRIESTS:
THE ROAD FROM HERO TO HUMAN

Man defending the honor or welfare of his ethnic group is a man
defending himself.

Milton M. Gordon

American Catholicism has been largely fashioned in the image and likeness of
Irish Catholic culture. In 1970, 52 percent of all active priests in the United
States were Irish Americans, 73 percent of all bishops, and five of six archbishops were Irish American at a time when only 17 percent of the Catholic
population was of Irish descent.

Even though the twenty-first century Irish and U.S. Catholic Churches
have experienced an unprecedented rupture of their indigenous clergy population and an influx of priests from a mixture of foreign countries—India,
Africa, China, Vietnam, South America, and Poland among them—the structure of the Catholic Church in the United States remains branded with the
stamp of Ireland. It is remarkable, but not surprising, how Catholicism in
both countries has been similarly devastated by the clergy sex abuse crisis
between 1995 and 2007.

The image of the priest and the presumption of celibacy, or the doubt of it,
are intimately interwoven in public consciousness. In the twentieth-century
United States, we note here five of those Irish American priests who cast
radiance and shadows that created images far beyond their own persons.

Father Francis P. Duffy, a New York clergyman, volunteered in the U.S.
Army as a chaplain during World War I. His consistent self-sacrifice and
indifference to risking his life ministering to the men of his Irish American

unit, the Fighting 69th, gained him their unswerving devotion and, in time, nationwide fame. A statue of him stands in Duffy Square, just north of Times Square in New York City. His example proclaimed that Catholic priests could indeed be patriotic Americans.

Youth groups called the Fighting Sixty-Niners were organized to honor him in grade schools across the country up until the 1960s. The members dedicated themselves to "heroic purity"—sexual abstinence—using the sixth and ninth as monikers for the two commandments that forbid sexual activity. This movement did not prevail in that form past the sexual revolution of the 1970s, one that gave a very different interpretation to the term *sixty-nine.*

After he founded Boys Town in Nebraska in 1917, Father Edward Flanagan won worldwide fame, admiration across all religious divides, and immense financial support for his work with homeless and wayward boys. His statement, "There is no such thing as a bad boy," became a mantra for generations of youth workers.

The incident of a young boy loaded down with another youngster on his shoulders appearing at the door of Boys Town on a snowy night has been commemorated in bronze. The saying inscribed at the base of a statue on the campus of Boys Town, "He ain't heavy, Father. He's my brother," worked its way into U.S. folklore and even popular music. Father Flanagan reached the acme of popular attention when Spencer Tracy portrayed him in the 1938 movie *Boys Town.*

The actor Pat O'Brien brought Father Duffy to similar fame in the successful 1939 movie *The Fighting 69th.* Father Duffy's statue still stands, and Father Flanagan's Boys Town continues its work into the twenty-first century.

Three other U.S. priests have achieved the status of media stardom on their own. In the 1930s, the Reverend Charles Coughlin used his mellifluous voice, a voice made for promises, to attract an audience of 40 million enthralled listeners to his radio broadcasts. He was a priest who would be heard.

In the 1950s, Reverend-Monsignor-Bishop Fulton J. Sheen provided his viewers with a vision of priestly glamour, enabling him to outdraw Hollywood stars in the television ratings. His penetrating blue eyes have been rivaled only by the likes of Paul Newman. He was a priest who would be seen.

In the 1980s and 1990s, Father Andrew M. Greeley, the priest-novelist, created a unique amalgam of sex and mystery informed by Catholic concerns, ensuring his books a consistent place on the bestseller lists. He was a priest who would be read.

Although their messages have been very different, there is no doubt that all of these priests have had a considerable impact on the idea that priest equals celibacy. They sold the image not merely by what they said but by who they were. Some of their efforts extended from the Catholic Church to U.S. society at large.

Father Coughlin made Americans aware that the Catholic Church indeed had a position on social issues. Bishop Sheen did much to legitimize the church intellectually in the popular mind during a time of widespread scientism. And Father Greeley opened a discussion of sexuality and celibacy as well as the nature and limits of church authority.

These very public priests reinforced the unexamined equation. Although the public unquestioningly presumed celibacy, in a very real sense, all of these priests gave their followers permission to refine their understanding of *priest* and eventually opened the way for a more informed discussion of clerical humanity: sex and celibacy.

Father Duffy impressed the public that priests can be heroes and men like any other soldier. When heroics are exposed, questions about the shadow side also arise because not all priests match the standard set by the champion. Heroes in a group raise the question of the possibility of antiheroes, too.

Father Flanagan gave the priest a human heart, even though it was supersize. His example raised the specter of human and tender relationships even beyond pastoral obligation. Bit by bit, the human side of priests was unveiled. The sexual abuse of minors, especially boys, stands in stark and shocking contrast to the example of Flanagan.

Father Coughlin sanctioned the labor movement generally and legitimized social activism by clergy, extending democratic dimension to the priesthood. Bishop Sheen permitted intellectual inquiry into basic religious concerns; he encouraged rational exploration of religious issues. Father Greeley encouraged Catholics to imagine erotically. Each of these Irish American priests has had a remarkable influence on the development of the twentieth-century U.S. image of priests, celibacy, and the Roman Catholic Church.

A reflection on the life work of three U.S. priests—Charles E. Coughlin, Fulton J. Sheen, and Andrew M. Greeley—and making a critical analysis of the autobiographical accounts of Sheen and Greeley have helped exploration of the reality of religious celibacy and the understanding of the system of which it is a part.

Although the tradition of religious celibacy is long, the list of autobiographical accounts is short indeed. Many revere Jesus Christ as a lifelong celibate, yet there is no scriptural evidence to disclose whether this was so. The astounding popularity of Dan Brown's *The Da Vinci Code* feeds on a deep and unarticulated doubt about Jesus's celibacy. That doubt is ancient but consistently discounted by dominant Catholic power and tradition. Perhaps there is divine wisdom in Scripture's silence on Christ's sexual/celibate integration. Saint Augustine, for all of the limitations of his times and understandings of sexuality, remains a giant in his witness to celibate integration. It would be unfair to expect contemporaries to meet his candor and theological witness.

Each of our contemporary autobiographical apostles of celibacy—Gandhi, Sheen, and Greeley—is admirable for offering his testimony, necessarily limited by his own personality and circumstances. Each has something valuable to teach about human sexuality and its varied expressions. Who can claim to have arrived at the full expression of celibate achievement and integration and at the same time have the talent to commit it to literary form? All witnesses to celibacy, almost of necessity, must be guilty of a few foibles that suggest some conflict along the road to the perfect and perpetual continence demanded by canon law for inclusion into the priestly caste.

Sheen avoids a radically honest self-analysis, and he projects an intolerance and superiority common in moral leaders. Greeley seems inadvertently self-revelatory in his ogling of women and teasing of his readers, which cover a deficiency, an intolerance verging on scapegoating. Even Gandhi, whose honesty and service to humanity outshone both Sheen's and Greeley's, nonetheless fostered intolerance for the lustful and manifested a lack of equal respect for women. Yet all three persisted in the pursuit of their ideal.

Perhaps this failure by all three to demonstrate complete integration— a radical honesty, humility, tolerance, and a sense of the oneness of all humanity—is the result of the public nature of both their witness and their vocation, the demands of their positions of power. Perhaps celibacy can be achieved fully only beyond the sphere of mass culture; perhaps it can find its testimony only in the most intimate of dialogues and writings. Such a conclusion would diminish the hope that such testimony will become widely available for the would-be celibate or the noncelibate who values the practice. For this reason, the genre of the novel could be the most likely vehicle of expression for an experience that is at once so intimate and yet of such deep religious significance.

The reality of celibacy, with all of its powerful contributions to culture as well as its aberrations and perversions, is a neglected area of the study of human sexuality. It is a far more vital area of life and culture than most people think. Our goal is to contribute to a deeper understanding of celibacy and to foster the development of a more adequate vocabulary for discourse.

Dialogue is essential because within every great institution reside the seeds of its own destruction. For the Catholic Church, the danger of potential demise is rooted with its power wedded to nonsex. The time bomb that has been ticking for centuries is religion's unresolved issues of human sexuality and religious celibacy.

Years of exploration have convinced me that celibacy is not just an incidental facet of Catholicism. Celibacy's image—its face—is not just another face in the crowd. Like the face of Helen that launched a thousand ships, celibacy has inspired men to heroic deeds in the name of love, and it has been capable of violent repression and destruction of human lives. It still has the capacity to inspire saints to selfless service. Celibate failure and hypocrisy, as in the past, still have the potential to ignite revolutions and reformations.

The reformation that is currently upon the Catholic Church owes its energy and driving force to the failure of the sexual/celibate system of the Roman Catholic Church—epitomized by priests and bishops who sexually abuse minors—and its inability to convince lay people that it has anything meaningful to say about their sexual lives. Celibacy's faithful portrait is painted in literature and its history written boldly in the lives of priests. Let us explore.

CHAPTER 4

THE RADIO PRIEST:
CHARLES E. COUGHLIN

The representation of defilement dwells in the half-light of a quasi-physical infection that points toward a quasi-moral unworthiness.

Paul Ricoeur

In 1930, Father Charles Edward Coughlin was the voice of the Catholic Church for many U.S. families. Father Andrew Greeley records a warm memory from his childhood home: Sunday dinners, with his family eating pot roast and noodles and listening to Father Charles Coughlin or Monsignor Fulton Sheen on the radio. He could not have imagined at that moment that someday he would join them as a star whose name would be widely recognized and whose ideas would be discussed around many U.S. dinner tables.

In truth, Coughlin was not a personal champion of celibacy—his practice has been severely compromised by history—but that made no difference in his public portrayal and reception. He was a priest. In the mind of his public, he had to be celibate.

Father Coughlin's fame was real in the 1930s; his tarnished reputation endures. His message of social justice and his legacy of organizing labor have been mixed with defilement. His celibate practice was imperfect. Unlike Sheen and Greeley, who both have written about celibacy in their autobiographies, traces of Coughlin's sexual/celibate adjustment have been pieced together from his school history, court records, and, most prominently, from the files of the Federal Bureau of Investigation (FBI) along with observations from his friend and parishioner, psychoanalyst Leo H. Bartemeier.

THE TIMES

In 1928, there were few, if any, prominent voices urging social justice or seeking vital social reforms. The novels of Upton Sinclair and Jack London, which had previously popularized the struggles of the poor, were replaced by writers who preached the doctrine that business should be left alone by government so that the forces of the market could work.[1]

Robert Hutchins, president of the University of Chicago, summarized the political consensus of the day in words that sound eerily timely in the early twenty-first century:

> The budget must be balanced annually, whatever the cost to the economy; the gold standard was sacred and must be preserved at all costs; socialism was the nation's greatest menace, and "free enterprise," if left alone, would provide jobs for everyone.... And finally, of course, business should run the country.[2]

The loudest voices in the 1920s belonged to advertising, public relations, and boosterism. Successful writers such as Ernest Elmo Calkins proclaimed that business was the world's greatest benefactor, and columnist Walter Lippmann agreed:

> [T]he more or less unconscious and unplanned activities of businessmen are for once more novel, more daring, and in a sense more revolutionary than the theories of the progressives.[3]

A Horatio Alger mentality prevailed, in which the businessman emerged as the hero of the age; the mood of the times stressed individualism. Collective bargaining was relegated to the trash bin; it was simply un-American. The outlook of the working class was that a man got ahead by himself and not by joining unions.[4]

Frederick Lewis Allen described the atmosphere in which chauffeurs, valets, nurses, cattlemen, grocers, motormen, plumbers, seamstresses, and speakeasy waiters were playing the stock market and listening to radios to follow their investments. When workers owned shares of stock, they preferred to think of themselves as businessmen.[5]

Realist novelists John Dos Passos and James T. Farrell wrote about ordinary people, plasterers, painters, and mechanics, dabbling in the stock market and quoting pamphleteers on salesmanship and positive thinking. As long as the prosperity of the 1920s held, the lack of a voice for workers and social justice was not felt keenly.[6]

After the stock market crashed on October 23, 1929, the attitude and atmosphere in the United States changed dramatically. The ordinary people who had bought shares of stock on margin were sold out, and so were those who had banked their money. The Bank of the United States, for example, which catered to poor immigrants, engaged in speculation; when the market collapsed, the bank officers passed their losses on to the depositors. The bank folded in the middle of the night on December 11, 1930.

Moreover, between 1929 and 1932, almost six thousand other banks closed, costing mostly working- or middle-class depositors almost $3 billion. Retail sales fell, merchants went bankrupt, and sales and production workers were laid off in increasing numbers. One insurance company reported that 23.8 percent of its policyholders in 46 large cities were unemployed in December 1930. Even though 76.2 percent of workers remained employed, the spectacle of 1 million people riding the rods and living in so-called Hoovervilles caused deep anxiety in a people who had expected prosperity to be a permanent part of their lives. Even in 1938, more than 10 million people nationwide, or 19 percent of the population, were still unemployed.[7]

Such were the times and the circumstances in which Father Coughlin was to raise his voice.

THE MAN

Charles Coughlin was born on October 25, 1891 in Hamilton, Ontario, Canada, the son of a third-generation Irish American family that had originally settled in Indiana. When Charles was a child, his father, Thomas, worked as a sexton at Saint Mary's Cathedral. His mother, Amelia Mahoney, had herself dreamed of becoming a nun; she dedicated her son to the priesthood even before his birth. Charles grew up literally breathing the atmosphere of the Catholic Church. Coughlin seems to have chosen the priesthood as a career early in life, and, like Greeley, he never looked back.

Amelia first dressed her son in girls' clothes and allowed his hair to grow in long curls; she even sent him to his first day of school in a kilt. Whatever the mother's motivation in cross-gender dressing (Ernest Hemingway was subjected to similar treatment), it did little to curb the young Coughlin's natural aggression. There are accounts of him roughhousing with his friends, yelling loudly, and ripping his clothes in minor scuffles in the streets. Distinct from Sheen or Greeley, Coughlin was a natural athlete; his aggression found an outlet in rugged sports: rugby, football, and baseball.[8]

After grammar school at Saint Mary's, Coughlin attended Saint Michael's College in Toronto. Saint Michael's was a minor seminary—a boarding high school—that prepared students for the priesthood. Like Greeley and Sheen, Coughlin proved himself to be an outstanding student; he studied public speaking and, like Sheen, excelled on the debate team. He capped his high school career as president of his class and starting fullback on the varsity rugby team.

After graduation, Coughlin enrolled in Saint Basil's Seminary. Priests of the order of Saint Basil the Great (known for scholarship) conducted Saint Michael's and Saint Basil's. Coughlin joined this religious group and was ordained a priest on June 29, 1916. After ordination until 1923, he taught English, history, Greek, and he coached football and drama at Assumption College near Windsor, Ontario.

Although Coughlin continued his excellent academic performance during his theological studies, his training with the Basilians had been interrupted by a brief and unexplained exile for a year to one of the order's high schools in Waco, Texas, where he taught philosophy and coached baseball. Another piece of the mystery in Coughlin's career was that his relationship with the Basilians was completely severed in 1923 when he joined the Archdiocese of Detroit.

As a diocesan priest, Coughlin served as assistant to pastors, first in Kalamazoo and later in downtown Detroit. He was appointed pastor of the small farming community of North Branch, where he served for only six months. In 1926, he was assigned to Royal Oak, Michigan. At the time, Royal Oak was a small and poor suburb of Detroit. Few parishioners and limited financial support coexisted with an additional obstacle to the development of a new Catholic parish: The resurgent Ku Klux Klan, with its nativist and anti-Catholic agenda, had an active chapter in the neighborhood.

Nevertheless, one of Coughlin's first acts on his arrival was to build a new church. This new structure, the Shrine of the Little Flower, with a seating capacity of 600, was much too large for the 32 Catholic families in the parish. But Coughlin led his parish to growth and prosperity even in the direst days of the Great Depression. He not only filled the pews and paid for his first church, he also built a larger, architecturally notable round church with the altar situated in the center. Coughlin remained in Royal Oak for 53 years until his death on October 27, 1979.

All of this would constitute an unremarkable biography of a suburban parish priest were it not for the extraordinary power, influence, and, ultimately, notoriety Coughlin achieved on the national scene by way of his radio ministry.

THE RADIO PRIEST

On October 17, 1926, Coughlin began a Sunday afternoon radio broadcast, *The Golden Hour of the Little Flower*, apparently to help finance his new parish, and he reaped almost immediate results. Even in the first weeks after his broadcasts began, people started to flock to his parish masses; mail was sent to him in the first years by the hundreds and, increasingly, by the thousands each week. Most of the letters contained small contributions.[9] By 1930, he had begun broadcasting nationwide over the CBS network. His reputation spread, the mail sacks multiplied, and the contributions kept coming in.

Part of the key to Coughlin's radio success was his voice. It was a deep voice that he could modulate into higher registers for effect. Coughlin would frequently manipulate his trace of an Irish brogue to add intimacy, warmth, and color. Andrew Greeley often employed a parallel technique in his later writings.

Frank Sheed who listened regularly to Coughlin described "a voice of such mellow richness, such manly, heart-warming, confidential intimacy, such emotional and integrating charm, that anyone tuning past it on the radio dial almost automatically turned back to hear it again... without doubt one of the great speaking voices of the twentieth century.... It was a voice made for promises."[10]

This voice could be heard regularly on radios throughout most or all the nation from 1926 until the end of 1940. His message, however, in the decade of the 1930s transmogrified from that of a kindly pastor expounding religious or biblical themes, often intended for children, into that of a shrill anti-Semitic demagogue and Nazi sympathizer. Although even his early broadcasts took an occasional shot at the Ku Klux Klan or at the perpetual enemies of Catholic sexual teaching—the proponents of birth control and abortion—Coughlin's voice was pastoral, nonpolitical, and noncontroversial.

All that would change with his January 12, 1930, broadcast, a stinging denunciation of Communism.[11] From this time on, the topics of his programs took a social and political direction.

What were the reasons for the shift? By this time, Coughlin had achieved acceptance, even wide popularity, and a degree of financial success. His mailbox parish drew comments and support from all parts of the country. People shared their plight, and he listened. Men in important positions in the church and business—for example, his superior Bishop Gallagher and Henry Ford—began to pay court and listen to the new media celebrity.

It would be unfair to assume that at this stage of his career, vanity alone emboldened Coughlin to speak out on political and economic issues. He had some genuine concerns for the weakened and vulnerable position of ordinary workers, an understanding of social encyclicals and Catholic teaching on the rights of the working class, the disposition of an activist, and now he had the power base.

In 1930, Coughlin knew that a large segment of the U.S. public was disenchanted with the language of business, deprived of the language of trade unionism, and unwilling to adopt the language of Communism. He was determined to speak for them in language everyone could understand; he would lend them his voice. Eventually, some 40 million Americans would listen.[12]

Although Coughlin's political message was vague at first, and his focus was initially blurred, he did zero in on the temper of the times. He preached that the real reason for concern was not the failure of business confidence but human suffering: the suffering of his listeners' unemployment, deprivation, and dispossession.

The Depression was not just a slump in the market, "but a problem deeply rooted in the economic system." He hinted that the solution "lay in a concerted effort to redefine the structure and goals of American society at home."[13] In his early political broadcasts, he lamented the economic condition of the country—millions of homes in the United States without adequate water, plumbing, electricity, and heat—but he did not propose an alternative.

Even in his exploratory attempts to help his audience find some understanding of their dilemmas and to define solutions for them, Coughlin generated emotion against an ever-widening circle of enemies. Communists—of the Bolshevik, intellectual, Jewish variety—were a frequent early target. The Left spoke for the most hopeless in the United States, for displaced Okies and black people, for immigrants and the starving. The Communist Party in particular proved tremendously attractive, not only to these classes but also to many artists and intellectuals. An editorial in *The New Republic* said that the Communist Party:

> Can offer an end to the desperate feeling of solitude and uniqueness that has been oppressing artists for the last two centuries, the feeling that has reduced some of the best of them to silence and futility and the weaker ones to insanity or suicide. It can offer instead a sense of comradeship and participation in an historical process vastly larger than the individual.[14]

BEYOND PASTORAL CONCERN

Coughlin's attacks on Bolshevism were political and economic, in contrast to Sheen's attacks on Cold War Communism that the latter saw as a spiritual enemy of freedom. Both garnered popular support from their sympathizers. The greatest numbers of anxious employed were terrified of Communism, which they associated with the violent overthrow of the government to be followed by the confiscation of private property, so-called race mixing, atheism, free love, and the destruction of the family.

Birth control was a consistent object of Coughlin's attacks, but because there were few effective methods in the 1930s, that subject was tolerated as appropriately Catholic, and it did not raise great controversy.

Negative reactions and controversy erupted immediately when Coughlin began to attack the power system: bankers, businessmen, international financiers, and U.S. capitalism generally. He blamed the economic power brokers for the social plight of the poor. Wall Street was the villain.

To help his listeners organize the contradictory and fragmented data that swirled around them, Coughlin constructed a narrative to make sense of their world. World War I served Coughlin as a convenient end point. That traumatic experience saw millions of Americans under arms for the first time in fifty years—more than 100,000 of them died and 200,000 wounded, gassed, or shell-shocked. Moreover, the war stimulated enormous changes in society, including the overproduction of goods, the change in the status of women, and the place of racial minorities in the workforce. Coughlin's choice of World War I as a starting point for the economic troubles of the 1930s thus made good rhetorical sense.

With moral indignation, Coughlin broadened the scope of his inquiry into the causes of the Depression to include the underlying conditions of class division and distribution of wealth. Coughlin was able to steal some of the Communists' thunder by first citing—and then denying—the reality of government overproduction to supply goods for Europe's war as a cause of U.S. unemployment. His references to Wall Street bankers and foreign interests are clear harbingers of the scapegoating that would soon poison his voice.

He proposed a corporatist economic program in which social classes are maintained, including a proprietary class, but in which everyone is guaranteed a slice of the pie. Coughlin attempted to satisfy both sides: the capitalists, by guaranteeing a right of ownership, and the workers, by guaranteeing public control over wages, working conditions, and benefits. Coughlin's words thus offered something to everyone at a minimal cost.

Although Coughlin's political economy was deficient, his demagoguery was masterful. Without a doubt, Coughlin was having a political impact. He was an important factor in the first presidential election of Franklin D. Roosevelt (FDR) and in rallying support for the New Deal. He was a principal in the formation of the United Auto Workers and influential in recruiting their membership. He taught and propagated the significant Catholic social teaching on justice, property, and the rights of workers, promulgated in the encyclicals of Popes Leo XIII *(Rerum Novarum)* and Pius XI *(Quadragesimo Anno)*. Coughlin was not just a parish pastor, he was a priest and social activist, and he was a star.

By 1934, Coughlin was a power broker. He had been a house guest at Campobello, Roosevelt's family home, before the presidential election; received a personal invitation to FDR's inauguration; could attract as many as twenty thousand people to a rally at New York's Hippodrome; and inspired his followers to inundate the White House with letters. Coughlin also took credit for the heavy turnout in urban Catholic areas in the November 1932 elections. Ten U.S. senators and 75 congressmen petitioned Roosevelt to appoint Coughlin an advisor to an economic conference in London.[15]

But Coughlin was not happy with the reforms of the political system. He was disappointed and angry at what he considered a personal betrayal and a series of rebuffs from FDR.

Coughlin's attacks on his so-called enemies became more frequent, direct, and shrill. His violence always tended to be directed against certain well-defined groups: Communists, the Ku Klux Klan, African Americans, bankers and financiers, the British government, the Roosevelt administration, and—especially—the Jews.

Coughlin's choice of these groups appears puzzling at first glance: He attacked both the Klan and African Americans, both financiers and Communists. And Jews included, in the 1930s, both Lord Rothschild and Leon Trotsky. Coughlin's social and economic program cannot be defended as the work of some kind of radical moderate, steering a middle course between rapacious bankers and wild-eyed Bolsheviks, between vicious Klansmen and "pushy" Negroes. Fascism is not a middle ground between capitalism and Communism, between race hatred and race mixing. Coughlin was not walking a middle ground between extremes. His star was out of orbit.

SOCIAL ORGANIZER

On November 11, 1934, Coughlin proposed the formation of the National Union for Social Justice. This date not only marked a definitive break with FDR and the New Deal, it was also a bid for greater power and a voice of command. This new phase ushered in an escalation of anti-Semitic attacks and mobilized the formation of a third party to post a presidential candidate in the 1936 election. Coughlin blatantly endorsed pro-Nazi propaganda, even plagiarizing speeches of Joseph Goebbels.

Coughlin's mellow voice became increasingly more strident in its political criticism and demands for its own brand of economic reforms. His National Union began to publish a journal, *Social Justice*, which was circulated until 1942. It would expand his sphere of pronouncements beyond the radio. The movement and the journal expounded his theories and organized cells to discuss social issues and promote activism. Coughlin's voice still had power, but it was becoming more disaffecting and less winning.[16]

Coughlin's tone turned bitter as his persona transformed from presidential advisor and New Deal promoter to demagogue. Coughlin's support and followers decreased in proportion to his exaggerated attacks and criticisms of the president. The caliber and quality of Coughlin's supporters also shifted dramatically from his first distressed but hopeful radio audience. They now became a rabble.

In mid-1938, *Social Justice* announced the formation of the Christian Front, which amounted to groups of followers who held chapter meetings, drank late into the night, praised Coughlin, berated the English, cursed the Jews, and ridiculed FDR.[17] The head of the Anti-Defamation League reported that many Jewish people were beaten by Christian Front members who screamed that they were "Father Coughlin's Brownshirts."[18] There is no doubt that Coughlin provided the ideological and inspirational foundation for the Christian Front, even though an FBI investigation into a 1940 armed conspiracy attempt by a New York chapter could not prove his direct involvement.

Protected by his priesthood, Coughlin could play it both ways. He could orchestrate mass demonstrations without appearing to have actual responsibility for any hateful outcome. A vignette from a Farrell novel serves as a more accurate description of his modus operandi than does any journalistic account. The scene is a rally; the priest speaks:

> "*They* didn't do the pick and shovel work to make America what it is today. Oh, no, not *they!*" The speaker gets an audience reaction. As his sarcastic tone increases, the audience becomes more attentive, and the speaker continues, "It was the Christian who did the pick and shovel work to build America!" the speaker yells, accompanying his words with flourishing gestures. The audience roars in agreement. As the applause dies down, a stout woman with a pudgy face cries out, "Name them!"
>
> "My fellow Christians, I don't have to name *them*," the speaker replies, smiling unctuously. A lean woman, whose face is beginning to crack with wrinkles, jumps to her feet. "I'll name them!" She shrieks in a shrill, high-pitched voice. "I'll name them! The dirty *Jews!*"[19]

The fiction of James T. Farrell also offers an enlightening contrast between Coughlin's early followers and his later ones. Thinly disguised as "Father Moylan," Coughlin is the subject of a street-corner discussion by the sons of Chicago's middle class in 1930. They conclude, "There's a man for you. Boy, what Father Moylan doesn't say about bankers, and the Reds, too."[20]

In a later work, *Tommy Gallagher's Crusade*, Father Moylan's xenophobic and anti-Semitic diatribes no longer interest ordinary well-adjusted youth. Only guys like Tommy, the maladjusted loner, chronically unemployed, a heavy drinker, and harboring hate for Jews and an admiration for Hitler, respond to Moylan's message. Farrell's fiction shows—with a power and precision that escape historical description—how Coughlin's changing persona first attracted, then alienated, the disaffected U.S. middle class and how at last Coughlin claimed only the weakest and most desperate.[21] The fictional portrait of the priest turns out to be more revealing and accurate than the priest in real life.

Fanatics had now replaced many of Coughlin's respectable followers. One by one, radio stations dropped Coughlin, and by the end of 1940 he found himself "with virtually no access to the air."[22] In spring 1942, the postmaster general refused to allow *Social Justice* to be mailed; even Coughlin's printed voice was silenced. At the same time, the attorney general of United States warned the archbishop of Detroit that Coughlin would face formal charges of sedition if his activities did not cease.[23]

For 30 years, from 1942 until 1972, Coughlin's voice was confined to the pulpit of his parish church. In Coughlin's career and his silence there are mysteries about his priesthood, his personality, and his celibacy that give important clues to understanding priests, sex, and celibacy in both literature and life.

FASCINATING MYSTERY

Father Andrew Greeley claims that priests are among the most fascinating men in the world and that it is their celibacy that makes them so. There are, however, other elements that add mystery and interest to the priest: one is his relationship to his church, his power vis-à-vis a veritable leviathan.

The priest is an organization man even more fully than any corporate executive or military officer. Theologically, he is another Christ; his commission is eternal. He holds the authority to forgive sins. There is a party line he is expected to support. All of this and more are under the direction and control of ecclesiastical authority.

When popes or bishops censure, silence, or discipline priests, the full weight of church control comes into public view. There are, however, multiple layers of power, intrigue, and ambiguity within the hierarchical system. This is the atmosphere in which the priest who is a star maneuvers. What mysterious, fascinating elements of power does a priest who has star status wield within the church system?

His religious superiors, even though many bishops, arguably most, were not antibusiness, anti-Semitic, pro-Nazi, or Fascist, never successfully curtailed Coughlin's mission and message. Of course, those elements were not the sum and substance of Coughlin's teaching. He did promote social justice and workers' rights. There was enough ambiguity and support of Catholic teaching in his message and sufficient support of his thinking in high places to save him from official censure.

Coughlin did receive criticism for his political involvement. After his first mutterings in 1930, William Cardinal O'Connell of Boston openly objected, but his opposition was to a priest speaking about politics at all rather than a rejection of specific ideas.

His Detroit superior until 1937, Bishop Michael Gallagher generally protected Coughlin in spite of controversy. Edward Mooney, who took over the reigns as archbishop of Detroit in 1937, soon after he arrived made repeated efforts to silence Coughlin. That autumn, when Coughlin attacked the Congress of Industrial Organizations (CIO) for supposed Communism and anti-Christianity, Mooney rebuked him. Coughlin knew that Mooney wished to censor his broadcasts; Coughlin's response was to cancel his radio program and appeal to the pope's personal representative in the United States, the apostolic delegate. In January 1938, the broadcasts resumed. Coughlin commented on his victory:

> The Archbishop had overstepped himself. I was more than he could take on. I had lots of friends at the Vatican, people who could not agree with me publicly. But they knew that I spoke the truth. They knew that I recognized the communist threat to the church. Well, they finally reached the Pope,

and when they did, he came to his senses and he saw the righteousness of my ways. So, of course, instructions were sent here to halt any restrictions on my activities.[24]

Coughlin was not merely blasting the establishment, he was popularizing papal teaching on social justice. This action garnered him support from some unexpected quarters, including some church liberals. Father John A. Ryan, who was professor of theology at Catholic University and one of the most prominent and influential Catholic liberals of the time, supported Coughlin to the extent that he "was performing a useful service by bringing the messages of the encyclicals to the masses."[25] And Coughlin got good grades from liberals for promoting labor unions.

Was Coughlin anti-Semitic? Yes, without a doubt. It is also clear that there was enough anti-Semitism within the U.S. church and in Rome during the 1930s to tolerate, and even support, Coughlin's preaching. In 1938, an Irish priest, Denis Fahey, published a book entitled *The Mystical Body of Christ in the Modern World*, which blamed Jews for every secular and liberal reform since the Renaissance.[26] Fahey saw these reforms as negative and destructive. Coughlin's anti-Semitism was at its most vocal when he discovered Fahey's "theology of history." Coughlin was inspired by yet another theologian to justify and reinfuse twentieth-century "scientific anti-Semitism" with long-standing medieval religious prejudice.

Was Coughlin a Fascist? Coughlin's economic program—private ownership, but the means of production rigidly controlled by government—was classically Fascist. He generally praised such avowed Fascists as Franco and Mussolini, and he broadcast and published what can only be described as German propaganda even in the months after Pearl Harbor. Coughlin's anti-Semitism dovetailed with the Nazi program.

Certainly, Coughlin never described himself as Fascist, and he never used the term in connection with the National Union for Social Justice, although he did endorse so-called corporatist economic policies under which everyone gets a piece of the pie but the government does the slicing. At the very least, Coughlin took a leaf from the success of the various Fascist movements, including the vilification of certain groups, including the Jews, to build a U.S. radical political movement that he would control. If Coughlin was not an actual Fascist, he was so close that it makes no difference.[27]

There were in the 1930s, and still are, Fascist regimes that support Roman Catholicism. This support of church interests merits silent acceptance if not outright endorsement in the Vatican. Fascism had been seen as a bulwark against Communism and other enemies of religion and a protector of the church's rights. Coughlin had support where it counted.

Coughlin held in his grasp the three elements of power needed to pave his way successfully through the authoritarian maze of his church—to maintain his voice. He enjoyed a broad-based popularity, even beyond a Catholic constituency. His message was ambiguous enough, no matter how offensive to some churchmen, to draw support at some elevated level of the hierarchy. And, importantly, he had significant and substantial means of independent financial support. In distinct synergies, these were also elements of the power at work in the careers of Sheen and Greeley.

By way of contrast to the hierarchical tolerance for Coughlin, Thomas Merton and Pierre Teilhard were famous priests silenced for periods of time by church superiors. They lacked the same unassailable power matrix of the stars.

COUGHLIN'S SECRET WORLD

Coughlin, like every Roman Catholic priest, was required to make a life-long promise of celibacy before his ordination. Coughlin left no written account of his thoughts on celibacy. Certainly, he never married, but throughout his public career, Coughlin was pursued by rumors of affairs with members of both sexes, and he left a considerable paper trail in his FBI file.

Coughlin biographer Sheldon Marcus cites several well-known accusations against the priest. It had been reported that Father Coughlin, as a young priest, was caught in the act of sodomy with another priest, who was defrocked.[28] The only documentation Marcus could locate was an unsigned, undated memo circulated within the Anti-Defamation League of B'nai B'rith.

Coughlin's mysterious conflicts within the Basilians—the interruption of his theological studies and his unexplained departure from the order—could have been the result of this incident or others like it. Although there is logic and precedent to give plausibility to such conclusions, one must be cautious in reading effect and cause into sexual affairs.

A court document from the income-tax evasion trial of Dr. Bernard Gariepy before a Detroit federal judge in 1949 records testimony that Coughlin paid Dr. Gariepy $68,000 over a three-year period for "taking liberties with Gariepy's wife."[29]

In more than seven hundred pages of FBI files that we obtained under the Freedom of Information Act, there are several references to Coughlin's sexual indiscretions. One tantalizing file is an unsigned typewritten note date-stamped October 12, 1937. The principal subject of this note is the questionable loyalty of composer Cole Porter and his valet. The note claimed that they listened to German propaganda every day at the Waldorf-Astoria in New York. But the last paragraph cites Coughlin: "How come that Father Coughlin, a Catholic priest, wears civilian clothes when he is in New York, and registers at a hotel under the name of Smith. And what parties—wine, women, and...."[30]

When the FBI anonymous informant wrote "wine, women, and…," it is clear that his ellipses referred not to "song" but to homosexual encounters.[31] The reports put Coughlin in the social company of the homosexual elite: Cole Porter, W. Somerset Maugham, and Noël Coward.[32]

Moreover, Coughlin did in fact sometimes travel under assumed names; in 1937, he journeyed incognito to England and Europe. A letter from the assistant executive officer of military intelligence to FBI Director J. Edgar Hoover reports that Coughlin visited Jackson, Mississippi, under the name "Eddie Burke."[33]

After 1942, all of the FBI entries about Coughlin concentrate on his sexual life. A memorandum dated April 15, 1942, from J. Edgar Hoover to Clyde Tolson, his assistant and close friend, cites a confidential source: "Father Coughlin at the present time was being treated by a reputable Detroit psychiatrist for certain sexual difficulties. It was also stated that Father Coughlin had in his employ a maid or a secretary with whom Father Coughlin had had relations, and who was also being treated by the same psychiatrist."[34]

J. Edgar Hoover conveyed the same information to the attorney general in a memorandum dated April 20, 1942. High-level memoranda flew in all directions. One operative reported to Hoover: "[A] confidential source [name deleted] told me that Father Coughlin was known to be a man of very unsavory repute; Reverend [name deleted]…had investigated Coughlin;…has proof that Father Coughlin has a mistress.…It is [source's] understanding that Reverend [name deleted] presented his evidence to some of the leaders of the church but that no action was taken."[35]

The FBI went to a great deal of trouble to probe these allegations. They conducted interviews in Toledo and Cleveland, Ohio; Washington, DC; and Boston. Obviously, the FBI and the Office of the Attorney General considered the source of the information credible enough to give him at least three extended interviews.

Can one guarantee the trustworthiness of anonymous and secret letters and FBI files? Hoover was out to curtail Coughlin's activity. It is clear that Hoover and some of his top aides took pains to investigate Coughlin, and they wrote reports clearly reflecting some knowledge of the goings-on in the Waldorf-Astoria and of Coughlin's penchant for traveling in disguise.

The "reputable psychiatrist" referred to in a number of the FBI reports was Dr. Leo H. Bartemeier. He and his wife were among the charter members of Coughlin's Oak Park parish. Even in the days before 1930, Bess Bartemeier often cooked for Coughlin to help the priest and his struggling new parish. In later years, Coughlin was a frequent guest at the Bartemeier table.

After Coughlin's death, Bartemeier revealed the key to Coughlin's thirty-year silence. It was not the threat of lawsuits by the U.S. attorney general, which were real but not daunting to Coughlin; he bragged he had better lawyers. Nor was it sudden obedience to his bishop, whom he had successfully defied for several years. That cover story was circulated in May 1942 by church authorities to explain Coughlin's retreat from public view.

Coughlin felt the effects of a voice more powerful than his own magnificent one. It was a voice that silenced Coughlin's in any public forum, on any subject, and shackled him to his parish pulpit as long as that voice survived. It was that of J. Edgar Hoover, who delivered a personal threat to Coughlin by phone on a February 1942 Sunday morning after Mass, at the same time trucks from the Office of the Attorney General were being loaded with files of *Social Justice* and all of Coughlin's other operations for transport to Washington, DC.

Coughlin rushed in a panic to the Bartemeier home to confer with his longtime friend at a juncture he felt was the greatest crisis of his life. Hoover had proof of Coughlin's homosexual activity. That proof, communicated in the verbal exchange between Hoover and Coughlin, was sufficient to silence Coughlin's public voice until May 24, 1972, when he gave his first unrestricted interview to *Heritage* magazine. J. Edgar Hoover had died just three weeks earlier, on May 2, 1972.[36]

COUGHLIN'S TRAGEDY

In another dimension, could one imagine Coughlin being cured of his violence and anti-Semitism by the sainted Sheen's reason? Or could one imagine that Greeley, the popular paperback writer, could transform Coughlin's life into a comedy of grace? Or is the irony of the mellifluous voice being silenced by the whisper of government blackmail too overpowering to be transformed into anything but tragedy?

This perspective is troublesome, but instructive. Tragedy is a Greek dramatic form. The place of the gods varies from portrayal to portrayal, but necessity and fate operate at the same time as man remains responsible for his acts of hubris. There is apattern: *korus*—a feeling of self-satisfaction—leads to *hubris*—an arrogant act—followed by *Ate* (the Greek personifiction of infatuation). Destruction results from the hero's embrace of *Ate*; he abandons reason for the "rash foolishness of blind impulse."

The priest-as-Prometheus imagery does have a certain delicious irony. Catholic tradition on the one hand—with its emphasis on grace and redemption—contrasts with the Faustian career of the Reverend Charles Edward Coughlin on the other. To understand, we must move temporarily from the language of religion, which emphasizes sin and salvation, to the language of behavioral science, which emphasizes causes and conditions.

The story of Coughlin resembles a Greek tragedy. Coughlin, the young, heroic voice, is blinded by his ambition and challenging forces greater than himself, only to end up out of control, pursued as a criminal, is isolated, and is finally silenced.[37] Beyond mere ambition, however, Coughlin's rise and fall depended on his historical circumstances, on his personal abilities and education, on his clerical status, and on his psychological makeup.

The importance of Coughlin's historical setting is clear. Had he been born forty years earlier, before the radio, before the Great Depression, and before the rise of modern Fascism, he might have become a clerical William Jennings Bryan, a gifted orator in the populist cause with a religious dimension. Forty years later, after the end of the Cold War, in a time when discourse defines itself as postmodern, he might have become a clerical Ross Perot, attracting millions of disaffected Americans. In neither case would his ministry have electrified, so to speak, such a substantial part of the U.S. public at a time of national emergency.

Coughlin's personal abilities and education also played a part in his tragedy. The 1930s produced a flood of angry orators. Many remained ineffective; others were ridiculous. Coughlin's power depended in large part on his beautiful voice and his rhetorical skill, honed by years of preaching, debate, and drama, at a time when radio communication was nearly universal.

Coughlin intuitively sensed the importance of a coherent social theory for a population in turmoil. He had the wisdom to offer a translation of solid religious teaching about workers' rights and social justice for popular consumption. Coughlin's status as a priest was important. He created the image of a strong authority figure, who gave permission to millions of Catholics, schooled in obedience, to question their society and their government, much as Greeley would one day give permission to his readers to question church teaching about sex.

The psychoanalytic quest—like the riddle of Oedipus, with which it is so closely bound—somewhat resembles a detective story. Something is dramatically wrong, whether in the individual's life or in the public life of Thebes. The task of the detective—whether analyst, king, or literary critic—is to discover the underlying cause of the blight. Coughlin is like a tragic figure in that he rose brilliantly but fell just as quickly in his hubris and his blindness, which raises the question: What was Coughlin blind to? The answer is: himself.

THE PERSONALITY OF THE STAR

Coughlin's personality characteristics are vital to his story. He was a man of action: impatient, always harboring a tendency toward aggression and violence. He hungered for attention and acknowledgment. He demonstrated a magical view of money and status; most important, he exhibited a pattern of wooing authority figures and then rejecting them. These impulses inspired Coughlin to strike out for new territory on the airwaves and in politics. Coughlin's situation thus virtually conspired to bring about both his rise and his fall.

Turmoil

A review of Coughlin's public life demonstrates his constantly troubled existence. Coughlin was frequently attacked and attacking, even on a physical level when, for instance, he ripped the glasses off and punched the face of a *Boston Globe* reporter for having the audacity to dispute his preposterous claim that Judge Felix Frankfurter was a Communist.

After a deranged attacker threw chicken feathers over him at a public rally, Coughlin began packing a pistol, "a thirty-eight caliber chrome Smith and Wesson revolver with a white pearl handle which he carried under his clerical garb."[38]

Authority

Coughlin enjoyed and used his clerical status to his own advantage, personally and professionally. Coughlin's relations with his ecclesiastical superiors, however, were far from smooth. At times, he openly defied them; at other times, he simply paid lip service to them and went his own way. Coughlin's obedience to his bishop depended on convenience.

Coughlin admired leaders he perceived to be strong, but there was an excessive and personal quality to his attachment to authority figures. In the case of FDR, Coughlin's overzealous adoption of Roosevelt was followed by an overzealous hatred of equal proportions. Coughlin fell in love, so to speak, with Roosevelt, only to reject him bitterly when Roosevelt did not return his fervor.

Coughlin's attitude toward dictators also betrays his love-hate relationship with authority. One biographer speaks of Coughlin's "admiration for strong, dictatorial rule."[39] Hitler was the "big man" whom Coughlin admired and feared.

Fiction helps us understand the dynamic: Writing of the motives of candidates for MI-5, the British intelligence service, John Le Carré's fictional Smiley notes that he eschews prospects who burn with hatred for Communism because such people are already half in love with the Soviet Union and will likely defect. Even Stalin, like Hitler and Mussolini *and* like Franklin Roosevelt, was for Coughlin one more hated and beloved father figure.

Coughlin's love-hate relationship with authority is key to understanding his attraction to violence—manifested in his tendency to scapegoat particular groups and mark them as targets for violence—and his grandiose thinking. All of these tendencies combined in his psychological underdevelopment and narcissistic attitude toward the world.

Enemies

The conjunction of Coughlin's anti-Semitism with his sadomasochism is very apparent in the way his anti-Semitism developed. At first, Coughlin complained not of Jewish machinations but of the preferential treatment accorded to Jews suffering in Nazi Germany and Fascist Spain while the suffering of Catholics in Republican Spain, Mexico, and the Soviet Union went ignored by the press. This grievance recalls a childish complaint that a parent unfairly prefers another sibling.

By 1936, Coughlin openly began to instigate violence by his followers against Jews. Coughlin pursued his enemies politically and personally and incited others to action.

His contemporary, Fulton Sheen, used his priesthood and power very differently. Sheen considered his opposition as intellectual adversaries and spiritual dangers. People, if informed, could reason and make free choices to improve conditions. The common features of Coughlin's groups of enemies are, first, their distance from or opposition to Coughlin himself and, second, their relative power. Greeley is clearly free and purified from Coughlin's racial and religious biases, but psychologically they share many common characteristics, especially in their treatment of enemies.

Grandiosity

As early as August 1936, according to FBI files, Coughlin was talking about sending an army to overthrow the anticlerical Mexican government. He bragged to a government agent that he could handle any opposition from Roosevelt.[40] Coughlin fantasized about vast wealth and armed might. Again from the FBI file, a letter dated September 10, 1940, notes a speech by Father Coughlin in Dubuque, Iowa, in June of that year, in which he recounts his opportunity to stop Hitler if the government had only listened to him. A news account quotes Coughlin:

> In 1933, March 4, there was an inauguration of a New Deal in the United States. Germany also had a New Deal with the inauguration of Adolf Hitler. There would have been no Adolf Hitler had the Democracies given Bruening [a German political opponent to Hitler] the 30 million dollars he had asked for. Now they can spend 30 billion dollars and Hitler will be their master. There is a page of history for you. I was in Washington on March 4, 1933. Some of Mr. Bruening's friends asked me to please plead with the administration for 30 million dollars from here. I did, and was refused. Hitler would not have risen to power if there had been one single grain of Christian charity in the treasury of the so-called democracies.[41]

In his own mind, Coughlin could authorize money from the United States Treasury as easily as he could command it from Germany.

At an earlier time, Coughlin had bragged that the big man, Hitler, had supported *Social Justice* with substantial contributions. In fact, Germany evidently did contribute money to *Social Justice* but not to the tune of hundreds of thousands of dollars, as Coughlin boasted. Records show that the government could prove payments of only $36 over four years by a German agent—little more than pocket change—in order to remain on Coughlin's mailing list and keep their clipping service current. Coughlin's grandiose boasting and his denial of actual responsibility for real crimes are thus opposite faces of the same coin.

Fantasy and Imagination

If Coughlin's boast of support from Hitler was mere illusion, perhaps encouraged on general principle by the German government, it is nevertheless interesting psychologically. Coughlin refers to Hitler as the "big man," an obvious reference to a childhood fantasy of a father at once terrifying and empowering. His boasts of vast wealth and an enormous armed following are likewise fantasies traceable to a very early period. The project of boasting itself indicates a difficulty of navigating among the real, the imaginary, and the symbolic, a difficulty arising early in the phallic stage of development.

Coughlin was absorbed with rhetoric on the practical levels of fundraising and demagogy, and he never rose to the literary level. Clearly, Coughlin failed to achieve the perspective necessary both to appreciate himself and to see himself in relation to others.

The foundation of Coughlin's stardom rested on a kind of bootstrapping. As a high school Greek teacher, he represented himself as an expert, though he was himself in the process of learning basic elements. His responsibilities undoubtedly encouraged him to remain a step ahead of his charges, and he succeeded. As a young pastor in Royal Oak, Coughlin built a 600-seat church on borrowed money, a church many times too big for his tiny parish, yet he was able not only to fill the church but to replace it with an even bigger one. And as a radio preacher, self-confidence and self-righteousness were quite literally his stock in trade; people listened to him to acquire a sense of power over overwhelming political and economic forces. Coughlin was, like Arthur Miller's Willy Loman, "riding on a shoeshine and a smile."

But on a level deeper than the sales pitch, Coughlin's imagination was rooted in violence and power, and his fascination was expressed in fantasies of military triumph. Such fantasies originate from early sadomasochistic desires. According to Freud, the fantasy of "a child being beaten" represents above all an incestuous wish for the father. A large, powerful father is a common image in Coughlin's discourse, particularly in his adulation of powerful politicians. This imagery contrasts with the status and person of Coughlin's biological father. Coughlin's repeated approaches to authority figures— and his repeated disillusionments—illustrate the incompatibility of childish fantasy with adult reality.

Some words resonate on such a deep level that they actually become violent; the courts have long recognized the reality of so-called fighting words. This continuum of words and actions may have made it difficult for Coughlin actually to distinguish between the fantasies that made him feel good, the words with which he attempted to communicate those fantasies, and their effects in the outside world. Coughlin, in other words, may not have been fully able to differentiate imagination from reality or to control completely his expressions of fantasy.

Narcissism

Coughlin reveals the depth of his narcissism in this comment on his own religious belief:

> Do you know how I would live—if I renounced religion and was illogical enough to disbelieve in a life beyond—in the real life? Why, if I threw away and denounced my faith, I would surround myself with the most adroit high-jackers, learn every trick of the highest banking and stock manipulations, avail myself of the laws under which to hide my own crimes, create a smoke screen to throw into the eyes of men, and—believe me, I would become the world's champion crook. If I didn't believe in religion and a happy beyond, I would get everything for myself that I could lay hands on in this world.[42]

Coughlin actually seems to have committed many of the enormities he catalogs. Sheldon Marcus records his abuse of his church's tax-exempt status to cover profit-making schemes, his speculation in silver and in the stock market, and his personal and political use of funds contributed for the relief of the poor.[43]

Coughlin profited politically from a cynical scapegoating of the Jews, and then he hid from responsibility behind flimsy equivocations. Apparently, he took advantage of his wealth and clerical status to conduct a series of sexual adventures. The surface of Coughlin's quotation tempts the reader to conclude that Coughlin simply did not believe in God.

But, as always, truth extends far below the surface of things. From a theological perspective, Coughlin's statement presents a startling outline. Dostoyevsky's Roskolnikov began from approximately the same theoretical position as Coughlin—with the proposition that if there is no God, then all is permitted—only to find such a philosophy literally unlivable.

Moreover, it is clear that committed atheists and thoroughgoing agnostics can be principled and upstanding people. Indeed, a certain atheistic conscience finds ethical conduct incumbent because it does not recognize a spiritual judge outside the individual.

On a level of common sense, Coughlin's syllogism does not hold up. From a Christian perspective, it is even stranger. Saint Anselm defined God as the greatest thought that the human mind can hold. If that definition is applied to Coughlin's quotation, the greatest thought, and hence God, is equated with the satisfaction of selfish desires. Greed and lust, for Coughlin, exist with or without an afterlife; the function of the afterlife is only to hold these desires in check. Coughlin's narcissism permeates his deepest religious convictions.

Coughlin came to assume, on some level, the ultimate deception of all discourse. The conflict between total mendacity and total truth implies a vitiation of the very opposition of mendacity and truth: There is thus neither lie nor truth but only the power of the voice.

How do the elements of Coughlin's life and work fit together? Which are of personality? Which are of priesthood and which of celibacy and celibate culture? If "priest equals celibacy" were not the accepted mantle of his work, would he have been allowed the same voice?

CHAPTER 5

THE TELEVISION PRIEST: FULTON J. SHEEN

Every theologian ought to be a saint.

Bishop Fulton J. Sheen

Andrew Greeley had a worthy predecessor on the center stage of U.S. popular culture. In the 1950s, the predecessor presented what was described as, "a vision of clerical glamour."[1] His name, though no longer a household word, was Fulton J. Sheen. Like Charles E. Coughlin and Greeley, Sheen was an Irish American priest who soared to ecclesial, financial, and popular success from humble family roots. Sheen sold millions of copies of the 60 books he wrote—only one-third the number of Greeley's titles. His radio broadcast, *The Catholic Hour*, spanned more on-air years than Coughlin's entire career as a radio star. But Sheen's preeminent claim to popularity and fame was by way of prime-time television.

From 1951 until 1957, Sheen's program, *Life Is Worth Living*, was one of the most popular television programs in the United States. What made it remarkable was that Sheen held the attention of 30 million major network viewers in prime time against some of the most popular entertainers of the day: Milton Berle, Gene Autry, Groucho Marx, and Lucille Ball.[2] In 1952, *Newsweek* and *Time* magazine both commented on the phenomenon, estimating that 14 percent of all of the television sets in the United States were tuned in to Sheen's broadcast.[3] That amounted to 2 million sets. By 1955, 5.5 million sets were fixed on Sheen's Thursday night ABC presentation. Sheen's books and videos of his television programs are still available, but they now appeal mostly to a pietistic segment of the Catholic audience rather than the broad spectrum of viewers in the 1950s.

Sheen, like Coughlin before him, reached a wide audience that included even agnostics and atheists; like Greeley after him, he was willing to address his audience on something like common ground instead of speaking to them from an authoritarian position, although that did not stop him from dressing himself in traditional ecclesiastical garb. Sheen's focus on this world of people and their problems rather than on the next world of eternity moved the discourse of U.S. Catholicism in a direction that anticipated the changes featured in the Second Vatican Council (1962–65).

Sheen's television ministry certainly changed the attitudes of millions of Americans about Catholicism and priests. He portrayed the Catholic Church as an institution that deserved toleration because it was accessible and did not need to be feared. He presented an image of priests as educated and reasonable.

THE MAN

Sheen was born on May 8, 1895, in El Paso, Illinois.[4] Perhaps he manifested a touch of characteristic vanity in his name selection. Baptized Peter, he later selected his mother's maiden name, Fulton, as his first name. John was his confirmation name, and he incorporated that initial into his adult identity.

He was educated in local parochial schools, where proved himself a superior student: Saint Mary's grade school, Spalding Institute in Peoria, and Saint Viator College, where he was a champion debater. He spent his first three years of theological studies at Saint Paul Seminary in Minnesota. Although admittedly a brilliant student of theology, some faculty and students judged him "too serious."[5]

Amazingly, one of the major factors that contributed to that impression was the amount of time he spent in the seminary chapel. During those first years, he took a private vow to spend one hour each day before the Blessed Sacrament.[6] It was a promise he kept until his death. But while in seminary, he did develop a stomach ulcer, left Saint Paul, and, after a period of recuperation, completed his theological studies in Philadelphia.

Sheen was ordained a priest for the diocese of Peoria, Illinois, on September 20, 1919. He took further studies in philosophy at the Catholic University in Louvain, Belgium, where he earned his PhD in 1923. Two years later, he was awarded the highest scholastic distinction the university could confer.

After serving one year as an assistant pastor in Saint Patrick's Church in Peoria, Father Sheen began to teach philosophy at the Catholic University of America in Washington, DC. He remained a popular professor there for the next 25 years, most of the time lecturing to standing-room-only classes. So, unlike Coughlin, who remained attached to one parish church all of his life, Sheen's congregation began in academia, but it was not grounded in buildings or confined to a pulpit. All three priests, Coughlin, Sheen, and Greeley, reached out to millions of people via radio, television, or novels, and they found their congregations in the mailbox.

By 1956, Sheen was to average between eight thousand and ten thousand letters per day, occasionally receiving as many as thirty thousand.[7] Some people dubbed his parish *the mailbox*. This volume, of course, did not equal Coughlin's mail, which at its height in 1932 exceeded the weekly mail sent to the president of the United States. Greeley has acknowledged with gratitude his own mailbox parish, and, in keeping with the changing times, he has expanded his outreach by way of his computer and Web site.

Early in his career, Sheen authored a respectable philosophical work, *God and Intelligence in Modern Philosophy*; it remains durable and credible in its professional area. *Three to Get Married*, *Peace of Soul*, and Sheen's autobiography, *Treasure in Clay*, were among his most popular books. Like Greeley after him, Sheen also wrote newspaper columns: "God Love You," syndicated in the Catholic press, and "Bishop Sheen Writes," for the secular press.

His speaking ability was showcased on the Sunday evening radio program *The Catholic Hour*, broadcast over 118 NBC stations from 1930 to 1951 and sponsored by the National Council of Catholic Men.[8] Fulton Sheen's voice was good, but it did not match the exceptional, magnetic quality of Father Coughlin's; but then how many voices could? What Sheen had was eyes and presence, wonderfully suited for the new medium of television, which was to be the venue of his popularity and fame.

As the prospect of Sheen's television career took shape, he moved to New York City. From 1950 to 1966, he worked there as the director of the Society for the Propagation of the Faith, a church-sponsored group that supported missionary work and charity throughout the world. During his entire career, he enjoyed a reputation as an excellent speaker, drawing large audiences when he preached at Saint Patrick's Cathedral and the Paulist Catholic Center. He continued teaching but focused on convert instruction. He received a good deal of publicity about the number of high-profile persons he ushered into the Catholic Church: the likes of Clare Boothe Luce, Louis Budencz, and Heywood Hale Broun.[9]

All of Sheen's work was conducted under a commission from superiors or sponsored by official church organizations. The institution he served honored and promoted him. In 1934, he was created a monsignor and later a papal chamberlain, and on June 11, 1951, he was consecrated a bishop. Coughlin and Greeley, in spite of their individual fame and power, always remained somewhat on the fringes of institutional borders and beyond bureaucratic control; ecclesiastical honors eluded them.

No one has ever questioned Sheen's loyalty to his church or his commitment to traditional priestly celibacy. Greeley credits celibacy and hard work for his productivity, factors that could well have been the keys to Sheen's productivity also. He was a driven man, working 17-hour days. Daily Mass, his Divine Office, and his hour of meditation before the Blessed Sacrament were his only regular daily respites. Naturally, there were those who criticized him. Some who lived with him, such as historian Monsignor John Tracey Ellis, found Sheen vain and ambitious.[10] Father Daniel Noonan, housemate and biographer, described Sheen as a consummate egocentric, who was frustrated by ecclesiastical ambitions and the tedium of administration.[11]

That, of course, was not the whole picture; it is not always easy to be objective about people who live closely, especially if they are famous. It is clear from many sources that Sheen was a brilliant man, impetuous, and entirely devoted to his church; he burned at any corruption he found within it. He was generous to a fault. Like Coughlin and Greeley, Sheen made millions of dollars during his career, and he gave literally millions of his own money to the charities for which he collected from the public. Greeley also exhibited a munificent spirit, but utilized incorporation and grants to his family as major ways to express his generosity.

All of these qualities made Sheen an effective priest. His intelligence and broad knowledge allowed him to deal comprehensively with the topics he chose to discuss; his impetuosity and spontaneity suited him for a series of half-hour telecasts, all conducted without a single written note or a tele-prompter.[12] His humanity inspired admiration and devotion among secular viewers; his ecclesiastical status and stardom compelled pride and respect among the faithful.

Sheen's final assignment from his church came in 1966. He was asked to serve as bishop of Rochester, New York. He threw himself into his duties with the added enthusiasm generated by the Second Vatican Council, but all of his earlier media and diplomatic experience were of little use in the daily administration of a small, economically divergent diocese manned not by intellectuals but by ordinary priests. His missteps were recorded in the national press. His fame followed him. His stardom was in the past. He suffered heart attacks and retired with dignity, continuing his charitable work until his death on December 9, 1979, at the age of 84.

In 2000, John Cardinal O'Connor, then archbishop of New York, gave permission to begin a study of the life and writings of Fulton J. Sheen, which could lead to his canonization, the long process whereby the Catholic Church declares a person to be a saint.

THE MEDIUM

Bishop Sheen was a man ready-made to be a television star. All of his teaching and preaching experience, his long series of radio broadcasts, his personal charm honed with enthusiastic college students and church dignitaries, and his intensity and personal good looks combined to make him a welcome presence in the burgeoning medium eager for new personalities to help it sell itself.

Sheen's on-camera strategy suited television. He was a salesman, creating a need in the minds of his viewers. Like the car salesmen of 1950s folklore, Sheen told his audience, "You can't afford to pass up this deal!" Although he never denied the cost of Christianity—and indeed spelled out the pain and separation of celibacy in his autobiography—his emphasis, like that of Greeley's novels, was on the good news of God's grace. Sheen sold peace of mind, hope, and freedom to reason about life and Catholicism to Catholics and anyone else who would listen. But to make the sale, he first had to get his customers' attention. Primarily, his own looks and manner accomplished this task: He appeared on television in his vestments, embodying what one commentator called, "a style of clerical glamour, his piercing blue eyes transfixing the viewer."[13]

The same writer elaborates:

Sheen's eyes were indeed striking, but it was his hypnotic half-mad use of them that made them really jive. Like a pretty girl without her glasses, he seemed to be gazing just at you, if not through you.[14]

Exceptional eyes were not unknown or unique among big-time U.S. evangelical preachers. Minister Charles Finney, a famous and captivating orator, held audiences of thousands spellbound, again giving the impression that he was speaking to each person individually. Many said his eyes had a hypnotic effect. "No man's soul ever shone more vividly through glance as did Charles Finney's."[15] He successfully sold salvation through fire and brimstone. But that was in the 1820s; no television yet existed to make audience contact available beyond the flaps of the revival tent.

Sheen flattered his viewers, oiling his discourse with laudatory references to popular themes and people: soldiers, mothers, the Irish, and the current hero, Dwight D. Eisenhower. He set his viewers at ease with humor and even corny jokes, "puns, jingles, alliteration," much in the recorded manner of Saint Augustine.[16]

Like the good pitchman that he was, Sheen situated himself in a common space and time with his audience, a space defined geographically as the United States; temporally as the modern world; and thematically as the province of mind and heart, marriage and the family, business, and practical decisions. In entering these regions, Sheen himself had to leave behind the sectarian Catholicism of ritual and authoritarianism. He brought many U.S. Catholics with him, anticipating the tone and agenda of the Second Vatican Council.

By 1958, when Sheen left his first television ministry, his ecumenism, his willingness to enter into dialogue, and his attention as a spiritual leader to the problems of this world helped change the U.S. mind about Catholicism.

It seemed as if when Sheen stepped before the cameras, at a distance from the old, stodgy, constricted, sectarian, domineering church and into the space of television, the old church, in reality, vanished behind him.

THE MESSAGE

Sheen established a common ground with his viewers, one of mutual respect. From this vantage point, he encouraged them to think for themselves, to reason, to figure out complex problems of life. He championed freedom. At the same time, he was not shy about stating his own views and rendering his own judgments. Invariably diplomatic, Sheen nevertheless had his designated enemies: not persons, but rather the enemies of reason and nature. These foes were not just enemies of religion, but of everyone. Sheen believed that the three greatest dangers of his time were Freudian psychoanalysis, atheistic Communism, and artificial birth control. All of Sheen's presentations were tinted to one degree or another by this bias.

The smallest category of Sheen's early telecasts addressed specifically religious or inspirational topics, which is not to say that religion played a minor role in his discourse. Quite the opposite. But he tended to downplay the religious, and specifically sectarian, aspect of his thought, emphasizing instead a kind of neo-Thomistic system of anthropology, economics, ethics, and politics: an Everyman's philosophy in which practical problems could be explored in terms of "the man" and "the woman."

By 1955, later in his television career, Sheen became confident enough of his reception by the general public to speak more frequently about specifically religious topics. His broadcast entitled "Angels" began with the observation that "our modern world does not believe in angels, regarding them as poetical and mythical creatures that tide over the transition from infancy to maturity."[17] He then inverted his observation to a critique of modern materialism and proceeded to a thorough discussion of the intelligence and function of angels. In the same series, he ventured into a discussion of biblical stories, such as that of the woman at the well featured in John's Gospel (4:1–30) and evangelists Matthew, Mark, Luke, and John. He even gave one presentation on the doctrine of the Trinity.

MODERN PSYCHOLOGY

The largest number of Sheen's television programs dealt with popular psychological issues involving marriage, the family, and child rearing. His program titles included "The Laws of Marriage," "The Training of Children," "How Mothers Are Made," and "To Spank or Not to Spank." He also focused on common stresses such as "Pain and Suffering," "Fatigue," and "Human Passions."

He devoted time to ethical questions, preaching on "The Meaning of Love," "Conscience," "Character Building," "Something Higher," and "The Cure for Selfishness," and the theme that permeated his philosophy, "Freedom." He featured specific problems such as "What Is Alcoholism" and "Cure for Alcoholism," and even psychology such as "Psychology of the Irish," all with an astringent antipsychiatric tone.

Anxiety, for Sheen, as distinguished from fear, is a purely psychological phenomenon, resulting from a preoccupation with the emptiness within a human heart. He proposed a spiritual solution: "Perfect love casts out fear."

Pain and suffering, like fear, present a double challenge to humans: on the one hand, pain forces one to look inward, which could lead to self-centeredness; on the other hand, this introspection could be a stimulus to faith.[18] Sheen chose as examples the two thieves crucified with Jesus. The thief on Jesus's left cursed his lot, whereas the one on the right begged forgiveness.[19] Pain and suffering are not then intrinsically evil; they become evil only when they serve as a stimulus to selfishness.

Modern humans, in Sheen's judgment, often invoke sickness as an excuse for selfishness, egotism, and impatience. Selfishness is the result of a choice to direct natural instincts inward to preoccupation with self rather than outward toward others and the world and its needs.[20] Similarly, fatigue results not from exhaustion but from stagnation. People grow fatigued when they are bored, and they become bored when they see no purpose to their activity.[21]

Sheen used his theme of boredom to join and attack his two enemies of moral freedom: Freud and Marx. He said that boredom frequently leads people to surrender to their philosophies:

> Marx holds that we are economically determined. Despite all the talk about freedom today, the plain fact is that many are bored with freedom. That is why they are willing to surrender it to a dictator as Marxism demands or else are willing to deny any personal responsibility as Freudianism suggests, by denying moral guilt.[22]

Human beings, Sheen said, must rise to the challenge of suffering and must not fail in their will. Sheen taught that alcoholism was one particular failure of the will. Alcoholics were to be distinguished from drunkards because drunkards enjoy the taste and the experience of alcoholic beverages, whereas alcoholics are driven to drink from mental stress and moral anxiety.[23] Eventually, however, the alcoholic is conditioned by his addiction and, to some extent, loses his free will.

To Sheen, alcoholism was not exclusively a physical disease but a complex spiritual and medical phenomenon.[24] The alcoholic can, however, cure himself by following the example of the prodigal son: He must recognize his powerlessness and turn to God, confessing his moral guilt without making excuses; he must make reparations for the damage he has caused, but foremost he must become reconciled to God.[25]

In Sheen's judgment, all of these psychic problems—fear and anxiety, pain and suffering, fatigue, and even alcoholism—ultimately stem merely from the failure of the individual to recognize that freedom must ultimately be directed to the service of God.[26] These observations seem dated and particularly unscientific compared with the sophisticated approach Greeley was to take when he commented on problems of the human condition and religion. But Sheen was specific about nationality when he said that the American people were basically good and moral, far more so than they gave themselves credit for. They needed spirituality, not Freudian explanations, for their condition. In fact, they had no need for psychiatry, for Americans were "Not As Queer As We Think."[27]

THE RED MENACE

Bishop Sheen devoted a great deal of air time to exposing and attacking the evils of Communism. In fact, more than a third of his broadcasts had anti-Soviet and Cold War themes. His take on Communism and his approach to his audience were dramatically different from those of Coughlin. Ever the dynamic teacher, Sheen kept his audience interested with historical background and instruction laced with practical and moral lessons. Communism had done nothing to alleviate human suffering; it perverted true brotherhood by reducing everyone to a one-size-fits-all mentality; it destroyed family values by advocating free love; it reduced the standards of living and morals. Communist evil was highlighted to inspire his listeners to do the opposite: increase compassion, reduce suffering, and promote democracy. After clearly defining Communist dangers, Sheen exhorted his audience to attack it by confronting the breakdown in our own order: by restoring the sanctity of U.S. homes and marriages, by raising children with discipline.

An example of this master's clever rhetoric is clear from one of his presentations on Communism:

> Fellow citizens, be not deceived. Remember, when Russia talks peace, it is a tactic, and a preparation for war. Russia says it wants peace. The peace it wants is a piece of China, a piece of Hungary, a piece of Poland. A peace overture of Russia will be the beginning of another Pearl Harbor.[28]

Sheen was generally careful to note that he was exhorting his viewers to attack evil in general and in themselves; he was not advocating a military attack on the Soviet Union specifically, but his choice of images—Pearl

Harbor, the swastika, the then immensely popular General Eisenhower—
tended to blur his message into a general sort of hawkishness. The threat of
Communism and the danger of the atom bomb it implied were worries and
drawing cards to many of Sheen's viewers in the 1950s, much as sex is a draw
and a timely concern for the readers of Greeley's novels. Sex, marriage, and
psychological issues were Sheen's other popular subjects, and they have retained a freshness in Greeley's sociology and fiction, but Communism has had
its day as a subject to hold popular attention. Many of Sheen's messages have
been marginalized by the fact that he zeroed in on very popular topics of his
day rather than eternal verities.

Nor, in retrospect, was Communism really much of a danger to the so-
called worried well who made up Sheen's congregation, an audience of white-
collar and secure blue-collar Americans. The Communist Party USA, which
had also been the object of Father Coughlin's ranting, never attracted more
than 50,000 votes in any presidential election and never succeeded in electing
a state governor or a congressman. The Soviets, for their part, were safely
packed behind the Iron Curtain, and Communists exposed few Americans to
any real threat, despite Senator Joe McCarthy and James Bond. In this sense,
Sheen's Cold War broadcasts were essentially psychological, translating perceived danger into moral motivation.

Coughlin had emphasized the threat of Communism for his own political ends, calling for the destruction of the entire system of capitalism. His
National Union for Social Justice would do away with exaggerated class
divisions—fodder for revolutions like those in France and Russia—at the
same time that it saved the United States from Communist domination.

There is no question that Sheen, the priest-philosopher, hated atheistic
Communism; however, he reassured his public that atheism was not a denial
of the reality of God but actually an affirmation of God. In a most telling
analogy, he explains that atheism is an experience of God, "just as much as
wife-beating is an experience of marriage. All hatred is love turned upside
down."[29] Sheen did predict that atheistic Communism would eventually con-
sume itself and turn to its opposite, re-Christianizing the West, a prediction
all the more astonishing because it was uttered in 1955.

For Sheen, Communism was an intellectual rather than a political affair.
He put words in the mouths of Communists and then caricatured and dis-
regarded their arguments. He ignored the central topic of Soviet public
discourse in the 1950s, which was the victory of the Soviet army over Hitler.
He ignored the importance of work in the Communist ethic. The possibility
of a Christian Communism, as expounded, for example, by the devout Roman
Catholic Ignazio Silone, was an oxymoron in Sheen's discourse. Communism
existed as an abstract and fallacious position in the debate about what was
most central to Sheen's philosophical and religious concern: freedom and
determinism.

FREEDOM AND REASON

Central to Sheen's philosophical and theological thought and discourse was the idea of freedom. He preached individual freedom and responsibility in the face of social degeneracy and national peril but with the assurance of God's grace and salvation.

In his broadcasts, Sheen argued that freedom was part of the nature of man and a necessary good, involving freedom from determinism and constraint. It demanded freedom for choice. Sheen's hatred of Freudian psychoanalysis was based on his belief that psychological determinism destroyed man's ability to choose. Freedom "for," in Sheen's schema, was equated with responsibility. He frequently said that psychoanalysis, so trendy in his day that it was part of mainstream culture, destroyed individual responsibility by absolving people of all guilt. At the time, many religious leaders judged it to be an intruder into the province of the clerical profession, the right to counsel and to hear confessions.

Individual choice, especially in matters of sexuality, should be in accord with reason and nature. Central to marriage and the family was the freedom to reject artificial means of birth control, which, in Sheen's mind, were against nature, reason, and love.

Sheen, like Coughlin, felt strongly about the evils of artificial birth control. He devoted much effort to making strong arguments for the soundness of his judgment. To lead viewers into an understanding of the importance of their personal choices and responsibilities and the assaults on their nature and reason, Sheen periodized history epistemologically; that is, he divided history in terms of how people knew the world. According to this scheme, there was the Age of Faith in an uncertain time of beginning that reached its apogee during the life of Saint Thomas Aquinas (1225–74). It was an ideal time of integration, and it was followed by the Age of Reason. The current Age of Sensation, in turn, followed this.[30]

But Sheen appeared not to be concerned so much with understanding history as with setting up an apocalyptic myth. According to this myth, the golden Age of Faith slipped into the Age of Reason. For Sheen, this was an organic process and complementary, as it was for one of his intellectual heroes, Erasmus. For each of them, reason implied faith and vice versa, but faith was always superior. The Age of Reason, through the action of wicked men such as Marx and Freud, became the current demoralized age. This Age of Sensation is degenerate and poses grave perils; nonetheless, good and faith will ultimately triumph.

According to Sheen's myth, the United States was portrayed as good and even divinely inspired. The United States under assault by external forces (atheism) and internal corrupting influences of materialism and sexual license (Freudianism) mirrored the individual consciousness under assault by the sensations of covetousness, resentment, anger, and, of course, sexual desire.

Sheen said that Satan—equated with Marx and Freud—would indeed triumph in the twentieth century if Americans were to the lose the importance of faith. Some countries of Eastern Europe, China, and Vietnam were examples of groups that had succumbed, and it was evident that individuals had also fallen by the wayside. Viewers, however, were assured a personal victory if they only had the courage to will it and to exercise their free choice.

These history lessons offered many of Sheen's viewers the gift of independent thought. To be sure, that thought was guided toward a predetermined end. Viewers knew that Sheen would end each broadcast by affirming the reasonableness of the values he proposed. The family, the United States, and Catholic Christianity would endure. This guiding of the meditation was one more aspect of Sheen's salesmanship; nevertheless, his broadcasts had the shape of independent reflection.

Sheen always began a program by positing some contemporary problem. He then defined his terms (to suit his own needs, to be sure) and proceeded through various thought experiments to imagine what it would mean, for example, for property to be held in common, for man to be without guilt, even for angels to have human intelligence.

Sheen, like Greeley after him, had a profound respect for the Catholic imagination. In his process of imagining, Sheen encouraged his audience, through his example, to explore novels and the great works of imaginative fiction. His list of authors was broad and bold, including Shakespeare, Malraux, Baudelaire, G. K. Chesterton, and even D. H. Lawrence. This choice held some interest because Malraux was, at the time, best known for *Man's Fate* and *Man's Hope*,[31] novels extremely sympathetic to Communism and anarchism; Baudelaire's *Flowers of Evil*[32] and Lawrence's *Lady Chatterley's Lover*[33] were even in an ambiguous legal position in the 1950s, and they were condemned in many jurisdictions for their depictions of sex and immorality.

To his credit, Sheen had the courage and the scope of vision to draw from them what he considered elements of truth. "Think for yourselves," he told his audience, "and by that route you will arrive at the same conclusions as Fyodor Dostoyevsky and John Cardinal Henry Newman."

Independent thought, however, is like a genie that can neither be controlled nor put back into the bottle. When U.S. Catholics applied freedom of judgment to problems of sex and marriage in particular, they came to conclusions that put them at odds with church authority and opened a gulf that only grew wider in the following half-century. This is the time and these are the areas in which Father Greeley's star would come into its ascendancy.

SEX AND MARRIAGE

Problems of love and marriage concerned many of Sheen's programs. He argued that true love between a man and woman implied body and soul.

He objected both to what he termed the *Victorian Error* of denying sexuality and the *Freudian Error* of focusing exclusively on sexuality.[34] If love between the sexes did not seek God, it was destined to seek death.[35] Following this logic, Sheen argued that Freud was correct in "equating Eros and Thanatos": a love that rejected the soul and God was destined for death. He quoted André Malraux's comment on D. H. Lawrence's Lady Chatterley, "She clings to sex in the face of disgust and death." To reinforce his point, he cited Baudelaire, who described soulless love as "sitting on a skull."[36]

For Sheen, marriage was the only natural goal of sexual love. Homosexual love was not a concept that he could even consider. Homosexuality was not a topic to be mentioned on television in the 1950s.

Once having embarked on marriage, Sheen predicted that husband and wife could expect their relationship to pass through three stages: an initial phase of infatuation, followed by a period of disillusionment, and, finally, maturing into a stage of fulfillment.[37] In the first stage of infatuation, which he considered a necessary biological state motivated by sexual desire, the wife believed her husband to be "the most wonderful man in the world." The husband considered his wife to be "an angel." This period leads to a second stage, one of disillusionment as "the repetition of pleasures" hardened into irritability. In Sheen's mind, this development was logical because the biological phase involved such a close and sustained encounter between two egos that the deficiencies in each individual would inevitably come to prominence.

Here Sheen's analysis unwittingly evoked Jean-Paul Sartre's *No Exit*, with its gloomy conclusion that "hell is other people." Philosopher Sheen, however, was no existentialist because, at the instant the two partners discovered God, they transcended the gulf that separated them and thereby reached the third stage of marriage, that of fulfillment.[38] Greeley's novels portray a far more complex and realistic process of sexual relationships, and his sociological study of intimacy, love, and fidelity in U.S. marriage, *Faithful Attraction*, supplies a detailed scientific bent to questions that Sheen could not approach through his medium.

When children arrive—as in Sheen's formulation of marriage they must—they are to be spanked soundly.[39] He argued that modern and Western ideas of child rearing led to license and juvenile delinquency.[40] Spanking, Sheen said, was a concrete symbol of the divinely instituted authority of parents over their offspring; indeed, the parent who did not care enough to spank his children did not love them. He preached that an error of the Western world was love without discipline, which produced softness. The Communist error was discipline without love, which fostered hardness. Sheen's principle of youth training was Freedom through Discipline. He made analogies to pulling up the weeds in a garden or breaking a colt. His goal was discipline to realize the glorious freedom of the children of God.

He was, of course, not advocating pathological child abuse. He also took pains to make it plain that parents' rules had to be reasonable and that parents had an obligation to listen to their children. But his harsh tone echoed the Irish discipline that James Joyce cited in *Dubliners* and his *Portrait of the Artist As a Young Man*. Although Greeley grew up in a typical Irish home with a strict father, there is no evidence in his writing of a harsh attitude toward children or young people. Greeley likes and trusts young people; he teaches by association.

Sheen argued that the rise in juvenile delinquency paralleled the decline of the razor strap and the woodshed. He yearned for the return of both. He also traced the causes of juvenile delinquency to parents: to drinking parents, doting parents, or discordant parents.[41] Needless to say, parents had an obligation to give their children religious instructions. His entire argument for discipline tempered by love was recapitulated in his condemnation of tolerance, which he thought was a by-product of psychoanalysis. Tolerance, in Sheen's vocabulary, referred to evil, not to persons.[42]

Strict discipline had an object: an approach to the transcendent. The philosophy was communicated in the simplest possible terms: Every human being, even a child, had a natural instinct leading it toward the transcendent.[43] This instinct was manifested in the achievements of the ancient Greeks and Romans in their philosophy and poetry and in the ease with which primitive peoples accepted Christianity.[44] Most important, it showed itself in the conscience, the sense of right and wrong experienced by everybody.

The innate hunger for the transcendent is a recurring theme in many of Greeley's novels, but he embraces more latitude in portraying it, unconstrained by the philosopher's grid. Also, he sees the hunger expressed and fulfilled between men and women in flesh-and-blood ambiguities. God is present in sex, not merely the object beyond it.

Sheen remained the philosophical commentator. For him, the natural instinct toward God had been perverted in the modern age, especially by sexual preoccupation. Man was shut up within himself. Sheen offered a way out, through study and through love. These two paths were viable because the soul had the faculties of knowing and loving.

In Sheen's view, humans were like animals inasmuch as they had sensations and passions. Knowledge and love were specifically human. Knowing belonged to man's intellect or reason; loving belonged to his will. The object of the intellect was truth; the object of the will was goodness or love.[45] Of these two faculties, will, therefore love, was infinitely preferred because, in the process of knowing, the subject of our knowledge was necessarily reduced to man's level. In the process of loving, the subject—ideally God or another person—was accepted without any attempt to dominate or reduce the subject.

This discussion of knowing and loving was basic to understanding the sharp distinction Sheen interposed between male and female and their modes of loving. Sheen's way of speaking about women was typical of the public discourse of his time. It related closely to his attitudes toward celibacy and sexuality, intellectual and clear cut and in sharp contrast with Greeley's generation's thoughts about the sexes.

Sheen's attitudes toward the sexes can now be seen as stereotypes. Men were concerned primarily with things; women were concerned with persons. Men talked business; women talked about how another woman was dressed. A man's interests were more remote; a woman's interests were more immediate. Men favored the abstract; women favored the concrete and intimate. Men were concerned with ends, goals, and purposes; women were concerned with something proximate, close, and near and dear to the heart.

This psychology was distorted but seemingly acceptable to at least part of his public. For instance, there was no outcry when he concluded that because men centered on things and women on persons, women were more inclined to gossip. "A woman does not believe everything she hears, but at least she can repeat it."[46]

Another difference Sheen listed between men and women was that a man's love was always tied to his intellect. A man needed to have reasons for loving, and he needed to justify his love. But for women, love was its own reason; she did not have to give anyone a reason for her love. This distinction presumed that personal defects interfered with a man's love for a woman, whereas defects in a man never hurt a woman's love for him.

Greeley's women are important players in many of his novels. Many of them demonstrate the characteristics Sheen attributes to women generally: they love unconditionally, and their nature is like God's, to save men.

Sheen's philosophical construct made all of sexuality problematic. His explanation of the process of knowing (the masculine principle) made an inevitable hierarchical conflict between the sexes:

> Whenever the mind or intellect knows anything that is below it in dignity, it elevates that thing by knowing it. Whenever mind or intellect knows anything that is above it in dignity, to some extent it degrades it. But when we know something that is above the mind in dignity, it, to some extent loses its nobility because we have to pull it down to our level...[47]
>
> The will, on the contrary, when it loves anything above it in dignity, goes out to meet the demands of whatever it loves.... We become like that which we love. If we love what is base, we become base; but if we love what is noble, we become noble.[48]

Beyond the evident stereotyping of men and women in Sheen's examples, it is patently clear that in his philosophy the act of knowing, proper to a man, "degrades" (Sheen's word) its object, placing her below the subject in dignity. At the same time, the act of loving, proper to a woman, ennobles its subject, raising her almost (but not quite) to the level of her beloved.

Greeley's sociological work seems free of gender distortion. The sum total of Greeley's novels, however, echoes a hint of Sheen's Thomistic psychology and reveals a population of female characters who can be divided into "whore" and "madonna."

Sheen mastered the medium of television to communicate his message and achieve fame, just as Coughlin did via the radio and Greeley would via the computer. Sheen set the stage for intelligent, educated priests who gave the impression of listening, without the requirement that the audience conform to their religious affiliation or political agenda and who could be respected for their openness and reasonableness.

THE NEW ERA'S CRUCIAL DIVIDE

Sheen firmly believed that reason and nature led inevitably to faith and, in Roman Catholics, to compliance with the reasoning of authority. He was truly the champion of freedom of thought, but he could not imagine that such freedom would lead U.S. Catholics to reject the sexual teaching of their church. By 1968, the Sheen era was over. Sheen's philosophy could reconcile itself to the birth control encyclical *Humanae Vitae*, but Greeley's sociology could not.

Father Andrew M. Greeley, who was to take the popular mantle from Bishop Fulton J. Sheen, was not a philosopher but a social scientist who studied changes in his church. Like Sheen, he approached the stage scientifically from academia. He examined issues affecting the church, including the influence of Catholic education, population migration from city to suburbs, the upward mobility of Catholics, and the interplay of ethnicity with the political, religious, and familial attitudes of Catholics. He applied statistical tests to the kinds of changes formerly cataloged anecdotally and by common sense.

One crucial issue to which Greeley paid close attention was the attitude of Catholic parishioners, priests, and bishops to the official church teaching on birth control. In 1960, Harvard professor Dr. John Rock, a devout Catholic and daily communicant, along with Dr. Irving Pincus, introduced Enovid, the first oral contraceptive for women.[49] Enovid was inexpensive, convenient, and, for most women, safe and relatively free of side effects. When taken correctly, it was nearly 100 percent effective. Because the Pill consisted of hormones normally present in a woman's body, it was judged by many to be a more natural method of birth control than barrier methods such as the condom and the diaphragm. Oral contraception quickly achieved tremendous popularity among U.S. women, including Catholics.

In 1964, Pope Paul VI appointed a commission to review the church's position on birth control generally and the Pill in particular. This group included experts in theology, medicine, sociology, and canon law as well as a U.S. married couple who founded the Christian Family Movement. The majority of the group issued a confidential report that concluded that the ban on artificial methods of birth control—all methods except rhythm and abstinence—could and should be changed. Pope Paul rejected the recommendation of his commission and reaffirmed the prohibition against birth control in his 1968 encyclical *Humanae Vitae*.

The document was greeted with a firestorm of protest and anguish. Archbishop (later Cardinal) Joseph Bernardin told Greeley, "Often I can't sleep at night because of what that goddamn encyclical is doing in my diocese."[50] Many bishops, priests, and most lay people did not simply accept the papal judgment in a traditional manner. Initially, many protests were staged around the world, and some remarkable objections were voiced on high levels. Most people became indifferent to church pronouncements; some intellectuals and scientists, like Dr. Rock who had served on the pope's commission, were deeply disillusioned by the pope's determination, but people did not leave the church in droves. Catholics simply continued to go to church and ignore the teaching. Greeley observed:

> A new era in Catholic life in the United States was dawning, an era of "do it yourself" or "selective" Catholicism, in which men and women would affiliate with the Church and engage in regular religious practice, but on their own terms and according to their own judgments, no longer listening to the church as arbiter of sexual ethics.[51]

During the final quarter of the twentieth century, U.S. Catholics were thinking for themselves and solving complex life problems with reason, just as Sheen, from the television screen, had encouraged them to do. Another priest, Andrew M. Greeley, was to become a force in the popular arena, gain fame, shape religious thought, and articulate the concerns of his time. The medium would no longer be radio or television, but the romantic novel.

CHAPTER 6

A MIXED MESSAGE:
FULTON J. SHEEN

If you have a sense of the hope in store for you, you will be delivered from all hurtful passions and you will put in your soul the image of God's love for man.

                                                    Jean le Solitaire

Gandhi may share an archaic model of human sexuality with Catholic clergy such as Fulton Sheen, but he makes no attempt to package that bitter pill in sugared rhetoric. He presents it with the simplicity of his own diet, challenging George Orwell and the would-be celibate alike to consider its savor and decide for themselves whether it is to their liking. Fulton Sheen chooses to offer the same ingredients with a different recipe.

The genre of autobiography raises the expectation of a personal narrative, and a narrative is a story of events in time. Yet temporality is entirely lacking in Sheen's account of his celibacy. The struggle for, and achievement of, celibacy appears to be a static balance of forces from the moment of intention and when one takes the vow until death or lapse ends the celibate practice. The process of change and progress toward achievement and integration of celibacy, which can be observed in every authentic celibate narrative, is either hidden or absent in Sheen's conception. Although such a flat and abstract narrative could be construed as an expression of permanent achievement, the recurrence of certain disturbing patterns in Sheen's description of sexuality suggests instead a failure to integrate celibate understanding fully as a lived rather than merely professed practice.

Sheen's claim at the outset that "celibacy is not higher, marriage is not lower"[1] forms the core of his mixed message about celibacy. Sheen demonstrated his perception that his contemporary audience expected a moral witness that upheld the democratization rather than the privileging of the spiritual vocation. He desperately tried to respond to their expectations with phrases. His arguments, however, belied his real convictions.

The failure of Sheen's witness reveals itself in his descriptions of his relationships with his inmost self, his God, and others, celibate and noncelibate alike. Sheen is caught in a religious culture in which spiritual relationships rely on vertical hierarchies called *states of perfection*. That stance is direct contradiction to the sense that "all are one," as witnessed in celibate maturity. Only at such a point can the sense of having transcended the self to a level beyond sexuality, beyond the distinctions between male and female, black and white, slave and free, become truly meaningless.

Sheen attempts to disguise this hierarchization with a kind of rhetorical shell game. Sheen accounts for celibacy in his autobiography[2] as if he were writing a promotional pamphlet, disarming his reader with conciliatory arguments while defending himself behind an abstract and metaphoric style of reflections rather than a narrative of witness, so unlike that of Saint Augustine.

The reader can choose either to be lulled by pleasant phrases into accepting Sheen's institutional coda, or he or she can go on the offensive, reading through the metaphors, listening for the double entendres, and exploding the simulated coherence of those pat arguments. That choice might appear to be simply one between a religious or skeptical reception of Sheen's message. There is another alternative, however. A critical reading allows the recuperation of whatever witness to the celibate life underlies this sermon. Applying the key that the author's title, *Treasure in Clay*, offers, the reader can sift the silt off of Sheen's rhetoric to discover what of real value remains in the pan.

Sheen's mixed message unfolds in two ways: First, there is the assertion of an ideal without any narrative of its practice, process, or achievement; second, there is the effort to distinguish the celibate from the herd through negative externals rather than a sense of inner worth. Sheen uses a chaste discourse that is charged with sexual innuendo and reveals the inadequacy of his model of sexuality.[3] He evades the reality of his own practice by tending to channel sexuality into a series of metaphors of unsuccessful sublimation. These become evident in his rhetoric of violence: violence toward women, toward self, and even toward Christ.

Violence toward women in Sheen's account of his celibacy takes two forms. The first is the catalog of misogynist clichés. Perhaps they can be understood as a cultural hangover from his Victorian past. Nonetheless, they promoted the antiwomen tradition, often identified with a celibate hierarchy.

The institutional nature of this violence is expressed by the quaint and un-original wording chosen by Sheen. Woman as temptress is a "hank of hair," a "Jezebel." Woman as bad wife is defined as not sexually fulfilling, "the shrew." Ironically, he contrasts her to "a lovely, beautiful wife," not a loving one.[4] This subtle linking of the bad wife and the temptress, in which both are given the blame for man's infidelity, runs throughout Sheen's imagery. He credits the husband who loves his wife intensely as having little problem with fidelity; the man subjected to constant quarreling is often in search of greener pas-tures. The guilt is quietly shifted to the woman as shrew and fallow field.

The second level of violence is more ominous, both because it is physi-cal and because it is expressed more idiosyncratically, giving a disturbing glimpse of Sheen's personal conception of the relations between men and women compared with a violation of celibacy:

> Any infraction of celibacy is always interpreted by every good priest as hurting Christ. A husband would never say, "I know I gave my wife a black eye; I also gave her a bloody nose; I beat her, but I did not bite her ear." If the husband truly loves his wife, he will not begin to draw distinctions about how much he hurt her.[5]

This analogy is made in the service of illustrating another even more sub-lime relationship: that of the priest with Christ. But the weight of the analogy with spouse abuse, in itself apparently unremarkable to Sheen, is maintained and, although not legitimated, is disturbingly normalized by the metaphoric sadomasochism of his love of Christ.

Sheen's favorite scriptural analogy for the priest's struggle is that of Jacob wrestling with the angel, the heavenly wrestler who finally touched the nerve in Jacob's thigh and paralyzed it, an image itself rife with sexual innuendo.[6] Similarly, the celibate struggles not with temptation but with Christ himself. The narration of this struggle combines metaphors of masturbation with a sadomasochistic interplay of pleasure and pain reminiscent of the anticlerical satires of the Marquis de Sade himself:

> So in our lives, Christ sets Himself up as our adversary in the dark night of the soul in which we are full of shame for what has been done. As we wres-tle with the great adversary...we hang our heads in shame....We grope around in the darkness and forget that even in the darkness He is wrestling with us bidding us to return.
>   The Spirit lusts against the flesh and the flesh lusts against the Spirit. It is not so much the wrong that we have done; it is rather how we have smeared the image.[7]

The crowning achievement of Sheen's struggle appears to be a love of Christ based on self-hatred: "It is because of His love that I loathe myself. It is His mercy that makes me remorseful."[8] The physical and sensual imagery of smeared images, fouled raiment, and groping in darkness accompanying the obsession with shame, wounds, and pain are psychologically provocative.

Gandhi's celebration of a similar renunciation of self and the senses opened the possibility for humility and a greater acceptance of human weakness in general. Sheen describes an experience of self-loathing tinged with contempt and thinly veiled condescension that seems to embrace the vast majority of his fellow mortals.

Sheen reserves sharp criticism for the lapsed celibate, those who reach a spiritual crisis when young in the priesthood and others who fail at a late age either from "weakness or defects" in their own character.[9] But he does not demonstrate either empathy or understanding of the developmental struggles involved in the various stages of celibate practice in spite of the personal implications raised by his reflections on the "dark night." He gives no clue to the developmental history of his own practice, but his use of the first person plural voice does not completely take away the impression that the voice of personal experience speaks through his analogy of a struggle.

Sheen's allegory of the cross in which "Heaven and Hell meet" also holds some personal hints. Hell is the realization of the part "our" infidelity played in the crucifixion. Heaven is "our" remaining faithful, or "our" return to ask pardon.[10]

The reader cannot ascertain what constitutes a celibate transgression, or slip, and what is a betrayal. The reader is simply told is that the author is one of "we priests who have never broken our vow."[11] Sheen's aggressive tone toward the imperfect celibate seems to be directed to those who abandon the priesthood rather than those who exist in some compromising situation still within the celibate caste. Is it a mechanism whereby he can pillory an isolated other while dissolving his own shame into the common pool of original sin?

The most disturbing mixed message of all, however, is the elaborate rhetorical ruse by which Sheen attempts to fool his presumably committed, though noncelibate, Catholic readers. Initially, he flatters their choice of worldly love. Sheen's essay on celibacy begins with the express goal of dispelling the assumption that marriage is less holy in the divine plan than celibacy. He boldly proclaims that both are good, complementary, and not competitive. Celibacy is not higher; marriage is not lower.

Yet, despite his professed stance, every one of Sheen's metaphors reestablishes a relationship of condescending superiority. Marriage belongs to the secular world, uses alternating current, travels by roadway, labors with hand tools and reason, and so forth. Celibacy, by contrast, deals with the spiritual world, uses direct current, travels by air, and positively vibrates with intuition, poetry, and dreams. The legitimate source of authority is clear. The attributes of celibacy are firmly aligned along a vertical axis, not horizontally.[12]

By contrast, Gandhi's blunt and insulting distinction between celibate and noncelibate seems refreshingly honest and a better, even if flawed, basis for achieving community between both groups. Difference, no matter how value laden the attributes of distinction, is still not a claim of superiority and, in this case, of being higher—that is, literally closer to heaven.

Sheen first implicitly, then explicitly, contradicts his claim that celibate and married loves share the same plane. He even constructs a new set of metaphoric connotations that claimed celibacy is sensually higher by pointing out that the libido has a potential for superiority and not merely a means of intensifying the unity of husband and wife.

Sheen attempts to use psychological arguments similar to the Victorian and Hindu theory of "spermatic economy," a quantifying vision of the libido through which it may be spent or harbored. He appeals to Carl Jung, who held that spiritual transformation involved holding back some of the libido that would otherwise be "squandered" in sexuality.

Sheen's positive understanding of this process of "holding back the sum of libido" is naive at best, manipulative at worst. Pop psychology, whether fielded by psychologists or priests, is consistently characterized by an evasion of the ambivalent nature of all sublimation. The sublimation involved in celibacy, rather than being simply superior, shares in a process connected with all human experiences of love.

The spermatic economy[13] thesis and its opposite, the optimistic thesis, which postulates genital gratification as the route to liberation or health, share a limited and mechanistic model of human sexuality. Both positions ignore the real basis for mutual respect and a shared reality between celibate and noncelibate: the ambivalence of sublimation as a universal human experience.

In his concluding paragraphs, Sheen's mixed message becomes clear. The argument with which he first woos the reader, that nether form of love is higher, dissolves before his testimony that "I never felt I gave up love in taking the vow of celibacy; I just chose a higher love."[14]

How can an observer square this statement with his "celibacy is not higher; marriage is not lower"? The reader is left with the disquieting sense that he has been following a shell game about human sexuality while Sheen slowly tilts the table from the horizontal to the vertical, attempting to disguise a spiritual hierarchy behind a spurious veneer of equality.

Pope Benedict XVI issued his first encyclical letter, *Deus Caritas Est*, on January 25, 2006. It is a meaningful statement about love that lacks any hint of misogyny or the double dealing demonstrated by Sheen. He points out the beauty of sex within a committed love relationship. Among other things, he suggests that sex within that love relationship fosters closeness, generosity, and service. He, of course, could not yet deal with the committed love relationship between homosexuals, but his openness does not put down charity in any forum or even hint at glorifying celibacy above married love. The playing field of Christian love is leveled a good deal by his statement.

The force of Eros was too big for even a great mind like Sheen to incorporate into a coherent picture, and the facets of celibacy were too complex to be so easily manipulated without exposing his mixed message. Pope Benedict XVI in his first encyclical letter attempted to approach Eros in a more sophisticated and rational way than Sheen. But the pope was not struggling to explain his own celibacy.

When analyzing Sheen's relation to his own sexuality, one wonders who is playing with whom. How much is a designed defense of a religious state and how much is an unconsciously determined avoidance of personal revelation of celibate struggle and achievement?

CHAPTER 7

THE PAPERBACK PRIEST:
ANDREW M. GREELEY

> An autobiography can distort: facts can be realigned. But fiction
> never lies: it reveals the writer totally.
>
> V. S. Naipaul

Andrew M. Greeley is a priest, sociologist, and storyteller. To those who
expressed amazement by quizzing the source of the voluminous productivity
that has brought him to public attention, his response is classic: "Celibacy,
hard work, and maybe a little talent, too."

Unlike Charles Coughlin, Greeley has no secular political agenda, nor
does he preach a volatile social message of hate. Clearly, Greeley is not anti-
Semitic; in fact, he has been frankly ecumenical. Greeley's expressed political
positions resist categorization. In a broad sense, though, he tends to be liberal on social issues such as racial justice and gender equality and libertarian
on economic issues.

Unlike Fulton Sheen, Greeley has not been known for a particular interest in missionary work. Although Greeley certainly preached in parishes on
weekends, he was not a televangelist, unlike Sheen. Like Sheen, however,
Greeley has commanded intellectual respect—not for philosophy but for social science. How then does Greeley fit in with a Fascist radio priest of the
1930s and a conservative television priest of the 1950s?

First, Greeley, like Coughlin and Sheen before him, has enjoyed tremendous popularity. Greeley is a literary figure; his readership, particularly of
his novels, is estimated at more than 20 million. At one time, Coughlin's
radio audience was estimated at 40 million, but his listeners could tune in

for free, and his radio career was limited essentially to one decade. Sheen's television audience, at its height, was estimated at 30 million. The programs' sponsors, too, treated his viewers to his broadcasts. But for the most part, Greeley's audience has had to pay for his words, and his novels consistently make best-seller lists. Each man extended his ministry far beyond any parish or institutional boundaries by way of the mail he received. With their huge followings, all three priests deserve to be called media stars.

Many authors and radio and television personalities have reached audiences in the tens of millions. How, then, do Coughlin, Sheen, and Greeley stand apart from myriad other media stars? One difference between Coughlin and the Lone Ranger, between Sheen and Milton Berle, and between Greeley and Harold Robbins is that each of these men has had something profound to say.

Nobody ever accused the Lone Ranger, Milton Berle, or Harold Robbins of profundity. But Coughlin, Sheen, and Greeley have made serious efforts to address current problems. Coughlin targeted political economy and the Great Depression as they related to the Catholic Church's stand on social justice. Sheen discussed the relationship of science and society to reason and religion. Greeley has considered the place of sexuality and democracy in the modern church. Coughlin, Sheen, and Greeley thus share not only popularity but also a serious concern with contemporary issues.

Finally, and most important, all three of these stars are Catholic priests. This special status has privileged their words for millions of listeners, viewers, and readers. Coughlin gave his listeners permission to act: to vote for Franklin D. Roosevelt, to join unions, to write to their congressmen in support of the New Deal, and later, regrettably, to attack Jewish-owned businesses and to engage in street battles. Sheen also gave his viewers permission to think logically, to define their terms, to consider root causes and to conduct thought experiments, and to integrate their conclusions into a coherent worldview. Greeley, through his novels, gave his readers permission to think about sexuality—even priests' sexuality—and about the authoritarian structure of his church outside the boundaries of the official moral teachings. He encouraged his readers to think analogically; specifically, to think about what, up to that point, could not be stated coherently in the language of the church.

Before proceeding, however, a digression is in order. The prospect of analogical thinking needs consideration because it is the key to understanding both Greeley's work and the man himself.

REASON AND MYTH

One of the weaknesses, as well as one of the great strengths, of logic as practiced by Aristotle, the Scholastics, Descartes, and Kant is that it cannot admit contradiction. Aristotelian logic corresponds very well to mathematical thinking, including Euclidean geometry and algebra. Throughout the Middle

Ages and the Renaissance, as mathematics grew ever more sophisticated, logic grew in importance and prestige. Moreover, when Newton was able to quantify physical theories—for example, of gravity and of celestial dynamics—the triumph of logic seemed complete. All that remained was for investigators to fill in the gaps linking physical phenomena to psychology, ethics, and politics.

Such, at least, was the project of La Mettrie, whose book *Man a Machine*[1] proposed the famous slogan "The brain secretes thought as the liver secretes bile." Condorcet[2] sought to apply mathematical formulas to political events. These systems, however, tended to break down almost as soon as they were proposed. Diderot's[3] *Jacques le fataliste et son maître* and *Le Neveu de Rameau* are direct expressions of his failure to construct a so-called scientific system of ethics and set in comic dramatic form. By the end of the eighteenth century, Kant used his famous antinomies to demonstrate that logic alone can say nothing about the ultimate nature of reality.[4]

At various times in its history, the logical view of reality appeared to conflict with Catholic religious teaching that glorified blind faith and obedience. The most basic problems of religion—problems such as the nature of Christ, the origin of evil, and the methods by which salvation is to be achieved—transcend the simple rules of systematic logic. How can Jesus be both human and divine at the same time? Why would a God of goodness permit evil in the world? Can individuals accomplish their own salvation? If not, what should they do?

Troubled by the apparent contradictions inherent in such questions, people in the ancient world tended to adopt radical positions and split off from the church. Such schisms, even expressed in civil war, were a serious problem during the first millennium of the church's existence. In the twelfth century, Averroës's commentaries on Aristotle, which postulated a difference between scientific truth and religious truth, provoked a storm of controversy in the universities, a storm that could only be quelled by the intellect of Saint Thomas Aquinas.

With the incredible advances in astronomy, geography, physics, and biology after the Renaissance, Saint Thomas's synthesis of reason and faith was itself called into question. Many thinkers, including the French Encyclopedists, solved the dilemma by denying any validity to religious thought. Although Kant refuted the totalitarian claims of pure reason, totalitarian claims of science still persist in Western culture. The psychology of B. F. Skinner expressed it as determinism. The philosophy of Jean-Paul Sartre expounded it as nihilism. Wittgenstein and Quine embraced it in positivism. Moreover, scientism has been in continual crisis since at least the last quarter of the nineteenth century, even as science continues to advance and to provoke serious questions for religion. It is fair to say that since Saint Augustine's era, the crisis of faith versus logic has been a constant in the history of the church.

One of the most reprehensible—but also, it seems, one of the most persistent—approaches to the conflict of reason and religion has been violence. Violent action was the approach favored by church authorities in ancient and medieval culture.

The Crusades and multiple anti-Semitic campaigns serve as horrific examples of the church's use of violence to control. Indeed, the Inquisition was a response to the threat of violence: The church had lost control of the princes, who in turn had lost control of the mob; both were energized by the heresies that challenged the ultimate authority of Catholicism. Violence in support of either reason versus religion or vice versa also fueled the wars that wracked Germany in the sixteenth and seventeenth centuries, the French, Russian, and Chinese Revolutions, and the Spanish and Mexican Civil Wars.

Violence, too, was the response Charles Coughlin elicited from his listeners, at least after 1936, when he encouraged them to solve the distress of the Great Depression by attacking Jews. And Greeley's mythical cleric, the fictional Blackie Ryan, repeatedly reveals his strong violent streak.

Sheen appealed to the neo-Thomistic mode of solving the discourse between religion and science. He was convinced that reason, thinking life through, would lead to the conclusion that "truth is one." He used a dialectical approach; he yoked reason and faith and resolved apparent contradictions by transcending them, leaving the logical system intact.

In the latter half of the nineteenth century, a kind of science of the concrete, as Lévi-Strauss called it, took shape in the new sciences of anthropology and psychoanalysis. These approaches enter into a metaphoric mode of thought, suspending, for a time, the rules of logic in order to allow the mind to operate according to its own rules. The language of dreams, the thought processes of children, and the evolution of myths all obey a logic of their own. This logic permits one object to be another object; it dissolves the boundaries between symbol and referent to permit the operation of magic. Myth represents a way out of the impasses of logic and point of view, not as a superior logic disclosed by the dialectic but as an immediate totality.

Contrasting scientific language with myth, the Egyptologists H. Frankfort and H. A. Frankfort write:

> Our modern desire to capture a single picture is photographic and static, where the Egyptian's picture was cinematic and fluid. For example we should want to know in our picture whether the sky was supported on posts or was held up by a god; the Egyptian would answer: "Yes, it is supported by posts or held up by a god—or it rests on walls, or it is a cow, or it is a goddess whose arms and feet touch the earth." Any one of these pictures would be satisfactory to him, according to his approach.[5]

The function of mythic discourse is profound. Myth eschews objective language for a coherent narrative that involves the speaker directly in a personal relationship with the universe. Its purpose is not mere entertainment. The ancient mythmakers did not intend to provide intelligible explanations of the natural phenomena; they were recounting events in which they were involved to the limits of their very existence. Their narratives reflected what they experienced directly. The images of myth are products of the imagination, but they are not merely fantasy. "True myth presents its images and its imaginary actors, not with the playfulness of fantasy, but with a compelling authority. It perpetuates the revelation of a *thou*."[6]

Mythic assumptions underlie all scientific approaches. Biologist E. O. Wilson acknowledges that the philosophers of science call these assumptions *paradigms*. In the physical sciences, these paradigms tend to be very much reduced so that almost anybody can supply the suppositions: cause must precede effect, an object is identical only with itself, no object can be in two places at once, the speed of light sets limits to time, and so forth. The myths underlying the physical sciences are abstract enough that researchers seldom have to worry about them.

In the case of the social sciences, such as psychology, sociology, and anthropology, questions of paradigm tend to be less obvious and more complex. Religion poses its perennial challenge to reason. But Wilson, in his search for a synthesis of ways of knowing reality, points out that "Doctrine draws on the same creative springs as science and the arts, and its aim being the extraction of order from the mysteries of the material world. To explain the meaning of life it spins mythic narratives."[7]

Greeley discovered myth—analogical thinking. By means of that discovery, Greeley was able to express his identity as a priest, sociologist, and storyteller. His life provides one key for understanding priestly celibacy.

THE PRIEST

Greeley was born on February 5, 1928, to a Chicago Irish Catholic family. Each of these elements is so tightly bound to Greeley's identity that he is unimaginable without any one of them. His sociological work and his novels revolve around or interweave these elements so consistently and profoundly that the stamp of his spiritual geography becomes a trademark.

Greeley was the first born of four children; a sister who followed died, essentially at birth, of spina bifida. His sister Grace, two years his junior, was chronically ill; Greeley supported her care and was personally attentive to her throughout her life. In his first autobiography, Greeley made the point that (unlike so many other Irish families) there is "no schizophrenia" in his family; close family friends, however, identify this as his sister's affliction.

Greeley, in contrast to Tennessee Williams, has not made use of the experience of an incapacitating illness of a sibling in any decipherable way in his novels. Greeley was especially close to his youngest sister, Mary Jule, her husband, children, and extended family. Early in his priesthood, they owned a beachfront home together. Both Greeley and Mary Jule received doctorates from the University of Chicago, he in sociology, she in theology. They co-operated on professional projects and coauthored books. Her affliction with Alzheimer's dementia (AD)—a fate similar to that of his parents—and her death were major struggles in his life.

Greeley's parents, married in 1927, were a hardworking couple who initially enjoyed enough prosperity to live in a substantial middle-class home in a good Chicago neighborhood. They were able to take a summer home on Grand Beach, Michigan, and travel, quite elegantly for the time, by train to Mississippi.

The Great Depression hit Greeley's family hard. It altered the family economy, necessitating a shift in employment and a move to more modest quarters. Hard work was the paramount family value, and excellence was an unwavering expectation. Greeley told a priest friend that, as a boy, if he brought home a grade of 99 on a school project, his father would ask him why he had not got 100.

Greeley's Catholicism is expressed in his priesthood that subordinates, or rather interweaves, all of the other elements of his identity. Greeley the man and Greeley the priest are indistinguishable. Greeley decided to be a priest when he was in the second grade. Certainly, his home was congenial to religious practice and custom, but he denies any overt parental pressure to be a priest like Coughlin experienced from his mother. In fact, Greeley's father was in general skeptical about the cloth, having known his share of unhappy, alcoholic priests, and he wanted his son to attend a high school that offered ROTC. But 13-year-old Greeley, acting on a decision made six years earlier, entered Quigley High School and began formal training for the priesthood. The scholastic aptitude that marked him the "smartest in the class" in grade school continued when he entered this minor seminary.

Greeley matriculated to Saint Mary of the Lake Seminary, in Mundelein, Illinois, on schedule to follow his studies in philosophy and theology. Like so many priests educated in the 1940s and 1950s, he found the seminary training regimented, rigid, sterile, and not intellectually challenging.

Seminaries in the era before the Second Vatican Council were so-called total institutions. The seminary allowed little freedom of choice, unlike universities, which offered latitude in course selection, lifestyle, values, friendships, daily routine, and schedule. The institution tried to mold and discipline the young mind and heart into a devout priest by controlling every element of his life. The mediocrity, misogyny, and air of juvenile peevishness that pervade some seminaries came also to mark some of the students who passed through its system of indoctrination.

Seminaries offered no direct instruction covering sexuality or celibacy. The system reasoned that its requirement of weekly confession and a designated spiritual director would imbue the student with all he needed to know about sex. Celibacy meant complete and perfect abstinence from all sexual thoughts and actions. Confession was the place to deal with any questions or lapses of control. The rest would come as the priest practiced his ministry and helped others deal with their sexual problems.

Greeley was ordained a priest for the archdiocese of Chicago in 1954. He was assigned as assistant pastor to a suburban Chicago parish, Christ the King. He was an enthusiastic, energetic, creative, and successful curate in every regard save one: his relationship with his pastor. Many young curates have empathy for Greeley's experience with his pastor, whom he found petty, tyrannical, and jealous.

A review of the full range of Greeley's works indicates that the great significance for Greeley in this curate-pastor conflict must have been rooted in his early family experience. He has demonstrated a lifelong desire and effort to please authority and an equally strong disappointment at being rejected. However painful Greeley found his 10 years of pastoral work, he permanently incorporated the role of parish priest into his identity, and a parish life similar to the one he experienced at Christ the King informs many of his novels.

The unpleasantness of the relationship with his pastor did not bridle or crush Greeley's creativity or intellectual ambition, nor did it deprive him of a firm footing from which to deal with authority. Quite the contrary; it drove him to look for additional outlets for his considerable talents. He asked for, and received, permission from his major superior, Cardinal Meyer, to study sociology at the University of Chicago. It was a bold move for both men; many religious leaders held the social sciences suspect in 1960.

GOD'S SOCIOLOGIST

Just as his advanced degree in philosophy offered Sheen an avenue into academia and beyond, so Greeley's 1961 doctorate in sociology opened a door to his future on the national scene. His early research was not a developed sociology of religion but rather a sociology of interest for religion. He began his career by studying Catholic education. He accepted as his thesis the prevailing assumption that the graduates of Catholic schools did not do as well professionally as graduates of public high schools; that was, they did not go as far in school, did not enter the professions in comparable numbers, and did not rise as high in their careers. Greeley found, however, that the conventional wisdom was false. In fact, graduates of Catholic schools performed significantly better than did graduates of public schools.

The results, published in 1966, as *The Education of Catholic Americans*, brought Greeley to national attention. In January 1969, *Time* magazine referred to Greeley, already three years on the full-time staff of the National

Opinion Research Center (NORC), as "one of the shrewdest observers of U.S. Catholic life."[8]

The Second Vatican Council, which Greeley attended as an observer in 1964, was crucial to his development and thinking. The council emboldened him to visualize the role of the priest as a facilitator and community builder rather than a lawgiver. He pleaded for the development of a sense of professionalism and intellectual curiosity among priests. Like Sheen, he preached that priests should think for themselves and not use obedience as a cover for dependence.[9]

Greeley defended the rule of celibacy for priests, but he recognized that some men join the priesthood to avoid the stresses of dealing with women. Along with others like Father Eugene Kennedy, Greeley began to write about sexuality as a reality of the priest's existence. This line of critical thinking plus Greeley's definition of contemplation as a "dreaming and imagining" conditioned by poetry, fiction, drama, music, and art already set his direction from sociology to storytelling, although it would be another decade before he published his first novel.[10]

Greeley had to complete some serious sociological studies before he found his role as a mythmaker. *Humanae Vitae*, the disastrous papal encyclical issued in 1968 that reiterated the traditional ban on artificial birth control, including the Pill, riled priests as well as the faithful around the world. Greeley used his training to investigate the effects of the encyclical. He concluded that the church teaching on sexuality had a negative effect on church attendance and financial support.

Greeley divined the trend of the times. Many priests and laypersons would reject the church as an authority in sexual matters; priests and nuns would leave their vocations in increasing numbers, and fewer men and women would enter religious life; and the hierarchy would suffer a crisis of authority. By the end of the century, all of these predictions had materialized.

Sociology gave Greeley a firm foundation to speak his mind about a variety of religious issues: priests, papal elections, schools, ethnicity, sexuality, myths, and the religious imagination. In his interests, Greeley never strayed far from the concerns of people in the pews. Early in his career, he wrote practical guides for young men and young women in the form of letters and a guide for adolescents. Greeley argued for a dynamic view of sexuality, one that opened one person to another and thus, eventually, to God.

Greeley's early model of sexuality was somewhat conventional and almost Victorian. He viewed a boy's naturally aggressive nature to be exaggerated by sexual attraction. As a result, the boy strives even harder to achieve in order to impress the one he loves. Greeley viewed the girl as "sweet and charming and all that" but giggly and superficial until she falls in love with a "real" man. Greeley evidenced no awareness of a homosexual stage in normal psychosexual development or of the homosexual component in normal male competitiveness.

The model of a sexual dynamic leading one to the love of God is appealing in itself and for the consistency it confers on the world. Greeley garnered the idea not from a theologian but from Paul Claudel's play *The Satin Slipper.*

This model remains constant in his early work. Some nervous caution on Greeley's part appears when he states, "Even if we pass over all the sins and the selfishness that pose under the name of love, we can't ignore the terrible narrowness that sexual attraction often introduces into the life of a young person." Greeley's novels and his extended experience of celibacy would later modify and refine his sexual model.[11]

Fidelity has been a consistent theme in Greeley's reflections on sex, celibacy, marriage, and even in his writings on sexual intimacy and playfulness. He participated in a major study about sexuality and marriage in the United States, published under the title *Faithful Attraction.*

Greeley maintained that the term *sexual revolution* is a mere metaphor, not a reality. He, of course, was part of both the metaphor and the reality. A celibate priest was surveying human sexuality, was expounding on the sacramentality of sex, the gender of God, revealing his own sexual fantasies in the context of his priesthood, for instance, in writing about the comely airline stewardess and her beautiful breasts as he praises God and turns in for the night in his celibate bed. It was a revolutionary approach in the discourse about celibacy and sexuality: powerful and effective.

The U.S. bishops, energized by the Second Vatican Council, set up a number of subcommittees to study the life and ministry of priests in the United States. They selected priest experts to direct segments: Monsignor John Tracey Ellis authored the historical survey; Father Eugene Kennedy with Victor Heckler directed the psychological study; and the NORC and Greeley conducted the sociological investigations.

The gap between the religious critique of social and psychological issues that bishops were used to (expressing what ought to be) and the social sciences (considering what actually is) was too great for the hierarchy to bridge. In effect, the bishops rejected their own studies, which had been commissioned with the admonition, "not to fear to speak the truth." Because the bishops did not have ears to hear the language of the social sciences when it conflicted with their notions of what ought to be, another language had to be used to express the same truths. Greeley already sensed that the discourse would continue in the language of myth, and the truth would be told in the form of fiction.

THE MYTHMAKER

Greeley's transition from sociologist to novelist seemed as natural and seamless as his movement from priest to sociologist mainly because Greeley remained Greeley. He passed intellectually from priest to sociologist to myth-maker without ceasing to be any of the three.

Greeley did not proceed immediately to compose novels. His study of myth was initially academic. His appreciation of mythic discourse grew as he explored the sociology of religion and felt the need for the development of an internal holistic approach in a field that favored external codifiable procedures. Greeley's study gave him an appreciation for the near universality of fundamental structures of religious experience and expression.[12] He learned a healthy critique of the limitations of the scientific method and that the "quest for truth was an exercise in model fitting."[13]

Greeley proceeded with his sociological training on three fronts: popular sociology written as literature, advanced consideration of models, and the writing of imaginative fiction. He used his sociological insights to describe the operation of mythic structures in religion—*The Jesus Myth*, *The Mary Myth*, *The Catholic Myth*, and *God in Popular Culture*—finally extending his observations by way of novels into the mythopoeic exploration of reality. Theologian David Tracy notes:

> In the course of his remarkable intellectual career, Andrew Greeley has illuminated the pervasiveness of symbols in our social and personal, our secular and religious lives.[14]

Although Greeley had written fiction since the 1950s, mostly inspirational stories for young people, by 1979 and 1980 he was ready to incorporate his experiences into novels. His first two works were not immediate commercial successes, but they were paradigms of all that were to follow. From the very beginning, Greeley crammed all of his theology, sociology, pastoral experience, and life into his stories. Of his first book, one critic commented:

> The Magic Cup, the Holy Grail, thus emerges as the central and most significant symbol in Greeley's writings, for, even more than the literary form of the romance (though inseparable from it), the Grail theme allows him to combine his two loves for the Catholic Church and his Irish heritage, while simultaneously permitting him to pursue the theological topics of the sacramentality of sexuality and the womanliness of God.[15]

Thus, Greeley passed from sociologist to mythmaker.

Greeley's second book was a mystery, *Death in April*. The setting: Chicago. The protagonist: a successful novelist. The theme: the courageous hero rediscovers and saves his first love. The mystery genre, which has included all of the elements of this novel, would later develop and come to full bloom in the character and escapades of Blackie Ryan, a fictional priest serving as a Greeley alter ego.

Before that, however, Greeley was to score a blockbuster commercial success with his 1981 novel *The Cardinal Sins*. It is the story of "Two Irish boys growing up on the West Side of Chicago, discovering themselves, awakening to desire, dealing with faith...then entering the priesthood. One rises to the center of power, the other remains a parish priest. Each must deal with the love of a woman—in his own way."[16]

Father Kevin Brennan is the narrator and "speaks at times" for the author. He remains celibately devoted to the church over the 33-year narrative. Patrick Donohue, proud and ambitious, becomes a shell of piety and a cardinal. As boys, they had experienced an agreeable adolescence, mostly focused on a lakeside resort. They struggled with the prospect of being priests and the issue of celibacy.

After high school but before seminary, the boys are allowed to date girls. They engage in flirtation and mild sexual experimentation. Kevin, for instance, goes skinny-dipping with Ellen Foley, a 15-year-old friend. Patrick's dalliance with Maureen Cunningham goes much further but ends short of intercourse.

These passages form a paradigm for the novel and Greeley's treatment of celibacy. A lake and skinny-dipping are recurrent images in Greeley's myths, representing a quasi-sexual but still sanctifying experience. Patrick's life-long sadomasochistic attitude toward women is apparent: He wants sex with Maureen in order to "teach her a lesson." When Maureen proves willing— "she gave up, as if resigned to losing her virginity"—he loses all interest in her and is filled with revulsion.[17] This passage echoes the behavior and feelings of J. T. Farrell's protagonist Studs Lonigan in the cab scene with Lucy. The reactions of these young men illustrate the ambivalence toward celibacy and sexuality typical of adolescent boys.

Greeley's Kevin and Pat move from summer vacation and the ill-defined and ambivalent world of adolescent sexuality into the homosocial world of the seminary. "If you lock up a couple of hundred lonely young men, attachments can get to be a problem."[18] Pat develops a problematic emotional attachment to another seminarian; Kevin rescues Pat's career by getting the other seminarian kicked out of school. Pat then turns his sexual attention to a girlfriend whom he frequently sneaks out to meet. When seminary officials suspect Pat's absences, Kevin again saves Pat's career by climbing into Pat's empty bed during bed check.

Pat is selected to study in Rome where he continues the predatory sexual behavior of his adolescence. He blackmails a married woman into having sex with him; as Greeley puts it, "He took her *brutally*. As he expected, *she loved it*. Back in his room, he sobbed in disgust and self-hatred, and murmured an act of contrition."[19] This pattern of cruelty and contrition escalates as he subsequently fathers a child with this woman, has a number of lovers, and develops a long-term affair with his childhood love, Maureen Cunningham. In contrast to Pat, Kevin keeps his promise of celibacy. He also maintains close and lasting friendships with Maureen and with Ellen Foley.

Toward the end of the novel, Greeley shifts genre, leaving the format of the introspective bildungsroman—novel of development, such as *A Portrait of the Artist as a Young Man* or *Of Human Bondage*—to become a novel of adventure, piling episode on episode with little space for reflection. All four characters are involved with Vatican and Mafia intrigues. Pat becomes a cardinal, but it is Kevin, the parish priest, who displays the real political power by circumventing authoritarian incompetence and enlisting a higher power to aid his efforts, to save the church from financial scandal and an inept pope, and to rescue Pat from blackmailers.

Greeley creates in Kevin a priest adept at using violence—a gun, explosives, karate, harboring murderous impulses—to further his ends of saving Pat and the church. It is the task of the woman, in another of Greeley's leitmotifs, to save the hero from his own murderous impulses.[20]

When Greeley says, "The principal theme of *The Cardinal Sins*—obviously and self-evidently, I would have thought—is that God's love pursues the four main characters through their human loves, sometimes licit, sometimes not, always with a sexual component, but never with a compulsion to sin," he is really describing the sacramentality of Kevin's love. Kevin's celibacy takes the direction of "vicarious sex": sexually abstinent himself, he is repeatedly involved with Pat's sexual transgressions, saving Pat from the consequences of his sexual activity.[21] Likewise, barred from actually having sex with Ellen, Kevin nonetheless manages to give her sexual satisfaction through an improved relationship with her husband.

All of Greeley's novels are peopled with a variety of priests, but the 1982 and 1983 novels have a priest as protagonist and the same theme as his 1981 book. Nowhere does Greeley come entirely to terms with his sexual tension and anxiety.

In contrast, James Joyce does in fact resolve his adolescent sexual conflicts in *A Portrait of the Artist as a Young Man*. But Greeley, having forcefully presented the nexus of sexual and Oedipal anxiety and celibacy in *The Cardinal Sins*, actually backs away from it step by step in his subsequent novels.

In *Thy Brother's Wife* (1982), sexual intercourse involving a priest occurs only once, and the character quickly repudiates his lover, returning to a celibate state. The central character in *Ascent into Hell* (1983) alternates sequentially between goodness (celibacy) and evil (sexual activity) without ever resolving the conflict.

Lord of the Dance (1984) externalizes evil (and sexuality). In place of the two priests of *The Cardinal Sins*—Pat, the sexually active "bad" one, and Kevin, the celibate "good" one, paired like halves of a single personality—Father Ace is entirely good and entirely celibate. This novel introduces seminarian Blackie Ryan as a personality. Elements of vicarious sex, the magical use of violence, the manipulation of the power system, and Greeley's characteristic mode of relating to fact and perception—denying the contrary of a proposition and thereby suggesting the proposition without ever actually stating it positively—become increasingly important in all of Greeley's myths.

After this set of novels, Greeley's priest characters tend to become increasingly abstract, remote, and bloodless, eschewing entirely the possibility of adult sexuality, whether as sexual love or as consolidated celibacy. Greeley's later novels become increasingly formulaic and avoid the essence of the sexual/celibate struggle.

Greeley presents his "good" mythical priests as rounded pastoral characters. Throughout, they can be seen praying, preaching, counseling the perplexed, mediating disputes, and supervising youth groups. They are troubled by doubts and fears, and they freely indulge in fantasies of a sexual nature; overall, however, they are hardworking and utterly devoted to their flock, to their church, and to their God.

But Greeley imagines his priests with an inordinate influence over their parishioners. The image of the parish priest is everywhere present, even in the bathrooms of his parishioners (at least in the minds of the attractive female parishioners!). These parishioners refer marital problems, choices of career, and intergenerational disputes to their priests, who usually counsel charity and restraint, seasoned by referrals to specialists for technical problems, such as seeking psychiatric help for depression or medical help for alcoholism, a more informed pastoral stance than that of Sheen.

In one of his pastoral works, Greeley proposes replacing the traditional authoritarian role of a parish priest with the model of a professor presiding over a graduate seminar.[22] He goes on to argue for the priest as the "Love Person" in the Christian community[23] and as the center of hope and vision in the parish.[24]

One concomitant of Greeley's parish-centered Catholicism is a type of insularity. Greeley goes out of his way to mock missionaries, for example, in explicit denunciation of the Maryknoll missionaries and liberation theologians who "have dirty fingernails, stringy hair, and bad breath." Greeley portrayed them as ineffectual and meriting the derision of a bishop who says, "Fuck the bastards, Blackie."

In one way, a concern with the parish becomes a kind of xenophobic attack on missionaries. Incidentally, this hostility to missions stands in sharp contrast to the career of Fulton Sheen, who served as permanent advisor on missions to the Second Vatican Council. Although Greeley is not hostile to all missionaries, his priests have an unmistakable tendency to focus on matters close to home, on family, parish, and community, and to regard the world outside the parish with a degree of detachment. The diocesan and even the Vatican halls of power appear in Greeley's works, but even then primarily as they relate to Chicago, the parish, and its parishioners.

Certainly, Greeley's stories inspire reflection on the meaning of Christian spirituality and sexuality, and they advance the discourse about the credibility of church authority in these matters, just as Jesus did. Marsden notes the association between Greeley's myths and the parables of Jesus:

> There is little doubt that Father Andrew M. Greeley is writing modern religious parables in his best-selling fiction which certainly seem to have found a large audience among both the Catholic and non-Catholic populations of the United States.[25]

Has Greeley's prolific production exacted a price in the quality and richness of his mythmaking?

Lévi-Strauss's view of the genre of the *roman feuilleton*—the serialized popular novel—may have relevance in reviewing the body of Greeley's myths. Lévi-Strauss claims that ultimately the *roman feuilleton* distorts the pristine freshness and originality of the myth. Greeley consciously eschewed irony in his mythmaking. His so-called comedies of grace necessitate a happy ending in which the good are rewarded and the wicked are punished. They run the risk of establishing a closed mythical structure in which "the hero of the novel is the novel itself. It tells its own story."

Precisely this mechanical winding down of the mythic substance, presented with such freshness in *The Cardinal Sins*, is what occurs in the fiction of Andrew Greeley. His investment in a few of his characters who appear repeatedly in his novels threatens to make his world claustrophobic instead of kaleidoscopic. Despite the recurring cast of characters, Greeley's paperbacks are not similar to the nineteenth-century French roman fleuve novels by Balzac or Zola, whose empathy and identification with even the most improbable characters lent a broad spectrum of colors and textures to their fictional worlds.

Homosexual orientation becomes a significant question in considering religious celibacy because it is frequently assumed, and validated by authoritative observers, that a larger proportion of gay men enter the ministry than exist in the general population. Greeley generally did not deal very deftly, either in his novels or his essays, with the subject of homosexuality in the priesthood. His attitude on the growing number of gays in the priesthood was to excoriate them and warn Catholics about the dangers of "lavender rectories." He acknowledged that good priests with a homosexual orientation could and do exist, but any gay priest character in Greeley's novels is invariably either defective or a villain.

Kevin, the priest hero of *The Cardinal Sins*, and Ellen experience a powerful sexual attraction that is portrayed as salvific for both: "God attracting us to Himself/Herself through our sexual attractions to others."[26] Greeley has not demonstrated that he can handle, mythically, the same celibate struggle between two men or between two women.

Not all novelists can portray gay characters with empathy. David Plante is one Catholic writer who can, and writers of varying religious and sexual backgrounds, such as Graham Greene, Willa Cather, James Joyce, Georges Bernanos, and Jon Hassler, have been able to deal with the reality of gay priests with sympathy, if also with some reserve and subtlety.

SEX AND THE FAITHFUL

In his novels, Greeley's concerns extend beyond the priesthood. In fact, one reason for his staggering popularity was that he raised a singular voice from within the authoritative ranks of the clergy, echoing the point of view of the lived experience of the people in the pews. His novels struggle with the religious problems of ordinary people: problems of sexuality and family, of job and community, of faith and practice, on their own terms and in their own language, as when a priest says, "Don't fuck with God!"

Greeley's characters are people with whom the reader can identify. Greeley's Chicago novels feature people like their readers, or, more precisely, people better off than most readers, but in positions the readers could realistically attain. Greeley's characters are all power figures; they work as psychiatrists, art dealers, judges, journalists, lawyers, investors, commodities brokers, and, of course, priests. Greeley's characters enjoy wealth and social status: They vacation in summerhouses, eat at elegant restaurants, and fly off at the drop of a designer hat to Rome or Ireland; they hobnob with the rich and famous.

But Greeley is no elitist; his characters attained their wealth by going to law school or medical school, by working hard, and by playing by the rules. His characters, like his readers, have extended families, ordinary families with ordinary problems, striving toward nuclear stability. In fact, most of Greeley's Chicago novels concern two large extended families: the Farrells and the Ryans. Together, these two families appear, at least as minor characters, in more than half of Greeley's published novels.

These families are multigenerational, commonly including a hero and heroine together with teenaged offspring. Older adults are on hand as advisers, and deceased ancestors are remembered, fondly or not, for their continuing impact on their descendants. Although Greeley himself describes his novels as comedies of grace, it may be enlightening to think of them as romances.

Northrop Frye divides classic works into four genres, corresponding to the seasons. According this scheme, comedy is proper to youth and analogous to spring. These stories are concerned with the struggle of young lovers to overcome obstacles placed in their way by a demanding elder.

The Ulysses myth—the hero trying to find his way home to his true love—informs the plot of many of Greeley's novels. Those novels, like James Joyce's classic, attempt to show a hero at the height of his powers seeking, in some sense, to come back to a mature heroine.

Greeley's couples are far from perfect; they stagger toward their goal of monogamy and family. Marriages fail as they do in the real world. Divorce is a common element in Greeley's stories—seen as the logical and reasonable outcome of the death of a marriage—in contrast to strict Catholic teaching.

Before and between marriages, Greeley's characters enjoy sexual relationships. Although they have sex with various partners, for the most part Greeley's characters are serially monogamous, sticking to one partner at a time. Moreover, most of the sexual relationships in Greeley's novels culminate in marriage and a nuclear family.

The specific sexual acts in which Greeley's heroes and heroines indulge are strictly, even aggressively, normal and idealized. Homosexuality occurs in the novels, but, as with Greeley's priest characters, it is always a mark of moral evil. Lesbianism marks a mother superior's evil. Similarly, a murderess is a lesbian. Only villains choose same-sex partners in Greeley's novels, and the virtuous are decidedly "healthy."

Masturbation is demonstrably the most universal sexual outlet for human beings, yet none of Greeley's men or women masturbates. To be sure, the characters spend a great deal of time fantasizing about sex, but they never seem to seek release from their tension through self-stimulation.

James Joyce, raised Catholic, could describe the experience that many young people suffer in a struggle with masturbation. Joyce's Stephen Dedalus is described in real pain: the pain of his "fierce longings" succeeded by his "secret riots" and the pain of guilt and a "humiliating sense of transgression." Greeley, for all his empathy for young people, is unable to deal with masturbation in any of his writings. Greeley and his young characters maintain sexual fantasy at a certain pitch of intensity, a strategy that protects them from the pain of sexual conflict felt by Joyce's hero.

Greeley was honored in 1993 by *U.S. Catholic* magazine for furthering the cause of Catholic women. His social stance is clearly pro-gender equality and antisexist. The epitome of Greeley's women is reflected in his assessment of a rectory's beautiful cook: "with her clothes off, God forbid, Brigid would be more devastating than any centerfold." Greeley's mythical women are indeed often idealized, but they are frequently subjected to pain, sacrifice, torture, and rape in the service of and love for a man, often a priest. The imagery of a woman in pain is a constant in Greeley's work; descriptions of women's feelings are shot through with sadomasochism. One character, for example, thrills to the image of herself naked on an auction block:

I should have been offended at that disgusting image of him buying me on the slave block. Instead, I reveled in it. I would be delighted to be naked before him, powerless as he played with me and fondled me, considering whether I was worth his interest or not. Absolutely vile and repulsive. Yet it aroused me even more. Like it is doing now. What is wrong with me?[27]

Greeley, seemingly unaware of the sadomasochistic undercurrent of many of his myths, goes to great pains to establish the health of his women, citing especially the Song of Songs and the mystical tradition that sexual love mirrors God's love for his people. Their asserted normative normality gives a clue to the ideal world Greeley imagines for his readers, a world where women revel in their status as salvific, if suffering, figures.

In Greeley's ideal world, questions regarding birth control and abortions do not arise. Yet both issues are relevant to the status of women. Greeley's adult women are sexually active, but unwanted pregnancies never occur. It must be assumed that they practice birth control. Birth control, in real life, is practiced and approved by the overwhelming majority of U.S. Catholics. Here, Greeley the sociologist and Greeley the mythmaker combine without direct rejection of official church teaching.

The question of abortion arises because, over the course of his novels, Greeley subjects a number of his women, including teenaged virgins who are presumably not taking birth control, to rape. Rape ties into the underlying tone of violence in many of Greeley's myths. The rape factor allows Greeley to submit his women to sexual dominance while absolving them of any responsibility for their sexual activity; they remain virgins and become martyrs. And although rape is not a particularly efficacious method of inducing pregnancy, in the real world, pregnancies nevertheless do result from rape. Fortunately, the question never arises for Greeley's women. As a result, Father Blackie and the other priests of Greeley's world are spared the very difficult matter of advising women faced with unwanted pregnancies.

Greeley's men and women turn to their priests for spiritual advice. It is noteworthy that Greeley's world, unlike Sheen's, does not exclude psychiatry as a source of enlightenment; indeed, one of his heroines is a psychoanalyst. Greeley renders his readers a considerable service by separating real moral guilt from neurotic guilt. Once the dross of mental illness is removed, however, there remains a residue of moral guilt, and it is this moral guilt that Greeley's priests address.

GREELEY AND THE CELIBATE MIND

John Blackwood Ryan—father, monsignor, bishop, Blackie—is a fictional priest-detective created by Greeley and featured in more than a dozen of his novels:

> Blackie Ryan serves as a contrast to the shallow, selfish, insensitive, mediocre priests who abound in these stories. Blackie represents the priesthood at its best, the ideals in the priesthood that originally attracted me.[28]

The person of the author reveals himself or herself most clearly in the telling of the story and in the mythopoeic values that prevail. In other words, what is revealed to be truly sacred and what has meaning? An author is the form giver of the inner struggles of the characters and the adventures to which they are subjected.

In more than a dozen instances, Greeley draws explicit comparisons between his character and the priest-detective Father Brown, created by Gilbert Keith Chesterton, a layman. Both fictional priests are important because each conveys to millions of readers an image of the Roman Catholic priesthood and Church. The insights garnered about the workings of the celibate mind that can be found in Blackie, however, are enriched by the fact that his creator is also a celibate priest. Any revelations are compounded by the fact that Greeley admits that his fictional creation sometimes speaks for the author.

Chesterton's Brown enters the world of crime and detection seemingly at random or stumbles onto the scene of a crime just by chance in the performance of his pastoral work. Father Brown is virtually without political power. His personal connection with a case rests either with his link to a former sinner or by apparent chance, and his entry into a case is motivated chiefly by a desire to move the criminal to repentance and reconciliation.

Father Blackie also holds a pastoral role in Greeley's stories, but, by contrast, the detective mostly enters into a case at the behest of a blood relative or a friend or client of the family. In other words, he comes into a case as part of an elaborate web of power involving patronage and obligation, as chaplain to one powerful Chicago Irish American clan. Father Blackie comes into the picture when this clan is threatened.

Each criminal puzzled Chesterton's priest because the culprit could look like anybody; the potential for evil lurks in every human heart. In *The Hammer of God*, when Father Brown corners the criminal, the following exchange ensues:

> "How do you know all this? Are you a devil?" "I am a man," answered Father Brown gravely; "and therefore have all devils in my heart. Listen to me."[29]

In Father Blackie's world, true crimes are committed only by the truly evil, those damned by their very nature. Greeley's villains can usually be identified by their appearance; oftentimes they are repulsive old men. In some sense, these characters are exaggerated caricatures of enemies and of the pastor who tortured young Greeley in the first years of his pastoral ministry. The satanic priest, Father Armande, has "breath like a sewer" *(Happy Are the Meek)*; drooling and senile Harv Gunther tortures young prostitutes *(Patience of a Saint)*; murderer Vinney Nelligan is a "dirty, kinky old man" *(Happy Are Those Who Thirst for Justice)*. Blackie can spot the truly evil, but he needs to figure out which dirty, kinky old man is to blame and then place him in the chain of causality.

Nowhere is the difference between Father Brown and Father Blackie more apparent than in the climatic scenes in which the culprit is revealed. Father

Brown, unlike Greeley's priests, abhors violence. His object is not to bring anyone to the gallows but rather to bring criminals to confession and reconciliation. Sometimes Brown simply allows the repentant murderer or thief to turn himself in or even to escape; he counters physical threat with moral admonitions. Father Brown is content to trust a sinner's conscience and God's mercy. An officer says, "'Shall I stop him?' when a criminal is in the process of escaping. 'No, let him pass,' said Father Brown with a strange deep sigh that seemed to come from the center of the universe. 'Let Cain pass by, for he belongs to God.'"[30]

Greeley's Father Blackie often acts as a kind of auxiliary to the regular police. He relishes political power and is privy to the Central Intelligence Agency and highly placed Vatican contacts. And, like Kevin in *The Cardinal Sins*, he is a man capable of physical force and violence. In a scene from *Happy Are Those Who Thirst for Justice*, Blackie recounts, "I jumped up, whipped the Beretta into position with both my hands, and jammed it across my desk into his forehead." Later, the priest emphasizes his violent reaction, "[If] he had moved a millimeter closer to the gun he was in fact carrying, I would have bashed him, weak old man or not, on the skull." The criminal is not led to repentance but to a mental institution—a hopeless case.

With regard to violence, Brown (the product of a married layman's mind) and Blackie (the product of a celibate priest's mind) are strikingly at loggerheads. The discourse of confession, a dialectical process aimed at discovering a sinner's true position before God, is at the heart of Father Brown's universe. Father Brown reveals his humanity over and over in his interactions with other sinners who, like himself, are in need of compassion. It is out of his shared humanity that he interacts vigorously and salvifically with the criminal.

Greeley's Blackie is a soul "hallowed by destiny." Blackie has more the quality of the dramatic hero who, by Lukács's definition, is passive and lacks interiority. Lukács holds that interiority "is the product of the antagonistic duality of the soul and the world."[31] Greeley's explicit desire is to show the church and the priesthood as instruments of God's love. But Blackie's struggles exist outside of him. He passively judges and brings others to justice. He is involved with tales of God's love and salvation mediated through human love, but vengeance, torture, and retribution also have a prominent place. In Blackie's universe, the demons are in other priests and are satanic, drunken, sandal wearing, misguided, unfaithful, or otherwise irredeemable—unlike him—or the villains are reprehensible, dirty old men.

The layman's priest, Father Brown, is the incarnation of Chesterton's understanding that there is even a Christian way to catch a criminal. The power of the sacraments and the sacramentality of human error and repentance captivate Father Brown. He follows clues with the sense of personal power conferred by simple lived truth or shared human struggle.

Author Greeley's vocation is to be a storyteller, and he embraces that vocation as both sacred and sacramental. He claims that all of his "novels are about God's love."[32] He embraces *sacrament* in the broadest terms as whatever discloses grace—especially water, fire, food, drink, and sex. Blackie is not the central character of all of the mystery series, but he is the element that holds the stories together. The celibate priest needs to coexist with power, money, and sex because they are essential elements of real life[33] and because "sex is edifying and religious and important."[34]

Central to every Greeley novel is his belief in the sacramental imagination that declares in word or picture that human passion is a hint of divine passion: "If God is love then surely S/He is present in sexual love."[35]

An understanding of Blackie Ryan is crucial to puzzle out Greeley's celibate mind. Greeley says that Blackie was a character who lurked in his imagination for a long time and who "sometimes speaks in the author's voice."[36] What, if anything, can the mind of Blackie Ryan and his creator, Andrew Greeley, reveal about the development and personalities of celibate priests?

GREELEY AND CELIBATE DEVELOPMENT

One basic question, and an area of justifiable fascination, is how does a man develop psychosexually without having any sexual experience? Greeley, Sheen, and Coughlin all began training for the priesthood during their adolescent years. Although none was bound by a promise of celibacy before ordination to the subdeaconate at around the age of 23, sexual abstinence was expected. Greeley denies any sexual love with a woman in his young life.[37]

Celibate development and adjustment are not and, by their nature, cannot be identical to adjustment that centers on sexual pair-bonding and/or parenting. An examination of the developmental picture of priests offered by priests and novelists becomes crucial to an understanding of celibacy because the Catholic priesthood and celibacy have, popularly and historically, become inextricably intertwined.

Greeley treasures the compliment of a friend: "You've always been a teenager, Father Greeley. You just never grew up."[38] One important key to understanding religious celibacy is evident by looking at adolescence itself. It would be naive to infer that this relegates celibacy to a state of immaturity. Pope John Paul II was nicknamed "the eternal teenager" as a young priest in Poland because he enjoyed the company and outdoor activities of his young students. Greeley has always enjoyed a good rapport with adolescents and is justifiably proud of this pastoral strength.

Adolescence is frequently understood as a period of transition between childhood and adult status. It would be incorrect, however, to equate adolescence with immaturity or exclusively as a stage in growth. Certain basic life tasks are resurgent during this period of life, including the need for intimacy, security, independence, work, peer relationships, and consolidation of identity and values—all fueled by hormonal and sexual changes. But these tasks and adjustments are lifelong challenges.

Religious celibacy capitalizes on the sets of personality tasks and opportunities common, but not limited, to this period of development called adolescence. These involve idealism, authority, consolidation of sexual identity, sexual themes, professional affiliation, and asceticism.

Idealism

The idealism of youth is legendary. This quality in adolescence is born of the sense of future and its seemingly boundless and eternal opportunities. In addition, a new and growing awareness of self positions one to participate in making the world better. Both qualities are beneficial for religious ministry and are clearly manifest in Greeley's storytelling. An I-can-do-anything attitude draws a man to noble tasks, creative enterprises, and original solutions.

Idealism can also lead a person to overvalue himself and exaggerate naive, healthy narcissism. A negative consequence of narcissistic thinking is idealization of the group to which one belongs. In the writings of Andrew Greeley, several of these groups appear. Irish Americans are most prominent, and they are said by their author to embody virtues of political ability, poetry, and (at least in the case of the women) unparalleled sexual attractiveness. Priests form another idealized group, although these priests must be of a particular stamp—not too stodgy, not too stupid, not gay, and certainly not Marxist—in other words, priests who agree with Greeley.

Authority

Questions about authority—one's own powers and the powers over one—are endemic to adolescence. The experience of one's independence, and the desire for it, motivates a man to seek the conditions and states that confer and enhance native endowments and minimize inherent limitations. The priesthood is an attractive prospect for many men precisely because it does offer an attractive power base.

James Joyce describes in elegant prose the ontic status and special powers of the Catholic priesthood as perceived by many young Catholic boys of his day:

> No king or emperor on this earth has the power of the priest of God. No angel or archangel in heaven, no saint, not even the Blessed Virgin herself has the power of the priest of God: the power of the keys, the power to bind and to loose from sin, the power of exorcism, the power to cast out from the creatures of God the evil spirits that have power over them, the power, the authority, to make the great God of Heaven come down upon the altar and take the form of bread and wine.[39]

Religious celibacy can and does exist outside of the priesthood, but within the priesthood it is subject to a strongly authoritarian structure and people who hold considerable authority over many of the elements of a man's life. A major task of adolescence is to balance one's own powers with and against the powers that be. The task is to make an honorable peace. The child-parent contest is the paradigm; the reality continues throughout the life cycle.

Greeley's conflict with authority figures is constant in his novels and in other writings, especially the autobiographical. He is not shy about depicting bishops as less than perfect or even despicable. Blackie, whom Greeley elevated to the episcopate in the course of his mythic career, is the embodiment of an ideal cleric. At the same time, Greeley has termed real-life bishops as a group "incompetent and stupid" and even psychopathic. The ongoing adolescent struggle between pleasing authority on the one hand and rebelling against it and subduing it on the other is alive in Greeley's writings.

Consolidation of Sexual Identity

Although adolescence is widely touted as the period of clarifying one's sexual identity, the reality of consolidation is far from contained within the parameters of teenage years and early adulthood. Certainly, many people discover aspects of their sexual geography during adolescence, but much of the topography remains to be mapped out in early adulthood and midlife. Even the wisdom of years is not immune from sexual discovery and fine-tuning.

Sexuality is a dynamic reality, comprising not only gender differentiation and sexual orientation, which in themselves have permeable perimeters, but the objects of excitation and the range and degree of sexual drives. Relationships, and the life experiences that one has been subjected to, influence all of these, as do the consequences of the choices one has made.

Sexual integration is no small accomplishment even under the most favorable of circumstances. Celibacy is a very special manner of sexual adjustment. Men who initiate celibate practice without sexual experimentation or with severely limited or skewed experience must find a variety of avenues to resolve natural sexual curiosity and establish and maintain sexual equilibrium. Sexual activity, let alone adventures, does not in itself assure integration.

Greeley advanced the economic theory of celibacy, claiming that celibacy itself plus training, practice of the ministry, and the grace of the priestly office give the priest "deeper insights into every human yearning," including the ability to support, advise, and assist married couples with their problems:

> For the Christian family, the example of the priest who is living his life of celibacy to the full will underscore the spiritual dimension of every love worthy of the name, and his personal sacrifice will merit for the faithful united in the holy bond of matrimony the grace of a true union.[40]

The priest, like every Catholic, is free to embrace his sacramental imagination: "a way of picturing reality in which God operates indirectly through the ordinary events of life." The paradox is that the celibant is deprived of one of the most important sacramental avenues in Greeley's schema of knowing the love of God: sex.

In his books, the priests can pace Greeley's imaginative process and difficulties in integrating sexuality with his celibate vocation. *The Cardinal Sins* depicts one idealized priest (underdeveloped in terms of Father Eugene Kennedy and Victor Heckler's psychological study of the priesthood) pitted against an aggressively sexually active priest (maldeveloped) whose sexual identity is undifferentiated but whose ecclesiastical career is successful.

Thy Brother's Wife tells the story of a priest who experiences one sexual lapse with a woman raised as his sister—mythically an act very close to incest. He abandons the woman to become a better priest. *Ascent into Hell* follows a similar pattern: A priest flees from grace and the active priesthood, returns, and resumes his celibate life. The priest's struggle between marriage and celibacy is explicit: "Had he been wrong all along? Had he sacrificed marriage for a historical mistake?"[41]

With the appearance of Blackie Ryan in *Virgin and Martyr*, however, the priest loses any real sexual/celibate conflict. He becomes a severed head, observing, judging, suggesting, fanaticizing, but never engaged in any sexual activity or any significant internal struggle with himself.

Greeley is on very solid historical and theological ground when he addresses God as male and female, with a preference for the female. The eleventh-century apse mosaic of the Cathedral of Torcello is inscribed "Deus Pater Materque"; that is, "God, the Father and Mother." Greeley claims to be comfortable with his anima—his feminine side—and addresses her as "Lady Wisdom." His myths demonstrate a greater comfort with the feminine than the masculine, not an uncommon feature in romantic novels or in the clerical psyche.

Greeley provides a strong indication of the level of consolidation within his own sexual/celibate differentiation in an incident he describes: He was sitting in a television studio in Tucson, Arizona, for an interview following the airing of *The Thorn Birds*. A cardinal in Philadelphia and a married priest and the priest's wife in Los Angeles, also participating in the remote hookup, were exchanging comments. The subject was celibacy. The married priest said his marriage was happy, and the wife agreed. Greeley later noted his own reaction: "I didn't think I would be happy married to *either* of them."[42]

Sexual Themes

Eight sexually related themes combine with remarkable economy in the writings of Andrew Greeley. His myths explore the common and primitive nature of the unconscious, which is yet accessible to language: Sexual anxiety

can reasonably be called *castration* because of its repetitious accretion of masculine prowess. The Oedipal drama is played out in the conflicts of the priests
with their authority figures. In the celibate mind, the primal scene is acted
out in the sexual adventures of others.

Many of Greeley's women characters are subjected to sadomasochism.
Although Blackie can demonstrate his strength with sadistic force, sexual
sacrifice is also a demand of the God who, by Greeley's definition, is like his
female character, Maria, "illusive, reckless, vulnerable, joyous, unpredictable,
irrepressible, unremittingly forgiving, and implacably loving." Maria must
give up her priest lover, and he must become celibate.[43]

The overall view of women in Greeley's novels is that of a virgin/whore
dichotomy, a common adolescent, imaginative solution to the threat of female
power. The tendency to narcissism in the novels is underlined by Greeley's
frequent explanations at the end of his books, underscoring for the reader
that they are about God. No matter if God or the priest or a woman is the
focus of the action, "The hero of the novel is the novel itself." The author is
"like God" informing all of the characters.

George Orwell observed that Graham Greene clothed theological speculation in "flesh and blood." Greeley can be said to wrap flesh and blood (sex)
in an elaborate theological myth.

Greeley is a good read; his celibate view of the world is attractive, in much
the same way that the adolescent process is engaging with its relative innocence, hope, enthusiasm, idealism, seductive fantasies, and freedom from
the ironies of human existence. Life can be imagined at a safe distance from the
sexuality that informs it. Greeley's imagination harbors a fund of knowledge
about celibacy; his myths tell the reader what he knows.

Professional Affiliation

The choice of work or professional affiliation in which one plans to settle
is regarded as an adolescent task. "What are you taking in school?" "What do
you hope to be when you grow up?" are cliché questions addressed to young
people. The choice of priesthood, like any profession, offers rich opportunities and makes special demands. Celibacy, a requirement unique to the priesthood for affiliation, can be attractive as well as daunting. The thought that
sexual conflicts and choices are settled once and for all, at least in principle,
provides relief from one basic human struggle. The achievement of any professional identity is a long-term process of internalization and individuation,
outlasting the original choice by a lifetime.

Asceticism

Self-control or self-mastery is one of the essential developmental tasks of
adolescence. Youthful athletic, intellectual, religious, and military conquests

all depend for success on the natural drive to conquer oneself, which is heightened during this time. Lack of impulse control and addictive traits undermine a person's ability to trust his own judgment. Choices made under stress are inimical to the achievement of celibacy. At the same time, an intuitive awareness of such a personality deficiency in himself can attract a man to a discipline and a system that he hopes will control him and his sexual instinct. Greeley describes some of these priests in his novels.

Prayer, work, service, and community bonding anchor celibate asceticism. Greeley demonstrates this asceticism in his life and in some of his priest characters.

Celibacy is an intriguing and valuable process. Novelists who have plumbed the depths of its richness provide a service to the understanding of human nature, religious striving, and sexual reality. Greeley reveals aspects of celibate development and reality in the myths he constructs from his imagination, from his sociological studies, and especially from his lived experience as a priest.

THE CELIBATE AUTHOR AND PERSONALITY

Does one type of personality predominate among the ranks of celibates? Life observation and the wide variety of priests portrayed in literature defy stereotyping. Greene's whiskey priest, Cather's archbishop, Power's Father Urban, Joyce's Father Flynn, Bernanos's curé, Voynich's Canon Montanelli, Ignazio Silone's Don Paolo, and the various priests of Farrell's and Greeley's Chicago all offer the reader a panoply of personality types from which he or she can distill images of priests. All are useful to the reader in constructing an understanding of men struggling to achieve the ideal of religious celibacy.

Have Greeley's personality traits affected his construction of myths and influenced his storytelling? It would be fruitless and foolhardy to attempt a reading of an author's life or personality from one of his novels. For instance, Bernanos's Nazi sympathies could not be discerned from reading his *Diary of a Country Priest*. Greeley offers readers a unique opportunity: He is a celibate priest constructing mythical priest characters at the same time that he offers an abundance of autobiographical revelations. What does the body of his work say about his celibate personality?

Greeley relates that some of his close friends and colleagues have called him paranoid. Certainly, from what Greeley writes, it would be unfair to use that as a diagnostic term. Greeley is the pioneer, the creator, the explorer whom Abraham Maslow describes as "generally a single, lonely person rather than a group, struggling alone with his inner conflicts, fears, defenses against arrogance and pride, even against paranoia."[44]

Every man who pursues celibacy has some personality type, a preferential psychic mode of coping with reality, reducing stress, establishing relationships, defining values, and channeling basic instinctive drives. Greeley's work is marked by his personality just as much as Coughlin's and Sheen's productions were.

Greeley has clearly been energetic, ambitious, hardworking, and competent. No one could question that he is intelligent and an intellectual. He says in his first autobiography that he had never experienced a depression or a "dark night of the soul"—a quite remarkable assertion for a deeply spiritual, celibate person whose life demands an essential loneliness. He says that he has always been conscious that he is different, a square peg.

Authority

Authority relationships have always been problematic for Greeley. He records in detail his conflict with bishops and pastors, and he does not mince words in pointing out their inadequacies. He is self-sufficient and has been resourceful in maintaining his autonomy within a highly structured organization. But he has experienced his own problems in exercising authority. Specifically, one of the greatest disappoints of his life was the small group community he had gathered around himself only to see it dissolve with acrimonious accusations that he was trying to dominate their lives.

Grandiosity and Projection

A hint of Greeley's grandiosity and projection of blame can be seen in the founding and breakup of his New Community, of which he wrote:

> It may well become a revolutionary development of the Church. It may represent a major step forward in the Christian life comparable to the appearances of the communities of hermits in the fourth century, the monastic communities of the sixth century, the friars in the twelfth and thirteenth centuries, and the congregations in the seventeenth and eighteenth centuries.[45]

Greeley vehemently resisted suggestions that he was in any way to blame, least of all psychologically, for the demise of the noble experiment. "They were either unable or unwilling to make the kind of religious commitment I was challenging them to make."[46] One favorite image, of himself as an "inkblot" for the entire Catholic Church, conveys with elegant economy Greeley's projection and grandiosity.

Hypersensitivity

Greeley claims that he has been "too trusting" and as a result has left himself open to personal hurts and betrayals. But the body of his writings portrays a personality type of the exact opposite bent. He is hypersensitive and easily offended. His attacks on book reviewers have been brutal and dismissive.[47] He was incensed when he felt slighted, for instance, by being left off the list of contemporary best-selling authors.[48]

Grudges and Enemies

Greeley holds grudges, and that is with a capital G. He devotes pages and chapters in both of his autobiographies to attacking his perceived opponents, and he relentlessly justifies his presumed misunderstood position and self. Irish humor fails him when it comes to the long list of his enemies: academics who impugn his scholarship, the Vatican bureaucracy, a list of popes, Cardinals Cody and Bernardin, pastors of the two parishes he served, Eugene Kennedy and other priests who leave the ministry, and even priests who stay in the priesthood. For instance, the National Federation of Priest Councils is "one of the worst collections of incompetent nitwits to whom it has ever been my displeasure to speak." A respected Catholic journal (*commonweal*) becomes "that mom-and-pop journal."

Greeley demonstrates a streak of self-importance and a shrill meanness and vindictive spirit toward anyone who ventures a criticism of his research, writings, wealth, and his sister Mary Jule, among others.

Narcissism

Greeley links Blackie with Anne Maria O'Brien Reilly, a character from his novel *Angels of September*, whom he identifies as one of his most mature heroines, "a laywoman who has been savaged by the church through much of her life." A colleague said: "Blackie and Maria are Andy's vision of God." Greeley agreed and elaborated: "The passionately loving and implacably seductive Maria" (fully sexually active) and the "ingenious, determined, mystery-solving Blackie" (celibate), "Only God is better, more lovely than Maria, more comic and resourceful than Blackie."[49] Greeley linked the sacramentalities of sex and priesthood (celibate existence) mediated by storytelling.

For Greeley, the status of mythmaker confers authority, in all senses of the word, including the right to define the world:

> I think I know a little bit more about how it feels to be God. For like God, a storyteller creates people, sets them in motion, outlines a scenario for them, falls in love with them, and then is not able to control what they do.[50]

The conglomerate of Greeley's personality traits has severely limited his capacity for intimacy. How much has this to do with his celibate striving and how much with his particular personality type? Celibacy does demand a special kind of aloneness, but given the range of observable celibates and the variety of novelistic interpretations of priests, a reader must conclude that Greeley's personality type is the foundation for, not the result of, his celibacy.

Coughlin and Sheen shared many personality characteristics with Greeley. Each also possessed a deep commitment to the church and a sense of a priestly vocation. Each was vigorously aggressive in promoting his chosen way of expressing his ministry and promoting it and himself. Each left a particular afterimage of priesthood and celibacy beyond his presentation. But the picture of the celibate personality left by Coughlin and Sheen is not entirely analyzable from their work alone. Greeley offers the student of celibacy an additional advantage by way of his mythic priests and people. His novels are projections of the mind of a priest-celibate. Every element of his personality can be deciphered from his stories. He *is* his stories.

CONCLUSION

Myth alone does not completely describe Greeley's stories. The reader must ask how much of Greeley's world is representational, depicting the real, observable, and quantifiable world, and how much is presentational, arguing for a world that might be. The line between these two modes of writing is fluid. There is an obvious representational dedication in the work of James T. Farrell, in contrast to the presentational effort of G. K. Chesterton. Farrell's work has a kind of photographic quality about it, extending from the everyday speech of his characters to their thoughts and dreams. Chesterton's work is allegorical. Each of these writers displays the reverse side of the coin, evident in Farrell's irony and in the morals illustrated by Chesterton's allegories, but Farrell's method remains representational and Chesterton's presentational.

Greeley's work is neither entirely presentational nor entirely representational. There can be no doubt that in his portraits of parish life, particularly those of the lives of his priests, Greeley is representational. Thus, priests do have sexual fantasies; some struggle successfully against their sexual instincts, and some fail; some are alcoholic, some demonic. Priests, bishops, and the church are open to some well-deserved criticism. U.S. Catholics really do practice birth control, live in families, work for a living, and attend church.

In other areas, Greeley is presentational: Most Americans are not part of the jet set. In general, however, even the presentational aspects of Greeley's work represent attainable and even laudable goals: People ought to be able to rise economically, and they ought to take church affairs seriously. They ought to take seriously the goal of a church that could concede the desirability of birth control and of premarital sex and the reality of divorce, a church that respects women (though it continues to deny them an equal share of power), and a church centered on family, parish, and priest.

Greeley seems to accept birth control but not, apparently, abortion. He accepts the inevitability of a certain number of failed marriages. He applauds a concentration of energies on injustice and suffering at home, on the beam in the believer's (or in the parish's) eye rather than on the mote in the world's eye. In all of these areas, Greeley is very close to the observed and quantifiable social reality of the Roman Catholic Church in the United States.

He is, moreover, just one tick off strict and accepted church doctrine. In a monolithic and hierarchical organization like the Roman Catholic Church, however, even this one tick can cause serious trouble for a priest. To Greeley, who has been subjected to the discipline of the church, receiving criticism and rejection from those he most wanted love has hurt him deeply and personally. At the same time, both psychologically and in the ontic system of the church, Greeley remains a priest.

Lack of maturity, indeed, may be said to characterize Greeley's novels. The novels themselves are almost literally adolescent: They are filled with energy and idealism, but they lack consistency and artistic distance.

More important than any literary deficits, Greeley gives his readers permission to imagine religion mythically and to consider openly their sexuality as a dimension of God's love. Whatever his motivation, he leads readers to question the celibacy and the sexuality of priests. Regardless of his own conflicts with authority, he reinforces and blesses his readers' doubts about the credibility of the teachings of the Catholic Church on human sexuality.

CHAPTER 8

Double Exposure: Andrew M. Greeley

The degree and kind of a man's sexuality reach up into the ultimate pinnacle of his spirit.

Friedrich Nietzsche

Andrew Greeley claims that priests possess a special fascination because of the celibacy associated with them. He is correct. Celibacy is a source of fascination. In his autobiographical account, Greeley delivers a double dose of fascination: first, in the rhetorical style with which he deals with sex and defends celibacy and, second, in the intriguing ways in which he reveals himself.

Writing fiction brought Greeley a serendipitous result. During the process, he discovered the anima of his personality in the women characters that he, "like God," created and fell in love with. Greeley posed Pygmalion as the positive myth for himself as a celibate at his time in history.[1]

According to the myth, Pygmalion set out to sculpt a woman more desirable than any mortal. A goddess invested his sculpture with life, and he received the object of unfettered male fantasy: a woman so completely his because she was so completely the creation of his own desire, the product of his own imagination. Freed from the imperfections of human relations, Pygmalion enjoyed both the godlike satisfaction of having created life and the self-centered gratification of keeping his sexual relations reserved for women of his own creation.[2] Although this myth is precisely the one Andrew Greeley appears to embrace so enthusiastically for himself, some readers find such a metaphor offensive when applied to the sexuality of a proclaimed celibate for whom celibacy is meant as a symbol of service to the needs of others.

There is a strong temptation when reading Greeley—especially within the often stultifying confines of traditional Catholic treatises on celibacy—to feel that he is refreshingly honest, contemporary, and direct. The writings of Gandhi and Fulton Sheen reveal a celibate tradition burdened by anti-sexual and misogynist prejudices. The components of Greeley's celebration of sexuality and women are neither so direct nor simple.

Achieved and integrated celibacy, wherever found, has been characterized by tolerance of others and modesty about oneself. The witness to the transcendent supports both qualities and a worldview in which all are as one.

Greeley's sexual/celibate world, like his rhetoric, is complex and difficult to measure. It is one of sharp distinctions between friends and foes, between men and women, between the righteous priests of his literary creations (who often speak for him) and the inadequate real-life church authorities who tolerate priest "pedophiles" and practitioners of the "gay lifestyle." He distinguishes between his own heterosexuality and the "orientation" of Joseph Cardinal Bernardin, about which, although he does not question, uninformed others "have their doubts."[3] Even the eroticized parts of women's bodies become distinct, quasi-religious icons in Greeley's hymns to "Lady Wisdom." Adolescents might more frankly and irreverently call Greeley's icons *T & A*—tits and ass.

Greeley shows one sign of a troublesome quality similarly exhibited by Gandhi and Sheen: an implicit superiority compared with noncelibates. Like Sheen, Greeley is reluctant to share any personal "weaknesses." Even though he does include some exonerating narrative of his celibate development—no adolescent loves and no adult love affairs—he, however, preserves and delights in his imagination on women, the objects of his seventh- and eighth-grade crushes. His frankness about his sexual fantasy life holds some of the charm found in the desert fathers, but he appears unnecessarily aggressive about proving their value and the adequacy of his "male hormones," as he puts it. The fact that strict church doctrine views lustful thoughts with as much abhorrence as the actual breaking of vows becomes conveniently irrelevant.

Greeley differs markedly from Gandhi and Sheen in that his use of these qualities is almost exclusively for self-acceptance. Gandhi's celibate discipline served one of the greatest ethical causes of our century. Even Sheen's mixed and defensive messages were deployed in the interest of the church as a collective institution. Greeley is a loner who has been at war with many branches of his own institution, conservatives and liberals alike, and his writings seek to enlist his readers in his cause through a bewildering combination of polemic, flattery, and scare tactics.[4]

Greeley's ability to combine contradictions—celibacy with flirtation, scientism with paganism, support of women's causes with antifeminism, requests for fairness with calls for purges—is a powerful and familiar rhetorical strategy used regularly by advertisers, religious preachers, and political demagogues.

Knowing how to use adjectives effectively, Greeley employs their full range of repertoires. For instance, a geographically scattered panel discussion of celibacy on *Nightline* after the airing of *The Thorn Birds* becomes "transcontinental." He becomes the "notorious sociologist from Tucson" who joins the panel. Father Ted Hesberg, president of Notre Dame, becomes a man answering questions from a "confused, conservative alumnus." John Cardinal Krol of Philadelphia becomes a "third-string sub" for Cardinal Bernardin, "who would not go on [the program] with me." A married couple is summarily dismissed—both parties—as unsuitable marriage partners for Greeley. In the end, he grants himself, generically to be sure, the potential of being the most "fascinating" man in the world.[5]

The core of Greeley's appeal is that, unlike Sheen and Gandhi, he claims to prefer a dialogic approach to the celibate tradition rather than a dogmatic defense of the discipline. He argues that unless church leaders accept the sexuality of priests and a "new" model for celibacy, "they will surely destroy celibacy in the long run." Although Greeley's argument is appealing, he seems reluctant to provide personal witness to what he preaches. If, as he says, celibacy is not served by denial or repression or pretense, why then does Greeley remain on the same allegorical level as Sheen when speaking of his own sexuality, merely exchanging Sheen's rhetoric of self-reproach with one of archness and titillation for the reader?

Revelations of Greeley's inner life are far removed from the witness of the desert fathers, who also shared their sexual fantasy life with their spiritual fathers; theirs, however, was marked with candor, distress, and concern that they could succumb to sexual compromise. Not so Greeley:

> So have there been women in my life…about whom I awake in the middle of the night with powerful hunger? With whom I can quickly imagine wonderful actions and fantastic pleasures? For that delightful delirium I am grateful, not ashamed…thus far the delights have led to no shattered promises or commitments.[6]

If masturbation indeed is his adjustment to celibate practice, as can be logically surmised from the revelation of his repeated nocturnal fantasies, why must it be denied in the first place, and why must it still remain an unspeakable word?

Greeley teases, yet at the same time archly blames his readers for the very thoughts he has conjured up:

> All abstract, you say? Anything less abstract than that, at this stage of the proceedings, you are not going to get, however much it might increase sales of the book. It would be telling, now, wouldn't it?[7]

The call for openness, never fulfilled, is typical of Greeley's clever rhetorical strategy, one that allows him to appear so much more direct than Sheen while still repeating the identical defensive moves. Both describe the celibate as the man who points to "that which is Beyond," only with this difference: Sheen served tradition, dogma, the church as an institution; Greeley's service is more self-limited under the guise of serving sexuality (Lady Wisdom) and woman, both cast in the mold of their maker.

Thus, Greeley's message, like Sheen's, becomes mixed with the relative values of marriage and celibacy in the sexual/ethical order. Sheen seeks to be a eunuch for heaven. Greeley prefers to cast himself as a platonic love person. Freed by his priestly vows from commitments to individual women, parish priest Father Greeley can be all things to all of the individual women in his flock.

Hermann Hesse wrote very insightfully about celibacy and fantasizing in *Siddhartha*.[8] In his novel *Steppenwolf*, the protagonist has a dream in which "All the Girls of the World Are Yours," a kind of mental theater in which the infinite potential love affairs with acquaintances and chance encounters are played out.[9]

Greeley has made his vocations as priest and writer similar theaters for safe sex. What is lacking in this totally understandable accommodation to celibacy is the sublimation of the erotic impulse into service, a resolution of negativity, and a manifest sense that all are one—essential elements in the model of achieved celibacy. Greeley's psychic investment, transferred from the literary women characters that he created, knew, and loved to the breasts and thighs of a passerby, is no more a sublimation of the libido than are the mental maneuvers of an immature noncelibate.

From the start, Greeley uses a highly overstated comparison to distinguish himself and celibates in general from all other men. Here is his definition:

> The celibate is the witness to the possibility of living in the world as a person powerfully attracted to women without being compelled to jump into bed with them.[10]

What a striking distortion. The measure of the celibate's relationship to women is measured against a behavior that, if understood literally (the only way that gives the comparison meaning), could be viewed as pathological.

Greeley suggests that his women parishioners and readers are getting the best of the celibate and noncelibate male companion in his kind of priest, the best of both worlds. The idealization of the married state and the bonding and healing role of sexuality within it stand in strange and inexplicable contrast to the image of the noncelibate man as an insensitive and unsteady companion for women.

For Greeley, the noncelibate is not equal to the celibate priest as a confidant and intimate companion of women, a point he argues from a bewildering range of positions. First, from the personal point of view, he repeatedly reassures readers that he is just as sensitive and probably more sympathetic to women that to most married men. He has so frequently stated that a confiding relationship between a woman and a "sensitive parish priest" actually benefits the couples' sexual relationship, that it has developed the quality of a mantra of reassurance.[11]

It is hard to accept that Greeley is not being disingenuous when he makes such a recommendation, particularly in light of research that finds considerable potential for these confidant relationships to become sexual. His exaltation in his celibate freedom runs the risk of mocking the confines of other commitments.

There is also a tone of cynicism when Greeley talks about the unmarried priest having extensive experience garnered from other peoples' lives and thus being able to give advice to married couples that he does not have to validate from his own marriage. The celibate is free to take risks that no married man could; he can say things to others about their relationships that he does not have to live up to. He is not obligated to practice what he preaches; the exact opposite in fact: He is forbidden to.[12]

The only measure readers have of the sexually charged nature of Greeley's one-on-one relationships with women is his deployment of rhetoric in the intimacy of the reader-writer dialogue. The archness and flirtation in some passages are surprising by any standard. His God is a woman with an Irish brogue:

Lady Wisdom:	Well, I'm not bad looking at all, if I do say so Myself. A lot better looking than that cabin attendant woman, though I'm rather proud of her too. I thought the arrangement of her curves was most ingenious. And the smile too, if you take my meaning—I get upset when people are too busy to admire my handiwork.
Me:	You put someone like that on every plane I board and I guarantee I'll admire her.
Lady Wisdom:	You dirty thing! But you're after missing the point. And that woman in the dining room? Wasn't I after outdoing Myself when I thought up her breasts?
Me:	You're the dirty thing, enjoying them that way.[13]

If this is a model for a real-life confidant relationship, it is a pretty strong come-on.

How does Greeley's game of flirtation fit with Sheen's tilt of moral superiority? Rather than make an unapologetic defense of his practice as a priest who indulges in enjoyable sexual fantasy instead of cultivating sublimation,

Greeley deflects scrutiny with a series of strategic appeals and covers. He hides the shrewdness of his sexual savvy behind a screen of suspended adolescent sexual development. His characterizations of women as followers and readers are sugarcoated with a superficial appropriation of feminism. He deflects attacks against his own ambiguous use of priestly "fascination"— privilege is more like it—by calling for a crusade against the "greatest threat to celibacy": homosexuality.

Again, his autobiography notwithstanding, the reader cannot speak of Greeley the person, only Greeley the writer. The latter forces the conclusion that he is a deliberate manipulator of contradictions. In the space of one page he can speak of "us" (i.e., men) as both mature and adolescent in their sexuality without acknowledging or exploring the implications of that simultaneity:

> The celibate and the married person both experience such…fantasy. Unless we, celibate or married, are early adolescents devoid of control of our most immediate urges, we appreciate the joy of such reactions and respect both ourselves and the other person and our other promises too much to permit our response to go beyond minor delight.…That a man could easily scream with desire for a woman who has smiled at him twice on an airplane flight.[14]

This fluctuation between mature and immature expressions of sexuality provides a kind of dissimulating cover; the adolescent persona allows him a way out of serious debate on sexuality/celibacy or his own celibate practice. It all seems as harmless and simple as the world in a teen magazine:

> So, those of you who were expecting "kiss and tell," eat your hearts out![15]

A kind of rhetorical double play reaches dizzying proportions in his absorption of feminist concerns into what is in essence an antifeminist worldview. It is tempting to accept him at his word when he says he merely wishes "to fend off the polemical feminist reviewer," but the adjectives are, in fact, inseparable. Although the author depicts himself as a defender of women within a misogynistic institution, this has considerably less to do with the emancipation of women than with the aggrandizement of their "champion." The alternating use of "He" and "She" for God remains fundamentally locked in strict gender roles. True egalitarians have urged non-gender-specific language for the liturgy.[16]

Although God can be a "She" when "arranging for the organs by which human neonates are fed," would the deity still be "Her" in the molding of Freud's universal signifier? These binaries may be structured as a dialogue, but the predetermination of appropriate gender behavior is still religiously— zealously—adhered to. Here is Greeley on the subject:

> We men perhaps may teach women about the captivating power of God, His imperious and loving demands that we surrender trustfully to Him and

give ourselves over completely to Him. They teach us about Her gentle, life-giving, healing grace.[17]

His description sounds like the same patriarchal ordering upon which power has been based for millennia.

When Greeley turns to sexual relations in his fiction, he uses oblique phrases such as "full-bodied sex person," and "a nubile member of the opposite gender," coupled with men's magazine clichés: "the mature, devastating, and delicious cabin attendant"; "the mature and tasty cabin attendant."[18]

These mixed messages seem part and parcel of a familiar rhetorical power game. Greeley's calls for enlightenment in the church's teachings on sexuality and for fairness to women are not only sensible but well put. This crusade on behalf of women is, however, to be carried out within the classical authoritarian power structure, headed not so much by men in general as by one man in particular.

When speculating on women's sexuality, Greeley seems to prefer mystical meditation to listening to (or reading) what real women have to say. He interrupts a reflection on the sexuality of various "persons" in order to remark:

Does the person of the opposite gender react analogously to you? Does she have her own fantasies while falling asleep? God knows.[19]

Greeley's final fierce attack on homosexuality does not cast him in a particularly flattering light, because it is confused. He identifies a scapegoat that can serve simultaneously as marginalized victim: the gay priest (and gay lifestyle). He confuses the evil victimizer (the pedophile) with the gay.

Sexual orientation is not identical with the object of desire. There is no evidence that gay-oriented priests violate their promise of celibacy any more or less than other priests. From his literary pulpit he can pour coals on the heads of sinners and under the feet of church authority by calling the church to account for their cover-up of sexual violations, especially of minors. The service of reform is mixed with the hysteria of his call for a purge of corruption, which forms a narrative with strikingly similar parallels to the concluding chapters of Sinclair Lewis's *Elmer Gantry*.[20]

Greeley courts women to join him in his campaign through a seemingly plausible, but actually tenuous argument:

[O]ne of the reasons for the continuation of Neo-platonic disgust for women in the Church is that some high-level leaders really dislike and fear women. They do not find them either attractive or tempting but repellent.[21]

Greeley defends himself and his mode of living celibacy by accusing the church of a double standard:

I find it ironic that my novels are thought to be "highly inappropriate" because of the shock they cause to those who haven't read them but who are troubled by the fact that I wrote, while the not only inappropriate but im-moral behavior of pedophile priests and the literally scandalous behavior of actively gay priests doesn't seem to create any problems at all.[22]

Greeley concludes with a veiled declaration of himself as the coming moral leader:

> Typical of the head-in-the-sand response of the church leadership to its gay lifestyle/pedophilia problem is the report on the state of the seminar-ies. You pretend, you cover up, you ignore, you pray it will go away. You do anything except act like a leader. I fear for the future. The celibate, to conclude where I began, is a man of fascination.[23]

Thus, the reader is led without explicit comment from the failure of the church's current leadership to the endangered future to the right man for the job. By this point the reader knows of only one celibate whose hands are clean, whose frankness is his sword and shield. And "God help those who are responsible."

Although Greeley is certainly an accomplished rhetorician and exposes the reader to a plethora of his own fantasies about sex and judgments on the state of celibacy in the priesthood, he provides little evidence to support the conclusion that he has completely integrated his sexuality/celibacy. Greeley also reveals his own exaggerated investment of being "a man of fascination."

PART II

FICTION, CELIBACY, AND THE SEARCH FOR TRUTH

CHAPTER 9

A Bridge from Autobiography to the Novel: James T. Farrell

Man defending the honor or welfare of his ethnic group is a man defending himself.

Milton M. Gordon

Chicago forms a kinship with thousands of people who have not been born or raised there; people who have never lived in Chicago or even visited there harbor deep feelings for the place. Chicago generates and invites a familiarity, so much so that many people, like me, experience a first visit as a homecoming.

A host of Chicago writers is responsible for this familial outreach. Each has peopled our imagination with characters, neighborhoods, and struggles that enhance our own family history. Among the most formidable of these writers are Theodore Dreiser, Carl Sandburg, Saul Bellow, Richard Wright, and James T. Farrell. In describing Chicago, each of them has in some sense described the color and texture of U.S. culture and of the U.S. family.

The novel form of literature can be a lens that focuses the problems of an age—or ageless problems—in a singularly powerful way. If a visual image—painting or photograph—can stun or haunt one's imagination into an awareness, the characters in a novel challenge one to action or transformation because they invite the reader to struggle through internal and social chaos endured in the novel. Such is the art of a novelist.

A scion of those who represent this artistic achievement is James T. Farrell, with his portrayal of society in transition in the person of Studs Lonigan. Studs Lonigan is one of those Chicago characters, like Dreiser's Sister Carrie,

Wright's Bigger, and Bellow's Herzog, who has become part of the U.S. literary landscape and family history. Studs is an urban Huck Finn who struggles
through home, school, and church; the streets and poolrooms of Chicago echo
the adolescent sexual development of Youth, Everywhere USA.

Farrell is the creator of Studs or, more accurately, the author who recorded
the life and death of Studs Lonigan in the trilogy *Young Lonigan, The Young
Manhood of Studs Lonigan,* and *Judgment Day.* Studs has an existence of his
own. He has joined the realm of the mythic, in which his persona transcends
his author or his author's life.

And *Studs Lonigan* is timely reading,[1] despite its dated slang. There is no
U.S. novel—*Studs* was the first published in 1932—that speaks so clearly to
the mood and the dilemmas of the final decade of the twentieth century. As
one analyst pointed out, "Behind the irreverence, the flaming youth, and the
artificial stimuli, were false patriotism, abnegation of ideals, the retreat from
sustained hope, and the use of sex as a palliative."[2]

Anyone who thinks that we are exaggerating Studs's relevance to the first
decade of the twenty-first century should reflect on Alan Friedman's evalu-
ation, delivered decades ago: "*Judgment Day* shows us a prostrate economy
that has not only terrified the leaders of industry and politics; it has sapped
the morale of the little businessmen and put fear and anxiety into the hearts
of the young generation."[3]

Certainly, the trilogy is a classic mirror of the past in which, if we look,
we can see our present condition in a clearer perspective. Margaret Zassenhaus, the German physician who saved scores of Scandinavian soldiers from
Nazi execution, said that the climate of the United States in 1992 was eerily
like the atmosphere of the pre-Hitler Germany she experienced.[4] The fate of
those who fail to learn the lessons of the past is apparent to all.

James T. Farrell, like Studs, was born and raised in Chicago. Irish parents
and Roman Catholic schools influenced both author and character. Farrell attended grade school at Corpus Christi and Saint Anselm's and high school at
Saint Cyril's. Unlike Studs, who dropped out of high school, Farrell attended
the University of Chicago for a couple of years. There he was deeply influenced by sociology, and much of his writing reflects his profound concern for
the social conditions of Chicago and the nation as well as their spiritual (and
material) poverty.

Farrell's *Studs* was branded as "filthy" because of its frank descriptions
of adolescent sexual development. Some scenes of masturbation were ex-
cised in early editions just as the scene of Bigger Thomas "polishing his
night stick" in the movie house was cut from Richard Wright's 1940 edition of *Native Son.* An English edition of *Studs* was issued in 1932 with the
disclaimer, "the sale of which is limited to physicians, social workers, teachers, and other persons having a professional interest in the psychology of
adolescence."

Andrew M. Greeley is a Chicago writer who can be compared with Farrell in the sense that he was deeply influenced by his Irish parents. His Catholic education extended through seminary and ordination to the Catholic priesthood, an alternative that Farrell considered briefly while he was in grade school.

Greeley is exquisitely sensitive to social conditions, and he often uses the Chicago setting as a metaphor for the social temperature and blood pressure of society, especially the society of the Catholic Church. He, too, was a student and even a lecturer in sociology at the University of Chicago. His books, too, have been branded filthy and sleazy (albeit equally unfairly) because of his frank portrayal of the sex lives of priests and bishops.

Greeley has done what no critic could presume to do: to compare himself not with Farrell, the Chicago Irish Catholic author, but with the life and character of Studs Lonigan, the prototype of Chicago Irish Catholic adolescence. When any author offers his readers such a personally profound and, at first glance, puzzling insight, it must be taken as a serious gift, a key to his own writing and person. Greeley makes the comparison, he tells us, after reading the novel and remembering it well.

At the critical juncture—in the first few pages of his autobiography, *Confessions of a Parish Priest*—when he is trying to introduce himself and his own life and to orient his readers, Greeley refers to Studs Lonigan's life at least six times. Greeley compares his own father with Studs's. His critical loves, he teases, could have been like Studs's Lucy. He confesses that the story of Studs and Lucy inspired tears, but he assures his bishop that there is no Lucy in his life. Greeley's revelation needs to be examined in detail to understand the celibate's comparison of himself with Studs.

Greeley familiarizes his readers with himself by taking his ethnic and economic bearings from Farrell's epic. Andrew Greeley was born in Chicago in 1928, a bare generation after Studs. Like Studs, he is a full-blooded Irish American: both sets of his grandparents were born within a few miles of each other in County Mayo. Of the Chicago of his parents' youth, Greeley writes:

> In the first two decades of this century the Chicago Irish were still, on the whole, poor, not perhaps quite as poor as they'd been in the world of Mr. Dooley's Bridgeport recorded by Finley Peter Dunne at the end of the nineteenth century but not yet quite as affluent and respectable as the painting contractor who was the father of James Farrell's Studs Lonigan.[5]

Moreover, he connects his father to Studs's father metonymically by beginning the next paragraph, "My father was..."

Greeley orients the reader to his own psychological valuation of relationships when he says (also in the first chapter of his autobiography):

> I don't cry much, but I did when I read James Farrell's story of the summer romance of Studs Lonigan and Lucy Scanlan, one of the most touching

accounts of love ever written....If ever there were a vivid portrait of what happens when grace is refused....Ah, but was there a Lucy Scanlan in my life? No.[6]

When Archbishop Joseph Bernardin asked him about the basis for some of his characters in *The Cardinal Sins*, Greeley responded that there was no Ellen in his life and concluded, "The storyteller in me realizes that a real-life counterpart of Lucy Scanlan or Ellen Foley would make it a far more interesting tale."[7]

There is a quadruple identification here. First, Greeley identifies personally and psychologically with the love observed (he cried). Second, Greeley the writer identifies professionally with *Studs:* he judges the work as a portrait of "grace...refused." *Comedies of grace* is a phrase Greeley uses frequently to describe his own novels. The third identification is frankly autobiographical and factual. He tells a bishop that there has never been a Lucy Scanlan (Farrell's character) or an Ellen Foley (his own character) in his own life. Fourth and most profoundly, Greeley teases the reader's imagination and encourages the reader to fantasize with him.

Here, the intuitive genius of Greeley emerges. He links himself, the storyteller, personally, intellectually, factually, and imaginatively with the protagonist of a great story told.

What follows here is a delineation of the comparison Greeley initiated. We will look at the Chicago, Irish, Catholic, sexual identity, and kinship manifested in Farrell's *Studs Lonigan* and in Greeley's autobiography and his novels.

CHICAGO

The Chicago of Studs Lonigan follows the axis of Fifty-eighth Street above Saint Patrick's parish and extends to Washington Park, with its lagoon (the parish is the geographic and mythic center). This is not so much geography as the topology of a culture, much as Sinclair Lewis's Main Street is an axis for states of mind and conflicts of values.

The poolroom is on Fifty-eighth Street, a street that is the spiritual center for the gang. Lucy's house is at Fifty-eighth and Indiana; Fifty-eighth and Michigan is where blacks are out of place.[8] The plight of black people is part of the Chicago streets, the site of the 1919 riots. Studs's Fifty-eighth Street is a world in transition. The streets of Chicago are the theater in which Studs plays out his life, where he repeatedly ends up drunk and sick, where his hopes are dashed, and where his deepest convictions are tested to the breaking point in arguments and fights.

The transition of Chicago is portrayed dramatically in one of the final sequences of the trilogy. Studs lies dying in his bed. His father Paddy (Patrick) goes to Saint Patrick's to pray for his son. Coming home from church, Paddy gets into his Ford and drives aimlessly from Fifty-sixth Street to the streets and neighborhoods of his own youth. They are streets now swaddled in poverty, boarded-up houses, closed factories, and still smelling of the stockyards. He stumbles onto a march led by the Trade Union Unity League, in which blacks and whites walk with one another and with children and Communist sympathizers of every brand (including the Irish Workers Club) parade through the streets where he grew up. They are no longer only Irish, no longer only white, and the neighborhood is no longer stable, predictable, or circumscribed.[9]

Many of Father Greeley's novels are set in Chicago, or they are at least centered there. Some of his books contain street maps such as those in *Angels of September* and *Patience of a Saint*, in which the John Hancock building, site of Greeley's apartment, is prominent. In *Love Story* and *Rite of Spring* are maps of Grand Beach and New Buffalo on the Lake Michigan shore, places similar to the site of Greeley's summer home. In *St. Valentine's Night*, Saint Praxide's parish is in a vague area of wooded hills described as a "magic neighborhood" and a "spoiled rich neighborhood," similar to that of Christ the King, Greeley's first parish assignment after his ordination. There are others.

But Greeley's characters do not explore Chicago's streets. His streets instead locate the halls of power: religious, economic, and political. The streets, for Greeley, are the grids that unite the powerful and that extend via O'Hare Airport to Washington, DC, and the Vatican. Greeley's axis is Lake Shore Drive, the northern suburbs with private homes and gardens, easy access to the lake and country club, and roads that lead to summer homes and to world travel, if necessary. But as in Studs's Chicago, there is an Irish Catholic parish church at the center of life in each of Greeley's novels.

IRISH

Andrew Greeley begins an essay, "The South Side Irish since the Death of Studs," with these words: "I remembered enough about the story of Studs Lonigan not to want to read it again. I knew it would force me to think once more about a problem that is too painfully close to me, both as a priest and as a human being—the tragedy of the Irish."[10] This essay is one of Greeley's most self-revealing pieces of writing; the revelation is both literary and psychological.

Studs moves in an Irish American universe. His father, Paddy, was born in Ireland and emigrated with his family when he was a child. His mother, Mary, was the child of Irish-born parents. Almost all of Studs's friends are Irish American: Weary Reilly, Red Kelly, Arnold Sheehan, Tommy Doyle, Paulie Haggerty, Three-Star Hennessey, Vinc Curley, Slug Mason, TB McCarthy, Elizabeth Burns, Lucy Scanlan, and Helen Shires (who is Protestant Irish).

The priests at Saint Patrick's, Father Gilhooley and Father Doneggan, are also Irish. In school and on the football field, Studs occasionally interacts with Polish Americans, and in the dance hall he meets a Swedish girl "with an accent." Two of Studs's crowd are Jewish: Davey Cohen and Phil Rolfe; Phil eventually converts to Catholicism and marries Studs's sister. For the most part, however, the people in Studs's world are Irish.

To be Irish American in Studs's Chicago meant to be part of an identifiable minority. It meant, in effect, to be assigned to certain neighborhoods, certain Democratic clubs, certain occupations, and even certain Catholic parishes: Saint Patrick's was known as an Irish church, and there were German, Polish, and Italian churches in other parts of the city. To be Irish meant to be part of a rising, relatively privileged economic group on a par with the Germans—above the more recently arrived groups from Southern and Eastern Europe but below the "old money." At the same time, some social stigma clung to the Irish. This social stigma frequently produced an aggrieved and defensive ethnic pride.

Like Studs, Greeley is an Irish American. Moreover, all of Greeley's novels concern Irish or Irish Americans. The heroes and the villains are Irish. Irishness is as essential to Greeley's identity as is his priesthood. He attributes both his success as well as some of his failures to these realities. When he was denied tenure at the University of Chicago for the eighth time, he attributed it to ethnic and religious bias. He wrote, "the sign 'No Irish Need Apply'...still hangs at the entrance to most intellectual literary circles and at the backs of most senior chairs in the country's major universities."[11]

Concurrently, in another article, Greeley commented on the same set of affairs by identifying himself as a "loud-mouthed Irish priest" and saying, "I am, damn it, still capable of standing by my own kind, come what may, and I wouldn't trade that for anything—not even for a membership in the National Academy of Science."[12] By "my own kind" it is clear that Greeley means the Irish Catholics. He expresses his pique in tones not unlike those Studs and his friends used toward their "enemies."

There is a poignant passage in Greeley's essay on the South Side Irish:

He is uncertain of his own emotions and the irrational powers, which he dimly perceives, that reside in the depths of his personality. But if his anger is ever given full vent, he is afraid that he will kill and destroy—especially the parents about whom he feels so ambivalent.

He is afraid of failure and thus leads a narrow, constrained, restricted life, which, while it guarantees that he will not fail, also prevents him from achieving the success that his talents and creativity would make possible. Like his predecessor Studs Lonigan, a contemporary South Side Irish male is the master of romance daydreaming, and, like Studs, he even understands vaguely that he has the capacities to make the daydreams come true. To put the matter bluntly, the Irishman will not and cannot be himself because his mother won't let him.

One suspects that it is not only the nieces and nephews of Studs Lonigan who are beset by strong self-destructive urges.[13]

Is Greeley also speaking of his own deep Irish self? John N. Kotre, Greeley's biographer, begins his work with a description of Greeley's "recurring dream" and speaks of Greeley the dreamer. The same biographer was cited in *The Wall Street Journal,* in which he speculated about Greeley's self-defeating cycles in institutions and with individuals. Whatever else, there is no doubt that Greeley is thoroughly Irish: a full-blooded Chicago Catholic Irishman.

Irish and Alcohol

Greeley makes another very telling reference to Studs Lonigan in this essay on the Irish. He identifies the destiny of the Irish American with Studs by way of alcohol:

Studs Lonigan loathed himself, and his whole life was a systematic effort to punish himself for his own worthlessness....None of this has changed. The site has moved from Fifty-eighth and Indiana to Beverly, but the self-loathing and self-destruction continue. South Side Irish—a marvelously gifted and creative people—have been bent on destroying themselves for three-quarters of a century. It looks as though they are beginning to succeed.[14]

Although Greeley drinks little himself, he is conscious that his identification as an Irishman is deeply aligned with drinking. Greeley, of course, is correct that alcohol is an essential part of the spirit and poverty in Farrell's novel, not merely in Studs's life but also in the Irish culture and family. Greeley's own grandfathers were both alcoholics.

Both Studs's father and brother are drunk at the moment of Studs's death. His father ends his tour of the neighborhood of his childhood in a speakeasy, and in his drunken stupor he speaks of "God's will" and the "dark angel" and says, "I had to get drunk. I'm not a drinking man. I had to. When everything a man has falls from under him, he's got to do something."[15]

Drink is a link between being Irish and being Catholic, certainly for Studs and clearly in Greeley's estimation. Jimmy Breslin describes a link with the meaning of being Irish in New York:

[T]here are great outward signs of Irishness. A network of neighborhood travel agencies keeps the Irish Airlines waiting room at Kennedy Airport filled with people taking advantages of low-cost tours. Saloon after saloon has a shamrock on its neon sign. And once a year everybody stops and goes to the St. Patrick's Day parade on Fifth Avenue. After these things it ends....Most people in New York with Irish names go back at least three generations before they reach Irish-born in the family. The heritage of being Irish is more a toy than a reality. A drink, a couple of wooden sayings, and a great personal pride, bordering on the hysterical, in being Irish.[16]

Drink was the death of Studs.

CATHOLIC

There is no question that *Studs Lonigan* is a religious novel in a way that is similar to the way Ernest Hemingway's *A Farewell to Arms* is a religious novel and Catholic. Hemingway's protagonist seeks salvation through his symbolic baptism (crossing the river to flee the demons of war) and his identification with Christ's passion and crucifixion (the bloody wounds he endures to save his loved one). Even if his final solution is nihilistic (God plays with humans only to torture them), the novel is a profound struggle demanding reflection on the place of religion in human destiny and on the irony of existence and its temporality.

Georg Lukács is correct when he insists that such reflection is the melancholy of every genuine novel.[17] I hold to the theory that every born-Catholic novelist is compelled to exorcise the religious demons of youth in at least one novel. For Farrell, it was *Studs Lonigan*. For Greeley, it was *The Cardinal Sins.*

The priests of Saint Patrick's Church hold a central but circumscribed place in Studs Lonigan's fate, from the opening chapters of the first volume,[18] which record his graduation from Saint Patrick's grade school, to the last chapters of the third volume, in which an anonymous "tall dark priest" anoints him on his deathbed.[19]

Farrell wrote that *Studs* was a tale of "spiritual poverty." Greeley says that all of his novels are comedies of grace; they are "about God's love...stories...of the 'breaking in' of God to the ordinary events of human life."[20] Later I will address each author's capacity for self-reflection. Here I want to compare the portraits of priests that each author paints.

Farrell's Priests

Father Gilhooley is the pastor of Saint Patrick's. Our first glimpse of him is as "he pursed his fat lips, rubbed his fat paws together and suavely caressed his bay front. A fly buzzed momentarily above him."[21] He speaks of "Gawd" in theologically correct terms: good and evil, the value of a Catholic education, the dangers of life (i.e., sex, the "primrose path to the everlasting bonfire").[22] But what really endures about his being is his obsession with raising funds to build his new Saint Patrick's Church: "Father Gilhooley was probably happy, thinking of what a collection he would get, and of how many parishioners had received Holy Communion," Studs opines at Christmas Mass.[23]

Father Doneggan is an assistant pastor. There is a detailed portrait of him during the same Mass. He appears quite admirable. He is devout, observant, but he is careful not to let his celebration become mere ritual. In his sermon, Father Doneggan offers his congregation a vision of Jesus as a baby, a vulnerable and powerless human being, a vision Studs cannot accept because he sees Christ as a stern judge.[24] Studs even senses that Father Doneggan wants to be his friend; he feels that the priest is "someone a guy could even have a drink with." Conviviality, however, is as close as Studs can come to true friendship and communication, and this limitation, no less than the bare stage of Studs's mental theater, reflects his own spiritual poverty as well as that of the priest/church to meet human needs.

Father Roney, another assistant pastor, is the moderator of the youth club, the Order of Christopher, the goal of which was to organize the "best stuff of Catholic American manhood." He stages a fake fight to teach lessons such as patience and fortitude. He administers the oath of "secrecy and the defense of his faith and his country" to the initiates for the protection of "Church and clergy wherever and whenever it may be needed."[25]

Father Shannon, "a plump bald-headed priest," along with Father Kandinsky, his sidekick, visits Saint Patrick's to preach a parish "Mission," the Catholic equivalent of a Tent Revival. He preaches an emotionally moving sermon that results in the youth of the parish coming to confession and communion in droves. Studs and some of the gang even swear off alcohol, briefly.[26]

Studs interacts with all of these priests, but his conversions are shallow. He ends up in the gutter, drunk, on New Year's Day 1929. Mental impressions of priests are lasting: Father Shannon accusingly appears in Studs's final delirium with Lucy Scanlan on his arm.

Then there is Father Moylan. On Sundays, Studs's father listens to Father Moylan on the radio, just as Greeley's father listened to Father Charles Coughlin on his radio. Greeley hastens to assure us, however, that "Dad did not buy Coughlin's anti-Semitism, by the way, not one bit."[27] We do not know what else of the radio priest's message *was* bought; inasmuch as Coughlin/Moylan was the most famous and powerful person outside government in the 1930s, claiming 40 million listeners each week, we can assume that there was in both Irishmen at least a modicum of approval.

Father Moylan was a man whose message exercised a powerful appeal for Studs's gang:

> "Well, Hoover is nothing but the tool of the international bankers, and he's the guy who put the country on the fritz," Red said.
>
> "That's just what Father Moylan has been saying on the radio," Mugsy said.

"There's a man for you. Boy, what Father Moylan doesn't say about the bankers, and the Reds too" Kelly said.[28]

A tall, dark priest precisely, solemnly, devoutly, and almost without personal interaction anoints Studs with the last rites (extreme unction). He is truly a man of mystery. He is an "outsider": religion personified. He is not of this world and not able to save or transform, unlike the social circumstances, such as the black population growth, that did transform both Saint Patrick's Church and Studs's neighborhood.

For Studs, the Catholic Church is not a religion or matter of spirituality as much as it is an identity, defining his family, his friends, his school, and his community. Studs was born into a Catholic family, and he is therefore Catholic, no matter what his beliefs, attitudes, or conduct may be.

Religion does intrude from time to time on Studs's consciousness, whereas spirituality and meaning do not. Studs does not apply the lessons of Jesus or the teachings of the church to his daily life—a life that consists for the most part of aimless wandering through the streets of Chicago, relieved by frequent squabbles with his family and his associates, binge drinking, and very occasionally, unthinking, almost anonymous sexual encounters.

Once in a while, Studs goes to confession and receives communion. These episodes are intimately connected with his conflicting feelings about sex and, not coincidentally, death and hellfire.

Greeley's Priests

In contrast to the priests in *Studs Lonigan*, who occupy a central but demarcated place, the priests in Andrew Greeley's works are diffused throughout the texts. Every one of Greeley's novels concerns a hero who either is a priest himself (as in *The Cardinal Sins, Thy Brother's Wife, Virgin and Martyr, Angels of September, Occasion of Sin*, and the Blackie Ryan mysteries) or is someone very like a priest: a priest on a kind of leave of absence from his vows in *Ascent into Hell* (during which he discovers sex), a weird oversexed priest in *The Final Planet*, or a former seminarian in *Lord of the Dance, Patience of a Saint, St. Valentine's Night, Love Story, The Search for Maggie Ward*, and *Rite of Spring*.

Other minor priest characters in each of Greeley's novels complete his tapestry. Priest/sex/church/social structure—all separate elements in Farrell's work—are woven into one seamless garment in Greeley's.

For instance, the life and destiny of Cathy, the protagonist of *Virgin and Martyr*, are inextricably bound to the love and torture she receives from her priests. Father Blackie, a Chicago seminarian/priest ministers to her via correspondence. Father Tuohy, a misguided liberal activist, whom Greeley most unfairly compares with the peace activists the Fathers Philip and Daniel Berrigan, marries and then divorces Cathy. He turns out to be homosexual.

Father Ed, a liberation theology priest in "Costaguana" loves Cathy, but he sells her to the local authorities to be tortured and raped. Finally Father Tierney, a drunken lecherous old priest, attempts to rape her. Only Father Blackie Ryan, Greeley's alter ego, intervenes, an action that sends Tierney to an asylum.

What emerges from the tapestry of Farrell's priests is a picture of human beings struggling, much of the time ineffectively, with the inexplicable conundrums of life and death: meaninglessness and powerlessness, racial injustice and anti-Semitism, social transition.

Farrell's refusal to judge priests or even Studs amounts, paradoxically, to a Christian attitude from a former Catholic/atheist/Marxist. *Studs Lonigan* demands reflection. It invites the reader to bring his or her own experiences and judgment to the struggles of the characters. The voices of the author and the characters are clear and distinct, leaving room for the reader to listen.

Greeley's portraits of priests are intimate. He produces a view of the world from the inside of the priest/church. Greeley's stories are tales of revelation, vengeance, judgment, warning, and power. "Don't fuck with God," says Father Blackie. Greeley assures us that Blackie is a character that sometimes speaks with the author's voice.

The church, even if ineffective, is a power, and its power is portrayed in intriguing and at the same time compelling imaginings that are not burdened by objectivity. The voice of the author and the characters merge and separate, somewhat indiscriminately. The result is more the musings of the author on a myth rather than an invitation to reflection. In fact, it is this very diffusion of character and voice that limits Greeley's power as a novelist.

Greeley argues correctly that his critics are unfair when they complain that his priests never pray. His priests *do* pray in every novel. What his critics mean, no doubt, is that the religious activities of his heroes—prayer, reflection, meditation, dialogue, and liturgy—tend to be eclipsed by their superhuman deeds. Greeley's priests engage in such exciting activities—electing popes *(The Cardinal Sins)*, making and unmaking saints *(Virgin and Martyr* and *Occasion of Sin)*, colonizing new worlds *(The Final Planet)*, solving murders *(St. Valentine's Night, Happy Are the Meek, Happy Are the Clean of Heart, Happy Are Those Who Thirst for Justice)*, undertaking love affairs *(The Cardinal Sins* and *Thy Brother's Wife)*—that it is easy to miss their religious activities. The rift between religious activities and spiritual meaning so gaping in Studs's life is not entirely healed in Greeley's novels, but both do seek to heal the chasm with sex.

SEXUAL IDENTIFICATION

Farrell

Studs is the epitome of adolescent struggle for sexual identification. His struggles are more explicit than those of Mark Twain's Huck Finn, but his goal of a firm sexual identity is no less clear. He masturbates, to be sure, but he does so with richer fantasy, more social awareness, and less compulsivity than Philip Roth's Portnoy.

As a 14-year-old boy, Studs idealizes Lucy Scanlan, the love of his life. This idealization emerges into a tender exchange of words and kisses in a tree in Washington Park, a scene in which Studs is tortured by the recurrent desire to "feel her up." However, Studs does not initiate his heterosexual activity with the girl he loves but does so rather with Iris, the "Anybody's" of Studs's neighborhood. According to Studs's friend Helen Shires, Lucy is jealous (or perhaps merely shocked) when she learns of Studs's escapade with Iris. Studs tries to seduce Helen even as she speaks of Lucy:

> Lucy! She seemed quite far away from him now. At times he liked her, and at times he tried to pretend to himself that he didn't. He wanted to tell it all to Helen, and the words choked in his throat. The time they sat in the tree! Helen said she could fix things up for him with Lucy. He wanted to say go ahead, but something stopped him....Lucy liked him, and it might do her good if she did a little worrying because he acted like he didn't like her....He told Helen that Lucy was all right, but he didn't think he was interested in girls any more.[29]

On both sides, the relationship between Studs and Lucy remains abstract, idealized, and imaginary for many years. There is a note of cruelty in the thought that it would do Lucy some good to worry. The ambivalence of adolescent sexual identity is betrayed in his thought that he "might not be interested in girls any more."

Studs maintains his idealization, but he wishes to show off before someone:

> Other guys had girls. Wished he had a girl, Lucy, a girl coming out only to see him play...goofy!...But he still loved Lucy even if he hadn't seen her in about four years.[30]

Studs's one chance to meld idealization/romanticism with mature sexual love ends disastrously. At a dance, his sister Fran arranges a date between Studs and Lucy. Studs's parents are ecstatic; Lucy is precisely the kind of girl they want for him. She is pretty, respectable, rich, and Irish Catholic. But at the dance, Studs behaves badly:

> He was surly....Lucy seemed to notice it.
> "You know, Studs, a girl likes to dance with different fellows. Variety is the spice of life," she said, during the next dance.
> "I didn't say anything."
> "I know that old dark look of yours."
> He tried to smile. He wanted it to be over, and him and Lucy to be alone.[31]

After the dance and before the cab ride to her house, Lucy says both insight-fully and indulgently, "You're just the same Studs...just like a little boy."[32]

The exchange in the cab ride home is focal for the understanding of Studs and his sexual development. At this time, he is well aware that he is suffering from an untreated case of gonorrhea.

Suddenly, he was French-kissing her. He dug through her dress and touched her breast. She froze up, turned her face away.

"I'm not that kind of a girl."

He tried, crudely, determined, unthinking, to pull her to him again.

"Please be careful," she said cuttingly.

He looked out the window. He saw the lake. He grabbed her hand. He kissed her. She opened her mouth on the next kiss. He felt under her dress.

"I won't hurt you. Come on," he said huskily. He didn't even think of his dose, all he had in mind was Lucy.

"I can't...no...not here. If my mother isn't home, maybe . . . "

"Why not?" he said.

"I can't...it'll be awful...I'll ruin my clothes...please wait till we get home," she begged.

He believed her. They kissed, and he felt her all the way home. She got out of the car rumpled, and rushed into the hallway. He paid the bill.

She opened the inside door, and stood holding it, blocking his entrance. She pursed her lips for him. They kissed. He tried to push open the door.

"No," she said.

She pushed his hat off, and when he turned, closed the door on him. He watched her go upstairs. She didn't look back.

He walked slowly out and away.

"That goddamn teaser!"

He felt that he'd been a goddamn chump, but realized what a bastard he'd been, trying to make her. He couldn't get her out of his mind.[33]

And "in his mind" is where Lucy stays, for her actual association with Studs comes to an end with this episode.

She appears in Studs's final delirium amid the phantasmagoric images of priests, nuns, his father, the pope (dropped on his buttocks, saying, "Do you receive the sacraments regularly?"), and his sister. They all dance around Studs accusingly. The vision continues: "Father Shannon, on the arm of Lucy Scanlan who was naked and bleeding from her young breasts, stopped before him and said, 'Be a man.'"[34]

Catherine, the pregnant woman whom Studs had planned to marry, loves him and recalls their sexual interaction as "beautiful." She is the faithful one by his dying side. But bloodied Lucy is the final vision of his dream, standing among those chasing him and shouting: "Stop thief!"

Studs sees himself running from them all and shouting, "Save me! Save me! Save me!" But there is no indication to whom his pleas are directed because all of the powers that be in Studs's world are accusing and pursuing him. The next person to speak is his mother, who announces, "He's dying."

Studs's relationship with Lucy is marked by its adolescent idealization, romantic exploration (the tree), devastating and incomplete sexual exchange (the cab), and the preservation of the image in cruel fantasy.

The final appearance of Lucy on the arm of a priest sums up poignantly Studs's experience that religion does not help one become a man despite its doctrinal demands. Studs remains an undifferentiated adolescent whose infantile sadomasochistic attitude toward women is never wholly absorbed by his masculine consolidation and ability to love the complementary sex.

Certainly, Studs is not a homosexual, but he languishes in a sexual developmental lag that is a cross between the normal homosexual phase of development, which is popularly termed *the gang age*, and deeper elements of latent curiosity. One cannot ignore these elements in Studs's character. "You were never one for the girls, Studs," one of the gang reminds him, and indeed he never was. Studs clearly feels more comfortable around men, around his gang, than he does around women, with the interesting exception of Helen Shires, who eventually comes out as a lesbian. Moreover, Studs is approached at least three times by men. One such approach occurs when Leon, an effeminate music teacher and acquaintance of Studs, pressures him to take private piano lessons.[35] The teacher's advances leave Studs with conflicted response. He has "no answer for Leon."

When an old man in the park makes a pass at him, Studs is frankly disgusted. Later, he finds himself "strangely interested" in a group of black gays who invite his companionship.

Studs's psychosexual struggles are intensified by the teachings of his church and the values of his gang. Both encourage his sexual conflicts to take the shape of a general violence—a madonna-whore view of women—and prolongation of a confused phase of sexual identity.

Farrell is merely putting Studs through the normal adolescent paces. The fact that Studs fails to negotiate successfully the sexual trek from childhood to maturity only heightens the reflective force that confronts the observer of Studs's journey.

Greeley

Does this journey have anything to do with Andrew Greeley, priest, sociologist, and, novelist? Yes, because he is a champion of the imaginative aspect of religion, of the reflective force of story and symbol. They form the bedrock of his sociological theory of religion. "We are reflective creatures; we must reflect on our imaginative religion."[36]

Greeley is explicit when he draws sexual images of the women and men (especially priests) who people his novels. It is his imagination, his experience of sexual development as part and parcel of the human quest, and the religious experience that he poses for his readers. His graphic sexual imaginations make it apparent how Greeley identifies himself with Studs rather than Farrell.

Adolescence and certain stages of celibate development both enrich and limit the sexual imagination. The mental productions of Studs and Greeley reflect the rich fantasy enlivened and circumscribed by lack of experience. Descriptions of sexual activities, feelings, and attributes occupy a very large place in Greeley's books. Greeley does not shy away from sacerdotal sex, a subject Farrell did not deal with and one Studs would find unimaginable.

Greeley practices celibacy. He clearly implies in his autobiography that he has never had sex with a woman. None of his writings betrays this truth. Accounts of sexual intercourse by an ordained priest in good standing are relatively rare in Greeley's books, occurring only in *The Cardinal Sins* and once in *Thy Brother's Wife* and in *Virgin and Martyr*. These are Greeley's most personally revealing novels. There are also allusions to, but not descriptions of, homosexual behavior by priests in several of his books. There are no scenes of masturbation in Greeley's writing, in contrast to both Farrell and Richard Wright, the latter's censored accounts from *Native Son* being published for the first time only in the 1991 Library of America edition.

Many of Greeley's characters are priests who are not in good standing with church authority or who are quasi priests: seminarians, boys preparing for the seminary, former seminarians, and a self-appointed saint (in the 1987 *Patience of a Saint*). These folk are given free rein, and their sexual activity is recorded.

Pain or torture of women is part and parcel of much of Greeley's sex. In its most demonic form, the woman is cruelly raped—often by the Mafia—as a sanction against her male relatives.

There is a special category of adolescent sexual play so frequent in Greeley's novels that it merits its own category: mixed skinny-dipping along with references to *Playboy* centerfolds. These events merit further analysis inasmuch as they are part of a system of recurring symbols in Greeley's writing along with water, fire, and the empty tomb.

Finally, all of the women in Greeley's novels, be they schoolgirls, nuns, or old ladies, are portrayed as sexually irresistible, with special attention given to sexually attractive bodily parts (legs, breasts, hips). One wonders where are the less comely, the less well endowed, the plainer women who people the real world? Only the uninitiated imagination clothes feminine beauty exclusively in a form worthy of *Playboy* magazine.

Greeley the author idealizes women. Nevertheless, there is an edge of empathy that Farrell the author consistently demonstrates. This element is just as consistently lacking in Greeley's novels. There is, for instance, a graphic rape scene that concludes Farrell's second volume. Weary Reilly rapes Irene[37] at a New Year's Eve party. One can be moved to tears for the victim. A rape scene in Greeley's *Virgin and Martyr*, much less explicit than Farrell's, leaves the reader cold and evokes little empathy:

> The commandante handed Ed a thick packet. Money? She thought. Father Ed sold me to him for money?
>
> She went unresistingly to the police car, too numb from shock to fight back.
>
> In the police station, Don Felipe was the first to rape her. She realized soon that he could not have sex without tormenting his partner. Only when he hit her bare buttocks with his riding whip was he able to force himself into her.
>
> As the whip cut into her flesh, she repeated over and over to herself the incredible words: Father Ed sold me, Father Ed sold me.
>
> Then the other police took turns raping and sodomizing her. Fifteen, twenty times. She lost count.
>
> And that was only the first night.[38]

Voices

When reading Farrell, it is fairly easy to distinguish the voices of the characters from that of the author. The characters do not fracture sexually; that is, there is a precision to their mythic existence that allows them to struggle freely even with their own sexual confusion, as Studs does. By contrast, Greeley's voice is quite frequently confused with that of his characters, both male and female.

For all of their elements of merchandising, book jackets do tell something about the contents of the book. A nude woman, seated, surrounded by ells of red velvet, graces the cover of Greeley's first novel. This cover, Greeley tells us, was his personal choice and decision. Images of beautiful languorous women in dishabille continue across 20 covers of Greeley's fiction. The packaging provokes some of Greeley's 20 million readers to attend to the word picture signaled on the cover.

Furthermore, if one compares the female body as presented by the two writers, one is quickly struck by their differing grades of objectivity. There is a nude scene in *The Lord of the Dance*[39] in which Irene Farrell is sitting in her bathtub and sipping a vodka martini: "Her body, a sponge for sensual pleasure, soaked up the reassuring warmth." We are told, "She had lost fifteen pounds" (without telling us what her original weight was from which the fifteen pounds were subtracted) "only she didn't really need to lose them. Irene turned away from the mirror, embarrassed as she always was by the image of her swelling breasts and full hips."

After Irene slips into an appealing bit of lingerie, her daughter Noele comes into the steamy-mirrored, powder blue–carpeted room. "'You're totally beautiful....I want you to be the prettiest mother in the parish.'" Greeley's voice and his personality seem to infuse with that of his character so that she is at once seen and seeing (as in the bathroom mirror), desired and desiring. One gets the impression that the author has somehow failed to understand the concept of detachment. Would Irene, who is embarrassed by her nakedness, even when alone in the bathroom, ever characterize her own body as a "sponge for sensual pleasure"? And who would be more likely to conceptualize the woman as being the "prettiest in he parish," the teenaged daughter or the parish priest?

This casual confusion of sexes pervades Greeley's writings, his nonfiction as well as his novels. For instance, in commenting on celibacy and sexuality in his autobiography, Greeley recounts an instance of sharing a television commentary with other notables such as Cardinal Krol, Father Hesburgh, and a person he lists as a "sometime priest." Greeley reflects on the experience with these words: "The sometime priest told how happy was marriage. His wife agreed. Secure in the tiny studio in Tucson, I noted cynically to myself that I didn't think I would be happy married to either of them."[40] *Cynicism* is perhaps the least significant element of that particular self-revelation.

Farrell wrote a nude scene that illustrates the distinction. In this interchange, Margaret, the daughter, is in the kitchen and is nude. Her mother comments:

> "It's a sin to be seen in your pelt," Mrs. O'Flaherty said from her bedroom off the kitchen, where she sat in her rocking chair, sewing.
>
> Naked, Margaret stood over the stove, waiting for the coffee in the white enameled coffee pot to heat. She was a well-built woman weighing about one hundred and thirty pounds, her hair brown and warm but not very thick, her eyes blue, her lips thin, her arms slender, her breasts small and upright, her pubic hair a large dark swab. The mother dropped her sewing, drew out a clay pipe, filled it, lit the pipe, stood in the doorway puffing, watching her daughter smoke a cigarette.
>
> "My mother, may the Lord have mercy on her soul, would have skinned me alive if I went around in my pelt," the mother said.
>
> Margaret went into the pantry by the sink and reappeared with a cup and saucer.
>
> "Shame! For shame!" the mother said.
>
> "What are you talking about?" Margaret asked, a rasp of anger in her voice.
>
> "I wouldn't be seen showing myself in me pelt."[41]

Farrell manages to withdraw from the scene almost completely, letting the women's billingsgate carry the weight of his argument. He rarely intrudes.

In particular, Farrell's description of nakedness is detached. Margaret weighs "about one hundred and thirty pounds." This is not a subjective or affective characterization but a measurement. Some of Farrell's other details are less impersonal but no less detached. Margaret is a "well-built" young woman, with brown hair that is "warm but not very thick," she has blue eyes, thin lips, slender arms, and small upright breasts. Even her pubic hair is represented anesthetically: It is a "swab," that is to say, a mop.

Margaret does not view her nakedness as erotic. At first, she does not even appear to know that she is naked or at least that there is anything remarkable in such a condition: "What are you talking about?" she asks her mother.

Sex and Society

The sexual struggle of Studs and that in Greeley's novels are central to the message of both authors. The church does not face up to or understand sexual reality. Authority is corrupt and ineffectual. Society must look elsewhere for salvation from its spiritual poverty.

For Greeley, the answer is in smaller community units that allow priest and people to make their own decisions regarding such matters as divorce, premarital sex, and birth control (cf. *Cardinal Virtues*). For Farrell, the remedy and the hope are in social movements that can relieve the poor and ensure social justice. In his own way, each author is saying that there is no salvation in the church as it is.

Greeley's popularity was at least partly based on his sensitivity to the sexual and social tension of the times. Greeley, like Farrell, does understand the common person and his or her discontent. This struggle is demonstrated repeatedly as Greeley puts his finger squarely on the pulse of the new U.S. proletariat that thinks of itself as "middle class," but it is a middle class that owns not businesses, not even houses and cars, but mortgages and loans. Of the housing shortage after World War II, the shortage that produced Levittown and thousands of suburbs like it, Greeley writes:

> It was easy for social critics like Pete Seeger a few years later to make fun of the "ticky-tac" suburban houses that were to spring up on the fringes of most of the cities of the country. But Seeger was a rich kid who went to Harvard; he never lived in a cold-water flat. So he never knew the joy of having for the first time your own bathroom and separate bedrooms for the different members of the family.[42]

Greeley's readers, his "parishioners" as he called them, live between the brat's squall and the boss's snarl and always in terror of the pink slip.

In fact, it may be that Greeley's novels, portraying the Chicago of money and glamorous settings, the commodities exchange, the power lunch, the yacht, and the characters with connections in the Central Intelligence Agency and the College of Cardinals, function as a kind of opium to his readers.

Nevertheless, in its mythic structure—its identity, politics, violence, and tortured sexuality—Greeley's vision steers uncomfortably close at times to positions described by Farrell's Father Moylan.

Greeley attributes the volume of his writing in part to his celibacy. Indeed, his novels are a witness to his sexual/celibate adjustment and his sociological expertise. Having said this, we are left with one final puzzle: How do we distinguish author and character and account for the kinship between the two?

KINSHIP, THE VITAL LINK

Three problems remain in understanding the kinship of Greeley and Studs. The first is the style employed in Farrell's portrayal of Studs in contrast to the style of Greeley's novels. Second, there is a problem of *spiritual poverty*, the term Farrell used to describe Studs's world. How could the spirit of an atheist/Marxist be linked with the spirit of a Roman Catholic priest? Third, what does the confusion or clarity of the voices of the author and characters have to do with the kinship?

Style

Farrell and Greeley have very different styles of writing, and they approach the Chicago Irish Catholic reality by very distinct methods. Farrell the author is an Andrew Wyeth of words. His characters are drawn finely with care and precision. The details of their inner psychic struggle are delineated clearly in their facial structure, gestures, carriage, expression, and in the atmosphere and settings through which they move.

Andrew Greeley the author is the Andy Warhol of the religious symbol: bold, pop, impressionistic, impulsive, and vague in depth. As Greeley said, "When I type, I talk aloud....I write what I hear....[W]hen I have a clear and powerful insight and I am writing with attention to it, the words fairly dance on the page before me. I say things I am not conscious of ever having thought before, in ways that surprise me."[43] This is reminiscent of W. H. Auden, who told an interviewer that he did not know what he thought about a subject until he spoke about it.

To extol one form of writing is not to denigrate the other. Respecting each approach—a consideration of style—can aid us in appreciating what each messenger has to say about the world in which we live.

Greeley's honesty is admirable when he states unequivocally in his autobiography that his motivation in writing his novels is primarily market driven (much like Warhol), and he describes the facility with which he can produce a book by dictation or computer in a matter of weeks.[44]

Farrell began writing the Studs Lonigan trilogy in June 1929 and completed it in January 1935. In the 1958 paperback edition of the work, he reflects on his motivation, especially in defense against those who claimed that his work was salacious:

> A man does not make sacrifices, take economic risk, put his future on the line, and give some of the best part of his years of young manhood to write a sensational shocker. Such books are hammered out in haste, often in a few weeks or months.[45]

Greeley's novels cannot be dismissed as pap merely because they are hammered out in a few weeks or months. Certainly, they lack the refinement of Farrell's novels, and none of his priest characters approaches the sensitively nuanced portrayals of Georges Bernanos, Ignazio Silone, Graham Greene, J. F. Powers, or Jon Hassler. Greeley's style is more reminiscent of Danielle Steele or Jackie Collins than of Richard Wright or Saul Bellow, and his production schedule is more like that of Joyce Carol Oates than of Farrell. Greeley can boast of "eight best-sellers in five years,"[46] a stark contrast to Farrell's trilogy, which sold a mere five thousand copies in a similar period. For all of his numbers, of course, Greeley has not produced an American classic.

If Greeley's style is breezy and thin, his intent and his themes are not. Greeley says repeatedly that his novels are about God, God's love, and God's intervention and revelation in people's lives. The Catholic Church and church people, especially priests, carry the weight of his argument. Bishop/Monsignor John Blackwood Ryan, PhD (Father Blackie), rector of the Cathedral of the Holy Name, is the one priest "character who has lurked in my [Greeley's] imagination for a long, long time, while sometimes he speaks in my voice he has an identity and integrity of his own."[47] Greeley attributes to Blackie his most memorable phrase, "[N]ever, I repeat never, fuck with the Lord God."[48]

Despite Greeley's style and intent, he does demonstrate an acute awareness of the spiritual poverty of church, priest, and layman. Greeley's piercing insight into human failings and the limitations of the sacred endear him to millions of readers and encourage many to think critically about religion.

Spiritual Poverty

What is the underlying link between the spiritual poverty that is expressed in such distinct styles? Farrell maintained that the spiritual poverty of Studs's environment limited his chances and conditioned his brain. What did Farrell mean by this remark? The term *spiritual poverty*, which might be remarkably appropriate from the pen of Greeley, seems a strange one from a naturalist writer like Farrell. Could it be that the Irish Catholic origins prevail?

Leave aside for a moment one of our basic assumptions mentioned earlier: that Farrell remains Catholic in spite of himself. We contend that a mutual grounding in sociology is the link between Farrell and Greeley.

The word *spirit* become less strange when we recall that Farrell was strongly influenced by Max Weber, for whom spirit was a basic principle of sociology. Weber's best-known book is titled *The Protestant Ethic and the Spirit of Capitalism*. And Farrell's study of Marx had led him naturally to the philosophy of Hegel, whose first influential book was *Phänomenologie des Geist*, literally, *Phenomenon of Spirit*; *Geist* is often mistranslated as "Mind." Hegel distinguishes between mind *(Sinn)* and spirit *(Geist)*, and he wrote at length about the evolution of the spirit, including, for instance, the spirit of peoples and of art and culture. Spirit clearly transcends mind for Hegel, for Weber, and certainly for Farrell.

The ideal of *mind* is clearly comprehended by *spirit*, and we begin to understand what Farrell meant by the term when we consider Studs's mental universe. Beyond the words that Studs hears in his mind—beyond, that is, the clichés that ricochet through his mental labyrinth like billiard balls—Studs's mind contains images of himself and of other people.

Studs cannot tolerate representations of himself as the child of privilege, as his mother's pampered firstborn, as a favorite of his sister Frances. He engages in a vigorous purge of such self-images. Studs wants to make sure that none of these unacceptable characters sneaks onto the stage, and he excludes any of their friends, allies, or relations. The only conscious self-image Studs permits himself is his fantasized self: "Lonewolf Lonigan," a tough guy with a gun, who, surrounded by darkness, hated and feared, wounded and in pain, has to fight the odds by himself.[49] The Lonewolf thus stands as the emblem of Studs's spiritual poverty.

Spirit, for Weber and Hegel, transcends mind. They, for example, speak of the spirit of a people and of an age. At the same time, however, this transcendent aspect of spirit is incorporated into an individual's consciousness and takes the form of a representation of other people and other consciousnesses.

For Studs, therefore, other people are very threatening. In his spiritual vacuum, he must represent them as cartoons. In Studs's deathbed delirium, when he is too weak to control and marshal his energies against these images, they rampage through his mind the way the furious mobs raged through Chicago in the racial riots of 1919: Studs's father, dressed in a clown suit, a fat priest in a black robe with a red hat, Sister Bertha with "the twisted face of a maniac in a motion-picture close-up," George Washington, the pope, President Woodrow Wilson, Father Gilhooley, Red Kelly and his father police Sergeant Kelly, Mrs. George Jackson (a woman Studs picked up in his brother-in-law's betting parlor), Mrs. Dennis P. Gorman "in the red robes of the master of ceremonies of the Order of Christopher," Father Shannon "on the arm of Lucy Scanlan," and Studs's sister Frances "in a transparent nightgown."

The mental riot, of course, occurs in the course of Studs's illness, but the cartoon other people are liberated only by Studs's loss of control. Indeed, throughout the book we can see Paddy Lonigan as a clown, Sister Bertha with the twisted face of a maniac, and Frances in a transparent nightgown. In fact, throughout his adolescence and young manhood, Studs devotes a good deal of energy to suppressing the inevitable riot, to policing his mental stage of these Bacchae.

Greeley, in his sober novels, gives form to the kinds of images that Studs could face only in his delirium or in his drunken bouts. The images of Studs's imagination, from his fantasized self, Lonewolf Lonigan, to the bleeding Lucy Scanlan, find echoes in Greeley's pages, where Father Blackie often finds himself in a similar position. Greeley understands Studs's spiritual poverty, and he gives it a new voice and continued reality.

Voices: Author's or Characters'?

Again, Greeley's voice tends to be diffuse, creeping into both male and female characters seemingly indiscriminately and in an undisciplined way. Perhaps this is the price of a Warholian style. Many Greeley novels demonstrate that he lacks the writer's naïveté and the novelist's objectivity, which Lukács considers necessary for the storyteller to produce a great novel.

Greeley has protested vehemently that all of his characters are the products of his own imagination; perhaps this limits his mythic differentiation and greatness. Both qualities are born out of long, hard, disciplined, and unfortunately necessary painful introspection wherein one knows oneself. In the words of psychiatrist David Berenson, the price of self-knowledge is the experience of "optional humiliation." A person who has paid the price therefore knows the nonself as well as the self, and he can transcend both in his characters. In other words, all of Greeley's characters are tools or aspects of his own striving, and therefore they cannot have lives of their own, as does Studs.

In his article on the Irish and Studs, Greeley demonstrates clearly his confusion of author and character when he writes:

> Dubious about his masculinity, harassed by his mother, nagged by his sister, lacking a confident father to imitate, and paralyzed by guilt, Studs was already bent on self-destruction when he graduated from St. Anselm's in 1916.[50]

Of course, Studs graduated from Saint Patrick's in 1916. Farrell graduated from Saint Anselm's grade school. The slip is symbolic of the deeper confusion of author and voice that pervades Greeley's own work.

Earlier in the same essay, Greeley mentions "St. Anselm's church, built by Father Gilhooley to 'save the neighborhood.'" Of course Father Gilhooley built Saint Patrick's.[51] Later, Greeley says ambiguously, "Who will celebrate the agony and the glories of Christ the King, the way Jim Farrell celebrated St. Anselm's?"[52]

From a literary point of view, what makes Greeley's ambiguity and confusion so striking is that he misses Farrell's personal transcendence in the work, his objectivity. Farrell does not confuse himself with Studs or his own past with that of Studs. Psychologically, what makes the confusion of character and voice so striking is Greeley's profound identification with Studs at the same time that he seems oblivious to the hopeful vertical transcendence implied by his identification. In other words, if one can effectively reflect on the fate of the tragic hero, in this case Irish self-destruction, one can avoid it oneself.

Greeley indulges a flight of fancy in which he imagines Studs not dead but moving to Beverly—a locale in several Greeley novels—to Christ the King parish, where Greeley served as assistant pastor for a time. Greeley endows his fantasized Studs with a summer home in Grand Beach, where Greeley himself has a home. Greeley's fantasy saves Studs from his fate—death at age 29—to make of him something he could never be, "a loyal parishioner, a fine father and husband, a distinguished citizen." Greeley would have Studs marry Lucy Scanlan rather than Catherine, his pregnant fiancée. "Yes, indeed," says Greeley, "Studs Lonigan, I know you well. What a shame we never met."[53]

We contend that the key to understanding Greeley's comparison of himself with Studs the character rather than with Farrell the author lies in the precision of voice in the latter and the diffusion of voice in the former.

Farrell as an author is consistent in his voice. Danny O'Neill speaks for him, not merely as a minor character in the Lonigan series but as a major speaker in Farrell's O'Neill-O'Flaherty cycle *(A World I Never Made, No Star Is Lost, My Days of Anger)*. Farrell can also point to the prototypes or inspirations for his characters from the friends, acquaintances, and situations of his youth. Studs is based on an admired schoolmate, a few years Farrell's senior. Because of Farrell's careful craftsmanship, the creation of his characters can arise, and they can take their mythic existence unimpeded by the person of the author.

By identifying with Studs, Greeley gives eloquent testimony to the greatness of Farrell's creation. Lonigan qualifies admirably against Georg Lukács's demanding criterion:

> The need for reflection is the deepest melancholy of every great and genuine novel. Through it, the writer's naiveté suffers extreme violence and is changed into its opposite. (This is only another way of saying that pure reflection is profoundly inartistic.) And the hard-won equalization, the unstable balance of mutually surmounting reflections—the second naiveté, which is the novelist's objectivity—is only a formal substitute for the first: it makes form-giving possible and it rounds off the form, but the very manner in which it does so points eloquently at the sacrifice that has had to be made, at the paradise forever lost, sought, and never found. This vain search and then resignation with which it is abandoned make the circle that completes the form.[54]

Farrell portrays the ironic struggles of "the making and education of an ordinary American boy."[55] His mythic garb, which makes him accessible, is that he is a Chicago Irish Catholic adolescent. Farrell reflects simply and profoundly on the melancholy of Studs, "There but for the grace of God go I.... There but for the grace of God go . . . many others."[56]

John Chamberlain draws on personal youthful Irish experience to reflect on the profundity of Studs. "We have no mere slice of life here," he writes. "If anything we have a sermon. 'The wages of sin is death.' But the sermon, like the politics, is implicit in the artistic arrangement of the material."[57]

Even though Greeley's novels lack the form-giving elements that Lukács says are necessary to complete the novel form and establish the melancholy reflection, he does identify with Studs. That intuitive kinship means that on some level he does understand the sermon. He has reflected and can embrace the irony instinctively even if he did not duplicate it in his own style.

Chicago writers have been generous in bestowing characters that challenge our need to be understood, empowered, and loved in this hostile world. We now need to turn to a wider group of writers who reflected the meaning of celibacy, not via autobiography or as priest-authors, but novelists who found the truth in their fictional priest characters.

CHAPTER 10

CHILD ABUSE IN THE OLD SOD:
JAMES JOYCE

The past is not dead.
In fact the past is not even past.

William Faulkner

People who think that sexual abuse of minors by Catholic priests is a U.S. problem and a phenomenon of the second half of the twentieth century have not paid attention to the literature of James Joyce. Nor have they tuned into the new Irish Catholic revolt that burst into consciousness as powerfully as any Irish Republican Army bomb in 1994 when Prime Minister Albert Reynolds and the government fell over their failure to extradite a pedophile priest, Father Brendan Smyth, from Northern Ireland.[1] Few Irish or Americans were surprised in March 2006 when the Irish government convened an investigation into how church and state authorities conspired, by negligence and design, to cover up decades of child abuse within the Dublin priesthood.[2]

James Joyce did not live long enough to witness the vital stirrings he cataloged so poignantly beneath the Irish paralysis he decried so bitterly. The work of Joyce, especially *Dubliners* and *A Portrait of the Artist as a Young Man,* illustrates sharply the fact of child abuse and its effects on the lives of Irish people and on Irish society at the beginning of the twentieth century.

First, there is the beating of children, so widespread that it scarcely occasions comment. "Counterparts" ends with the brutal beating of a little boy by his father. In "Ivy Day in the Committee Room," an old man remembers nostalgically how he used to beat his son, now grown too big for beating.

His friend remarks that beating is the only way to bring up children. And in *A Portrait of the Artist as a Young Man*, Stephen is unjustly beaten with the "pandybat."

Sometimes, this beating shades into sadomasochism. "An Encounter" describes a strange man who is fixated on whipping schoolboys; his fantasies excite him so much that he masturbates in front of them. The villain of "An Encounter" shows many similarities with Father Flynn of "The Sisters" as well as with Father Keon of "Ivy Day in the Committee Room"; we may reasonably infer a sexual dimension to Joyce's priests' relationship to boys. (This sexual dimension is reinforced by a scene in the "Circe" section of *Ulysses* in which Father Dolan, who beat young Stephen in *A Portrait*, springs out of a coffin like a jack-in-the-box.)

In Joyce's Ireland, the entire family is complicit in the oppression of children and adolescents. "The Sisters," for example, is the story of the adult world's incomplete efforts to hide an unseemly truth about Father Flynn from the narrator. Mrs. Mooney of "The Boarding House" encourages her daughter Polly to carry on a sexual relationship with her lodger in order to land Polly a good husband; Polly's brother enforces the mother's decision with the implied threat of a beating. Mrs. Kearney, of "A Mother," ruins her daughter's chance to perform at a concert by quarreling over a four-shilling difference in her honorarium, and the mother of the little boy in "Counterparts" is in church while he is beaten.

The children, beaten, browbeaten, and seduced, learn their lessons well: not lessons in the history of the Roman Empire or of France or Ireland, but lessons in silence, violence, respectability, paralysis, and simony. Maria of "The Clay," for instance, has shrunk almost to invisibility. Mr. Farrington of "Counterparts" beats his son as he was (and is) beaten. Eveline cannot grasp her one chance for happiness, standing paralyzed on the docks. Mr. Kernan, of "Grace," literally bites his tongue. Corley, of "Two Gallants," sees in his girl's love the chance to cadge a few shillings as Mrs. Mooney grabs at the chance of a steadily employed son-in-law.

Over the years, Joyce has been treated primarily as a symbolist, or as a psychological realist, so the images in his stories are said to represent states of mind or psychic processes. But this view is contrary to Joyce's own aesthetic, according to which characters, events, locations, and things are both real and symbolic. In fact, one of Joyce's purposes was to show a certain view of Irish reality.

Vasily Aksyonov once remarked that censorship is not entirely bad for a writer because censorship forces reader and writer alike to approach texts with meticulous attention, concentrating not only on the explicit meaning of statements but also upon metaphor, metonymy, and process to reach levels of meaning beyond the denotative. All of the writers of the Soviet period, as well as such Western writers as James T. Farrell, Henry Miller, D. H. Lawrence, Theodore Dreiser, and Gustave Flaubert, worked under the eye of the censor.[3]

James Joyce, as we know, was subject to very severe censorship and on many levels. Much of Joyce's work was banned as obscene and was subject to criminal prosecution; publication of *Ulysses*, for example, was illegal in the United States until 1934. Beyond criminal sanctions, though, Joyce's work was subjected to the far more effective censorship of the marketplace. Joyce's early success with the stories that were to form *Dubliners* was cut short when H. F. Norman, editor of *The Irish Homestead*, which had published "The Sisters," "Eveline," and "After the Race," declined to accept any further stories because of the number of complaints from readers.[4] Publisher Grant Richards asked Joyce to make changes in *Dubliners*, omitting "Two Gallants" and "An Encounter" entirely as well as the use of the word *bloody*. Joyce did make some changes, though with the greatest reluctance.[5] Beyond these immediate levels of censorship, however, there remains the constraint of discourse as a social space: Language is only communication if it can be understood on some level, and some of the topics Joyce wished to discuss were literally unspeakable in the language of his day. One of the topics was sexuality—remember the furor that greeted Freud's first discussions of the topic at the turn of the century—and another was the suffocating power of organized religion. We can only imagine what would have been the public reaction to any mention of the problem of priestly pedophilia, though the data we have been able to glean from oblique references as well as available comparisons suggest that there must have been such a problem.[6] The historical and current reaction of the church to questions of such abuse—denial combined with a condemnation of the accusers—gives us a hint as to the reaction Joyce might have faced had he articulated a statement such as "I once knew a priest who was sexually attracted to young boys." We believe that Joyce dealt with the difficulty by a process of meiosis, splitting out the explicit pedophilia from "The Sisters" (and leaving a mysterious hole in its place) and resetting it in its own story, "An Encounter." In this way, the original unity of the statement "I once knew a priest who was sexually attracted to young boys" is split into its two halves: "I once knew a priest who was..." and "X was sexually attracted to young boys," and both enunciations acquire the motive discontinuity proper to myth. In the process, each story is given an importance and a suggestiveness that reaches beyond the unity of the original statement. "The Sisters" becomes, literally, a Euclidean gnomon, suggestive of mystery itself, whereas "An Encounter" (which retains its integrity, like the parallelogram separated from its larger original shape to leave the gnomon) illustrates the loneliness characteristic of perversion (in the Lacanian sense).

Our reading is marked by three assumptions:

1. Although "The Sisters" eschews direct statement, it nevertheless allows
    meaning to shine through a web of silence, ellipsis, and contradiction
    via various indirect mechanisms.

2. The narrator of "The Sisters" and "An Encounter," though unnamed, is
    a child, with a child's limited perspective; knowing that the narrator is
    a child, the reader is expected to fill in the spaces in his narrative.

3. The stories are not to be read in isolation but rather in a reciprocal rela-
    tion to one another as well as to the other stories in *Dubliners* as well as
    to *A Portrait of the Artist as a Young Man*.

THE PUPPET SHOW

"The Sisters" unfolds in a series of incomplete scenes before the boy narrator's gaze, each ending when the shutter is slammed down by the adult
stage crew. As the story opens, the narrator studies the sickroom window
of his friend Father Flynn for a clue as to the old man's hour of death. He is
fascinated and horrified by the priest's paralysis and also by the word *paralysis*, which he conflates with the equally incomprehensible words *gnomon* and
simony. When the boy arrives home, he stumbles into a conversation already
begun, a conversation involving Father Flynn but with an obscure text. On
retiring, the boy passes the last conscious moments of the day trying to deci-
pher the meaning of Old Cotter's mysterious speech, and he passes from this
perplexity into a mysterious dreamworld and hence to a state of amnesia.
The next day, persuaded at last of Father Flynn's death by a printed death
notice, the narrator proceeds to a new level of mystery as he struggles to
reconcile his sense of freedom with the sadness he should be feeling. Casting
his thoughts on Father Flynn, he remembers chiefly that the priest had made
the familiar strange, posing difficult questions on purpose, emphasizing the
secrecy of the confessional, and only smiling when the boy "could make no
answer or only a very foolish and halting one." After viewing the body, the
boy accompanies his mother as she talks with Father Flynn's sisters, Eliza
and Nannie; here, so to speak, the narrator leaves us, in our own perplexity.

But the mystery in "The Sisters" appears deliberate, enforced like a conspiracy or a state secret, by the adult world against the boy narrator. The
checks to understanding in "The Sisters" operate like doors quickly slammed,
like window shades dropped over disturbing scenes momentarily glimpsed.
Old Cotter drops a hint about Father Flynn's character: "No, I wouldn't say
he was exactly...but there was something queer...there was something uncanny about him. I'll tell you my opinion."[7]

Old Cotter never gives his opinion; instead, he rephrases slightly his
empty insinuation: "'I have my own theory about it,' he said. 'I think it was
one of those...peculiar cases....But it's hard to say.'"[8]

Next comes the news of Father Flynn's death, news delivered obliquely but (this time) with unmistakable meaning:

> "Well, so your old friend is gone, you'll be sorry to hear."
> "Who?" Said I.
> "Father Flynn."
> "Is he dead?"
> "Mr. Cotter here has just told us. He was passing by the house…"[9]

This interchange between the narrator and Old Cotter marks the first time information is actually conveyed. Note the baroque shape of the statement: when the boy asks, directly, "Is he dead?" Cotter refrains from denying the death, in effect affirming it. This nonnegation is one important way information is actually transmitted in the story.

The information regarding Father Flynn's death is followed by a somewhat scandalous, though again abstract, implication: "'I wouldn't like children of mine,' he said, 'to have too much to say to a man like that.'"[10]

One interesting feature of this remark is that Old Cotter is enjoining to silence: He does not say "I wouldn't like children of mine to be seen with a man like that," but "I wouldn't like children of mine to have *too much to say* to a man like that." Old Cotter's utterance is so vague (as well as so disturbing) that the narrator's aunt asks him to explain it; Old Cotter begins to cite some problem involving the disparity of age between the priest and the boy but ends by throwing the question to the narrator's uncle who changes the subject. The narrator confesses himself baffled by these hints: "I puzzled my head to extract meaning from his unfinished sentences."[11]

This puzzlement is succeeded by a dream in which the boy sees "the heavy grey face of the paralytic" following him and trying to confess something in a murmuring voice through a smile and "lips…moist with spittle." The dream, itself mysterious, dissolves in amnesia: "I could not remember the end of the dream."[12] It seems that the narrator's psyche is in league with the keepers of the secret.

The following morning, the narrator sees a printed death notice containing a vague hint of something wrong, as Father Flynn is identified as a former pastor of Saint Catherine's. The qualification can only mean that Father Flynn was removed from office.

Another check to understanding comes in the use of cliché by Eliza, one of the eponymous sisters of the story; the clichés contain further clouds in Eliza's malapropisms. Following the string of clichés are two cryptic half-admissions:

> "Mind you, I noticed there was something queer coming over him latterly. Whenever I'd bring in his soup to him there I'd find him with his breviary fallen to the floor, lying back in the chair and his mouth open."

She laid a finger against her nose and frowned, then continued.

"He was too scrupulous always," she said. The duties of the priesthood was too much for him. And then his life was, you might say, crossed."[13]

Of Eliza's laying her finger alongside her nose, in the first quotation, Jackson and McGinley's note reads, "Body language: say no more in front of the boy."[14]

The narrator's aunt presses Eliza: "'And that was it?' Said my aunt. 'I heard something...' Eliza nodded."[15]

This nod is the closest Eliza will come to a positive statement; in effect, she appears to affirm what the narrator's aunt heard. The nod is, however, equivocal, because Eliza may be affirming that "that [the breaking of the chalice] was it" rather than conceding what the narrator's aunt had heard.

Eliza next proceeds to an equivocal digression on some fault in Father Flynn, in which each statement but one is immediately contradicted: "It was the chalice he broke.... That was the beginning of it. Of course, they say it was all right, that it contained nothing, I mean. But still... They say it was the boy's fault. But poor James was so nervous, God be merciful to him."[16]

This mass of contradictions—containing another cryptic and disturbing hint in "they say it was the boy's fault"—is followed by the tale of a search ending only in incomprehension:

> So then they got the keys and opened the chapel and the clerk and Father O'Rourke and another priest that was there brought in a light for to look for him.... And what do you think but there he was, sitting up by himself in the dark in his confession box, wide-awake and laughing—like softly to himself.[17]

This tale, so like *Heart of Darkness* in miniature,[18] is interrupted by aposiopesis: "She stopped suddenly as if to listen."[19] But Eliza's silence is answered only by the silence of the house and of the dead man, a silence succeeded by Eliza's meaningless repetition: "Wide awake and laughing—like to himself.... So then, of course, when they saw that, that made them think that there was something gone wrong with him."[20]

"The Sisters," indeed, operated almost as a catalog of checks to clear statement in the blank window shades, the incomprehensibility of foreign words, abstract and fragmented speech, "relinquishing the floor," changing the subject, dream speech, amnesia, half-truth, cliché, malapropism, encoding, equivocation, aposiopesis, and circular statement. Only four so-called facts emerge regarding Father Flynn's character:

1. Old Cotter would prevent children from speaking to him on the basis of some peculiarity or incommensurability or because he might somehow lead them astray (through overeducation, at least).

2. Father Flynn was removed from office.

3. The narrator's aunt heard a rumor of some behavior more serious than the breaking of a chalice.

4. They say it (whatever it was) was the boy's fault.[21]

Four facts only, but what facts!

A CONSTELLATION OF TEXTS

Taken by itself, "The Sisters" operates indeed as a hermetic system of silences and checks to understanding, disclosing only that there was something odd about Father Flynn, that he was removed from office, that "they say it was the boy's fault," but "The Sisters" need not be considered in isolation. "The Sisters" is followed immediately by "An Encounter," a story that presents both metaphoric similarities and metonymic links to "The Sisters." The dynamic of "An Encounter" is very much like the dynamic of "The Sisters." In "The Sisters," the boy, confronted by the mystery of death, seeks words that will explain, heal, and make whole the paralytic, the simoniac, but he finds only secrecy, silence, and distance. In "An Encounter," the boy seeks the fullness of an adventurous adult life suggested to him by penny dreadfuls, and although he finds a real adventure, he is left as mystified as ever.

Besides the similarity in structure, there are many accidental (in the scholastic sense) links between the two stories. The action of "An Encounter" centers on an excursion by two schoolboys to Irishtown; as Jackson and McGinley note: "[T]he boys go south into Irishtown, the childhood home of Father Flynn of 'The Sisters.'"[22]

The strange man who approaches the boys wears a "suit of greenish black," Jackson and McGinley note "a clear echo of Father Flynn's attire in 'The Sisters.'"[23] Father Flynn regaled the narrator of "The Sisters" with stories of the catacombs and of Napoleon,[24] whereas the stranger in "An Encounter" talks of "the poetry of Thomas Moore.... The works of Sir Walter Scott and Lord Lytton":[25] Each man entertains a boy with stories of adventure. Of the stranger's "yellow teeth," Jackson and McGinley write, "They are clearly reminiscent of Father Flynn's "big discoloured teeth" and are also like Stephen's "mouth of decay in [*Ulysses*] Proteus."[26] Of the stranger's discourse on the attractions of girls, the narrator observes: "He gave me the impression that he was repeating something which he had learned by heart or that, magnetized by some words of his own speech, his mind was slowly circling round and round in the same orbit."[27] "Something which he had learned by heart" could easily apply to the words of the Mass, as taught by Father Flynn: "Sometimes he used to put me through the responses of the mass, which he had made me learn by heart."[28]

Moreover, the stranger's variations on his theme suggest precisely the tropes of the Mass. Jackson and McGinley note, too: "The mystery and ritual of sex are added to those of religion from 'The Sisters,' a process comparable with the explanation of the mysteries of the Mass. All sorts of unexpected things are 'complex and mysterious.'"[29]

Although there is no suggestion of sadomasochism in "The Sisters," there is a clear connection elsewhere in Joyce between priests and beating. In *A Portrait of the Artist as a Young Man*, for instance, schoolboys are beaten with a "pandybat." "An Encounter" also suggests the confessional: "[H]is voice, as he led me monotonously through the mystery, grew almost affectionate and seemed to plead with me that I should understand him."[30] In its juxtaposition within *Dubliners*, in its deep structure, and in its many accidental attributes, "An Encounter" parallels "The Sisters."[31]

There is, besides, as Lucinda Boldrini has written, an information of "The Sisters" by Dante's *Inferno*.[32] Boldrini notes, first, the Dantean echo of "There was no hope for him," which, moreover, introduces the story (and the volume) in the same way that the inscription "Abandon all hope" introduces Dante to hell. Boldrini sees a parallel between the boy's puzzlement over certain words and Dante's incomprehension of the same inscription: "Master, their meaning is hard for me."[33] Boldrini believes that a comparison between Father Flynn and Virgil is ironic and that the true comparison is between Father Flynn and Brunetto Lantini, Dante's former teacher, who is being punished for sodomy.[34] Boldrini observes that both Dante and the narrator of "The Sisters" retain a filial affection for the punished soul as well as in a certain social dimension: Brunetto warns Dante to keep clear of the sins of Florence (sodomy), as Father Flynn's paralysis warns the narrator to keep clear of the "simony" and paralysis of Dublin.

Beyond these accidental links and parallels, however, it is the confessional moment in "An Encounter" that most profoundly ties "An Encounter" to "The Sisters" and raises our understanding of the two stories, for, as the stranger "confesses" to the boy, he makes the boy his priest and completes the circle. In "The Sisters," too, the boy becomes a priest: In his dream, the narrator is followed by the gray face of Father Flynn: "I understood that it desired to confess something."[35] On other levels, too, there is an identification among the boy, the priest, and the stranger. Jackson and McGinley note that "the boy's formula for saying goodbye is identical to the man's formula for saying hello."[36] We note, too, a certain ambivalent attraction of the boy toward the old man: "I pretended that I had read every book he mentioned so that in the end he said: 'Ah, I can see you are a bookworm like myself. Now,' he added pointing to Mahony who was regarding us with open eyes, 'he is different. He goes in for games.'"[37]

Here the boy eagerly participates in the exchange with the old man, partly perhaps to impress Mahony but partly to ingratiate himself with the stranger. The narrator notices, besides, the old man's good accent.[38] The boy suffers the old man's peculiar monologue with remarkable patience, though he experiences some "agitation," not surprising, because it is clear to the reader that the old man's attentions are directed at him:

> The man asked how many [girlfriends] had I. I answered that I had none. He did not believe me and said he was sure I must have one...[39]
>
> And if a boy had a girl for a sweetheart and told lies about it then he would give him such a whipping as no boy ever got in this world. He said there was nothing in this world he would like so well as that.[40]

When the boy stands up, he is afraid that the old man might seize him by the ankles; might this fear not also be, on some level, a wish? The narrator is clearly aware of, and disturbed by, the identification between himself and the old man: "I can see you're a bookworm like myself." In a similar way, the similarities between the old man and Father Flynn help explain Old Cotter's counsel: There is some apparent affinity between the narrator of "The Sisters" and Father Flynn, and this identification is to be discouraged. Old Cotter and the uncle admit as much, even as they pretend that the fault to be avoided is "overeducation" (and we are struck once more by the fact that the stranger of "An Encounter" uses books for bait).

We can certainly see on the psychosexual level a connection between the old priest, the stranger, and the young boy's conflicted images of himself. In connection with the rest of *Dubliners* and with *A Portrait of the Artist as a Young Man*, we can view "The Sisters" as a gnomon of the paralysis with which Joyce identifies celibacy and of a kind of simony in exchanging the life of the artist for the outward show of the life of a priest, the "empty chalice" Father Flynn breaks. One standard reading of *Dubliners* is that kind of auto-biographical thought experiment: Ellman cites Joyce:

> The order of the stories is as follows. The Sisters, An Encounter, and an-other story [Araby] are stories of my childhood; The Boarding House, After the Race, and Eveline, which are stories of adolescence; The Clay, Counterparts, and A Painful Case, which are stories of mature life; Ivy Day in the Committee Room, A Mother, and the last story of the book [Grace], which are stories of public life in Dublin.[41]

In this citation, Joyce is clear that "The Sisters" and "An Encounter" (to-gether with "Araby") are autobiographical; afterward, his wording indicates an increasing tendency to fiction proper. In 1905, the date of the letter cited, "The Dead" was as yet unwritten, but from the conflation of the character Gabriel Conroy with Joyce's father and with Joyce himself, we may assume that Gabriel Conroy is what Joyce imagines he would have become had he re-mained in Ireland: bitter, frustrated, ineffectual, and paralyzed. Joyce's most obvious symbol for paralysis is, of course, Father Flynn. Ellman notes: "Although he never allows himself to say so in the story, he makes the priest's actual paralysis a symptom of the 'general paralysis of the insane' with which Ireland was afflicted."[42] Father Flynn is not only paralyzed, he is paralysis itself, and that paralysis is contagious.

Joyce's identification of paralysis with the priest is clear, but to understand the mechanism of the identification, we need to consider that other mysterious term, *simony*. Simony is, of course, the exchange of a sacred office or property for gain; it takes its name from one Simon Magus, reported in Acts to have attempted to buy the gift of the Holy Ghost from the apostles. When we combine the terms *gnomon, paralysis*, and *simony* to form a rebus, we may say that that Father Flynn (attached to the rebus at the term *paralysis* in the opening paragraphs and at the term *simony* in the dream sequence) stands as a gnomon of the simony of paralysis. This rebus is to be understood in terms of Joyce's theory of epiphanies, of the moments of grace that art can discern in the mundane: Grace is to be apprehended by art alone, and the claims of religion are empty chalices, sham, simony (the censored word *sodomy*), paralysis, gnoma (in the sense of incomplete figures). This explanation is supported by the crisis of conscience of Stephen Dedalus in *A Portrait of the Artist as a Young Man:* Shocked by the intensity of his feelings after a sexual encounter, Stephen withdraws into an ascetic piety until he has sufficiently matured to integrate sexual attraction as beauty.

When I Was a Child, I Thought as a Child

Priest or artist? The dichotomy is, of course, false. Many men have combined the two callings: Gerard Manley Hopkins and John Henry Newman may stand as two examples, Vivaldi and Rabelais as two more. Further, most people are neither priests nor artists.

The dichotomy is not to be taken at face value. Indeed, to insist on a literal meaning would be contrary to Joyce's (implicit) theory of the sign.

Portrait "Words"

Signs mean not only their referents but also serve as symbols of a psychological moment: the struggle between latency and adult sexuality.

Inscape

Finally, from what we know of Joyce's view of Irish society, we can say that he viewed it not so much as a patriarchy but as a repressive system of paralysis enforced by women molded by a mother church (and Catholic priests).

CHAPTER 11

FATHER AND FATHERHOOD: ETHEL VOYNICH AND GRAHAM GREENE

If the achievement of celibacy is one of the most potent symbols of spiritual grace and self-mastery, the birth of children is certainly a sign of the power, biological and spiritual, of the relationship between a man and woman. Both conditions, celibacy and parenting, are associated with the greatest and most intimate human responsibilities (as well as the greatest betrayals of trust), and both make commensurate demands on the emotional and intellectual resources of those who shoulder them. Yet what happens when both conditions coexist in the lifeworld of a single individual, making their demands felt with simultaneous force? After all, one cannot be celibate and involved in a sexual relationship at the same time, but children remain long after vows are broken and renewed.

In two works apparently written from opposed points of view, this issue of currently celibate clergy confronted with their emotional bond to the natural offspring of an earlier lapse is treated with great sensitivity and surprising similarity:[1] Ethel Voynich's *The Gadfly*, labeled by supporters and detractors alike as a classic of anticlericalism, and Graham Greene's *The Power and the Glory*, a novel condemning the persecution of the church in revolutionary Mexico. In both novels, the clergy protagonists are brought to their greatest spiritual crisis by the confrontation with their natural children at a moment of intense political conflict. The power of their emotions as parents directly diminishes their ability to wield the spiritual and temporal power vested in their vocation. Whether the outcome of either crisis represents a spiritual triumph or merely surrender and collapse poses a difficult challenge for interpretation.

Irish-born Ethel Voynich wrote *The Gadfly* in 1897. This fast-paced historical romance draws equally on her experience of work with political radicals
in Italy, Russia, and Poland and on her powerful and romantic imagination.
Largely ignored in the West, the novel had its greatest success in Russia and
later in the Soviet Union, a fact that, together with the career of its author,
earned the novel the pejorative label *political.* This categorization is probably
most responsible for its being taken as anticlerical. What else could a novel
about revolution in Italy that was canonized in the atheist Soviet Union be?
But no careful study of its plot, characters, and conflicts could substantiate
either label as sufficiently descriptive.

First, the plot is far more psychological than political. The political conflicts between the Young Italy movement and the Austrian and papal authorities are melodramatic, even comic opera, alongside the intensity of the family
drama and the love story. The most intense scenes of political struggle are
always subordinated to correspondingly more intense episodes of psychological struggle. If *The Gadfly* is a *roman à thèse* (novel of ideas), it dramatizes
the theories of Freud more than those of Marx.

The opening pages of the novel introduce us to an idyllic scene: In the
seminary of Pisa, Montanelli, a kindly and learned priest, and Arthur, his
young and devoted English assistant, retire to the seminary garden to rest
from their research and to converse. But *et in Arcadia ego.*[2] The young man
confides to his father confessor his desire to join the cause of Young Italy,
a commitment—a vocation—he believes to be entirely in keeping with his
Catholic faith. In fact, he considers it the sincerest expression of his faith,
despite the political ambivalence of the Vatican. The priest's reaction is so
profound that he is rendered inarticulate. He turns ashen and begs Arthur to
reconsider, but he offers no intellectual or ethical reasons against the political movement itself. He merely tells him, "I cannot argue with you tonight....
But...if you, die, you will break my heart."[3] After Arthur leaves, Montanelli
broods on the biblical story of David: "For thou didst it secretly, but I will
do this thing before all Israel, and before the sun; the child that is born unto
thee shall surely die."

Arthur is Montanelli's son. His mother was Polish and the wife of an
English merchant based in Leghorn. Married to a Protestant, she had attended church alone for many years. The sensitive young priest offered her a
companionship lacking in her marriage to a wealthy foreigner.[4]

Events move quickly. Montanelli is promoted to bishop of a mountainous
border region. Arthur attends clandestine political meetings where he meets
and falls in love with a young English woman, Gemma, a friend of his family. Her infatuation with a young Italian revolutionary enrages him; driven
by guilt over his jealousy, he relates the story to his new father confessor,
Montanelli's replacement at the seminary, who, by his concerned inquisitive-
ness and knowledge of politics, appears to be an ally of Young Italy. When

Arthur and his political colleagues are subsequently arrested, he realizes that his confessor is a police spy: "[W]hat did Christ know about a trouble of this kind? … He had only been betrayed…. He had never been tricked into betraying" (56). But he is even more crushed by his family's revelation, an outburst occasioned by the public disgrace of his imprisonment, that he is the love child of Montanelli and his dead mother. Arthur avenges himself on Montanelli for hiding the truth from him and on the church for betraying his trust by declaring suicide, casting his hat into the Arno, and stowing away on a ship bound for South America.

When the narrative resumes 13 years later, we are reintroduced to the protagonist, now totally transformed. Felice Rivarez, known as "the Gadfly" for his stinging satirical attacks on the church, is, like his contemporary in the Young Italy movement, Garibaldi, returned to Italy from mysterious adventures in South America. Disfigured and crippled by wounds and famous for his bitter wit, the Gadfly seems the very incarnation of revolutionary commitment and sacrifice. But as he confides his history to Gemma, now a professional revolutionary herself, he reveals his adventures in exotic lands to have been the descent into hell of a naive and sensitive youth. His disfigurement has been the result of beatings in bars and brothels, his cynical humor the protective shell secreted during years of enslavement and humiliation on plantations, in mines, and, perhaps worst of all, in a traveling circus.

The radicals attribute his assault on the church to deep political convictions and his special malice toward Montanelli, now a cardinal and spokesperson for the progressive wing of the church, to a revolutionary scorn for liberal reformers. But the expression of the Gadfly's malice is too irrational to be so construed. Its idiosyncratic nature becomes most evident when it is revealed that the Gadfly is writing both the attacks on Montanelli and the anonymous columns in his defense.

Although the Gadfly appears the very figure of commitment in a series of gunrunning missions to guerrillas fighting against Austria, his route through Montanelli's diocese expresses his personal obsession. Disguised as a pilgrim to the cathedral, the Gadfly crosses paths with Montanelli, taking full advantage of the opportunity: "[W]ould Your Eminence receive a man who is guilty of the death of his own son?" (164). The same evening he is praised by the guerrillas for his skills as an actor: "[Y]ou nearly moved His Eminence to tears" (165). When questioned by another, an admirer of the cardinal ("he's too good to have that sort of trick played on him," 165), why he risked drawing so much attention to himself, the Gadfly points out that it was the best means of establishing his cover. But this so-called professional explanation is belied the same night when he goes back to the cathedral to torment Montanelli further, almost bringing the encounter to the point of a full confession.

The climax of the novel is reached after the Gadfly's imprisonment during another mission. When Montanelli hears that the authorities plan to try him unconstitutionally by military tribunal in order to hurry his execution, he decides to intercede on behalf of this scourge of the church. Although there is no doubt that he has the temporal power to effect a pardon, Montanelli conducts several interviews with the prisoner, urging him to renounce violence as a means of political change.

As the Gadfly, afflicted by his old wounds and mistreated in the prison, sinks into a dangerous illness, his self-command begins to dissolve, and a confrontation with his father becomes inevitable. On Montanelli's side, the ongoing political crisis of his vocation—between his pacifism and his hatred of the regime—comes to a head in the case of the Gadfly. How can he, in good conscience, urge the pardon of a man who openly upholds the use of violence, a man, whom the authorities claim will, if given the chance at a fair and public trial, foment riots costing many lives? In desperation, Montanelli offers the Gadfly a choice: to renounce violence or to submit to a secret execution. Faced with this ethical paradox, the Gadfly loses his calm:

> "And you talk of cruelty! Why [the governor] couldn't hurt me as much as you do if he tried for a year; he hasn't got the brains. All he can think of is to pull a strap tight, and when he can't get it any tighter he's at the end of his resources. Any fool can do that! But you—'Sign your own death sentence, please; I'm too tender-hearted to do it myself.' Oh! It would take a Christian to hit on that." (227–28)

Montanelli regrets the arrogance with which he had set the terms, but he does so in a manner that draws out the deeper revelation: "I never meant to shift my burden on to you.... I have never consciously done that to any living creature" (228). Arthur, the son, speaks to that: By submitting to the church, he argues, Montanelli forced him, still a youth and nearly an orphan, to make all the hard decisions for both of them.

Now it is his turn to set terms, cutting short Montanelli's joy and amazement: "You have come back—you have come back at last!" "Yes...and you have to fight me, or kill me" (229).

Montanelli tries to dispel the political conflict in light of their reunion: "Oh, hush, carino! What is all that now? We have been like two children lost in the dark" (229).

But it is not the political conflict that is motivating Arthur's terms; rather, it is a primal sense of betrayal, the betrayal of the responsibilities of a father by Montanelli's choice to remain loyal to the church, to renew his vows, and only father his son in the guise of confessor, teacher, and church father of all orphans. For Arthur, they cannot have the innocent reconciliation that was possible with Gemma, this reconciliation of "two lost children," because the

failure of a parent to a child does not imply the same kind of mutual responsibility involved in broken peer relationships: "When you had finished [your
prayers], and kissed the crucifix, you glanced round and whispered: 'I am
very sorry for you, Arthur; but I daren't show it; He would be angry'" (230).

The original hard choice presented by Montanelli to the Gadfly, the revolutionary, is now turned against Montanelli by his son: free Arthur, leave
the priesthood, and acknowledge him publicly or consent to the governor's
request for a secret execution of the Gadfly. From the time he had recognized
his son, Montanelli had no doubt of having him freed but not at such a price, a
price he had already paid many times psychologically in order to become the
best of priests—generous, devout, loving, just—the model of the attainment
of celibacy as "a commitment to universality of accessibility," as a charism.[5]
Furthermore, his faith had been a great consolation after the disappearance
of his son: "Arthur, how can I help believing in Him? If I have kept my faith
through all these frightful years, how can I ever doubt Him any more, now
that He has given you back to me?" (230).

But Arthur retreats behind the rhetoric of the Gadfly's sardonic anticlericalism: "And I accept no favours from priests. I will have no more compromises, Padre; I have had enough of them, and of their consequences. You
must give up your priesthood, or you must give up me" (232).

Montanelli wrestles with this impossible choice; his decision, his verdict, is
pronounced in an unlikely way, yet one that is deeply significant, through an
observation he makes more to himself than to his son: "You have your mother's eyes!" (233). The previous double movement of commitment and betrayal
of commitment to a greater family at the expense of his own is recapitulated
in the moment that past and present are collapsed through resemblance.

The court-martial and execution are narrated with a solemnity and realism in striking contrast to the earlier mood of adventure that had surrounded
the political events of the narrative. It seems as if there are no longer any
grounds for simple oppositions in this earthly realm and, therefore, no need
to paint the combatants in simple terms as manifestations of the forces they
represent. Even stock villains are humanized:

> There was something almost like pity in the Governor's face. He was not
> a cruel man by nature, and was secretly a little ashamed of the part he had
> been playing during the last month. Now that his main point was gained he
> was willing to make every little concession in his power. (235)

Ironically, this mood of regret is the cause of a messy and prolonged death
agony before the firing squad: "Each man had aimed aside, with a secret hope
that the death-shot would come from his neighbor's hand, not his...they had
only turned the execution into a butchery, and the whole ghastly business
was to do again" (238).

Montanelli arrives in the midst of this ugly scene, and the psychological impact it has on him is narrated in the final chapter in which Montanelli breaks down during Mass. Collapsing the sacrifice of sons by his God and himself, he rants at the parishioners that their self-assurance in salvation is the mark of their guilt in the murder and hurls the Host into their midst as "twenty hands seized the madman" (253).

In Graham Greene's *The Power and the Glory*, the politics are reversed, but the ambiguities, also brought to a close before a firing squad, remain much the same. The protagonist, the last surviving priest of an anticlerical purge in one of Mexico's revolutionary provinces, flees from village to village in the backcountry, whether motivated more by a sense of duty or by fear of capture is impossible to say. This priest is not the unequivocally heroic martyr described in the Catholic propaganda of the time, snatches of which we "overhear" a mother reading to her children at key points in the book. Although Greene's priest most often receives the epithet of "whiskey priest," his propensity for alcohol is of less significance to his spiritual crisis as a priest than the result of one drunken indiscretion: a bastard child, a young daughter.

The importance of this daughter to the priest's inner struggle is felt in three passes, three symbolic encounters with a living memory that coincide with three encounters with his pursuer, the police lieutenant. In this way, the daughter's significance is felt at those moments of the most intense quickening of spiritual life, that is, when he comes in closest proximity to his physical annihilation.

The first occurs when he hides out in the hut of the mother of the child, during which the police catch up with him and search the village. The second occurs when he is arrested for drinking and dealing in contraband wine and is imprisoned under the guard of his very pursuers. The final agony coincides with his deathwatch at the conclusion of the novel.

When he arrives at the hut of his onetime lover, Maria, disguised in peasant clothes, he confronts the child he has not seen in six years, "feeling the shock of human love" (65).[6]

> The child stood there, watching him with acuteness and contempt. They had spent no love in her conception: just fear and despair and half a bottle of brandy and the sense of loneliness that had driven him to an act which horrified him—and this scared shame-faced overpowering love was the result. (66)

But this love is not reciprocated; instead, the daughter, Brigitta, pays him back for six years of abandonment with a maliciousness as much a projection of the guilt-ridden priest as it is an expression of a child's bitterness:

> He caught the look in the child's eyes which frightened him—it was again as if a grown woman was there before her time, making her plans, aware

of far too much. It was like seeing his own mortal sin look back at him, without contrition. He tried to find some contact with the child and not the woman. (67)

His last image of his child in this encounter is a grotesque collapsing of time, the symbol of an annihilated childhood: "The seven-year-old body was like a dwarf's: it disguised an ugly maturity" (68).[7]

This depressing encounter finds a disquieting contrast in the role Brigitta plays in saving him from the police. She tells the lieutenant, the man obsessively committed to destroying the "corrupt" priesthood in the name of the children, the future generations, that the priest is her father: "That's him. There" (76). The priest is so moved, he attempts to give himself up, to save the villagers from providing a hostage or other reprisals, but he does this so clumsily that the police refuse to take him seriously:

> He could feel all round him the beginning of hate. Because he was no one's husband or son. He said, "Lieutenant . . ."
> "What do you want?"
> "I'm getting too old to be much good in the fields. Take me."
> The lieutenant said, "I'm choosing a hostage, not offering free board and lodging to the lazy. If you are no good in the fields, you are no good as a hostage." (78)

The will to sacrifice himself quickly fades, if it had ever been truly present. The police leave with another hostage. "I did my best," he says, defending himself from an unspoken accusation.

This episode concludes with a last encounter with the daughter, one that forces the priest to consider the nature of her special challenge to his responsibilities as the last representative of the church in this province. He meets her in the village rubbish dump, her eyes "red-rimmed and angry." He recognizes her vulnerability, her inevitable victimization, a victimization no worse than his own but one for which he shares the blame. The conflict between father and Father makes itself felt:

> He prayed silently, "O God, give me any kind of death—without contrition, in a state of sin—only save this child."
> He was a man who was supposed to save souls. It had seemed quite simple once, preaching at Benediction, organizing the guilds, having coffee with elderly ladies behind barred windows, blessing new houses with a little incense, wearing black gloves. . . . It was as easy as saving money: now it was a mystery. He was aware of his own desperate inadequacy. (82)

But at the moment he seems about to realize that it is precisely because of his divided loyalties—to self and community, now incarnated in the presence of his daughter—that he can save neither this one nor the many, and certainly not himself, from spiritual struggle or corporeal death, the priest finds solace and self-worth through an abstract comparison with his political opponents:

> He said, "I would give my life, that's nothing, my soul…my dear, my dear, try to understand that you are—so important." That was the difference, he had always known, between his faith and theirs, the political leaders of the people who cared only for things like the state, the republic: this child was more important than a whole continent. (82)

The irony is that his love for this "soul," worth more than a continent, is not what makes him unlike the political men—after all, the lieutenant finds the justification of his anticlerical purge in the person of a young boy he meets in the street—but what makes him like any loving parent, ready to put his child before all else. He leaves the rubbish dump denying the truth of the encounter, but the central conflict has been defined for the reader.

The thought emerges only half formulated much later when he is again facing the scrutiny of the lieutenant as an imprisoned drunk. He notices an old photograph, used by the police to search for him, on the office wall: "What an unbearable creature he must have been in those days—and yet in those days he had been comparatively innocent…. Then, in his innocence, he had felt no love for anyone; now in his corruption he had learnt" (139).

The thought is forever interrupted by the interview with the lieutenant, during which he again goes unrecognized, but its ambiguity raises the question again of the origin and object of his deepest spiritual feelings. He has just found communion with his varied cellmates, even the most dissipated, but the reference to his own corruption cannot fail to remind us of its result: a daughter and a profound parental bond. At this point, his increasing fellow feeling seems to be growing alongside the discovery of a personal love, but they cannot merely reinforce one another ad infinitum.

In the final episode, the priest confronts this conflict head on as he awaits execution by firing squad the next day. Drinking brandy given to him to make the wait more bearable, he attempts a confession, but while dwelling on the absurdity of his "mortal sin" with Maria, it seems to go nowhere; then the significance of his lapse strikes him:

> As the liquid touched his tongue he remembered his child, coming in out of the glare: the sullen unhappy knowledgeable face. He said, "Oh, God, help her. Damn me, I deserve it, but let her live for ever." This was the love he should have felt for every soul in the world: all the fear and the wish to save concentrated unjustly on the one child. He began to weep; it was as if he had to watch her from the shore drown slowly because he had forgotten how to swim. He thought: This is what I should feel all the time for everyone, and he tried to turn his brain away towards the half-caste,

the lieutenant, even a dentist he had once sat with for a few minutes, the child at the banana station, calling up a long succession of faces, pushing at his attention as if it were a heavy door which wouldn't budge. For those were all in danger too. He prayed, "God help them," but in the moment of prayer he switched back to his child beside the rubbish dump, and he knew it was for her only that he prayed. Another failure. (208)

Although he dies a public martyr, we the readers are left with his final ambivalent meditations on love and saintliness.

In these two novels, the themes of fatherly and priestly love are played out in all of their metaphorical and psychological intensity. Despite many differences in detail, the force of their private love of their offspring directly erodes the spiritual and temporal powers of both priests. The differences in their cases reinforce the similarity of this underlying theme.

Montanelli's love for Arthur's mother and his lifelong relation to his son stand in striking contrast to the fleeting squalor of the Mexican priest's drunken sexual encounter and abandonment of his offspring. Yet the emotions and choices remain the same. Voynich relies no less than Greene on the almost instinctual bond between parent and child, an instinct arising just as forcefully from a rich intellectual bond as from a brief and awkward physical reunion.

Likewise, although Montanelli is a powerful cardinal and the Mexican is a fugitive, both are publicly viewed as figures of mystery and meaning to their people. And though both are driven to a similar despair by the irreconcilable conflicts of fathering, biological and priestly, it is perhaps ironic that the more powerful of the two, the cardinal, is publicly destroyed, whereas the weaker, the fugitive, suffers only privately, dying a martyr and the symbol of spiritual strength.

In this conflict between father and Father, the meaning of celibacy is perhaps best represented for what it is—the sublimation of personal affections for communal ones—thereby providing a more significant exploration of the theme than could be accomplished through narrations of sexual temptation. The latter can lead to lapses yet be assimilated on the path to the achievement of celibacy or provoke a choice to leave the priesthood for married life. But the child remains present, physically or psychologically, with much more profound consequences and requiring much more profound choices.

Because of the press of political circumstances, neither Montanelli nor Greene's priest can make a lasting choice. Nevertheless, in both characters we see the potential of celibate achievement emerging from the parent-child bond and the risks to both that this entails.

CHAPTER 12

VOCATION, LOST AND FOUND:
J. F. POWERS

> How can one avoid becoming a manager of souls in a social context that demands such an office?
>
> Jacques Lacan, *Écrits*

In his novel *Morte D'Urban*,[1] J. F. Powers took on the difficult project of narrating the struggle for meaning, and social meaning at that, in the inhospitable climate of the world of commerce in the United States of the 1950s. That he chose as his protagonist a Catholic priest—and a priest in a monastic order no less—by no means mitigates this aim of grappling with what Max Weber called "the disenchantment of the world" in such a calculating society. In fact, the "man of mystery" in a disenchanted world becomes Powers's ideal vehicle for testing that society's apparently infinite power, its "necessity" as the medium of human interaction.

A tense double irony, one much closer to Cervantes's style than that of Malory—the somber medieval muse evoked by the title—is maintained between the search for meaning and its worldly impossibility through the problematic character of Father Urban. He eschews the withdrawal from the world through which some of his colleagues attempt to insulate themselves from a world without mystery—their pathetic otherworldliness being the only mystery left—and instead he practices a vocation based on the church's history of worldly engagement as an institution.

Of all of the chapters in this book, this one has been the most difficult for me to write. First, the irony and humor of Powers are so balanced and subtle, analysis is daunting in any but his terms and his narration without distortion. Beyond that, he deals with a fundamental corruption of the institution, the Catholic Church, disguised as one priest. I am reminded of Dorothy Day's comment, which was often repeated by her and appeared in her autobiography *The Long Loneliness*: "[T]he church is my mother. Sometimes she acts like a whore, but she is still my mother."

Mary Gordon neatly sums up the materialistic context of Urban's vocation (symbolized by sectarianism) in her introduction to the novel:

> Urban's reasons for joining the priesthood and the Clementines are revealing: the boy Harvey Roche became the man Father Urban because he perceived at a young age that the best of America was reserved for Protestants. The one man Harvey meets who seems to have it made like the Protestants is the visiting Father Placidus, a Clementine who spurns rectory hospitality to "put up at the Merchant's Hotel, where bootblacks, bellboys, and waiters who'd never seen him before seemed to welcome him back." So Harvey becomes Urban, not because he is called to serve God but because he sees the priesthood as the easiest way to stay in the best hotels, to meet the best people, to live like a Protestant. (Introduction)

The narrative of Father Urban's ambiguous travels proceeds between two allegorical tableaux. The one is his fantasy of the good life of the perfect social animal: the successful businessman, the indifferent agnostic, the carefree family man with no children and no regrets. Urban knows that despite his social facility—his golf game, his affability, and his business acumen—he has the tragic-comic flaw of using such worldly talents in the service of otherworldly ends.

That tableau of a life in perfect harmony with disenchantment, dreamed in the ironic enchantment of the castle on Belleisle, his monastery, stands opposed to an ominous tableau from scripture. The exegetical key to the novel is chapter 16 of the Gospel of Saint Luke. Powers's novel can be read as a sermon, one Urban scrupulously avoids composing, on that paradoxical parable.

That parable and Urban's relationship to it will start us down the road of Urban's vocation. Along the way, we find the sociological context of vocation in Urban's world, a context so omnipresent in the novel that it precludes any direct speculation on what the ideal of spiritual vocation might be for Urban. This is in striking contrast to Ignazio Silone, who makes Spina's spiritual vocation clear. Powers allows instead only room for a hypothesis about its possibility and the role of celibacy in Urban's vocation. Finally, the significance and meaning of Urban's "death" becomes key to understanding him. Here a new question is prominent: Are we still on the road to vocation (i.e., meaning), or is it simply the end of all roads, all quests?

THE ROAD TO ETERNAL HABITATIONS IS PAVED

And I say unto you, Make to yourselves friends of the mammon of unrigh-
teousness; that when ye fail, they may receive you into everlasting habitations. (Luke 16:9)

Ye cannot serve God and mammon. (Luke 16:13)

In Luke,[2] two alternative allegories of the spiritual vocation are set forth
side by side without any narrative effort to reconcile or compare them. Only
the reader or hearer can bridge this gap and decide the fate of vocation in
such a world, for the world of Luke 16 is surely as disenchanted as any sociological or economic analysis of our own "iron cage of rationality."

In the chapter entitled "Twenty-Four Hours in a Strange Diocese," the
reader accompanies Urban burning up the pavement in a red Barracuda
sports car to Mirror Lake, where the good father will have ample opportunity to study his reflection. In his essay on the so-called mirror stage in ego
formation, Jacques Lacan concludes in words that express Powers's narrative
process in the scene at Mirror Lake:

At this juncture of nature and culture psychoanalysis alone recognizes this
knot of imaginary servitude that love must always undo again, or sever.
For such a task, we place no trust in altruistic feeling, we who lay bare the
aggressivity that underlies the activity of the philanthropist, the idealist,
the pedagogue, and even the reformer.[3]

One objection to such a formulation would be to question why psychoanalysis alone should claim a monopoly in that function that so precisely describes
that of the novel and, with a surprising congruence of details, the narrative
of *Morte D'Urban*.

At Mirror Lake, Urban meets two classic American cranks, the letter-to-
the-editor writer and the devil's advocate, in neither of whom does he see the
slightest resemblance to himself. They are the Red and the Black that Urban,
the consummate status quo man,[4] so carefully avoids. But unlike the heroic,
if corrupted, Red and Black of Silone's world, these opponents, lounging in
the comfortable surroundings of Mirror Lake, are merely ridiculous. The
Catholic beer tycoon Zimmerman, with "a larger-than-life photograph of the
late junior senator from Wisconsin" on the wall of his writer's cabin (211),
is the reactionary "black clericalist" in this narrative world. The corpulent
and slovenly Mr. Studley, an argumentative atheist with a bright red World
War I airplane decorated with "heraldic devices" and on which "appeared the
words 'SIR SATAN'" (217), is its man of the people.

But in this scene, Urban also enters forcefully the register of biblical
allegory. In keeping with the novel's parody of the medieval theme, it is
thoroughly carnivalesque in style. Accordingly, Zimmerman and Urban must

play, respectively, the nervous shopkeeper and the humorless Pharisee to Studley's witty Lucifer.[5]

From the start, Studley has Urban dancing to his tune, driving a playful wedge into the opening offered by Urban's public relations man affability:

> Mr. Studley laughed. "Say, I hope you won't mind if I don't call you 'Father.'"
>   "That's entirely up to you, Mr. Studley," said Father Urban.
>   "I'm not a Catholic myself. I'm not much of anything, as a matter of fact. But you know what it says in the Good Book. 'Call no man thy father.'"
>   "Yes. Well, it's O.K. with me."
>   "I see you don't wear the collar, Mr. Urban."
>   Father Urban could do without the "Father," but that didn't mean he'd take "Mister." Nothing was better than that. "Up in the car," he said slowly, "with my coat." (215)

Confronted with such an interlocutor, eager to talk shop with a priest, Urban finds he has an uncharacteristic problem with speech and is barely more articulate than the dull Mr. Zimmerman.

At Studley's cottage, a place much like the Zimmermans', Urban must join the roster of priests who have made this questionable pilgrimage:

> "Now you have to sign my guest book," said Mr. Studley.
>   Father Urban, tempted to sign himself "Father," wrote "Rev." and hoped that was all right. "Now I'll show you something," said Mr. Studley.
>   "Here, here, here," he said, pointing to other names in the guest book. "And over here. And here. All priests like yourself." (218)

Urban finds himself in the awkward position of the friar in the Summoner's prologue of the *Canterbury Tales* who, while touring hell like Dante, finds a disquieting number of his fellow religious already residing there.[6] Significantly, Urban feels more comfortable signing this guest book than the one proffered to him by the reactionary Catholic, which he finally signs under the alias "Pope John XXIII" as he leaves (224).

He and Studley return to the Zimmermans', where the topic of Luke 16, the morning's Gospel reading, is introduced. That is the passage in which the steward called the master's debtors together and wrote off the debts. The rich master oddly praises the steward's action (219).

Urban, who had preached that morning, prides himself on his handling of this difficult text. He read dutifully but segued into an Old Testament text he could make more acceptable. His sermon on financing the temple was one of his better jobs.

But Urban's professional pride is hurt when he realizes that nobody had mentioned his sermon. Despite his efforts to explain the reading, "Mr. Zimmerman, like many before him, was worried about Luke XVI, 1–9."

What apparently troubles the wealthy shopkeeper is the idea of con-
doning an employee's mismanagement and theft of his employer's property.
Urban tries to reassure him but is soon confused by the playful pedantry of
Mr. Studley:

> "Our Lord," said Father Urban, "isn't commending the steward for cook-
> ing the books, or even condoning this. You'll note this man is called 'the
> unjust steward.'"
>   "Yes, I know." said Mr. Zimmerman, but he still didn't like it.
>   "And I think you'll find 'unjust' means 'inaccurate,'" said Mr. Studley.
> "There's a difference, you know."
>   "Well, I don't know about that," said Father Urban. "I know there's a dif-
> ference, yes." Where they were now, Father Urban didn't know. Mr. Studley
> not only made it seem that he and Father Urban were together but that he,
> Mr. Studley, was, of the two of them, the sounder man. (220)

Urban is so off track in his approach to the text to begin with that Studley's
play on a single word derails his apologia. Studley is able to manipulate the
discussion so easily because the others are so eager to ignore the crucial ethical passages of the reading.

> And the lord commended the unjust steward, because he had done wisely:
> for the children of this world are in their generation wiser than the children
> of light. And I say unto you, Make to yourselves friends of the mammon
> of unrighteousness; that, when ye fail, they may receive you into everlast-
> ing habitations. He that is faithful in that which is least is faithful also in
> much: and he that is unjust in the least is unjust also in much. If therefore
> ye have not been faithful in the unrighteous mammon, who will commit to
> your trust the true riches? And if ye have not been faithful in that which
> is another man's, who shall give you that which is your own? No servant
> can serve two masters: for either he will hate the one, and love the other;
> or else he will hold to the one, and despise the other. Ye cannot serve God
> and mammon. (Luke 16:8–13)

The difficulty of the text lies in its paradoxical assertion of two contradictory morals: first, "Make to yourselves friends of the mammon of unrigh-
teousness and Ye cannot serve God and mammon." The first moral appears to
gain subtle support in the 11th verse, which urges faithfulness to unrighteous
mammon as a sort of test of one's general ethical soundness. The knottiness
of this paradox begins to unravel, however, when one considers the rhetorical
context of the parable's utterance and the relative position of the transcendent in measuring the ethical significance of the worldly allegory.

Jesus tells this parable in the context of responding to the derision of
his ministry by the Pharisees.[7] His audience in Luke 16 is not the people in
general but his disciples, troubled by the mockery of religious authorities.

This rhetorical context, in turn, structures the allegorical positions of the characters in the fable. The "lord" is none other than God, the owner of "the true riches." The "unjust" (or, equally appropriate, "inaccurate") steward is the guardian of those riches, the priest or Pharisee. The debtors are those sinners who receive their worldly accounting only from God's steward.

With the transcendent clearly positioned, the ironic delivery of the lesson becomes lucid. The Lord (God) commends his steward (the priest) for being wise in mundane matters with the sarcastic qualifier "in their generation." In the same vein, the Lord advises that the steward/priest make friends with the Lord's debtors, the unrepentant sinners, so that when you fail with Me, they may receive you into "everlasting habitations"—that is, in their residence in hell. "Ye cannot serve God and mammon."

Mr. Studley, contentedly pulling out tufts of Mr. Zimmerman's grass, understands this message full well, but he prefers to play the devil's advocate and draw out his devout neighbor's obsession with worldly interests. By proposing a spurious liberation theology reading of the passage,[8] Studley exposes Zimmerman as the polemical spokesperson for mammon:

> Mr. Studley yanked up a nice handful of Mr. Zimmerman's grass and threw it away. "Look at it the right way or not at all," he said. "You people are always looking at things from your own view point. You'll never get it that way, I can tell you. Look at it from the employee's viewpoint. Christ was always on the side of the employee—the little guy. That's what Christianity means. That's what all your great religions mean. That's why we fought two major wars. Ask him," said Mr. Studley, referring to Father Urban.
>
>   Mr. Zimmerman started again. "If somebody in bookkeeping tried something like that on me, I'd prosecute. I'd have to—or set a bad example. See what I mean? That's my point," he said, looking to his two friends for support. (220–21)

Even when it is not costing him, Zimmerman closes ranks with his class interests, and he is so concerned with the punishment of the employee that he fails to note the obvious gaps in Studley's reading, which ignores the applicability of this moral to the story and the comparisons in verses 10 and 11, which hardly condone the employee's theft. But, of course, Studley's real interlocutor is none other than the steward himself, "Mister" Urban.

No longer able to steer the conversation, Urban reflects on his own understanding of the passage, one that, like his general spiritual outlook, contains insight but is nonetheless hopelessly fragmented:

> "I'll grant it's a difficult text," said Father Urban . . . and let it go at that. Father Urban had some ideas of his own about this text. Our Lord, in Father Urban's opinion, had been dealing with some pretty rough customers out there in the Middle East, the kind of people who wouldn't have been

at all distressed at the steward's conduct—either that or people had been a whole lot brighter in biblical times able to grasp a distinction then. It had even entered Father Urban's mind that Our Lord, who, after all, knew what people were like, may have been a little tired on the day he spoke this parable. Sometimes, too, when you were trying to get through to a cold congregation, it was a case of any port in a storm. You'd say things that wouldn't stand up very well in print. (221)

Although he implies recognition of the text's meaning—its construction of a subtle distinction—he ends up deriding, though more sympathetically than the Pharisees of the Gospels (Luke 16:14), the Lord's failure "on the day he spoke this parable." The scene at Mirror Lake concludes with a carnivalesque repartee in which Urban's equivocations are mercilessly parodied:

The man whose wife had brought the shortcake said, "Father Tom just skips it. 'Every year,' he says, 'I come to it and I just skip it. It does more harm than good,' he says. 'So I just skip it.'"
"Who's Father Tom?" said Father Urban.
"I think I've met him," said Mr. Studley, from his prone position.[9]
"Our pastor. He just skips it," said Mr. Shortcake.
"Too bad Father Prosperus isn't here. He'd be able to tell us a thing or two, I'll bet." This from Mrs. Potato Salad.
"I guess he could at that," said Mrs. Zimmerman. "Who's Father Prosperus?" said Father Urban.
"Our son," said Mrs. Zimmerman.
"Your son's a priest?"
"Yes, he's a Dolomite father," said Mrs. Zimmerman. (221–22)

Instead of recognizing his reflection in Mirror Lake, however, Father Urban merely mimics it:

That did it for Father Urban. There hadn't been much reason before to hope that Mr. Zimmerman would make a benefactor for the Order of St. Clement. Now there was none. (222)

In all fairness, Urban only went to Mirror Lake to befriend the mammon of iniquity, not to contemplate his vocation. This theme of his vocation is strongly sounded in the closing melody of the overture:

And still he found the time and energy to make friends, as enjoined by Scripture, with the mammon of iniquity. (10)

Urban uses his native intelligence: "[P]erhaps it was a job for the Jesuits" (8) to weave a clever theology, complete with edifying historical examples, around this mission. That at least one critic follows Urban in his interpretation that he is doing "as Jesus advises in the puzzling passage from Luke that informs the novel"[10] reveals that he is in good intellectual company and explains part of Urban's dazzling appeal, both to his fellow fictional beings and the novel's readers.

The theological and historical rationales that Urban uses to gird his concept of vocation could be summed up as "the middle way":

> Charity toward all, even when a few sharks get in among the swimmers, is always better than holier-than-thou singularity. That, roughly speaking, was the mind of the Church. (97)

In practice, this means husbanding a diplomatic relationship with the rich and powerful:

> Not running off the mouth at every opportunity, but knowing when to cast one's pearls, and how—that, in the best sense of the word, was priestcraft. (14)

Urban is planning to write a book on "this aspect of ecclesiastical history" to accompany his own history of conquests. Even his Brother Clementine, the saintly and humble Father John, or Jack, reminds him of the pedigree of such behavior: "[T]here were a number of occasions when Our Lord dined with the rich and well-to-do—Pharisees and the like" (24).

Urban sees church history in terms of such diplomatic successes and blunders:

> Father Urban felt that Clement VII had been the wrong pope to deal with Henry VIII, and he wondered what the feeling was in Heaven on this point. Centuries later, Pius IX, who had begun so well, had thrown down his cards in a fit of self-righteousness, and the Church was still trying to get back in the game. A bad mistake, that, since it had left the other players at each other's mercy—and thus had prepared the way for World War I, the Russian Revolution, Mussolini and Hitler, World War II, and now the bomb.[11]
>
> Father Urban had preached a great many thrilling sermons on saints who had really asked for the martyr's crown, but he believed that there were others from whose lives we might learn more. (276)

It is with just such bait that Urban hooks his big one, Billy Cosgrove:

> Billy...had warmly praised the sermon—in which Father Urban had roared and whispered and crooned about Francis of Assisi and Ignatius of Loyola and Clement of Blois and Louis of France and Edward of England and Charles of the Holy Roman Empire—it was he who, you might say, owned and operated Europe but who, in the end, desired only the society of monks.

Billy becomes Urban's Charles the Bold.

In his early encounters with Billy's egoism and violence, he remembers that some of the most powerful figures in history had been spoiled children like Billy, and he hopes to make Billy a Constantine whose legions would come later, now there was only his chauffeur (14). Urban later dreams that Mrs. Thwaites, another rich conquest, is an old queen in late medieval times. That was a time of uncertainty when church and state were mingled, when kings and prelates were "selling out right and left." He imagined himself as a tall handsome cleric "on business of church and state" (247).

These powerful figures, Billy Cosgrove and Mrs. Thwaites, are the two debtors of his Lord to whom Urban ministers his discounted bills of ethical credit. Right from the start, Urban catches glimpses of the price involved in befriending the mammon of iniquity when riding with a recklessly driving Billy. Stopped by a squad car, Billy:

> smiled at the officers and—pointed to Father Urban in his clericals. The squad car dropped away and the red convertible went on for a while as before. "I hope you didn't mind that," Billy said presently. He was now driving at a reduced speed, and Father Urban took this into consideration. "Oh, I guess not," he replied, with a laugh. He had minded, though, and still did. (2–3)

Nevertheless, Urban hews to the middle way and keeps the situation in the hazy focus of historical distance. That moment recalls Ignazio Silone, with an ironic ethical inversion, Spina's fear of hearing the confessions of the peasants and their hopeless lives of poverty. Urban reveals the myopia required by his methods:

> Billy, a widower and childless, didn't seem to have a problem in the world. In a way—because so many problems were simply insoluble—Father Urban was glad. (5)

Keeping his benefactors in this sort of moral limbo is the only possible basis for continuing the relationships, but even a priest as cynical as Monsignor Renton draws the line at a Mrs. Thwaites:

> Father Urban felt that Monsignor Renton was probably right about Mrs. Thwaites—up to a point. After that, there was no knowing, and, in any case…"Who are we to judge her?" he said. "What if she is only motivated by old age and fear of the Lord? That's enough, thank God. It takes all kinds to make the Church."
> "God is not mocked."
> "The woman's a daily communicant. That should count for something."
> "*God is not mocked.*"[12] (138)

Urban, however, continues to discount her ethical debt, recalling that he had heard Mrs. Thwaites's confession once: "[He] had talked over her chances in the next world, giving her all the reassurance he could—which wasn't quite enough, he felt" (165).

The reward for all of his good intentions is to be given a tour of Mrs. Thwaites's "eternal habitation," her underground bomb shelter, as if to say he too will be received there after failing in his vocation (244).

In his use of Luke 16, Powers constructs a narrative sermon on its meaning. This exegesis, however, is performed in the same sort of earthy medium Jesus chose for his parable of the two vocations for stewards, the hard-edged realities of the business world: The one is clear and compromised; the other is merely suggested and amounts to a negation of compromise beyond narrative representation. That makes up the repertory of spiritual vocations after disenchantment.

VOCATION AFTER DISENCHANTMENT

> They (the Clementines) were like the blind men in the fable who, touching the elephant's body here and there, could not agree about it. The elephant, in the case of the blind men in the upper room, was their vocation. (139)

Carol Iannone, writing about Powers's novel, makes what is perhaps the most damning criticism one can inveigh against a serious novel: that it falls short of universality.[13]

> It cannot precisely be said, however, that Powers transcends his Catholic material to give it universal applicability. So closely is the novel bound to the history of the Church, to the perennial antagonisms among levels of its hierarchy, to the relationship of priests to their vows, to certain insider jokes, and so on, that probably few would recognize Father Urban as Everyman.

Although Iannone blames this failure on the quantity of church-related details in the narrative, the judgment follows hard on her major qualitative reading of the novel. She argues that the novel concludes with a vertical transcendence of the protagonist, an interpretation that I would see as itself an adequate basis for dismissing its claim to universality in the radically secular context of a "disenchanted" social world. But the issue of Urban's "death" in the final section of this chapter renders a different conclusion. Iannone's criticism of the novel's bonds to the church, however, does raise serious questions about Powers's choice of protagonist. Is a priest—and not merely a priest, but one in a particularly obscure monastic order—an appropriate vehicle for a social novel of "middle-class America in the age of Eisenhower?"[14]

Lukács observes that the narration of a unique individual's accommodations to his or her world is only of factual interest unless the process reveals the possibility of the conventional world's being penetrated by meaning. Powers's choice of protagonist reveals much more than the idiosyncrasies of "this poor specialist," as Urban refers to himself and as some critics like to think of Powers:

> Powers specialty, moreover, is not merely the priesthood per se but the priesthood as practiced in the cities and small towns of Minnesota and the Midwest.[15]

However, Mary Gordon writes in the introduction to the first edition

> J. F. Powers is one of those master writers whose genius expresses itself in the description of a small area perfectly understood.

More than that. The Clementines are no more simply a broken-down religious order than Sinclair Lewis's *Main Street* is a story about a Minnesota town. Urban and his fate constitute a portrait of the Catholic Church in the United States painted with such subtle hues and comic grace that one is tempted to laugh before one realizes whose picture it is.

Powers's choice is an intuitively brilliant response to both the crisis of the social novel and to the disenchantment of the world. Urban is not only a representation of an archaic and dying institution, the Order of Saint Clement, he is also a person capable of dreaming perfectly a successful life and making us believe he could have attained it—a life with no regrets and, hence, with no meaning either. But something unspoken drives Urban to combine his striving for success with a desperate desire to "enchant" the world.[16] His fantasy world suggests a romantic imagination on a par with the "knight of the doleful countenance." This active imagination is easily overlooked as Urban wheels and deals his way through Minnesota, but it is the narrative's literary anchor.

The problem for the social novel, and one that grew considerably more acute with the growth and prosperity of the middle class in the 1950s, was that of maintaining its orientation to meaning and its significance beyond that of mere satire.[17] Through the figure of the Clementine father, Powers seeks to restore to the social novel the comic status, in which humor serves meaning as well as critique, so central to the novel's history as a form. There is much satire in *Morte D'Urban*, but the comic balance of the narrative keeps the double irony of the novel form active.

To comprehend Powers's dilemma fully, compare his social world and his choice of genre with those of Silone. In the 1930s, Silone could still find his U.S. reflection in John Steinbeck or Michael Gold, but in the 1950s United

States, Powers may have been the only echo possible. Certainly, Silone's world, both social and spiritual, seems remarkably enchanted compared with that of Powers. Perhaps it would be unfair to Silone to say that he ends up playing Feliciano de Silva[18] to Powers's Cervantes. Nevertheless, if Silone could narrate spiritual vocation as an ideal, Powers can only do so as the Unseen.

There are two aspects of this unseen elephant of vocation. The first is Urban's dual desire as a white-collar cleric to combat the U.S. religious climate dominated by a Protestantism so closely integrated with economic patronage and to fight the disenchantment of the world through an odd combination of public one-upmanship and private escapism. The second aspect is the possibility of spirituality through withdrawal—now given the social status of failure—a possibility only briefly glimpsed in the novel and in the vocation of the novelist.

WHITE COLLAR

> But one must ask every man: Do you in all conscience believe that you can stand seeing mediocrity after mediocrity, year after year, climb beyond you, without becoming embittered and without coming to grief? Naturally, one always receives the answer: "Of course, I live only for my 'calling.'" Yet, I have found that only a few men could endure this situation without coming to grief.[19]

At the heart of every novel lies a paradox: In *Morte D'Urban*, it is Urban's loyalty to the Clementines. Harvey Roche seems to have been driven into the unlikely vocation of Father Urban by a brief, almost perverse mood of resistance to the domination of Protestantism in the midwestern United States. Although this may explain something of Father Urban's origins, it does not explain his fascination, his charisma as a novelistic protagonist. Rather, this relationship to Protestantism shapes the context of Urban's ambition and his sense of limits. His vocation, on the other hand, is a comic quest to find a space for mystery within that world, a quest that is comic because Urban seeks mystery in the hopeless form of enchantment, in fantasy rather than in the Unseen.

In his essay on "The Protestant Sects and the Spirit of Capitalism," Max Weber exposes the mutual influences between changes in religious institutions and socioeconomic structures. Whereas the rise of Protestantism can be clearly linked to the shift from a traditional feudal and guild economy to one based on the market and profit, changes within the institutions of the Catholic Church can be viewed as a related struggle to adapt. Urban certainly feels that the church has not done enough in this regard. Father Urban could not see how the Catholic Church among large corporations could be rated second to Standard Oil in efficiency, as *Time* magazine had reported.

Urban struggles with Father Wilfrid, the steward of his monastery—"the Hill." His confrontations give parodic expression to this frustration. Urban cannot help comparing the economy at the Hill with that of "real" institutions when Wilfrid argues at length about saving 30 cents by phoning station-to-station rather than person-to-person. Wilfrid was also a monk who felt that money should be no object when it comes to national defense (45–46).

The comparison, however, leaves little room for meaningful ethical action. Later, when the Hill is threatened by competition from other orders—the Jesuits and the Benedictines—Wilfrid longs for a return to a more feudal socioeconomic order. He wants borders to protect "their territory" (62). When it comes to the struggle for economic power, Urban knows that the Protestants must serve as his role models.

Weber analyzed both the theological and practical reasons for the success for which Urban envies them. Theologically, Protestantism took a more ascetic attitude toward this world than Catholicism. This attitude led to the devaluation of earthly beauty and good works. The ironic result was a higher valuation of rational behavior and professional success as emblems of one's grace.[20] Over time, however, Protestant sects became intimately connected with the world of commerce in a way that could yield economic rewards for their members. This interconnectedness became most pronounced in the United States where no previous economic and social norms prevented the simultaneous competition of sects and businesses. But the question, "To which church do you belong?" is telling to determine one's credit worth.[21] Similar to, "To which country club do you belong?":

> Admission to the congregation is recognized as an absolute guarantee of the moral qualities of a gentleman, especially of those qualities required in business matters....Only those men had success in business who belonged to Methodist or Baptist or other sects....He found not only easy contact with sect members but, above all, he found credit everywhere....A fairly reputable sect would only accept for membership one whose "conduct" made him appear to be morally qualified.[22]

Why then, aside from the obvious ethnic prejudices, were the Catholics at a disadvantage? Protestant affiliation "meant a certificate of moral qualification and especially business morals. This stands in contrast to membership in a 'church' into which one is 'born' and which lets grace shine over the righteous and unrighteous alike."

Affiliation with the church that one is born into is obligatory. Alone it proves nothing about the member's qualities. To make matters worse, Catholic mores were harshest in regard to those areas of personal conduct least oriented to business conduct: contraception, masturbation, and remarriage, for example. Weber notes that, "religious organizations that facilitated remarriage had great attraction."[23]

Urban knows that relations between confessional affiliation and business matters are not so smooth or dependable in his church. Father Urban tells the rector of the monastery that it can sometimes be a mistake to count on a Catholic concern (54).

But even if Urban cannot share in the same material rewards—business contacts and creditworthiness—as the Protestants, he can still create the illusion that he belongs to the same exclusive club. Urban is obsessed with competition between Catholic orders and even other denominations for "the higher type" of patron and convert. This snobbishness even applies to vocations, although here Urban meets with dubious results. The novice master talked of "beefing up" the Order. Father Urban's idea was to raise the tone "by packing the Novitiate with exceptional men. He had overshot the mark on occasion—two of his recruits had proved to be homosexual and one homicidal" (9).[24]

On his excursions beyond the church, it is unclear whether Urban is acting like a Protestant to win over non-Catholics or whether he is using his status as a priest (but a "friendly" one) to escape the confines of the church. This infatuation with the "public vocation," one that puts him in close company with Fulton Sheen, with whom he is twice compared (27, 113), and Andrew Greeley, also ranks him alongside the Protestant evangelists such as Billy Graham and Oral Roberts, with whom he is also compared. His specialty, like that of his mentor Father Placidus, is oratory. Again, it is Weber who notes that along with the market and democracy, the West has seen the rise of the "demagogue" as a figure of moral and political authority.[25]

In one particularly revealing scene, Urban, who tries to talk and smile at the same time, "a thing he'd noticed Protestants did better than Catholics" (175), speaks to the Great Plains Commercial Club, in which he takes their side against Wilf's campaign to "put Christ back into Christmas." During the question period, he distances himself farther and farther from his church to win over the audience to him personally. In response to every question, he begins, "I'm glad you asked that." Even when the questions turn to church authorities, he is accommodating and gracious until the discussion turns on belief that it is "going to rain because the Pope says so?" At that point, Urban had reached his limit of endurance:

[T]he question was tasteless and irrelevant, but Father Urban smiled....
He had no choice but to shoot the woman down. "As a Catholic—that is,
as one who respects proper authority—I'm afraid I'd be more inclined to
trust the weather bureau in such a matter." (86–88)

Urban's sermons generally reflect polished Protestant oratory; this, however, also reflects a deep bitterness toward the dominant society under his interdenominational style. That bitterness, with its origin in Urban's

youth—the Ku Klux Klan cross burning he witnessed comes to mind (68)—
is expressed here in his contempt for the very audience he is trying to win
over, whether Protestant, agnostic, or mainstream Catholic.[26]

Urban always combines a thirst for applause and respect with aggression—
a trait common in the clergy—toward any convenient victim. He tortures
them publicly when possible, privately when he cannot. This resentment toward society that which his desire for popularity finds archetypical expression
in his reaction to the reception he gets in Duesterhaus: "[I]f this was how the
town welcomed a priest...there was plenty of work to do there" (30). Father
Urban has no intention, while avenging himself on society, of being a little
Tarcisius martyr for the church or any cause.[27]

So why is he a monk? Powers tells us that he fell under the spell of a certain Clementine father, but what is the symbolic significance of that choice
in the novel? At the sociological level, Urban's vocation puts him in the awkward position of being a success-oriented "white collar" while wearing the
Roman collar. This double signification of the collar suggests deeper homol-
ogies between the church and a hostile Protestant society than are evident in
"the Harvey Roche story."

Historically, the monastic orders first cultivated a rationalized life of economic production as a basis for ethical contemplation much like that which
became the basis of the Protestant ethic. Nevertheless, the monastic order is
closer to the medieval guild, with its emphasis on a collective economy, than
to the Protestant churches, which measured worth and wealth in individual-
istic terms.[28] Urban has little in common with either of these ways. He mocks
the economy of the novitiate and "a little bit of community life went a long
way with him" (7). And he hurls the harshest epithet he can throw at the
Protestant ethic and his fellow clergy—*Puritanism*—implying a narrowness
of both mores and economic vision (16, 231).

What Urban strives to be is a good company man, combining the loyalty
to the collective required of the white collar with the individualism of an
employee seeking to be a winner within the company.[29] By striving to be a
successful white-collar man as a monk, Urban seeks the only form of resistance to his society he can find: a strange sort of have-your-cake-and-eat-it-
too form of revenge. Ironically, it is not society that fights him, but his own
church, and it does so in two ways: by the incompetence of his colleagues
among the Clementines and by the hostility and competitiveness of other
Catholic institutions.[30]

The rule of mediocrity and incompetence in the Clementines, which Urban
finds so limiting, is, in fact, a function of an institution that seeks to subordi-
nate (rather than exploit) individual ambition to an appearance of a consen-
sual will. Weber noted this as a structural element even in papal elections in
which the cardinal thought to be the favored candidate seldom wins.[31] As the
ancient saying goes, "He who enters the conclave a pope exits a cardinal."

Urban finds this pattern to hold true throughout his order, from the inexplicable election of Boniface to his feeling that "indigence was too often a cloak for incompetence" (35). This cynicism—"Father Urban had long since stopped looking to his superiors for gratitude" (177)—eventually feeds a resentment on his part that poisons his sense of vocation. He harbors a malicious attitude even toward the survival of the order. He is willing to go down with it (84).

Urban's attitude of social superiority shows itself in his regard for the people who come to his retreats, whom he demeans as "Teutonic and Central European" types. Instead of the wealthy audience he wants, he draws only "the ham-and-sausage-supper horseshoe pitchers" who set the wrong tone (179).

But almost as discouraging to Urban as his own order's incompetence is the resistance the secular clergy accord his efforts. In the course of the novel, he enters two such conflicts: the one with Monsignor Renton over building a new church at Saint Monica's parish (chapters 7 and 8) and the other with the bishop over the ownership of the golf course at the Hill (chapter 11).

Although he wins both, he does so without any sense of satisfaction. The reward for winning is never worldly success. Rather a sense of loss is the result of both encounters: the death of Father Phil and Urban's dismissal from Saint Monica's in the former and the concussion and permanent headaches from the bishop's golf ball in the latter. Urban's entrepreneurial and public-relations skills win him momentary applause but no institutional recognition. So what keeps Urban and, of greater importance to the significance of the novel, the reader interested in serving the church?

Max Weber diagnosed the ambiguous position of the church in our disenchanted time in a way much more true to Powers's (and Urban's) worldview than to Silone's. For Silone, both spirituality and history are rendered enchanted with meaningful possibilities. Precisely because of his clear-sighted disenchantment, Urban stands squarely in the abyss of that ambiguity, thereby offering Catholic and non-Catholic, believer and nonbeliever, a sympathetic yet challenging vantage point from which to observe their world.

More mysterious and significant to the force of the novel than the question of his conversion at the end is Urban's faith throughout the narrative. If he often seems to lack faith, it is because of his need to measure up to workaday existence. Weber saw this confrontation between faith and the demands of socioeconomic structures as a struggle between Christianity and a disenchanted polytheism:

> Today the routines of everyday life challenge religion. Many old gods ascend from their impersonal forces. They strive to gain power over our lives and again they resume their eternal struggle with one another. What is hard for modern man…is to measure up to workaday existence.[32]

Urban, a priest with a gift for sociological insight that surpasses even his entrepreneurial skill, is an appropriate protagonist for the narration of this struggle. Urban applies this social insight with the rigor of an ethnographer in the field when he makes his appraisal of parish life in the United States. Parishioners resist a pastor who encourages them to think for themselves as Sheen encouraged his TV viewers. Pastors resist people who try to raise the status of parishioners as Greeley encouraged his readers. These agitators are products of higher Catholic education or converts. He discounts the so-called ideal parishes.

> The most successful parishes were those where more was going on than met the eye, where, behind the scenes, a gifted pastor or assistant pulled the strings. God, it seemed, ran those parishes, which was as it should be. Wherever parishionership became a full-time occupation, whether it consisted in liturgical practices or selling chances on a new car, the wrong people took over. (152–53)

Similarly, a sociologist could have written his assessment of the U.S. seminaries. They are institutions, "Turning out policemen, disc jockeys, and an occasional desert father" (167). In it, too, however, is the crucial recognition and respect for the mystery still adhering to our "godless and prophetless time."[33] In the light and comic yet striking addition of that "occasional desert father" resides the last refuge of the irrational and the Unseen. The source of Urban's own power, it adheres in his loyalty to the Clementines as a vehicle for a quixotic struggle against disenchantment.

Urban's desire for enchantment takes two forms, the one comically absurd, the other containing the grain of truth that keeps the scales of judgment hanging over him in perfect balance. The first is his refusal of our time, his retreat into a medieval fantasy world "when saints were bold" (294). The second is his subtle yet conscious awareness of the charism lurking within his vocation.

Urban veils his mission to the mammon of iniquity in a fantasy of feudal relations between clergy and benefactor. In Billy he thinks he has found the perfect King Arthur to serve, the charismatic warlord whose power is not yet rational and managerial but still personal, arbitrary, and, therefore, in need of spiritual guidance. Billy conducts himself with the noblesse oblige of a Dark Age seigneur and barbaric independence—drowning a deer with his bare hands. He is hardly recognizable as a modern businessman. The only glimpse we even get of his business is an oblique reference to his having "the heavy stockholder's loyalty to the railroads" (270). Is he a racketeer? Urban asks no questions.

Billy treats Urban as his personal priest, and Urban cultivates this archaic relationship, even though he recognizes the inadequacy of Billy's noblesse oblige in practice. Billy sends his broken model railroad trains, which he enjoys crashing, to another set of his dependents, the invalids in the veterans' hospital.

Nevertheless, Urban accepts Billy's feudal contract. He supplies the office space in Chicago, a color TV set for the "invalids" at the monastery, and a check made out to Urban for the entire cost of the golf course in exchange for three cords of oak firewood annually and prayer. More ominous is Billy's desire to perpetuate relations of dependence. He teases about ways the Order could make money, like the Dalmatian fathers who were selling hams. But Billy had no confidence in priests who went into "business" (4–5).

On one disastrous fishing trip, Urban discovers another such feudal patronage system, one in which Billy and "Doc Strong" subsidize Henn's Haven in return, it appears, for sexual favors from "Mother." Doc Strong has access to the late Mother Henn, while Billy is the current lover of Honey Henn (262, 272–73). This arrangement and the Tarzan-like attack on the deer prove too much for Urban's overstrained powers of imagination.

Urban makes a similar effort to cast a spell of medieval enchantment over Mrs. Thwaites, with similar results. In addition to his fantasy of being a papal emissary, he tries to play Saint Francis for her benefit. He wears his cassock and walks under the trees on her estate:

> When he saw Mrs. Thwaites watching him from one of her windows, and tried to get a squirrel to take a green acorn out of his hand, but it wouldn't, nor would a dove. (244)

In these episodes of theatrical medievalism, Powers represents Urban with Cervantean irony. Only in the golf tournament with the bishop's champion, Father Feld, does Urban fully share in that ironic self-consciousness. Here, Urban recognizes that the metaphor of an Arthurian joust may be accurate, but it does not serve any kind of spiritual vocation:

> In Father Urban's mind, informed as it was by a good deal of solid reading, the match between him and Father Feld took on the appearance of a judicial duel. Victory for Father Urban in the field, however, would not mean victory for his cause. That was the hell of it. Father Urban had read of many ordeals by combat (in the dim past even religious men, unfortunately, had sometimes appealed to the God of Battles for justice), but he doubted that history would reveal a parallel case. (234)

Although he can never succeed in becoming, like Twain's Connecticut Yankee, the "boss" in this archaic court, Urban allows himself to be inspired by his mentor's all-American slogan—"Be a winner!" (236)—and in this key moment we see the subterranean connection between his medievalism and his Americanism. They combine in a mutual irony that can hardly serve his vocation.

What does serve Urban's vocation, at least according to its own ambiguous logic, is his sense of its charisma and mystery. Even some skeptical clergy must concede him this point. When Urban brags about his ability to preach a "clean mission" without "razzmatazz," one assistant priest agrees. Another assistant also responds, "Yes, and that's why I can't understand it" (28).

Urban may not have the compensations of the successful businessman nor the support of a rational institution, but he does have a blend of personal and religious charisma that he hopes to use in the last resort to turn his wealthy charges onto the path of righteousness. No matter how ruthlessly or cynically pursued his projects, Urban never loses sight of the fact that they are ultimately selfless and otherworldly. Whether he is dealing in real estate or souls, Urban, like Andrew Greeley, lends the patina of transcendent mystery to all of his activities. We get a glimpse of this blend of self-confidence and altruism in Urban's attitude toward the young novices with whom he took time to walk and talk in the hope of breathing quality into them. "He could hope and pray" (199).

Urban's consciousness of the value of this charisma also helps explain his choice of vocation. When he encounters the hostility of the secular clergy, he pays homage to the advantages of being a Catholic priest and a monk. The "lower clergy" were seen as lukewarm "less traveled, less learned, and less spiritual" than the monks:

> In short, they know that they suffer from a deficiency of mystery and romance, as the Protestant clergy do, compared with them. (178)

Here, Urban's medievalism finds a more substantive, if subtler, basis. The monastic order has that special charisma of the male community. They are the Knights Templars, the Arthurian Round Table. In his essay on the Arthurian romance, Erich Auerbach observes the special charismatic appeal of the knightly ethos:

> [I]t has a great power of attraction which, if I mistake not, is due especially to two characteristics which distinguish it: it is absolute, raised above all earthly contingencies, and it gives those who submit to its dictates the feeling that they belong to a community of the elect, a circle of solidarity.[34]

The possibility of attaining this ethos provides the veiled object of Urban's desire and the key to Powers's use of the Arthurian reference. Urban's grandiose hope for a vocation that is both meaningful and successful, however, is the source of Urban's isolation and his tragic-comic "death." Urban's fate is that of a self-conscious Quixote as Auerbach points out:

> Don Quixote's first setting forth...is a perfect parody—precisely because the world which Don Quixote encounters is not one especially prepared for the proving of a knight but is a random, everyday, real world. (137)

It is the "supplementing" Urban is forced into doing that gives Powers's novel its force and Urban his picaresque appeal.

Powers found his protagonist, his problematic hero, in the type of the modern so-called organization man situated in an archaic order of a premodern institution. But he does not leave the definition of vocation solely in his protagonist's hands. Urban is only one of the blind men around the elephant, albeit the one through whose hands we most feel what it is like. If there is an ideal of spiritual vocation comparable with that in Silone's world, it resides far off at the margins of the narrative, just as it does in the society narrated. Out of focus as it may be, this ideal still has a determinant influence on any understanding of the life and death of Urban. I call it, with intended Weberian overtones, *failure as a vocation.*

FAILURE AS A VOCATION

> The fate of our times is characterized by rationalization and intellectualization and, above all, by the "disenchantment of the world." Precisely the ultimate and most sublime values have retreated from public life either into the transcendental realm of mystic life or into the brotherliness of direct and personal human relations. It is not accidental that our greatest art is intimate and not monumental, nor is it accidental that today it is only within the smallest and intimate circles, in personal human situations, in pianissimo, that something is pulsating that corresponds to the prophetic pneuma, which in former times swept through the great communities like a firebrand, welding them together.[35]

When Urban refers to himself as "this poor specialist" (200), he is playing to the crowd, and his modesty rings false. His goal in such self-presentations before the world is summed up in his success with the housekeeper at Saint Monica's: "If he in any way fell short of the ideal (and of course he did), Mrs. Burns didn't know it" (146–47).

But what is this ideal he falls short of? It is not the heroism of Monsignor Morez who, "admonished a hooded mob from the porch, then fired off a shotgun, which did the job as words hadn't, and then broke a bone in his foot kicking over the fiery cross" (68). That sort of act was only possible in a lost age of heroes as remote from Urban's world as Homeric Greece. The ideal is expressed only in the pianissimo still, small voice of God.

Urban certainly does not recognize the presence of any ideal in the Order of Saint Clement as an institution. Its failings are the result of a merely worldly incompetence. He thinks they live under a "curse of mediocrity": "The Clementines were unique in that they were noted for nothing at all" (8–9).

Their social failure is not the result of an excess of spirituality either. Urban recognizes a certain basic pettiness at work in his superiors: "[T]here are those who resent excellence of any kind, having none themselves" (72). Urban harbors his own resentment.

Between the resentment of thwarted success and the resentment of the incompetent lies the humility of failure as a vocation. Father John—Jack—is the exception to the rule of resentment among the clergy in *Morte D'Urban.* Jack is the one Clementine "for whom, in a way, [Urban] had a lot of respect" (15). Even while pitying him—really a hidden form of self-pity—Urban recognizes without qualifications that "of course, his spiritual life was good" (94). Jack has the crucial role in the novel of suggesting the presence of a lived spirituality, even if it is often unseen and always difficult to discern. Its nearly invisible quality, to Jack as well in his holy naïveté, is symbolized by Jack's own blindness: Without his bifocals, "he was almost blind (15). Nevertheless, he is the only one of the "blind men . . . touching the elephant's body" who at least sees his own limitations.

Jack's spiritual accomplishment is played entirely in pianissimo "in simply cultivating plain brotherliness in personal relations."[36] The power of his spirituality finds full expression in the chapter "A Couple of Nights Before Christmas" in which he gives the resentful "star" and the resentful "incompetent"—Urban and Wilf respectively—a lesson in the meaning of Christmas that has nothing to do with its exploitation by shopkeepers or preachers.

As in Silone's novel, game playing becomes a useful allegory through which to reveal the limitations of man-made rules and the truly human capacity to transcend them. Wilf and Urban are locked into a gaming mentality in which all is measured by victory and defeat. On this occasion, it is Wilf who shows a greater awareness of what is at stake between them when he enters a discussion on chess and checkers. Urban and Jack are playing checkers but have never played chess. Wilf claims that although the boards are the same, the counters are different. "Altogether different. It's a different game." Urban intends to up the ante by saying, "I'd say the principle's the same." Wilf has the last word. "I'd say the principle's the same in all games." "Father Urban couldn't think of a single exception, try as he might" (94–95). That principle is none other than Urban's cherished motto, "Be a winner."

Then Urban discovers that he and Wilf are engaged in a fierce competition, one that began with Urban's betrayal before the Commercial Club of Wilf's campaign to "put Christ back into Christmas." When Urban begins proudly to survey the nativity scene Billy sent him, he realizes that "the bambino was missing" and wants to know why. Wilf replies, "He's not born yet" (98), and thereby lets Urban know that he has gotten revenge by taking Christ *out* of Urban's Christmas. Urban is immediately engrossed in this phase of the game initiated by Wilf. Urban does the only thing could do: nothing; he sits down (98–99).

At first, Urban, like a child, resents and is angry at Jack's passivity and "blindness." Why does Jack not say something? He is chicken; he hates trouble.

When Jack starts to investigate the scene of the crime for himself, Urban snaps at him, "You can *see* it's not there." But when Urban, waiting for "Wilf's move," resumes playing checkers with Jack, he ponders his friend's qualities:

> It occurred to him that Jack would have been an entirely different sort of person if he'd handled himself as he did his checkers. Jack could have been a big success in life—and not a very nice person to know. (99)

Urban realizes that the Jack he wishes were on his team would no longer have the very qualities he cherishes in him.

Jack, however, is in the game, and his first move is not absurd chatter but a subtle feint. At this point, Urban, and the reader, cannot grasp the method in Jack's apparent madness because Jack is playing by a set of rules based on a different principle than that of "Be a winner." Jack muses toward Wilf:

> "I see what you mean, Father," he said, and cleared his throat again. "But I've been wondering if the shepherds should be present yet. Or even Mary and Joseph—in the attitudes we see them in, I mean. And the Magi. The animals, yes, but not running around in circles." (99–100)

Baffled and feeling defeated, Urban asks himself what he was doing there: "Why had he been cast into outer darkness, thrown among fools and failures?" But to Urban's surprise Jack has actually turned the tide in Urban's favor: "Wilf reached up into the branches of the tree and brought out the bambino and put it back where it belonged."

Urban is not grateful, however, because Jack has set things right in a way that precludes any division into winners and losers. Wilf makes his next move. Plugging in the crib, he says, "Just shows how wrong we can be sometimes." Father Urban rejects any thought that "We had been wrong" and continues his game of checkers with Jack with a vengeance, only to realize that Jack let him win. Jack was satisfied. There was peace even Father Urban could accept (100–101).

In this intimate scene, Jack reveals the ideal of spiritual vocation, an ideal that can only be played in pianissimo in Urban's world. This scene is also the only time Urban grants Jack such charism. Usually, his resentment gets the better of him, as, for example, in their encounter after both have received notice of their transfers to the monastery. When Urban witnesses Jack's humble resignation, he knows it is the better way, but he thinks it is easier for Jack, who has nothing to lose. Jack mistakes Urban's bitter mood as a show of sympathy and brotherly love:

> I just want to say that in a thing like this I don't much care what happens to me, but it's nice to know somebody else does. (22)

Even then, Urban belittles his generous companion and quickly buries the glimmer of the spiritual ideal he sees under a contempt for worldly failure (25).

Later, after the Christmas chapter, Urban and Wilf begin another rivalry, but this time Urban dismisses Jack's peacemaking as simple ignorance. Wilf tries to steal Urban's thunder when Billy Cosgrove gives the monastery a TV set. Jack attempts to make peace, but Urban will have none of it, this time dismissing him: "You mean well, I'm sure." Jack did not know Billy Cosgrove (110–11).

Although Jack's wisdom still peers through, he is beginning to disintegrate (his rattling cup) under the ironic gaze of the narrative itself.[37] This narrative must strike a bargain, like Urban, with a disenchanted world and its often mocking principle of "Be a winner," if it is to exist at all.

This narrative irony joins forces with Urban's acerbic wit (always an irresistible invitation to the reader to laugh along), pushing Jack beyond the pale of sympathy:

> [A]t the mention of Our Lord, Father Urban saw Jack drop his hands and take leave of his senses. (114)

At such a point, we remember Jack as the man who gets chewed out for putting on another man's trousers (108) and who sets out to write a scholarly children's edition of *Le Morte D'Arthur* (246) rather than as the Yuletide saint of the fifth chapter. In the visible social world of *Morte D'Urban*, Jack's vocation cannot avoid a quixotic appearance.

URBANE CELIBACY: GOOD CARS
AND EVIL WOMEN

> He got out of the car, took off his coat, rabat, and collar.... Then he got in, started the motor, which had a plummy sound he loved, shifted himself into a slouch, and, with his head resting easily to one side as if he were dreaming...[38]

Father Urban loves good cars. He also loves power. Cars are the ultimate expression of possessive individualism. Father Urban's missions to the mammon of iniquity always begin with cars being put at his disposal and always end with the withholding of that privilege at an especially awkward moment. But cars also symbolize sexual power in *Morte D'Urban*. Urban's celibacy meets sexual temptation in the sensual seats of sporty cars.

Perhaps the most difficult area of Powers's novel to explore is the structure of celibacy and the vision of sexuality implicit in Urban's vocation. Iannone argues that there really is not that much to look into. She observes:

> Powers' priests do not suffer from sexual repression or from closet homosexuality. They are manly (or boyish) men with mostly real if not always

very inspired vocations who enjoy smoking, drinking, sports, and a good game of cards. They like being priests, mean to keep their vows, and try to handle temptation when they are able to see it.[39]

This is very much in accord with the public-relations picture the church still strives to project even after the crisis of sexual abuse of minors has disabused most of the public of that asexual scene.

Urban's celibacy, however, hardly conforms to Iannone's simple and un-problematic summation. The centrality of the scene in the tower with Sally Hopwood alone would suggest great significance and complexity lurking behind Powers's only apparently offhand representation of sexual conflict.

First, the institution of celibacy holds an uncertain position in Urban's disenchanted social world. Urban does have attitudes and strategies that he uses to support his practice of celibacy, but his supports are not those of an achieved and integrated celibate. His practice is maintained with difficulty and much regret.

There are two sexually charged relationships in the novel, both between Urban and the women with good cars. His flirtation with Sylvia Bean reveals the workaday practice of Urban's celibacy, and the critical encounter with Sally Hopwood exposes, through its magical, dreamlike narration, the depths of Urban's spiritual crisis through the allegory of a failed celibacy—not failed in the flesh but in the spirit.

When Powers introduces the poverty of the Clementines, he subtly reminds us that the church's sexual teachings have been left behind in a world of economic prosperity and liberalizing mores. The old building occupied by the Clementines had been in receivership for years and looked it, looked condemned, in fact. The Clementines were on the fifth floor. The previous tenant, a publisher of sexual-science books, had prospered and moved.

The same forces that are driving the church to rationalize its administrative and economic structure have called into question the legitimacy of the doctrine of celibacy. Early Christianity, which came into being in a major spiritual revolution, saw celibacy as an extraordinary charism that no set of rules could either mandate or contain.[40] The transformation of the church into a dominant institution of society, however, required the discipline and laws Weber calls "the routinization of charisma."[41] As an institution whose legitimacy, like that of the other power centers of feudal society, was based on traditional and patriarchal authority, the church needed to consolidate its sexual teachings as a regularized body of law that was incontrovertible and one that served the lines of a patriarchal control outside family lineage.[42]

To survive the transition from a feudal to a capitalist society, a traditional institution like the church had to shift its legitimacy to a more modern basis. Even if the content of the church's teachings remains based on mystery, the management of the church as an institution had to become administratively bureaucratic and economically rational. The difficulty for the doctrine of celibacy in this transition is whether it, too, can find a rational basis in a new economic and social order. For this reason, the debate around celibacy in today's church often takes the form of a struggle between "traditional" and "rational" positions.[43]

Urban's own rational practice of celibacy is based on his recognition of the power and charisma it can lend to the supposed celibate. Erving Goffman has noted the value of systems of self-concealment—mystification, manners, and, we might add as an especially rigorous case, celibacy, in which the individual's sexuality remains a secret world, as tools of establishing personal power. "Self-concealment serves, among other purposes, that of preserving a sort of ascendancy over the unsophisticated,"[44] or what could be called the *uninitiated*. Urban maintains his celibate practice with the organization man's loyalty, a loyalty that seeks institutional rewards in return for personal sacrifice. These personal rationalizations of celibate practice force Urban into a lonely struggle with the irrational aspects of traditional discipline—what he calls the church's *Puritanism* and with an internalized set of conflicting supports for that practice.

Urban rejects Puritanism in favor of a casual sociability with Catholics and non-Catholics alike. But behind his sociability lurks one of the same attitudes typical of that Puritanism: a profound misogyny. The use of misogyny as a defense, a sign of an immature sexuality and a fragile celibate practice, combines dangerously with his gregariousness, propelling him into sexually charged and destructive relationships with women so common among Catholic priests.[45] This reality is diametrically opposed to Greeley's romantic assumption that a woman who has a confiding relationship enhances the relationship of her and her husband.

Urban gives the impression of having been previously able to avoid such situations through a highly mobile lifestyle supported by a confident sense of achievement in his work. The crisis that opens the novel, however—his transfer to the Hill—removes these superficial supports of celibacy, and women become threatening to him.

At the age of 54, Urban has had no positive mature relationship with any woman, or with any male friend, for that matter. Although he is worldly and insightful enough to be able to imagine a balance between work and sexual life—in his fantasy of being a businessman (292–95)—he has found no way to strike such a balance as a celibate salesman. Achieved celibacy is, after all, a form of sexual life, not the mere negation of sexuality.

One of the reasons Urban is such an effective protagonist is the sympathy he can win from the noncelibate reader through his sociability and worldliness. He is true to his clerical role model, Father Placidus, "who would sing such ballads as 'Kiss Me Again' and 'I'm Falling in Love with Someone' in mixed company" (70).

Urban offers the mixed audience, Catholic and non-Catholic, in Great Plains a nonthreatening yet attractive image of the celibate:

> "Differences of opinion can occur in any organization human or divine, large or small—yes, even in the best-run families, between husbands and wives, so I've been told anyway." Laughter. People who, perhaps, hadn't entirely trusted the speaker…were now in a mood to get cozy with him. (88)

Nothing rankles Father Urban more than the idea that he might be seen otherwise. Even Billy considered Urban to be very unworldly:

> This was an idea that many people had of the clergy, and perhaps the clergy indulged them in it, as did the major communications media, but Father Urban didn't see how he could have conveyed that idea to quite this extent. (275–76)

Urban tries hard to distinguish himself from those clergy who project a lack of sexual savvy or, worse, an outright prudishness. He even explains his major conflict with the bishop over ownership of the Hill through a contrast of his own tolerance and modern outlook and the hypocrisy behind the bishop's Puritanism.

The conflict centers on attitudes toward the golf course that the monastery owns. Women wearing shorts used it, and one laughed at the bishop, "teeing off on his first visit to the course, had swung and missed the ball completely. Father Urban wondered if a thing like a woman's laugh might not be at the bottom of the man's desire to seize St. Clement's Hill" (227).

His confrontation with the bishop reveals itself to be a fairly straightforward power struggle over turf behind a sexual front like the need to install toilet facilities to accommodate women and other improvements.

> "There'll be some changes here next year, Your Excellency," said Father Urban…. "Everybody except yourself, that is," said the Bishop. (230–31)[46]

In fact, the bishop's threat strikes much closer than his views on lay sexuality to the supports of Urban's celibacy. Urban's success as a career man is at stake.

Urban could practice celibacy successfully as long as he moved irresistibly forward. As Andrew Greeley has observed, celibacy is not impossible if priests are happy in their work. But what happens when that happiness is threatened? On his transfer to Duesterhaus, Urban immediately realizes his vulnerability, not only as a celibate but also as a person, not only as Father Urban but also as urban man. Urban resists the temptation to drink, although he had a silver flask in his attaché case. He reminded himself:

> Many a good city man had gone down that drain. Yes, and even worse fates, it was said, could overtake a city man in desolation—women, insanity, decay. (13)[47]

The kind of work that Urban exults in is just one of the physical elements that I observed as supporting achieved celibacy.[48] Work is only part of a celibate life built on service, community, and spirituality. Urban's exile to Duesterhaus does not cut him off from any of these aspects of the spiritual vocation per se. As far as service is concerned, however, Urban specializes in managing the souls of the rich and powerful, a specialty ill suited to such an assignment. He does have a spiritual life—a key point raising him above the status of an Elmer Gantry—and one without which his vocation would be entirely impossible. Over the years, however, it has receded to a secondary position. He knew that it was easy to neglect prayer living at the pace he had; now he "reminded himself to spend more time before the Blessed Sacrament" (37).

Finally, his view of community life is one more firmly based on the U.S. success ethic and individualist responsibility—that is, with work, narrowly defined—than it is on love. Urban criticizes Wilf for the inadequate job he was doing as rector (116).

As in all of his cynical soliloquies, Urban is saved—as a protagonist, if not a priest—by his ability to comprehend the social truth of his spiritual poverty. Father Urban is a priest James Joyce would recognize.

Morte D'Urban is not a world of easily achieved celibacy but one of secrecy. Powers demonstrates great novelistic rigor by remaining on the social plane. He narrates only what is visible in this secret world. When we do obtain glimpses of the private lives of priests, they are far from unproblematic. Wilf is hiding something—we never learn what—from Urban. Wilf "covered the clutter of papers and photographs on the desk with a newspaper" (39). Wilf, in turn, suspects Urban of having a girlfriend (117). There is homosexual activity among the Clementines (9, 38). The description of the activities of Dickie Thwaites among the Dolomite fathers suggests both heterosexual and homosexual possibilities (162).

Powers's subtle awareness of the gaps between discipline and practice are captured by Monsignor Renton's deadpan remarks about canon law "that made Father Urban think" (226).

It would be a serious enough mistake to equate these understated glimpses of the difficult sexual lives of priests with an unproblematic view of celibacy, but Powers is quite explicit about the limitations of Urban's celibate practice in the narration of his exploitative and misogynist relationship with Sylvia Bean. Urban himself recognizes his regrets in the tower of Belleisle.

Misogyny has become a major negative support of Catholic celibacy since its routinization as a required discipline of the clergy. Rather than building celibacy on the positive sublimations of community and service, contempt for women—portraying them as more evil and less human and spiritual than men—has been used to ennoble celibate practice as purification. When celibate practice lapses, it becomes logical to cast the blame on women.[49] Of course, this tendency is compounded by the general misogyny of the society as a whole. The church's failure in this regard is one of not rising above an attitude that has a less than spiritual basis.

As Urban's excitement about his work and his sense of success become threatened, he falls back on this misogyny as the central support of his continued celibacy. Given his ability to rationalize and equivocate on so many other ethical matters, it is noteworthy that Urban manages to handle temptation at all, but his resistance has a price. He cannot resolve the sexual tension in any productive way but must simply externalize it and, failing that, flee from it.

When Urban's confidence erodes, so, too, do his sociability and worldliness, and, in their place, an increasingly unbearable sexual tension arises. Even though his relationship with Sylvia has been built since the beginning on Urban's manipulation of the sexual tension between them, he abruptly breaks off his contact with her out of a sudden fear but projects the fear onto her. It is really a failure of Urban's self-confidence. Later, at Henn's Haven, he repeats this uncharacteristic gesture of flight before attractive women in his first encounter with the second Mrs. Henn:

> She was dark, perhaps part Indian, and so attractive that Father Urban was relieved when she left them for the kitchen. Her scent remained, however. Father Urban moved away from it. (263)

The next evening, Urban begins talking with a Mrs. Inglis, "not a bad-looking woman," but he pulled out of the conversation "after she said she was going to tell him a secret if she wasn't careful" (272). Although such defensive reactions could be a necessary part of someone's personal adjustment to celibacy, they are clearly a new development in the practice of the once sociable Urban.

Urban's nervousness around attractive women would only be an honest admission of new limitations if it were not based on a subtle contempt for women and a consistent tendency to see them as the source of the problem. In *Morte D'Urban*, both clergy and laymen use the woman as temptress as a metaphoric motif of their everyday speech. Urban considers the difficulty of using the medium of television for evangelism in these terms: Even Bishop Sheen had not been able to "make an honest woman of a whore" (112–13).

Likewise, Father Louis, who had spent all but one of his seminary years with the Jesuits, sees his unfortunate career with the Clementines as a sexual indiscretion with a fallen woman:

> He had met Father Placidus and joined the Clementines on the first bounce, as a divorced man takes up with the first floosie he meets, so he'd once told Father Urban. (188)

The handiness of such metaphors extends well beyond the clergy and moral lessons. Billy's golfing expert, Mr. Robertson, laces them into his own mundane sermons about the golf course:

> She'll be a little jewel in a few years.... Always remember a golf course is like a fancy woman—you have to take care of it. (198)

His final word to Urban: "And don't think you can cheat your course" (198). Although these clichés may seem harmless enough in the mouths of specific characters, they are reflected more ominously in Urban's general attitude toward women.

Urban is at best condescending and at worst contemptuous in his relations with women. His positive reactions, like Andrew Greeley's, are almost exclusively limited to compliments on physical appearance. When he agrees to speak to a Catholic business and professional women's group, an invitation he had previously declined with only veiled derision—"How do I know it isn't just this woman's idea to have me come and give a talk? How do I know the Bishop would be there for it?" (119)—he delivers a talk with rather ambiguous implications for precisely that audience. "The Hand That Rocks the Cradle Rules the World" (171) may flatter some, but it seems to suggest that the listeners would do better to return to mothering as a vocation. Even women in the church come in for a similar dose of male condescension: "nuns could coo their way out of difficulties" (226).

But Urban's scorn for women who fail to meet his ideal—the upper-middle-class society woman—is as sharp as his other observations at Saint Monica's and much more acerbic when he considers the squalor in which so many of his parishioners live. It was not a slum, just households miserably neglected by women who drink coffee and eat pastry together—"trousered queens"—and disregard or do not care about keeping house. They could never guess what he thought of them, "so courtly was his manner. 'Ladies, the pleasure was all mine.'"

He does not limit his blame to them: The U.S. male had gone soft. And he guesses the source: "another green-eyed European, another G.I. who'd married an Asiatic" and the Mexicans who had no sense of time (148–49).

The audacity of the kind of racist and ethnic slurs that come naturally to Urban ("Mighty white of you, Cal," 180) can be understood from the biography of the author. J. F. Powers was a civil rights advocate, short story author of "The Trouble," "He Don't Plant Cotton," and "The Eye." To the end of his life, he was faithful to the pacifism that had cost him four years in prison. In this area, there is no ambiguity concerning the narrative point of view. This *is* the secret world and communications of Powers's Catholic priests.

Powers's disdain of prejudices and priests who harbor them seems at times to ignore ethical implications in favor of dramatic effect. The slurs against

Eastern Europeans are clearly Urban's prejudices; Father Wilfrid is a ste-
reotyped Bohunk. Billy's racism—"Grow up, Greaseball"—is acceptable to
Urban as is the reference to the "blackamoor coffee boys" in the Pump Room
(22–25), but the use of Honey Henn as an image of animal ("scent") seduc-
tiveness because she is "part Indian" combines clichés of race and gender
based on notions of nature versus culture (263, 279).

The question of the relationship between the narrative point of view and
the character is an open one but, as we shall see in the case of Silone, inescapable once the ethical issues around celibacy are raised. Although Silone's
second version addressed itself precisely to these concerns, only later novels
and stories of Powers's can be examined by way of a comparison. Certainly,
in regard to *Wheat That Springeth Green*, Powers has been criticized for one-
sidedness and didacticism, but of a decidedly different stripe. Iannone, again
missing the sense, says:

> [The] ending seems shockingly cheap, hitting the hitherto exhilarated
> reader like Father Urban's golf ball, but without any spiritual payoff
> afterward.[50]

In the case of Urban's relationship with Sylvia Bean, the irony is present but still gentle enough to be ambiguous. What maintains the narrative's
edge of critique in this subplot is the use of the car as a symbol of power
crossing the sexual and the social. Urban is so bewitched by the privilege
of driving the Barracuda that he only breaks with Sylvia when she herself
becomes, in his eyes, a witch of seduction, Urban's Morgana. Through the
middle two-thirds of the novel, she is his Maid Marian: "[S]he was Robin
Hood's girl friend, whatever that might mean" (191). We do learn, however,
what that means for Urban. He plays the celibate martyr, trapped between
the irresistible, though permissible, temptation of a good car and the illicit
temptation of an "evil woman," but his martyrdom is only the refuge he seeks
after failing to control the woman through his celibate allure.

Sylvia is the devout, attractive Catholic woman Urban chooses to "shoot
down" in order to win over the non-Catholic members of the Commercial
Club (87). When he discovers that his cruelty only increased her interest in
him, he begins, "after her husband had acted as matchmaker"[51] (123), subtly
to manipulate her intellectual masochism. First, he savages *The Drover*, her
favorite Catholic magazine:

> In no other paper would you find everything that was wrong with the
> Catholic press. "The Drover" had it all, all the worst features of the bully
> and the martyr. (124)

Despite his rudeness—behavior he would never indulge in with a well-
to-do man like Sylvia's husband—Urban has no intention of driving her out

of his life (125). In fact, he soon learns that she is quite willing to play the martyr to his bullying. His refusal of her offer to host a pair of charlatan preachers, the Shrapnel Brothers, at Saint Monica's—"Over my dead body, Mrs. Bean"—only quickens her ardor (155).

In the next stage of their relationship, Urban shifts from bullying to exploiting her. Powers introduces this shift with great subtlety, presenting it in a manner that is strikingly offhand when Cal's Body Shop shows up with Phil's repaired car:

> Father Urban was sorry to see it. For two days, he'd had the use of Sylvia Bean's little English sports car—a Barracuda S-X 2. (179–80)

The use of Sylvia's car, which is apparently only an exceptional event, turns out to be a regular occurrence. Again, this important fact is presented in the most passing sort of way:

> [W]ith Wilf's permission, and with Sylvia Bean's little Barracuda, Father Urban became the Hill's roving ambassador of good will. (202)

In the chapter in which he meets Mr. Studley, Urban is tooling around in her car as if he were a teenager showing off his graduation gift. He even drag races a group of teenage hot-rodders (223).

> Urban, enjoying the feel, the roadability, of the little Barracuda, thought of Sylvia. (208)

In this reverie, Urban flatters himself both as a handsome and charismatic man and as a priest true to his vows, while revealing a thoroughly misogynist view of women: their intellectual inferiority, their lack of self-consciousness, and, in contradiction to the first two attributes, their craftiness. She had asked him to read just one verse of a poem. He did:

> An intellectual hatred is the worst,
> So let her think opinions are accursed.
> Have I not seen the loveliest of woman born
>   Out of the mouth of Plenty's horn,
> Because of her opinionated mind
> Barter that horn and every good
> By quiet natures understood
> For an old bellows full of angry wind?

When he finished, he said to her, "Is that what you mean?" And yes it was—the poet had put it very well.

Yes, and so had Father Urban. But Father Urban, with and without benefit of poetry, had been through this sort of thing with too many women. He was afraid Sylvia might be building herself up for a letdown. In effect, by asking him to read the poem, she had put words in his mouth he might think but would never speak. In the privacy of her imagination, Sylvia might distill pleasure of an illicit nature from the words that might be said to compromise him. And "loveliest woman born" was pushing it some in her case. "Damned attractive redhead" would have been more like it. Experience had shown Father Urban that a handsome priest could not be too careful with women.

Even though Urban "is worried about her" and cannot "be too careful," he chooses to keep using her car for the supposed good of his ministry, and "he'd be lost without it" (208–9). Certainly, Urban cannot be expected "to give up his little trips" to the mammon of iniquity. They are the core of his vocation.

When Billy invites Urban to go fishing, Urban is expected to provide the car. He has a problem. He tried and failed to get a response from two laymen (253). The third possibility is Sylvia, but we learn only now, *post factum*, of their significant parting. Powers again handles the most sexually charged episodes in an offhand and understated way, almost as an afterthought or flashback. In this case, Urban reminds himself that he has not seen Sylvia lately; in fact, not since a trip to Ray's farm. They had arrived just as two hired men were about to breed a mare. Father Urban's first concern was for Sylvia's sensibilities. But, much to his surprise, Sylvia got right into the act. "She was crying encouragement to the stallion and being cross with the mare." Father Urban had not seen Sylvia or Ray or asked for the little Barracuda since that day (254).

The importance of having a good car for his ministry is revealed simultaneously with the fate of his relationship with Sylvia, who, it turns out, has gone too far. She upset the convenient balance Urban had established between them.

The balance between his sexual/celibate power and her material possessions collapses when she tries to exact the price he can only pay at the cost of his mystique. A vocation based on the courtship of power, of sexual mystique and the mammon of iniquity, is an extremely fragile one. The fishing trip destroys the balance, first by Billy's petulance over Urban's failure to provide a car (255–58) and then by stranding Urban at Henn's Haven (279–80).

In the final dramatic confrontation of the novel, Urban meets the united threat of sexual seduction and economic power in the figure of Sally Hopwood, the daughter of his benefactress Mrs. Thwaites. Sally is "a small, finely made, attractive woman in a white convertible," who arrives on the scene of his recent defeat with Billy. Powers, the layman, elicits modest verbal descriptions of women that stand in stark contrast to Greeley's lush "Playboy" vocabulary. Ironically, as Urban departs with Sally, he has a final encounter with Sylvia. She drove by in her Barracuda. "Father Urban waved, but Sylvia cut him dead" (280–82).

In the episode about Sally, Powers shifts from an offhand, deadpan narration of Urban's sex life to a highly direct and probing one. Urban eats forbidden fruit on the way into the tower of Belleisle:

> He'd hesitated ... about eating one of the tiny red berries from a bush by the castle door. The berry had tasted sweet and then bitter. (286)

Inside, he sees Sally in her literal nakedness and himself in his spiritual nakedness:

> In a matter of moments, she was standing before him, before the fire, back to him, wearing nothing but her shoes. They were high-heeled shoes. Calf. Golden Calf. Lovely woman. No doubt of it. (297)

The "Golden Calf," however, is not what she is but what Urban has been worshipping in place of lovely women. Sally tells Urban the truth about all of his spiritual charges among the mammon of iniquity: Dickie Thwaites "isn't very well off"; Mrs. Thwaites "is a hard, hard old woman"; his relationship with Billy "is all wrong"; and she herself is simply "not a religious person" (287–90). But, worst of all for Urban, she tells the truth about him:

> "Has it occurred to you that people might be disappointed by you and your reasons, and even more by you?"
> "I'm not sure I know what you mean," said Father Urban.
> "I mean you're an operator—a trained operator. And an operator in your heart—and I don't think you have a friend in the world."
> Father Urban smiled. "Now you've gone too far." "Name one." (291)

After Sally strips away his pretensions, Urban imagines an alternative vocation with a surprisingly precise vision of its sexual life:

> Father Urban just sat there, sipping scotch and seeing himself as he might have been.... Until his marriage, he'd played around a lot, but he'd never touched waitresses, stewardesses, receptionists, the wives or mistresses of his friends, or anybody who worked for him in the office.... His life hadn't been quite right, though—he'd known it all along—and so he'd fixed that. He'd married late, but not too late. Always partial to mature women, he'd married a widow. Lovely woman. Not beef and not pork but woman. Her throat not as full as it had been, perhaps, but otherwise she was good as new.... He had no children, so far as he knew, and his wife had none by her first marriage. No regrets. (292–94)

It is difficult not to recognize this fantasy as a more appropriate sexual life than celibacy for a white-collar man like Urban, and Urban sees this alternative life with more clarity than he sees his own.[52]

When Sally strips away her clothes, however, there is a danger that she will be read simply as another bewitching temptress when the significance of the act lies in its being the final attempt to hold a mirror up to Urban:

> "You've got me covered," he said, and took his eyes off her, and kept them off, commending himself. It was like tearing up telephone directories, the hardest part was getting started. (297)

The reader is left to ponder whether his looking away is an act of looking inward or merely the continuation of his blindness. In any case, there is more at stake than Urban's ability to "handle temptation."[53] Is Sally then "the best of the lot," as Urban puts it, before getting into her convertible, or is she "the best of a bad lot," as Monsignor Renton says? Is she evil (like her mother) or only a mirror in which evil sees itself? In the Catholic allegorical tradition, temptation may take physical form for the sake of visible representation, but its meaning always concerns the struggles of interiority.[54]

The problem that Powers has in following the allegorical tradition, especially in the genre of social and psychological realism, is that of reproducing, even if for symbolic reasons (e.g., to represent Urban's venality), a misogynist view of women with a long pedigree. It perpetuates a confusion of antiquated sexual mores—with which the church is rife—and a view of women as closer to evil with both the eternal and contemporary evils of society. Powers's explicit views on these controversies remain mysterious, but his general outlook, even if it fails to inform every moment of his narrative, can be gleaned from his more openly satirical passages.

These archaic sexual views of the church are cleverly parodied by the efforts of Jack and Urban to edit Malory into conformity with Catholic doctrine. How to handle their tendency to initiate a pattern of ethical equivocations? The biggest problem for Jack was Sir Lancelot. He had not been married to Lady Elaine, and he was under a spell when he fathered a child with her. Elaine, the evil woman, had no such an excuse.

That left a problem of Lancelot's relationship with Guinevere. In some children's editions, they referred to it as "sinful love." Jack thought of calling it "untrue love" or, as Urban suggested, "high treason." Jack, however, did not regard Sir Lancelot guilty as charged:

> There's good evidence that Sir Lancelot, on the night he was surprised by Sir Agravaine and others, was innocent. I could show you where.

In the end, after considering the text, Urban is inclined to agree with Jack. It was true that Lancelot's past performances with the queen were against him. Yes, even if, as Malory said, "love that time was not as is nowadays," Sir Lancelot had "brast" the iron bars clean out of the window to Guinevere's room on one occasion and had taken his "pleasance and liking" until dawn. But on the night he was surprised by Sir Agravaine, Sir Mordred, Sir Colgrevance, and others, Father Urban found him not guilty. Jack was relieved when Urban said Lancelot "says he's innocent, and I, for one, believe him." That solved Jack's problem, and he could write that Sir Lancelot and the queen were "wrongly accused of high treason on this occasion" (306–9).

Keeping Jack's symbolic relationship to his fellow writer (our author) in mind, we can understand to what extent Powers recognizes the absurdity of trying to force the ways of narrative to conform to a doctrine too narrow to contain it. The results of such an effort, which include reversals of the ethical tradition such as preferring high treason to sinful love and reducing ethical questions to legalistic quibbles, can only lead to the disintegration of the church's teachings as a coherent and meaningful worldview.[55]

In *Morte D'Urban*, the ultimate significance of Urban's celibacy remains implicit in and subordinated to the broader issue of the very possibility of spiritual vocation in such a society. The satirical use of the Arthurian allegory has more to do with the meaning of death, the *Morte* of Arthur, than it does with the sexuality of Lancelot.

Now is the time to take up this question of change in Urban's vocation: his conversion and death.

DEATH OF A SPIRITUAL SALESMAN

And no man who comes to die stands upon the peak that lies in infinity.... He catches only the most minute part of what the life of the spirit brings forth ever anew, and what he seizes is always something provisional and not definitive, and therefore death for him is a meaningless occurrence. And because death is meaningless, civilized life as such is meaningless; by its very "progressiveness" it gives death the imprint of meaninglessness.[56]

When Malory wrote *Le Morte D'Arthur*, he stood, in the last decades of a philosophically—if not politically—unified Christendom, at the disintegrating edge of the medieval worldview. Malory defends rather woodenly the meaning of death in chivalric and Christian terms. Cervantes writes the epic parody of that world in which only death may retain any meaning. The question here is whether for Powers, who writes his Cervantean version of Malory at the far end of the process of disenchantment when it is easier to fantasize about a distant Middle Ages than to live up to workaday existence, the death of his protagonist could still have that meaning for his readers.

Does Urban's death represent a conversion, the embracing of the transcendent? Is it a reconciliation, after which he can die satiated with life? Or is it only a premature decay, the retirement of a man of the world tired with life?

How does one read the final dirge of the novel? Mary Gordon sums up its meaning with the same confidence that some Catholic writers read the death of Don Quixote:[57]

> *Morte D'Urban's* great distinction is that it is a conversion story told in comic terms. Urban's peripeteia takes place in the context of a virtuoso display of Powers' talent for recording American kitsch. And instead of being knocked off his horse on the road to Damascus, he is knocked out by a bishop's golf ball. He finds his soul, but at a cost. (Introduction)

Carol Iannone concurs with Gordon and sees the loss of his material success as a gain for his spiritual life. His humiliating trials purify and elevate him.[58]

Terry Teachout, however, finds in the end of the novel only Powers's rigorous use of negation: pursuing meaning by exposing its absence. When Father Urban is hit on the head by the bishop's stray golf ball, his life takes a sharp turn for the worse. He loses his nerve and becomes fearful and uncertain. Teachout sees Urban's election as the father provincial of the Order of Saint Clement's as triumph. Is the death of the old Father Urban "the product of inward contemplation or a delayed effect of concussion by golf ball"? The question is deliberately left vague. It is Powers's sense of literary grace that allows him to leave the question unresolved (73).

Although the text itself only supports Teachout's argument for its ambiguity, none of these interpretations explores Powers's complex handling of the alternatives. The death is not an either-or proposition. It is an interpretation of the hermeneutics of the visible and the invisible that structure the practice of the spiritual vocation in a disenchanted world. The either-or of the critics revolves around their reading of the comic incident of the golf ball, but, in focusing on that scene, they overlook the importance of the Tower of Belleisle in shaping the novel's conclusion.

The Enchanted Tower

> Thou art saved, thou art on the way to the goal. None of thy follies wilt thou repent; none wilt thou wish to repeat; no luckier destiny can be allotted to a man.[59]

The golf tournament expresses Powers's Cervantean irony toward the chivalric epic;[60] nevertheless, the stark contrast between medievalist fantasy and disenchanted reality in *Morte D'Urban* would suggest only a satire motivated, in this case, by religious rejection of the mundane if Urban's will to worldly reconciliation were not so engaging. After all, a contest between

Malory and Cervantes would be too uneven to hold us in suspense. The real struggle for meaning occurs in the more subdued register of the prosaic itself, the world of modern middle-class aspirations and failure. The image of the tower may be the most blatantly Arthurian gesture in the novel. It recalls a mediating literary reference: Goethe's *Wilhelm Meister's Apprenticeship*. There, the enchanted tower is an openly fantastical device that allows an optimistic reconciliation. The resolution is not based on the poles of the Cervantean universe, utopian illusion, or transcendence with the prosaic world of commerce.

Meister, the upwardly mobile—through marriage to an heiress/young theater director, who has rejected the middle-class world of his parents—becomes reconciled to a life as a successful man of commerce by means of a magical, dreamlike revelation in the tower of Lothario's castle. According to Georg Lukács, this device allows Goethe to portray bourgeois society as a world of convention "partially open to penetration by living meaning," but at the same time revealing the limitations in such a forced and magical reconciliation.[61] Goethe introduced the fantastic apparatus at the end of the novel, the mysterious tower, the all-knowing initiates, and their providential actions:

> He absolutely needed these methods in order to give sensuous significance and gravity to the ending of the novel, and although he tried to rob them of their epic quality by using them lightly and ironically, thus hoping to transform them into elements of the novel form, he failed.[62]

By comparison, Novalis's rejection of his contemporary Goethe and his willful attempt to enchant the world à la Malory represents a more consistent, more rational, if also failed, pursuit (Novalis was the pseydonym for Georg Phillipp Frederick Freiherr von Hardenberg [1772–1801] was an author and philosopher of early German Romanticism):

> Novalis' own harking back to the age of the chivalrous epics was not accidental.... [He] wanted to create a totality of revealed transcendence within an earthly reality...this fairy-tale reality as a recreation of the broken unity between reality and transcendence became a conscious goal.[63]

Lukács says this is precisely why Novalis could not achieve a decisive and complete synthesis and that the artistic fault he detected in Goethe is even greater and irreparable in his own work.[64]

Powers restages the revelation in the enchanted tower but in a manner that refuses both Goethe's desire for reconciliation and Novalis's escape to the magical. Like Meister, Urban discovers the only possible "good life," that of the successful and married businessman, while dreaming in the tower. It is precisely the sexual imagery of the phallic tower and its role in generating meaning by penetrating the world of convention—all of which remains implicit and symbolic in Goethe, Meister's route to success lying through the sexual union of marriage—that becomes an image of Urban's impotence: his symbolic phallus; that is, his sexuality, the tower of Belleisle, is only a kitsch counterfeit of Lancelot's tower, or even Meister's, for that matter, whose castle is authentic, if a bit archaeological. Although sexual potency may seem a quality whose absence would be peculiar to complain of in a priest, it is in fact the very basis of a productive celibate vocation. Because Urban's sexuality is not integrated with his vocation beyond the success ethic, because it is not harnessed in the service of meaning, it remains only a weakly repressed regret. Thus, the narration of his dream life, punctuated repeatedly with the coda "no regrets," is the mirror opposite of his experience as a priest (292–95).

Meister's revelation in the tower is the turning point in his *Bildung* (formation) when he changes from a romantic and idealistic youth into a productive and mature man of the world. Urban's revelation comes too late for *Bildung.* His only way out is vertical transcendence, the conversion the critics search for in the novel's concluding chapters. But there is no visible indication of grace, only of Urban's loss of the mundane. He leaves his dream life of worldly happiness behind, like his shoes while escaping the tower:

> Life here below…was shoes—not champagne, but shoes, and not dirt, but shoes, and this, roughly speaking, was the mind of the Church.

Without his dream life, Father Urban is left only a shadow of himself (298–99).

On the Road?

The ending of *Morte D'Urban* is unresolved. The question that remains open, however, is not where Urban has arrived, but where he is going. The reader is left stranded like Urban, without a car, between a visible world of decay and the invisible one of death. Urban takes on the responsibility of being father provincial, but he has shed all costume-drama fantasies of the late Middle Ages and accepts simply prose, for the order means the decadence of his own historical time. Any grandiosity that remains is laced with irony, as when he is reading the speeches of Winston Churchill, he comes to the passage:

> "I have not become the King's first minister in order to preside over the liquidation of the British Empire," he thought, "No, nor did Mr. Atlee consider himself so called, but such was his fate." (323)

Like all those who measure themselves against worldly criteria of success, Urban can only be represented in his peripeteia as a victim of premature decay. This decay is not, however, the exceptional fate of a tragically anach-ronistic hero.

Applicable here is the observation:

> When men reach the age of forty or fifty they tend to observe a curious change…show signs of degeneration. Conversation with them becomes shallow, threadbare, and boastful. Previously the aging individual found mental stimulus in others but now he feels that he is almost the only one to present objective interest.…Men of the world are not excluded from this general rule. It is as though people who betray the hopes of their youth and come to terms with the world, suffer the penalty of premature decay.[65]

In his mission to befriend the mammon of iniquity, Urban immerses him-self in a social world that is precisely "shallow, threadbare, and boastful" as described. His conversations turn on smoking, "What d'ya smoke?"; makes of cars, "What d'ya drive?," "How d'ya like it?"; and parking facilities in small towns, "What're you doing about parking in your town?" "Where you from?" (270–71).

When he finally despairs of making his way in this life of shoes, Urban is reduced to silence, a silence expressed by a jolting shift away from the domi-nant presence of his consciousness in the narrative point of view. The final chapter of the book is entitled "Dirge." Iannone comments:

> Powers almost seems to move outside of his character's consciousness, as if to indicate that Father Urban has himself moved beyond the glad-handing accessibility of his former self. It is an uncompromising ending, oddly warm and chilling at once.[66]

The final chapter is a mystery not unlike Spina's physical disappearance at the end of Silone's novel. Spina's total invisibility at the end of the narrative suggests the accomplishment of transcendence. Urban's shadowy presence is less dramatic but no less convincing that "He who would save his life must lose it." In his monastery, beyond the material-political world he had once trusted and pursued so relentlessly, he embraces the Gospel that is "scary, dark and demanding."[67] And he finds his vocation at last. The narrative gives a hint that there is a greater spirituality residing in this diminished presence:

> He gained a reputation for piety he hadn't had before, which, however, was not entirely unwarranted now.[68] (324)
>
> Oddly enough, although for many years he'd traveled out of Chicago, he seemed to think of the Hill as his home. (326)

Urban had come to a full realization that a man truly cannot serve two masters—God and mammon. He had tried. He was content in his failure.

As I knew J. F. Powers, I think that he experienced the same triumph.

CHAPTER 13

WILL THE REAL PRIEST PLEASE STAND UP: IGNAZIO SILONE

No word and no gesture can be more persuasive than the life, and if necessary, the death of a man who strives to be free, loyal, just, sincere, disinterested. A man who shows what a man can be.

Ignazio Silone

INTRODUCTION: THE SPIRITUAL VOCATION IN A SECULAR WORLD

Ignazio Silone's *Bread and Wine* and J. F. Powers's *Morte D'Urban* are predominantly social novels of the spiritual vocation. These novels share sensitivity to the problem of practicing such a vocation in a society hostile to it, understanding that practice as both a product and a reaction to social context. Nevertheless, they narrate that problem in quite different ways. Silone writes about the spiritual and, quite clearly, priestly vocation under the apparently secular guise of the political activist. Powers presents the story of a nominal priest whose vocation seems indistinguishable from the professions of his white-collar "clients." Yet this is only the most superficial and obvious level of contrast.

In each, the relationship of the spiritual vocation to its social context unfolds according to a guiding principle by which the individual relates to social norms: *Bread and Wine* is a narrative of resistance, whereas *Morte D'Urban* is one of conformity. Furthermore, these relational principles are intimately connected to the status of death in both works. Although the gulf between social success and spiritual realization remains a constant in both works, the meaning of death, the crucial measure of the presence of the possibility of transcendence, is radically different.[1] The spiritual vocation, therefore, finds its most profound expression at this divide in the tension between the structured repetitions of society and the existential imperative of the novel to narrate the universality of the unique.

In *Morte D'Urban*, the pursuit of the priestly vocation was undermined by Urban's struggle to measure his vocation by the norms of his society's success ethic. The book's motto, "Be a winner," stands in ironic commentary over this attempt to conform to incompatible standards. By contrast, the ethic of resistance guiding the narrative in *Bread and Wine* allows the spiritual vocation to be promoted precisely by the presence of social norms hostile to it, the same conflict between the spiritual and social that stultifies Urban's vocation.

These opposite points of departure should not be understood, however, as the product of either opposing worldviews on the part of the authors or of opposing psychological dispositions on the part of their protagonists. The specific political and economic structures of each society—Fascist Italy for Silone, the white-collar United States for Powers—have much more to do with the so-called necessity of each author's representation of the conflict between the existential quest for meaning and the limits imposed by society and of the role of death in mediating that conflict.

Illustrating this point simply requires posing an imaginary reversal of principles and settings. The novel of a priest trying to conform to Fascism, while an interesting exercise in clinical narrative, is almost unthinkable as a novel of spiritual vocation. On the other hand, a novel about active resistance to the relatively tolerant ethic of the postwar United States is even more difficult. The so-called hidden hand of the market exerts a much more indirect and depersonalized but no less coercive control over the heart and mind of U.S. culture. It would be easier to produce a thinly disguised polemic, a roman à clef as Greeley's did in *The Cardinal Sins*, or a dramatization for some memorable cause célèbre.[2] Another alternative is the production of narratives of personal paranoia and isolation in which the social function of tolerance makes the resister more eccentric than ethical, more victim than martyr.

The surest measure of this narrative necessity, however, is the status of death in each novel. In Silone's world, the nearness of violent and premature death guides the protagonist to spiritual realization. Personally it marks the end and goal of the ethical lie under a dictatorship. Socially it allows the achievement of an inspirational martyrdom. In the world that Powers describes, death is a purely negative sign, marking the ultimate meaninglessness of all forms of social success and the senseless obscurity of any who refuse to play the game. Urban's tragedy is to be a priest in a context that allows only a choice between a success that will eventually be cut short by death—a condition exacerbated by the celibate's lack of family—or a re-sistance indistinguishable from that of the harmless and incompetent U.S. eccentric, the crank (the definition ascribed by Urban himself to most of his fellow clergy).

Despite these oppositions, between conformism and resistance and be-tween death as failure and death as realization, both authors present the practice of spiritual vocation against the constant of hostile, if different, so-cial contexts. Each narrative uses a reversal of expectations to expose that dynamic. Silone's protagonist, Pietro Spina, disguised as the false priest Don Paolo Spada, is one of the most fully realized representations of spiritual vo-cation in the secular genre of the novel. Powers's Father Urban, on the other hand, ranks with Willy Loman as a tragic protagonist in the confrontation between white-collar conformism and spiritual alienation. Taken together, these novels offer a broad and insightful examination of the social practice of such a personal vocation.

At the level of the relations between individual and society, the contrast between these novels would remain a simple and self-evident one. But our goal is to explore one of the most mysterious and ambiguous aspects at work within and between these novels: the role of celibacy in the practice of the spiritual vocation.

Celibacy is a particularly implicit problem in social novels of vocation; it is not confronted directly because their focus is not on the crises of the in-dividual as an individual. The celibate priest always has an aura of mystery about him, but in the social novel, the protagonist, the individual per se, often assumes a mantel of mystery as well relative to the exposed mecha-nisms of society. As a result, the dynamics of the celibate practice are doubly shrouded. Fortunately, both the literary and theological modes of inquiry recognize such an obstacle to direct analysis as the potential route to greater understanding. The mysterious hero of Edward Albee's first play *The Zoo Story* (1958) puts it well: "[S]ometimes a person has to go a very long dis-tance out of his way to come back a short distance correctly." Only close readings of the texts can draw out the subtle handling of celibacy in each novel, but some general parameters of the celibate vocation in each can be cited by way of introduction.

Again, as with the spiritual vocations of each protagonist, the hostile so-cial context serves Spina's practice of celibacy while threatening Urban's. As a hunted outlaw, Spina has little inclination or opportunity, outside of a few significant episodes, to pursue romance, and the class difference between him and the peasants as well as the religiosity of the women and the expectations of a priest in a Catholic culture conspire to construct Spina's celibate voca-tion: Where there's a way, there may turn out to be a will.

Urban, on the other hand, is a worldly operator, a political animal, and, therefore, a frequent socializer with noncelibate men and women, Catholics and non-Catholics. What is more, he carries the anachronistic trappings of his vocation almost as an afterthought or a quirk of fate into the United States of the 1950s, a prosperous world little concerned with spiritual matters. It was a world already in the upswing of the sexual revolution. The cure of syphilis "ushered in for one brief Camelot-like era a pause in the human medical record when every known sexually transmitted disease was curable."[3]

The difficulties of analyzing the psychodynamics of celibacy in the two protagonists are also of a different magnitude because, on closer scrutiny, Powers's novel reveals itself to be the more sociological of the two. That *Bread and Wine* is more the novel of private vocation is another reversal of expectations. Silone was closely associated with the political movements of the 1930s and is considered a master of the novelistic genre of social realism. Powers's work tends to be received as a hybrid of Catholic confessional literature and the dominant genre of 1950s U.S. fiction, psychological realism. Although Marx and Augustine might appear as appropriate mentors for Silone and Powers, respectively, as novelists Silone explores the concerns of existentialism, Powers the terrain of critical sociology. Thus, the difficulty in analyzing the inner structure of each of their protagonist's celibacy is the result of quite different narrative contexts. Urban's celibacy is almost entirely taken for granted; Spina's is only an implied expectation of either his political practice or his spiritual vocation.

The complexity of these contrasts between the handling of vocation and celibacy in the novels requires a two-stage approach. We analyze the implicit structure of each protagonist's celibacy separately, attempting to construct case histories, but placing special emphasis on the ambiguities and lacunae in each text concerning celibacy. After that, we return to a comparative mode to explore the interaction of genre, social context, and vocation in the novel. The object has been to suggest what insights these novels offer the study of celibacy as a psychosocial reality in clinical and empirical research.

There are methodological problems in attempting to uncover the presence and meaning of celibacy in Spina's vocation. The first concerns the riskiness of applying literature to a question extrinsic to the literary per se, in this case the study of the practice of celibacy. This problem is a generic one for all the studies we have been dealing with, and it is invoked here only as a sort of fair warning to "ye that enter."

The reconstruction of fictional elements can only be done within the narrative structure of the literary text. These elements are not freely available for alternative narration as, for example, a coherent life history built around the problem of celibacy. This can be done in psychotherapy and is the backbone of our ethnographic study. The life of Pietro Spina is already as much a reconstruction of mythical narratives—the Gospel, the lives of martyred saints, the secular hero, the revolutionary—as it is the construction of a believable or realistic life history based on the experiences of the author and his contemporaries.

Under the explicit rubric of fiction, the novel is simply the most obvious vehicle for understanding that all experience of the celibate vocation will reach us ensconced in the structure of a narrative, a narrative of a particularly complex way of life.

The problem peculiar to the case of *Bread and Wine* is the existence of two finished—that is, published—versions of the novel. One is tempted to follow the path of most scholars and choose either the earlier or later versions as the better version.

Scholars focusing on the work's intrinsic literary merit and most critics responding to *Bread and Wine* since the appearance of the substantially revised version have chosen the later edition, because it is, as the author argues in the new preface, significantly improved in terms of aesthetic economy and discipline. The contrast between the two versions reveals a fascinating pattern of what remained constant in Silone's views of the spiritual vocation and what underwent development and change. Silone's development is, in fact, a quite stirring allegory for the potential future of the church and its teachings on sexuality.[4]

Silone's success, as both a thinker and a novelist, in eventually resolving the apparent tensions and contradictions that pervaded the presentation of each in the first version (which also pervade the present-day Catholic Church's teachings on sexuality, its view of women, and its inflexible and defensive attitude toward change) makes his work extremely valuable to any consideration of these issues. In this process of refashioning a coherent worldview from the conflicted fragments of his Christian upbringing and secular education, Silone seems to have succeeded, at least within the world of his novel, in seeking God without abandoning the search for understanding, the elusive task so desired by his character Murica (263).

THE IDEAL OF THE SPIRITUAL VOCATION

In *Bread and Wine*, Silone's ideal of the spiritual vocation as an existential and social practice unfolds through the narratives of three people—Don Benedetto, Pietro Spina, and Cristina Colamartini—as they approach a common conception of what it must be in their society. Each appears at first as an exemplar of one of three possible practices of the Christian, used here synonymously with spiritual or ethical, life: service to society within the institution of the church (Don Benedetto), withdrawal from society into monastic purity (Cristina),[5] and ethical resistance to society and, if necessary, the church (Spina).

Both clergy and secularists also represent each ideal in the novel, whether as mildly or severely compromised practitioners of it. They contribute to the shaping of the ideal negatively by exposing the dangers of rigidity—and even more, instrumentalism—in the name of serving ethics. Don Benedetto and Cristina are eventually disabused of belief in the possibility of living their ideals under Fascism. It is left to Spina to develop his own path as the only possible ethical life available to them in such times. For this reason, he emerges as the spiritual leader, predominantly through example, for the others, albeit with strong mutual influences at work in their dialogues.

When Don Benedetto, Spina's elderly teacher, is first introduced, he has already handed over his lifelong career as an active priest to the Piccirillis and Girasoles, priests capable of accommodating themselves to Fascism. At the opening of the book, Spina is living in a condition of almost hermitlike withdrawal, the result not of spiritual need but of his having been dismissed from his teaching post. Nevertheless, his equilibrium in this condition of internal exile is steadied by the same powers of sublimation that supported his lifetime of spiritual commitment and his adjustment to the internal solitude of celibacy: his love of nature and literature, his regimen of prayer, the support of his sister, and a strong faith in Providence (4–5). Strongest emphasis is placed on his need for the timeless value of beauty: "Don Benedetto… lived in seclusion in his house above Rocca dei Marsi…devoting himself to his beloved classics and poetry and plants, to everything that beautifies the world and does not change with changing fashions" (5). In the appreciation of beauty both secular and spiritual, interests in ethics have found a common and visible sign of a celibate's faith.[6]

Don Benedetto, however, had also intended to spend his life in the service of others, one of the greatest supports of a celibate vocation. As his sister puts it: "[H]e who has the good fortune to live at Don Benedetto's side receives a thousand times more than he gives" (13); yet now she is the only one with the courage to receive his gifts. Don Benedetto's commitment to service within the institution of the church had never been easy. Even as a young priest, he had upset his family and the church authorities by holding his first mass in a prison (235). Don Girasole recalls to Spina that "His brusque way of flying in the face of public opinion worried his superiors even then. For that reason they were unwilling to intrust [sic] him with a parish and he was sent to teach in a school" (236). Even this compromise between personal vocation and institutional demands became impossible under Fascism, and he was dismissed.

During the course of the novel, Don Benedetto undergoes a radical change in his practice of the spiritual vocation. He begins in enforced but resigned solitude—"he took no interest in politics" (5)—but, under the influence of his reunion with Spina, he becomes such an active resister of the government that he meets his martyrdom at the hands of assassins.[7]

Cristina Colamartini, the young woman Spina meets in Pietrasecca, who becomes both a romantic interest and a spiritual interlocutor for him, is committed at the outset to entering a convent and practicing the spiritual vocation as a withdrawal from a fallen world. Unlike Don Benedetto, who has been exiled to such a position, she believes withdrawal to be her vocation of choice and debates its merits with Spina in two key scenes near the beginning and end of the novel, respectively (79–81, 289). These dialogues on withdrawal versus engagement are paralleled and parodied by two carnival-allegory vignettes in which Spina encounters the monk, Brother Antifona; the first follows Spina's first argument with Cristina, the second shortly precedes his final debate with Cristina on the subject of vocation.

The monk is a minor character in the realist narrative of the novel, but he gains significance for his symbolic role in Silone's construction of the ideal of spiritual vocation. The carnival-allegory absurdity of his name, Antifona, which has the double meaning of a contrapuntal melody in music or a repetitive response litany during the mass, implies that he plays the counterpoint melody to Spina's dominant. At the same time, he represents an ethically inspired yet inflexibly formulaic response to the corruption of human societies.

In the first encounter, a balance is struck between their positions as Spina finds a surprising congruence of values between himself and the monk.

> "In a monastery you live badly, too, but you are safe," said the Capuchin. "You have no family life, but you have no fear, either. Moreover, there is hope."
>
> "What hope?" asked Don Paolo.[8]
>
> The monk pointed towards heaven.
>
> "It's not a way for everybody," said Mastrangelo. "We can't all become monks."
>
> "The demon of property lures people," said Brother Antifona.... "How many people is it sending to damnation!"
>
> "So in your opinion one ought not to work?" Mastrangelo said.
>
> "When I'm not going round collecting alms I work, too," said the monk. "Behind the monastery there is a large expanse of fields, which are cultivated by the monks. We don't live well, but in security." (124–25)

The monk's valorization of work over property is an echo of the common 1930s apologia for the Soviet Union that people do not live well there but have their needs met. This and his desire for hope make him a sort of spiritual mirror of the socialist Spina. The recognition of their commonality, however, breaks down in a brief but pointed comedy of errors:

> "Good-by," he said to Don Paolo. "If we do not meet again down here, we shall at any rate meet above."
>
> "Above? Where? In the mountains?" the priest asked.
>
> "I mean in heaven," said the monk.
>
> Don Paolo admired this way of making appointments. (125)

Although the monk is apparently lampooned for his literal religiosity, an unavoidable impression given the sympathy commanded by Spina's dominance in the narrative point of view, there is, in fact, an awkward standoff if one considers the lack of synthesis in Spina's own sense of vocation at that time.

When next Spina encounters the monk, the synthesis has already transpired within Spina himself, through both the tempering of his revolutionary adventurism and his profound encounter with his Christianity during his meeting with Don Benedetto. Thus, the medievalist withdrawal of the monk can be fully dismissed as a parody of the spiritual vocation, one that is even susceptible to pathetic forms of collaboration. In this final meeting, Spina finds Brother Antifona hustling medals of Saint Francis, "for the protection of the life of combatants," to poor peasants whose sons have been conscripted for the war against Ethiopia. The monk appears to have lost the values he shared with the socialist in proportion to how fully Spina has accepted his Christian heritage:

> The priest and the monk walked along the road up to Pietrasecca.
> "Are the medals selling well?" the priest asked.
> "Not badly," the other replied. "They would have gone better if we had started on mobilization day. But the Church is always late. The father provincial is too old and does nothing but pray. Our father superior, who really has the nose of a saint, wrote to him months ago and said: 'War is coming, and what are we doing?' 'War? What war?' the old father provincial replied. Thus time was wasted and we were taken by surprise." (286)[9]

Because withdrawal from society can never be perfect, Silone sees the vulnerability of such an inflexible vocation to debasement.

Cristina, however, is the more challenging interlocutor in this debate. If she does not succeed in persuading Spina of her choice, she certainly engages him in a dialogue on the spiritual vocation that shapes the development of both characters over the course of the narrative. We will examine the significance of those dialogues in the definition of Spina's vocation in the following section on his struggle and development. Suffice it to say that Cristina, like Don Benedetto, decides finally that the social realities demand the search for a meaningful engagement and the abandonment of the search for a pure withdrawal, an option left to the shallow medievalism of Brother Antifona.

In Cristina's case, however, the goals of such an engagement remain unformed, lost in an alpine wilderness of hungry wolves and icy cold. The final scene gives symbolic expression to the hard lot of the woman who chooses resistance in such a brutal social world. Which is harder, that or the lot of Annina, raped by the police (187–88), or Chelucci's wife, who is abandoned to poverty by the other Communists after her husband's arrest (182–84)? Despite any difficulty, Cristina attempts to follow Spina's dangerous path.

Spina's choices call into question both the opportunism and corruption that must inevitably result from the church's adjustment to the social context of Fascism. That is an adjustment that will lead every servant of the institution either to conform or lose his career. Also, the search for a pure spiritual withdrawal, always a difficult goal, risks becoming compromised as well when pursued under Fascism. Spina gives impassioned voice to the latter contrast in his efforts to persuade Cristina:

> [W]e are in…a country in which there is great economic distress and still greater spiritual distress.…Do you not think that this divorce between a spirituality which retires into contemplation and a mass of people dominated by animal instincts is a source of all our ills? Do you not think that every living creature ought to live and struggle among his fellow creatures rather than shut himself up in an ivory tower? (80)

But when the normal institutional avenues to such an ethics of engagement, such as the church and democratic political parties, are absent or corrupted, what structures remain to shape and support such a lonely vocation? Silone proposes that a life lived according to ideals rooted in human experience will reveal deeper structures of support than those offered by institutions.

Silone's ideal of vocation emerges in the course of the narrative as a practice based on noninstrumental human communication. The intimacy of companionship and the altruism of teaching express the highest values of his ideal of spiritual vocation: friendship and truth. In his last encounter with an agent of his political movement, Spina raises questions about their practice that are equally relevant to church and Comintern:

> "And if the truth is demoralizing?"
>   "It is always less demoralizing than the most encouraging lie." (301–2)

The Kantian ethics of treating people as ends in themselves rather than more or less useful tools and of using only what is true as a point of departure are the only appropriate means for a movement that claims to serve humanity. The cornerstone of such a practice is an intimate knowledge of one's fellows and one's social context.

Intimacy is repeatedly contrasted to the ethical compromises of a public vocation built on the hypnotic powers of rhetoric and images. Spina knows that for pragmatic reasons he cannot be a public agitator or preacher while hiding from the authorities in Pietrasecca. At the same moment, he realizes that there is something inherently wrong with such a means of communicating his beliefs.

The ethical superiority of intimacy over other forms of communication is expressed throughout the novel in his relations with Cardile (24–25), the deaf-mute (111–12), Pompeo (157–59), and, to be sure, with Christina, Murica, and Don Benedetto. Intimacy is also valorized by the negative representations of public oratory. The mass hypnotic effect of the war rally, inciting an irrational consensus for violence in the crowd (200–204), and the chameleon use of rhetorical skills by the ex-socialist Zabaglione in the service of new masters (209–11) cement the connection between oratory and ethical degradation in Silone's world.[10] Human intimacy and the manipulation of the public are juxtaposed within the circles of the Comintern as well: The intimacy of a clandestine group gives Murica a "purely human pleasure" (256–57), whereas the agent Bolla uses people and language as mere instruments (301). The spiritual value of intimacy is expressed perhaps most forcefully in Don Benedetto's relation to God, who speaks not in the roar of wind, earthquake, or fire but in a "still, small voice" (243).

The conclusion Spina arrives at concerning the modus operandi of the spiritual vocation is nothing less than a modus vivendi. Preaching must be subordinated to a way of life, the life of the free man under a dictatorship: "No word and no gesture can be more persuasive than the life, and if necessary, the death of a man who strives to be free, loyal, just, sincere, disinterested: a man who shows what a man can be" (250). Later, Spina calls directly for revolutionaries "who would be recognizable not because they wore emblems in their buttonholes or a uniform, but by their way of living" (284).[11]

Spina is inspired to find more creative ways to awaken the critical spirit in the new society beyond the sheltered intimacy of school or the open pulpit. "Nothing was more repugnant to him than to present himself as a master and as an initiate" (159). In the famous scene of the card game[12] (116–19), Spina suggests to the peasants that they can make their own rules and laws, their own history, through the parable of replacing one card, a king, with a particularly lowly one, the three of spades. In essence, he is teaching them to replace their "king" with a democratic process for arriving at mutually agreeable values and rules, but he does so indirectly, merely by raising questions and posing analogies.

Silone constructs his ideal of the spiritual vocation from this dialectic as a practice based on intimate community, an ethical way of life, and the teaching of a critical spirit. In this way, Silone attempts to draw together the lessons of the Gospels, early Christian resistance, community, the Reformation's critique of institutional religion, Enlightenment freethinking, and Kantian ethics in order to suggest a way out of "a world abandoned by God."[13] Yet Silone chose to express this ideal in a novel rather than a treatise because its compelling power resides not so much in its abstract simplicity as in its unfolding development: the narrative of Spina's struggle to attain it as a lived vocation.

SPIRITUAL VOCATION AS A NARRATIVE OF STRUGGLE

Next, the key passages marking Spina's initiation into the spiritual vocation and the crises he experiences in the process of developing his commitment and practice need to be highlighted. *Bread and Wine* is not the literal narrative of a man's entry into the priesthood, so it is difficult to identify the precise stages in such a process, such as the moment of taking vows. My working assumption, one based on taking Silone's device of taking Don Paolo's alias at its face symbolic value, is that Spina takes the step from novice to priest at the moment he dons the robes in the presence of his school friend Dr. Nunzio Sacca.[14]

There is, in addition to its manifest symbolic quality, a very real social determinant in Spina's donning of the priestly disguise. It is from that moment that everyone treats him as a priest, forcing him to respond according to peoples' expectations. Spina's quandary is not really so different from that of any newly ordained priest, who is less convinced of the reality of his being worthy of the grave step he has taken than are those who adopt an attitude toward him based on his collar. Nevertheless, the compressed form of fictional narrative makes it a hybrid of realist reportage and mythical allegory.

Spina's initiation to his priestly role occurs in chapter 2 and begins with the recognition of his aptitude for the spiritual vocation by others. The worker Cardile tells Dr. Nunzio Sacca about how his friendship with a mysterious traveler began and developed.

Cardile recognizes Spina's charism in one simple fact: He wants nothing in a practical way from others. Perhaps even more significantly, he awakens in Cardile the awareness that he, too, could desire such a noninstrumental companionship with the man "I enjoyed talking to." Such an otherworldly quality, recalling the Taoist allegory of the tree whose use is to have no use, has long been the mythical measure of both the spiritual and, for humanist ethics, the purely human. Cardile, however, draws a sharp distinction between his encounter with the man of mystery and his experiences with men of the cloth and other representatives of institutions. Spina's capacity for living this ideal of human interrelatedness is the sign that he is ready to begin the process of vocation.

Sacca recognizes Spina's suitability to a spiritual vocation and responds to Cardile: "I can imagine who it was." But in his case, this vocation is equivalent to that of the Catholic priesthood. Although Spina had been outside the church for many years, he has scruples about the disguise and does not want to be irreverent. He feels that would be inconsistent with his character. Sacca then makes a semiserious speech, one that links Spina's disguise to the eternal myth of initiation into the mysteries of vocation:

> "These vestments," he said, "are descended from the primitive mystery religions, from the priests of Isis and Serapis, as, of course, you know. They were inherited by the first monastic communities in the Catholic Church, who tried to preserve the Christian mysteries from worldly contamination and to assure the essential charismatic virtues to a minority living apart from the world and opposed to the world. Thus do usages outlive the age

in which they were born, and pass from one religion to another. And now, here are you, a man dedicated to the new revolutionary mysteries, to the mysteries of revolutionary materialism, donning the dark vestments that have been the symbols of sacrifice and supernatural inspiration for thousands of years." (36)

Here, Sacca invokes in ironic phrasing the underlying theme of Silone's work: the interchangeability of costumes and names under which one may practice, or fail to practice, that most human of all vocations.

The ironic ambivalence of this initiation scene reemerges in Spina's first crisis during his stay in Pietrasecca, his first so-called parish. The forced idleness of his convalescence from tuberculosis and the need for clandestinity, as well as the desire he feels in the presence of the young women, Bianchina and Cristina, combine to threaten his surety of purpose. This dissatisfaction comes to a head during a conversation with Cristina in which he seeks to talk her out of her intention of entering a convent. While debating this choice with her, he begins to have an inner debate about his own vocation:

> Cristina's voice recalled Don Paolo's own internal dialogue between the adolescent and the revolutionary in him. Thus he had himself been greedy for the absolute and in love with righteousness when he had cut himself off from the Church and gone over to Socialism. But much time had passed since then. What had remained in him of that generous impulse towards the masses of the people?...He had broken with the old world and all its comforts, cut himself off from his family, abandoned his favorite studies, set himself to live for justice and truth alone, and entered a party in which he was told that justice and truth were petty-bourgeois prejudices....Had he, perhaps, taken the wrong road? (80–81)

Cristina has the last word: "You cannot serve two masters" (81). Spina is left alone to ponder the contradictions of his situation, a situation surprisingly similar for both red and black in Italy's *Guerra civile*.[15]

In his room, Spina's reflections on his dialogue with Cristina lead him to a Weberian insight into the conflict between the social norms of professionalism and institutionalism, on the one hand, and his personal desire for spiritual purity, on the other:

> Alas for all professions that have for their ultimate aim the salvation of the world! For the sake of saving others, you ended by losing yourself....Don Paolo saw clearly now that his return to Italy had been at heart an attempt to escape from that profession...."Have I escaped from the opportunism of a decadent Church only to fall into bondage to the opportunism of a party?" (83)

Spina's crisis deepens with his reflections, and he begins to recognize an inner lack, the lack of interiority, the knowledge of self and the inner peace that support one through such difficult trials:

> There was a kind of cleavage in him, dividing his being into two. As long as he had been active the two parts had coalesced and dovetailed, giving an impression of solid strength. But no sooner was he immobilized than the two parts fell asunder. Here he was, with inactivity thrust upon him, and the woodworm of his brain took advantage of it to gnaw obstinately at the weak cartilages that still linked the adolescent to the revolutionary. (85)

In this uncertain frame of mind, he delves deeper into the sociological connection linking priests and revolutionaries beneath their costumes and rhetoric. These reflections trouble him so deeply that "he became obsessed with the fear of going mad" (86). In the midst of this crisis, Spina arrives at a profound recognition of the social truth of the spiritual vocation. It is based on a radical alienation from the natural order of the universe: "If only I could go back to real, ordinary life. If only I could dig, plow, sow, reap, earn my living, talk to other men on Sundays, read and study; fulfill the law that says, 'In the sweat of thy face shalt thou earn thy bread'" (87).

His personality still poised uncomfortably between the ethical demands of the adolescent and the rational materialism of the mature intellectual, Spina is not ready to admit to the positive and active side of his alienation, his striving for meaning, for the transcendent, for the invisible. Spina seeks to resolve his crisis, as many clerics do, through immersion in his work, through action in the world. Chapter 6 narrates his efforts to preach among the peasants. It is extremely significant for Spina's later development that he begins his ministry by rejecting, like Jesus, the institutional hypocrisy of the dominant church, especially that central ethical mechanism of Catholicism: confession. Confession works to the advantage of those with power in this world and the next:

> What's the Church for? Does the Church forbid the carabinieri to shoot? . . . You said that at Pratola the carabinieri shot at the peasants. That means that afterwards they confessed. But what about the dead peasants? Who confessed them? In this life they suffered from cold, and in the next they'll suffer from fire. (108)

The poor learn the lesson of their masters well. They, in turn, use the confession as a cynical cover for their pathetic crimes. At this point, confession symbolized for Spina only a well-suited support for a social system that is utterly corrupt and corrupting. Spina keeps trying to awaken the critical ethical judgment of his parishioners against this institutionalized hypocrisy in the manner of Jesus through parables.

He begins to formulate his concept of vocation as the example of a different way of life, but he does so with a nagging sense of self-doubt. He is afraid
that he might be "seeking refuge in action because he is afraid of thinking"
(129). But his success with young people leads him to regain a measure of
(over) confidence in rhetoric and to greener pastures for his talents in Fossa
and Rome (chapter 7).

Spina requires a confrontation with the extreme limits faced by his secular
comrades under Fascism before he can integrate the entirety of that myth,
its tragic events, and the lesson of humility it contains for those with worldly
aspirations. In his fellow socialist Uliva, he is faced simultaneously with the
harsh realities of his comrades' lives and confirmation of his own desperate
reflections during his sojourn at Pietrasecca (Dry Rock). When he enters
Uliva's apartment, he enters a scene almost identical to the one Georges
Bernanos's country priest discovers at the flat of the ex-priest Dufréty. In
fact, the scenes and their implications for vocation and its alternatives are so
similar that it is worthwhile to note the congruence of details: Both Uliva
and Dufréty live out of wedlock with poor and uneducated women in squalid
walk-ups; both exhibit signs of ill health and despair; both enter into intense discussions with their student friends, in which they try to debunk the
other's illusions through contrast with the ugliness of social reality; and both
seek to hide the real depths of their despair (173).[16]

Uliva describes to Spina, in the same cold sociological terms in which
Spina saw his vocation while at Pietrasecca, the hopeless marginality of the
ethical life compared with the totalizing world of social convention and institutions: "There has never been any other alternative for us. Either you serve
or perish. He who desires to live disinterestedly, with no other discipline than
that which he imposes on himself, is outlawed by society, and the state hunts
him like an enemy" (173).

As he delivers his oration on the hopelessness of the struggle, Uliva simultaneously turns his piercing vision on Spina's own inner conflict:

> "But I know you," said Uliva. "I watched you when we were in the Socialist
> group. Since then I have discovered that fear is what makes you a revo-
> lutionary. You force yourself to believe in progress, to be optimistic, you
> make valiant efforts to believe in free will, all because you are terrified of
> the opposite." (177)

Spina's secular theology of progress is suddenly confronted with its dark
other, the rigorous secularism of the nihilist. He can admit that he believes in
the liberty of man or at least in the possibility of it and therefore progress.

On leaving, Uliva delivers the final slap when he whispers, "Life can control man, but man can control death." Suicide and murder called war.

Spina is heartsick at the horrors of war: the beatings of innocent protestors, the futility, disillusionment, and discouragement of fighting back

symbolically by writing graffiti. He doubts himself and disparages his disguise as a priest in iodine makeup.[17] He despairs at the popular frenzy for war that grips all classes. In this mood, he seeks out his former teacher.

This meeting with Don Benedetto finds the latter on the brink, like him, of despair. Yet, from their ability to give sincere voice to the same essential question, Don Benedetto is able, through his ability to express the continuing presence of God and the transcendent in his life, to reassure both himself and the younger man:

> "I started asking myself: Where then is the Lord? Why has He abandoned us?"
>
> "That is a very pertinent question," the young man said. "Where is the Lord? If He is not a human invention, but an objective spiritual reality, the beginning and the end of all the rest, where is He now?" His voice was not that of an atheist, but that of a disappointed lover.
>
> "There is an old story that must be called to mind every time the existence of the Lord is doubted," the old man went on. "It is written, perhaps you will remember, that at a moment of great distress Elijah asked the Lord to let him die, and the Lord summoned him to a mountain. And there arose a great and mighty wind that struck the mountain and split the rocks, but the Lord was not in the wind. And after the wind the earth was shaken by an earthquake, but the Lord was not in the earthquake. And after the earthquake there arose a great fire, but the Lord was not in the fire. But afterwards, in the silence, there was a still, small voice, like the whisper of branches moved by the evening breeze, and that still small voice, it is written, was the Lord."
>
> Meanwhile a breeze had arisen in the garden, and the door of the room in which the two men were sitting creaked and swung open. The young man shuddered. The old man placed his hand on his shoulder and said, with a laugh, "Do not be afraid. You have nothing to fear." (243)

In the intimate circle of this faith, Spina is finally able to confront the harsh truth Uliva sought to teach him:

> "We have reached a point at which it can be said that only he can save his soul who is prepared to throw it away."
>
> "There is no other salvation than that," the old man said. (245)

Don Benedetto offers Spina an exit from the paradoxes of Uliva's cynicism by offering him a vision that has united the ethics of Christianity and secular humanism: the dialectics of "I and thou." Jürgen Habermas has argued that this simple discursive construction guarantees the truth of our value system:

> The human interest in autonomy and responsibility is not mere fancy, for it can be apprehended a priori. What raises us out of nature is the only thing whose nature we can know: language. Through its structure, autonomy

and responsibility are posited for us. Our first sentence expresses unequivocally the intention of universal and unconstrained consensus.[18]

Thus, the very materiality of our language expresses our highest ethical ideals, our relationship to "the still, small voice of God."

Don Benedetto concludes by describing the ideal of the spiritual vocation
discussed in the previous section: "the life . . . of a man who strives to be free,
loyal, just, sincere, disinterested; a man who shows what a man can be" (250).

When the younger man expresses his impatience with things as they are
("I do not think it is enough"), the older man responds: "One must respect
time" (250). Spina returns to Fossa and announces his renewed sense of vocation in the simple phrase: "I no longer wish to go [abroad] now" (251).

In chapter 11, Spina begins his ministry in earnest and discovers how
much more he must still understand about others and himself and how profound the problem of faith can be. As a true parish priest, one who hears the
confessions of others and grants them absolution and, thereby, hope, he must
learn to accept a humanity he previously held at an intellectual distance.

His first trial is hearing the confession of Judas himself, the young man
Murica who became a government informer and betrayer of the small group
of socialists who had befriended him (256–59). In the process, he learns to
value his humanity: "For the first time he saw before him the writhing soul
of a poor man in whom everything human and decent had been soiled, tarnished, and trampled underfoot" (260). Through Murica and his act of confession, Spina is forced to reconsider his view of that practice as merely a
hypocritical prop of social corruption.

Murica began to escape the grip of his fear through witnessing the example of others:

> "After glimpsing the possibility of another life that would be clean, honest,
> and courageous, after that frank communion with another and those lovely
> dreams of a better humanity...I passed from dread of being punished to
> dread of not being punished." (262)
>
> "My confession lasted five hours, and at the end I lay prostrate and
> exhausted on the floor....He taught me that nothing is irreparable while
> life lasts, and that no condemnation is eternal. He told me also that...good
> was often born of evil, and that perhaps I might never have become a real
> man without the calamities and errors through which I had passed....I
> was no longer afraid." (263–64)

Thus, Murica has learned the deeper lessons of confession and shares them
with Spina:

> I did not come here to seek pardon or absolution....There are wounds that
> should not be bandaged and hidden, but exposed to the sun. The usual

ritual and sacramental confession, generally carried out behind a grating, is a ceremony towards which I have reservations, but a confession of one man to another can be like the cauterization of wound. (264)

Murica accomplishes for Spina, through allegory, a synthesis of the en-lightenment project ("exposed to the sun"; the medical metaphors) and the meaning behind ritualized Christianity. Spina is able to recognize that the ethical origin and potential of confession lie in this honest and intimate communion. That is what allows faith in God (forgiveness) without blind-ness to the existence of evil. Spina then confesses his true identity to the man who was an informer and "the two men dipped the old bread in the new wine" (265), performing the ancient ritual of communion that connects you and me, old wisdom and new understanding. Murica concludes their encounter: "I have been making my confession.... Now I am ready for any-thing" (265).

In the final chapter (chapter 12), Spina is ready to accept the personal and intellectual synthesis that will support the next stage of his struggle to live his vocation. Rather than resolve the conflict between his secular rationalism and Christianity, he can now see the proper place of each:

"It seems to me now that for fifteen years I was only half alive," Don Paolo confessed. "During that time I never ceased trying to smother and repress my deepest impulses, solely because in my youth they had been bound up with religious symbols and practices. I tried, with an obstinacy and a de-termination that sprang from my loathing of the Church, to substitute logic and intellectual ideas taken from the world of economics and politics for those deeper forces which I felt myself compelled to distrust. . . . Don Benedetto's words penetrated to the depths of me. Within a few days all that remained alive and indestructible of Christianity in me was revived: a Christianity denuded of all mythology, of all theology, of all Church con-trol." (281)

At the same time, he can accept what he has learned from "the world of economics and politics" as enrichment rather than a threat to his ethical impulses:

He had not forgotten that the social question is not a moral one and is not resolved by purely moral means. He knew that in the last resort the rela-tions established among men are dictated by necessity and not by good will or bad. Moral preaching did not suffice to change them. But there came a moment when certain social relations revealed themselves as outworn and harmful. Morality then condemned what had already been condemned by history. A sense of justice caused the slaves to rise, put arms into the hands of the advance guard, kindled the souls of martyrs, inspired thinkers and artists. (290)

No single system, intellectual or theological, can explain the complexity of human experience and choice. The only hope lies in a critical dialogue and, in times of crisis, a mutual support between the search for understanding and the desire for justice.

Silone implies that the full acceptance of the spiritual vocation means at least a partial exit from the historical register to that of the mythical:

> In all times, in all societies, the supreme act is to give oneself to find oneself....He is saved who overcomes his individual egoism, family egoism, caste egoism, does not shut himself in a cloister or build himself an ivory tower, or make cleavage between his way of acting and his way of thinking. He is saved who frees his own spirit from the idea of resignation to the existing disorder....In a society like ours a spiritual life can only be a revolutionary life. (289–90)

Silone's intuitive sense as a novelist expresses itself most strongly in the ambiguous and open ending of *Bread and Wine*. Once Spina has his vocation so well in hand, he truly becomes the man of mystery, more myth and ideal than protagonist, and he simply disappears into the wildness of the mountains. The price paid in rejecting a corrupt society for the elusive transcendent, however, is clear: "[S]piritual life and secure life do not go together" (291).

SEXUALITY, WOMEN, AND THE CHURCH: SILONE'S FIRST DRAFT OF CELIBACY

In neither the first nor the second version of *Bread and Wine* does Spina take a vow of celibacy, yet in both texts he remains chaste despite the presence of sexual desire and possible lovers. Only in the first version is celibacy explicitly upheld as a structural part of the spiritual vocation even as an ideal (284). In both versions, the most persuasive argument for celibacy is expressed by the example of Don Benedetto, a priest who has achieved celibacy and has integrated it to a remarkable extent.

Spina, on the other hand, passes from a highly conflicted and uneasy relation to his sexuality and its place in his vocation to a much greater tolerance of both human sexuality and his own sexual self. This development does not, however, transpire over the course of the narrative but is the result of the changes Silone himself underwent in the more than ten years that passed before his writing of the second version.

Both Spinas are chaste, and their chastity bears enough of a relationship to their vocation to be labeled "celibacy." But it is the Spina of the first version whose chastity is as much the product of sexual underdevelopment and repression as it is the support of his vocation. His associations of sexuality with depravity, irresponsibility, and the animalistic and egoistic aspects of humanity are quite similar to the sexual teachings of the Catholic Church, both of his time and our own.

In what follows, I will examine the construction of Spina's celibacy as it develops in close relation to his views and experience of sexuality. Then, I will explore two sets of views that reveal a deep connection to this sexual/celibate process: Spina's attitude toward women and his attitude toward the established Catholic Church. Although his views of women tend to mirror the structural misogyny of the church[19] and many individual celibates, Spina's hostility toward the church functions literally as a mirror, turning the church's antisexual dogma back at itself in an institutional portrayal of the church as sexually corrupt, hypocritical, and pagan. In the section that follows, these aspects of Spina's personality in the first version of *Bread and Wine* will be contrasted with the handling of sexuality, women, and the established church in the second version.

In the first version, the tension between the practice of celibacy and the presence of sexuality grows over the course of the novel, as if the effort of maintaining the practice requires the support of a rejection of the sexual as inherently compromised ethically, the repository of evil. Although it is quite easy to recognize Silone's authorial viewpoint behind the ideal and practice of Spina's spiritual vocation, the congruence of author and protagonist seems to come apart, not so much over the need for celibacy as over Spina's hostility toward the sexual. In fact, the author is so absent from these scenes that the reader is somehow abandoned between the character's prejudices and the objectivity of the social-realist narrative, for Spina never seems so much the object of a narrator's critical scrutiny, never so much a clinical case study as an exemplar for the reader and a mouthpiece for the author as he does in the scenes dealing with the evils of sexuality.

In the first half of the novel (chapters 1–6), Spina maintains a fairly balanced view of sexuality and accepts his own desire in a conscious and psychologically productive way. This disposition lasts through his first visit to Pietrasecca, and its collapse appears to be part of the adjustment that follows his first major crisis (chapters 4–6).

In chapter 2, Sacca at first fails to recognize Spina because "he had treated his face with a special iodine mixture, in order to give himself the lines, wrinkles, and complexion of premature old age, and thus make himself unrecognizable to the police" (28). Spina's sexuality and the beginning of a celibate vocation are introduced simultaneously in Sacca's reaction to his self-disfigurement, a reaction that equates that act with a renunciation for ethical reasons (although Sacca cannot label them so, preferring the pejorative term *sectarianism*) of an active sexual nature:

Dr. Sacca looked in astonishment at the disfigured and aged face of his contemporary. Pietro Spina had never been considered good-looking, but his impetuous nature and his sincerity had always made him attractive to women. He had never been an idle petticoat chaser, but he had the reputation of having a passionate temperament and of being a violent and tenacious lover. Dr. Sacca found it hard to understand how political sectarianism could have driven him to disfigure himself. (28)

Spina reinforces this connection between "serious aims" and sexual renunciation in his kidding of the surprised doctor:

When the average young Italian stops wanting to become the lover of every American or Swiss tourist and starts applying himself to more serious aims, perhaps it will be necessary to open an artificial disfigurement institute for the handsomest and daintiest dandies, to take the place of the present beauty parlors. (28)

Although the scene passes quickly, it reveals a deep contradiction in Spina, one that will return ever more forcefully, between a serious and almost dangerously ("violent") passionate nature, on the one hand, and an affected scorn, though still lighthearted, for sexual relations as frivolous and secondary, on the other. If Dr. Sacca were his analyst, perhaps he would have lingered longer on Spina's words and his act of self-mutilation.

If the disfigurement symbolizes Spina's vows of celibacy, his first trial as a celibate comes in chapter 4. The same idleness that sets off his spiritual and intellectual crisis also makes him prone to his sexual urges. When Bianchina, the young woman he comforted when she appeared to be dying of an illegal abortion (45–46), arrives, they begin a flirtation that has its predictable effect:

"If I make love, is it really true that Jesus is angry?" she said. "Why should He be angry? Who tells him to be angry?"
    "Let us change the subject," the priest suggested.
    "All right," said Bianchina, laughing. "But lovemaking is so nice that I don't understand how anybody can do anything else. Don't you agree with me?"
    "Listen Bianchina," answered the priest. "I am sorry, I am really very, very sorry, but I do not belong to this diocese."
    "You mustn't think ill of me," she said.
    Round her neck, under her chemise, she wore the scapular of the Madonna del Carmine. She unbuttoned her blouse, opened her chemise and showed it. The scapular was green and her breasts were milky white. Don Paolo felt his heart beating faster at the sight, after long abstinence, of this tender and fresh fruit of his own country. (70–71)

He feels even more strongly drawn to his spiritual interlocutor, Cristina, addressing her in his diary with "the tender expressions of a lover" (84), and it is his physical desire for her that makes him understand that he has taken up a celibate path. Although he had dismissed his desire for Bianchina on purely pragmatic grounds—"It was a pity, it really was a pity, that he had to be prudent"—his desire for Cristina seems to threaten his ethical vocation itself: "Cristina was washing the floor. Don Paolo scarcely dared look at her. He discovered what purity meant; what it meant to make chastity the guardian over one's body" (98).

When he seeks "to escape the boredom of the female atmosphere around him" (106), he surely is seeking to escape more than "boredom." Despite this light irony, Spina seems able to weather the trial as a celibate while maintaining a generally enlightened belief in sexual openness. His kindness to Bianchina during her postabortion illness reveals his hostility to the church's outmoded positions on sexuality: "[Y]ou are forgiven. What will not be forgiven is this evil society that forced you to choose between death and dishonor" (46).

Spina also attempts to defend the lovers Bianchina and Alberto from the intolerance of the village and even Cristina (103–4). Spina's sexually enlightened worldview is also expressed during his efforts to preach to the peasants. He is irritated with the difficulty of getting past their sexual mores to talk of important political issues:

> "Have you ever suffered from lack of liberty?"
>
> "Liberty?" he said. "There's only too much of it. Once upon a time a girl was not allowed to be alone with her fiancé before marriage."
>
> "I am not talking of that," said Don Paolo. "I am not talking of the behavior of engaged couples."
>
> "I see, sir," he said. "You are talking of married people. With us things have remained as they were, but down in the plain there's only too much liberty."
>
> "I see," said Don Paolo, and gave up trying to go on with the conversation.

He is even more disturbed to see these mores, long inculcated by the church and manipulated by the Fascist schoolmistress to foster hatred of other nations:

> The last announcement the schoolmistress read out was about the coalition of the Protestant countries against Italy.
>
> The schoolmistress told the story of Luther.
>
> "Luther was a monk," she said, "and he had taken the vows of obedience, chastity, and poverty. One day he made the acquaintance of a nun, and fell madly in love with her. He asked the Pope's permission to marry her, but the Pope refused. So Luther started protesting. All the monks who found the vow of chastity vexatious joined him, and that was the origin of Protestantism."

It is puzzling that the same frustration with this manipulation of rhetoric that leads Spina to seek vocation in a way of life also leads him to equate sexuality with evil and irresponsibility, thereby adopting the same restrictive mores he had earlier condemned in others.

The suddenness of this change is only comprehensible if the passages concerning his views on sexuality in the first chapters are reviewed and more carefully scrutinized. Even his most direct attack on the moralistic dogmas of his society and the church, during his absolution of the autoabortionist, is noncommittal on sexuality itself. In the prudishness of the new Spina, we realize that the old one had never come to terms with the specificity of sexual desire; that is, he never had a theology of sexuality.

The Protestants should not be hated, but there is no commentary on their repudiation of celibacy; Alberto and Bianchina should be allowed to marry, but there is no opinion expressed about their desire for free love. This non-committal attitude, which the secular or progressive reader can easily conflate with his or her own views, can also be easily supplanted by a dogma close to that of the Vatican.

What runs as a constant theme through the novel is the contrast between the "animal" (all that has to do with survival) and the "truly human" (that which is purely disinterested). Sexuality is too easily subsumed under the first category, the "animal instincts" Spina speaks of with Cristina (80), and becomes, therefore, a sign of all that inhibits the spiritual life: social and biological necessity. This contrast between sexuality (animal) and celibacy (truly human) undermines any possibility of arriving at a synthesis of the animal and the human, sexuality and celibacy, the worldly and the spiritual. As I argued in the previous section, however, Spina does accomplish a significant synthesis between his intellectual and his spiritual views, and it is precisely between that synthesis and a fragmented view of sexuality that the largest contradiction in the novel looms. Before examining Silone's response to this contradiction after the publication of the 1937 edition, let us survey the specifics of that conflict.

Even more striking are Spina's personal and visceral expressions of contempt for the physical side of human sexuality. Spina again lets his disgust for the physical details of sexual desire take over his moral vision while he listens to the cowherd recount the story of his perverse relations with the baroness.

Toward the end of the novel, the evil and ominous connotations of sexuality seem to have become embedded in the mythical structure of the narrative itself. Spina has an unexplained reaction to a strange vision: "On the windowpane the priest saw two flies on top of one another, surprised by death in the act of love. Outside it was raining. Don Paolo shuddered" (270). His shudder seems to foreshadow, like the contrast between Cristina's virtue and the "love-making of wolves," a terrible fate in which sex and death, the inescapable powers of nature, are inseparably linked.

If Spina is openly conflicted about sexuality, the narrative point of view expresses a more objective ambivalence, one that is perhaps "beyond good and evil" in its novelistic rigor. (This point of view cannot be equated with that of the author; Silone was profoundly concerned with questions of good and evil, but, as a novelist, he usually succeeds at critical moments to submit himself to the genre's structural imperatives of ambivalence and irony.) This ambivalence unfolds in three crucial episodes: the story of Annina and Murica; Spina's second crisis of celibate vocation; and the sexual tension of Spina's final meetings with Bianchina and Cristina, his two "lovers."

In his encounter with Annina (chapter 8), Spina reveals both a belief in the value of celibacy, even for secular political activists, and suspiciousness toward sexuality, even in its most positive manifestations. Spina expresses himself with uncharacteristic malice and sarcasm:

> "Listen," said Spina. "We revolutionaries are few and weak. Against us there is a whole world of self-interest and fear. To hold out and not allow ourselves to be annihilated we must concentrate our energies, support each other in every way we can. Instead, we waste our best strength on sentimental stupidities."
>
> "Our friendship did not in any way diminish our participation in the work of the group," the girl said. "On the contrary, we were among the most active. We organized excursions and reading evenings, and chose novels dealing with social questions for the discussions. We even gave up marrying, setting up house, and having children, in order to have more time for the group."
>
> "I can imagine the rest," said Spina. "Love faded, and with it all interest in the group."
>
> The girl's mind was elsewhere and she did not hear Spina's interruption. (185–86)

In this brief exchange, Spina expresses a dogmatic view of sex now shared by the institutions of church and party. Despite Annina's comprehension of what is at stake in her vocation—they gave up family life in order to serve— Spina demands more, mocking their relationship as a "sentimental stupidity." What we see is the materialist version of moral Puritanism; despite early Communist endorsements of sexual enlightenment, and even free love (e.g., the glass-of-water thesis), the party under Stalin began to promote sexual restraint and traditional family values for all and, for party cadres, the foreswearing of the "bourgeois attachments" of romantic love and even abstinence.[20]

Although the dark side of sexuality destroys the lovers' relationship— Murica rejects Annina as a "whore" because she allowed the police to rape her in order to protect him (187–88)—the narrative ambivalence toward their sexual love is expressed in the irony with which Spina's view is presented. He becomes so spiteful that the reader cannot help condemning his inflexibility and looking for the good in their relationship. In narrative, over-statement always suggests its opposite, but in Silone's novel the counter to Spina's view finds its own positive expression during Murica's confession in chapter 11.

Between his castigation of Annina and his hearing of Murica's confession, Spina has himself passed through a second crisis in his celibate vocation. Although emphasis is on his despair over the war enthusiasm, Spina regrets his sexual abnegation, "ruining his face with iodine" (225),[21] and briefly con-siders a new life with Bianchina, whom he has begun to regard again with desire (224).

In the critical scene with Don Benedetto that follows, Spina renews his ex-plicit commitment to his vocation and an implicit one to celibacy. This latter receives small yet significant support from Don Benedetto, who remains in the church precisely to preserve his reputation as a celibate, the loss of which he censures in others:

> In the last fifty years every priest who has left the Church has done so because of some scandalous infraction of the rule of celibacy. That is suf-ficient to give an ideal of the spiritual condition of our clergy. If the news were spread in the diocese that another priest, one Don Benedetto, of Rocca dei Marsi, had abandoned the priesthood, the first explanation that would naturally occur to the faithful would be that yet another priest had eloped with his housemaid. (248)

This impulse to censure the decisions of others, one of the most troubling aspects, partly because of its apparent ubiquity, of celibate practice, is car-ried over to Spina's rudeness to Bianchina (the temptress?) as he prepares to embark on his vocation with new confidence. In this "thoughtlessness," Spina's inner sexual conflict remains unintegrated, projected unto others rather than mastered.

In the final chapter, Spina makes an explicit call for celibacy as part of the vocation of the new revolutionaries:

> "You cannot conceive what it would mean to a country like ours," said Don Paolo, "if there were a hundred youths ready to renounce all safety, defy all corruption, free themselves from obsession with private property, sex, and their careers, and unite on the basis of absolute sincerity and absolute brotherliness." (284)

The unresolved tensions and ambivalence underlying this confident call, however, emerge in his final confrontations with Bianchina and Cristina. The former reveals a very real psychological tension in Spina's personal-ity, whereas the latter touches on the central mystical ambivalence of celi-bate theology. His admission amounts to a confession that he is unable to confront the sexual or help others resolve their sexual problems, much less his own, a problem implied in his flight from the confessions of the villagers in chapter 11.

When Bianchina gives voice to her selfless love for him, however, Spina's fragile celibacy seems to shatter. She asks quite simply, "Can we spend the night together?" and Spina replies even more simply, "Yes" (307), a reply that remains utterly mysterious because no such opportunity presents itself in the last pages of the novel.

In fact, we are left with the mystery of Spina's celibacy, and of celibacy itself, in the concluding encounters of the book. Spina has demonstrated a sexual/celibate charisma—the sexual power of the man of mystery—in his relations with both women; both give up everything for him.

Nevertheless, the significance of celibacy in the novel remains bound to Spina's conflicted sexuality. The harmful aspects of this inner conflict manifest themselves most clearly in a tendency toward misogyny. The narrative point of view maintains, as in its relation to Spina's prudishness, some ironic distance from Spina's attitudes toward women, but much less so because of the tendency of all the female characters to confirm Spina's attitudes in their words and actions. Like the church, Spina gives women two roles to play: Mary Magdalene before and after meeting Jesus.

Spina's uneasy relation to his sexuality leads him to project the problem onto women, seeing them as prey to their desires—the depraved baroness being the extreme example (215–17)—and not, therefore, truly human. The threat their presence poses to his chastity (chapters 4 and 4) leads him to dismiss the value of their companionship (106). In his meeting with Annina, Spina also hints that she carries the blame for the flagging of their political commitments: "Love faded, and with it all interest in the group" (186). In both of these episodes, the narrative portrays Spina in a strongly ironic light. The narrative point of view does not distance itself, however, from Spina's construction of female subjectivity as one suited to a more passive form of resistance through devotion to a male spiritual model.

Spina's conflicted sexuality not only has these unsurprising effects on his relations to women, it also exacerbates his hatred for the established church. Just as a Catholic clergyman might find support for his problematic celibacy in church dogma, Spina seems to seek support in an antichurch dogma; both rely on an association of concupiscence with evil. Throughout the novel, the church is revealed to be steeped in hypocrisy, from the use of the confessional as a cover rather than a confrontation with sin (108–9) to its self-interested endorsement of the war: "'The bishop is going to bless the Avezzano conscripts today,' said the other. 'The death ray will open the way for the Pope's missionaries'" (192).

The war rally becomes a pagan and barbaric ritual, complete with patriotic fetishes, unintelligible cries and chants ("CHAY DOO"), and a symbolic

"Witch-Doctor," which is presided over by the church (200–203). Spina's rage against this hypocrisy is sharper than his anti-Fascism and finds expression in the graffiti he writes on the church steps: "Down with the Pope who's in favor of the war!" (218). This connection between the church's evil and a re-version to paganism is also suggested in the appearance of Don Benedetto's assassins: "One man wore a piece of snake skin in his hatband against the evil eye; another had some badger's hair tied to his watch chain" (278).

Celibacy is clearly the one unsuccessfully integrated element in Spina's vocation; even as his vocation reaches higher levels of integration with each crisis, the conflicts in his sexual adjustment are, if anything, exacerbated. As a narrative of the struggle for celibate achievement, *Bread and Wine* would seem to suggest that celibacy should be jettisoned from the ideal of spiritual vocation, if it were not for the example of Don Benedetto. Although Don Benedetto's vocation undergoes significant transformations from service within church institutions to withdrawal and, finally, resistance and martyr-dom, his celibate achievement remains a constant that is never questioned. It exhibits the earmarks observed by me of a fully integrated practice: ap-preciation of beauty, intellectual curiosity, tolerance of others, and respect for women. He is at first the unconscious then the explicit priestly model in-spiring Spina's vocation, a crucial element in a young man's decision to take up such a difficult life: "Men will follow Christ if they can find persons who have already done so with honesty and joy. Nothing is more powerful than example. Nothing exerts more authority than simple truth lived."[22]

With astounding insight into the process of celibacy, Silone contrasts Don Benedetto's achievement of celibacy with Don Girasole's uneasy prac-tice of it. Don Girasole hints at his uncomfortable adjustment to his vocation through the mouthing of an old cliché: "'The man of God must always be tired,' he said. 'For idle thoughts occur in idle moments, and behind them lurks the Evil One, who is always on the watch'" (233). At first glance, this modus operandi seems harmless enough, and it may even be regarded as part of a rich life of service to his parish, if it were not soon revealed to be a cover for moral lassitude:

"By the way," said Don Paolo, "what do you think of the war?"

"A country priest has many things to do and little time to think," Don Girasole replied. (233)

When Spina probes into his repudiation of Don Benedetto, that "very rash man of God" (235), and his refusal to condemn evils in society, Don Girasole murmurs: "O God, O God, why do you torment me?" (238). Don Girasole's resigned pessimism and his need to be busy are ways to hide from his sexual-ity and, by implication, his social responsibilities. To be able to resist social injustice effectively, as Don Benedetto does, the celibate cannot be hiding from his sexual nature and desires but must master them. In Don Benedetto's person, the successful conscious resistance to the demands of sexuality (his natural destiny) becomes a metaphor for the strength needed to resist human oppression.

It is Don Benedetto's achievement of celibacy rather than Spina's conflicted sexuality that guided Silone's reworking of the narrative between the first and second versions.

HOPEFUL REVISIONS: SILONE'S SECOND DRAFT OF CELIBACY

In his preface to the second version of *Bread and Wine*, Silone relates an anecdote that he credits as the origin of his revision. He notices that a Swiss woman sharing his train compartment is reading his novel, and he becomes riveted on her progress:

> It was a strange sensation to be faced with a stranger to whom I was secretly telling a long story.... In fact a strange uneasiness came over me. The page she was reading did not satisfy me at all; indeed, at the moment it struck me as actually absurd. Why had I written it? If I had foreseen that a person like this was going to read the book, I said to myself, I should certainly have cut that page, as well as others, besides giving much thought to certain expressions.... Perhaps I had never before felt so immediately and so acutely the privilege and the responsibility of being a writer. (2nd ed., xiv)

Which page was it that he wished so badly to cut? Were the revisions limited to tightening the narrative? Silone implies as much in his only statement about the results of his editing project:

> As critics have noted, the structure, the moral essence, the vicissitudes of the characters have remained unchanged; but these books have been stripped of secondary or non-essential material and the basic theme has been deepened. (2nd ed., xv)

That basic theme certainly did remain intact, a theme that is succinctly captured in Silone's statement about his responsibilities as a writer: "The only commitment that deserves respect is that of a personal vocation" (2nd ed., xvi). Nevertheless, the revisions are by no means limited to so-called extraneous elements. What has been most noticeably eliminated are the episodes and scenes, at times mere lines, that made up the narrative of Spina's inner struggle with a prudishness that linked sexuality to depravity, evil, and irresponsibility and his corollary treatment of women's subjectivity as a threat and the church's compromises as a metaphor for concupiscence.

Although Silone makes no direct commentary on the fact, one cannot help being struck, in light of the revisions he made, that the encounter that motivated him to make the changes was that of the woman reading his novel. He notes that earlier some workers had questioned him concerning the meaning of certain lines but that this had not been sufficient to convince him of the need to revise it. When we examine the substance of the changes, however, the significance of his embarrassment before a female audience—"a person like this"—becomes understandable. Perhaps there is nothing more disconcerting to a mature man than having a woman discover the adolescent within him, especially if it is exposed in the printed page.

The discussion of the revision and its thematic results would be limited almost exclusively to a cataloguing of deleted scenes, a trimming that goes far beyond matters of artistic economy because their absence reveals a newly conceived understanding of the role of sexuality in the spiritual vocation, if it were not that these cuts found a substitution in Silone's addition of a crucial new scene at the beginning of the novel. That scene, in which Spina attempts to seduce a peasant woman living near his hiding place, establishes the sexual issues at stake in his initiation to vocation, and especially the idea of celibacy, much more vividly and subtly than the combination of symbolic (the disfigurement) and rhetorical calls for celibacy in the first version.

Spina meets a woman beside a stream and sets up a liaison with her for the same evening. In his desire for her, he seems to forget everything to do with his mission; He is impatient and rude with Cardile (2nd ed., 39–40) and risks exposing himself to capture: "[H]e...made straight for the water trough, without worrying about hiding the direction from which he came" (2nd ed., 40).

After an initial idyllic rendezvous, their conversation turns to Spina's real identity, and the woman, Margherita, reveals that she knows that he is wanted by the police. Spina's reply expresses his cynicism about women, a cynicism that was present throughout the first version, but he meets an active resistance and dignity in Margherita that makes explicit what was only shrouded in vague irony in the figure of Bianchina. Although the disfigurement remains, though now more subordinated, the explicit call for celibacy (284) was cut. The invisibility of the disfigurement to women, however, is still a mystery, especially in the added scene.

As both a lover and as a celibate, Spina ceases to see in women his human peers. In this symbolic initiation to celibacy, which precedes the initiation scene of donning the priest's robes, Spina is also initiated to the subjectivity of women. Thus, in the second version of *Bread and Wine*, celibacy is not the continuation and exacerbation of an immature sexual development; rather, it is the beginning of the possibility of true relationships with women. In the physical distance that Margherita establishes, Spina obtains a space for reflection and understanding.

In the development of the second version, the ambivalence in Spina's generally enlightened view of sexuality from the first half of the novel now remains focused throughout the text on the productive tension within celibate sublimation. Rather than degenerating into a conflict between sexual perversion and prudishness, Spina's sexuality intensifies alongside his growing appreciation of female companionship as more of a support than a threat to his vocation. As a result, the final ambivalence about the love between him and Cristina gains in mystery, meaning, and power.

After the scene with Margherita, this change of perspective is expressed mainly through what has been cut. Missing in the second version are the scenes linking sexuality to moral corruption: Achilles' seductions (and Spina's disgust at the physicality of sex); the story of the depraved baroness; and, most important, Bianchina's turn to prostitution and Spina's disgust with her and pornography. Even the sexual descriptions of the Ethiopian women are toned down. Perhaps the change is most powerfully felt in the revised dialogue during Spina's visit with Annina.

In the final scene with Murica, Silone not only drops the call for celibacy, he even portrays Spina as respecting, if not envying, the relationship of the reunited lovers:

"When does Annina arrive?" Don Paolo asked.
   "Perhaps tomorrow," Murica said. "She writes to me every day."
   "She's a marvelous girl," Don Paolo said. "I'm certainly jealous of you."
(2nd ed., 256)

Closely bound with this altered view of sexuality is a revised view of women's subjectivity, evident in the added lines in the dialogue with Annina and in the character of Margherita, which is expressed with particular force in the revision of the concluding scenes of the novel. Not only is the entire encounter with Bianchina in Rome, with her fall, her self-effacement, and Spina's attempt to play the pedagogue cut, but Silone also adds a significant scene between Spina and Cristina. Their dialogue is much richer in the preceding pages than it was in the first version, and Cristina seems much more aware of the world, much less childlike and dependent (cf. 288 and 2nd ed., 249). They then confess the sexual nature of their affection for each other in a veiled but forceful way. The scene over the loom that follows reveals to Spina the deep connection between his spiritual vocation and the active influence of women in his life and his desire to recapture their community.

In an almost perfect inversion of Spina's efforts (in the first version) to play the pedagogue to Bianchina, in which he attempts to bequeath to her the abstract world of male philosophy,[23] Spina now offers Cristina instruction based on the learning he received from women. This new world of intersubjectivity and exchange across gender lines was also expressed in perfect complementarity by Margherita, who tells Spina that she learned from a man, her father, to protect the persecuted, inverting in turn the gender determinism of the scene in the first version in which Spina makes the distinction between the good of woman, who resists the war passively, instinctually, and the evil of male careerism. This cycle of cross-gender sharing makes possible a sphere of honest affection.

Here his return to Christianity is connected, in striking contrast to the first version in which it leads to prudishness and misogyny, to memories of the affectionate bond with women in which work and companionship weave a world of shared feelings and intersubjectivity. In addition, he can share that affection with Cristina in a way apparently beyond him in the scene with Margherita and, most significantly in the paranoid world of a Fascist society, let the truth come out. As a result, the final scene of Cristina's martyrdom, while still steeped in mythical and symbolic imagery, gives way to a more vivid poignancy, a more real sense of human loss.

This higher integration of sexuality and celibacy, vocation and affection, is accompanied by a greater forbearance for the foibles of institutions, church and party, that claim, yet fail, to serve ethical ends. Silone cut the scenes in which the monk sells medals to make money on the war and Spina mocks the church as constipated. When he writes graffiti against the war, Spina no longer writes one against the pope. And by cutting the melodramatic martyrdom of Don Benedetto, Silone also frees the church from implication in his murder. Even the party is handled more gently; both as a representative of the party (in his meeting with Annina) and as its critic (the scene with the agitator Bolla, which was cut), Spina seems less trapped between moral absolutes and rank opportunism. Although one could take issue with these decisions, arguing that both the church in Fascist Italy and the Communist Party under Stalin are hardly deserving of forbearance, it is clear that the more tolerant mood is the result of both Silone's greater distance from the events and a more integrated ethical system, one with less need for resentment toward others as a form of self-justification.

In the process of revising *Bread and Wine*, Silone appears to have found a smoother integration of his Christian and secular values through an allegorical process of integrating the ideal of celibacy with the realities of human sexuality and the subjectivity of women. That his is achieved largely through cutting heterogeneous[24] materials, however, suggests that some problems were avoided rather than resolved, an observation that holds for both the disturbing aspects of the sexual and the depth of gender conflict in a male-dominated society. Perhaps the truth of ambivalence has been lost: Is the result too perfect an ideal? Is Spina no longer a truly literary figure, the "picaresque saint," as one critic named the protagonist of the first version, but only an edifying, and perhaps impossible, role model? What is certain is that this most difficult process, the process of achieving celibacy itself, is absent from each separate narrative; that process is only restored by reading both versions as a single narrative of celibate struggle and achievement.

Silone's successful integration of such issues as sexual freedom and women's liberation to both a fairly timeless standard of Christian ethics and way of life and an implicitly positive presentation of celibacy suggests reason for optimism about the possibility of synthesizing Christian ideals and celibacy as a mode of practicing the spiritual vocation, with a modernized anthropology of human sexuality and the contemporary values of gender equality and multicultural tolerance not only without losing the meaning of the former but, in fact, with much to be gained all around. We can only hope that Silone's optimism is not an illusion of that value system, known generally as humanism, which upholds the potential of human consciousness and actions to create and maintain its values against the apparent limits, the necessities, of natural and social structures.

There is perhaps a Christian tradition better able to endure the threat of an implacable necessity, one more grounded in the acceptance of the fallen condition of the world and original sin than any activism. It is such a Christianity that weathered the Dark Ages, the Black Death, and much more. And it is such a Christianity that sustains J. F. Powers in his effort to narrate the life and death of a priest in a hostile context: postwar United States.

Whereas Silone's novel is triumphant, especially from a Christian point of view, Powers's is tragic, but it is not the tragedy of a single individual, the priest who attempts to succeed, nor, by any means, is it the tragedy of Christianity, which is content to "fail," to endure in the minds and souls of those incompetents and cranks who submit to it with humility. It is the tragedy of a society.

In these two great social novels of the spiritual vocation, *Bread and Wine* and *Morte D'Urban*, society and vocation are handled with the most striking contrasts for their significance; yet celibacy, as a mediating structure between society and individual, remains surprisingly constant in its practice, limitations, and potential.

As I have sought to demonstrate, the radical contrasts between the novels express less the differences between the outlooks of the authors than a response to two very different societies. Heroic resistance to social norms and a meaningful death are still possibilities for Spina because his world, that of rural Italy and, oddly enough, dictatorship, is still enchanted; that is, it still offers a realm for meaningful action.

Even if Powers had desired to produce such a narrative, he could have done so only as a latter-day Don Quixote, the victim rather than the wielder of Cervantean irony. His white-collar world, as a quintessentially disenchanted one, defies the visible representation of meaning, forcing the writer to suggest the presence of meaning only in the Unseen. Neither Max Weber nor Georg Lukács predicted the last heroic age of the novel, its engagement as a literary form in the anti-Fascist struggle, but their foresight is all the more striking in the work of someone like J. F. Powers.

Although celibacy is pursued differently in the two novels, its structure remains the same: Whereas Spina seeks to tap into a sublimated sexuality to build greater affective relationships with his community and with meaning, Urban manages only to sublimate his sexuality to a success ethic. Spina's celibacy deepens as his commitment to service outside institutional measures and rewards grows. Urban, however, loses the very meaning of celibacy when his ambitions collapse; thus, his final resignation to vocation occurs in a post-sexual state, in a dirge of age, illness, and death.

Neither novel allows for the narration of the achievement and integration of celibacy within their limited time frame, that of a single year. In Silone's case, however, the 20 years that elapsed between the two versions of the novel reveal the process of achieving celibacy in an almost magical way. In both versions, Spina is still the same young man, but in the second one he seems to have acquired 20 years' experience as a celibate priest, eschewing his earlier misogyny and prudishness for the firmer supports of community, service, and hope. Urban has had that same time span to grow with his vocation, but his faith in mundane success reveals a celibacy ever in crisis, still needing the crutches of misogyny and institutional gratification.

These two novels comprehend the sweep of twentieth-century Western society, in which, at one moment, resistance and a meaningful life and death appear still possible and, at another, only conformity or failure seems to be an option. In both cases, however, spiritual vocation functions as a litmus test of the possible, and the actual practice of celibacy is one of its most telling signs.

CONCLUSION

This book represents an excursion—literary and psychological—into the discovery of a long noted, but little explored sexual backwater—religious celibacy. *Sexual backwater* defined as "a place or situation regarded as cut off from the mainstream of activity or development and consequently seen as quiet and uneventful or unimportant and dull" seems to me an accurate characterization of celibacy in the minds of many people today.[25.] Idea associations with 'energy withheld' and even 'stagnant and sewer-like' situations complement this notion.

Religious celibacy has been touted as a sign of the most supreme altruistic human achievement at the same time as receives the label as the 'greatest sexual perversion.' Both claims may very well be true.

This book does not pretend to solve the contradictions or expose the range and depth of this sexual adjustment either individually or socially.

What I have done is look for the revelations and half-hidden knowledge and awareness of celibacy wherever I could note them in the hope that the results will contribute to the welfare of individuals and society—especially in groups that hold sway over peoples' lives and exert immense spiritual power precisely because of their perceived purity.

For near half a century I have labored to construct an accurate account of this form of sexual adjustment because I think it is important for the welfare of many people who find religion an important element in their spiritual striving. The odds and powers set against this process of discovery and reconstruction are daunting from the idea that "there is nothing to talk about" to accusations of disloyalty, and outright instances of "blackballing" and attempted character assassination because of the work have, in the end, proved minor 'excommunications' if major annoyances.

No entirely reliable research tools to study human sexuality are currently available. People tend to misrepresent themselves (read lie) on sociological surveys about their sex lives. Nonetheless, these, too, can be of use in putting an accurate picture of sex and celibacy together. Neurobiology, evolutionary psychology, and plain, sturdy, reliable human curiosity will provide new challenges and opportunities for discovery in this very important area of life. I have chosen clinical observation and ethnographic means to describe some of what I have learned.

Extending observation into literature and autobiography is simply an extension of my clinical and psychoanalytic bent—old fashioned as that may be. My work has been like putting a mosaic (or a tapestry) together. That method is not executed on a continuous surface like a canvas nor advantaged by possibilities of nuanced color blending and shading at a stroke. Piece by uneven piece is assembled and placed adjacent to other isolated pieces allowing the picture to emerge from the interrelationship of all the discrete pieces. The work has meaning only from a distance. A tapestry, too, takes time and faith that the final pattern will emerge even if it cannot be comprehended or appreciated in the process.

To return to my original metaphor of my work as an exploration: this book is not the end of a search. It has led me to three elements of celibacy/sexuality that need to be examined in greater depth—they are elements of *mystery*, dimensions of *myth*, and the effects of celibacy as *miasma*.

Religious literature is rife with the idea of mystery in relationship to celibacy. Indeed, celibacy is puzzling way to live out one's sexuality. In my experience it has moved some men and women to the heights of universal love, service, and self-giving. It is also often posited as a "divine grace" and therefore unquestionable by any spiritual person, and unquestionable to anyone else. Purposeful or not, the assertion of mystery is off putting for examination, discovery, and discourse. This represents a loss for religion and society.

Mystery is not an answer. It is a puzzle to be struggled with and solved. Mystery should not be used as a "No Trespassing" sign to keep anyone from searching the meaning of sexual human nature, the persistence of celibacy as a practice, or the real character of altruism. Nor should mystery be a prerogative of any religious discipline; to make it so is an impediment to spirituality and can make the claim of celibacy a cover for perversion.

Myths related to celibacy abound in the Roman Catholic tradition. The most remarkable is that celibacy irreversible linked to priesthood raises a man to a state of perfection. James Joyce recorded his interpretation of the Catholic teaching on the place of the priest in society—not less than the angels. He was accurate in his account of what the church teaches on the basis of declarations of the reform Council of Trent.

Belief is one thing; to be respected, even if disagreed with. Behavior is another separate question. One of the most obvious defects and ideas detrimental to religion is the myth that every man or woman who claims celibacy is, in fact, abstaining from sexual gratification or practicing celibacy. Of course, the shadow myth that no one claiming celibacy is actually abstinent is equally dubious.

According to figures published in the 2005 *Annuario Pontificio*, 410,695 Catholic clergy were committed to celibacy as of 2003. In addition to priests that number includes 4,695 bishops, 745 archbishops, and 190 cardinals. In 1993 Cardinal Jose Sanchez, at the time secretary of the Vatican Congregation of the Clergy, was asked by a reporter for the BBC what was his reaction to studies that claimed that at any one time 45 to 50 percent of Catholic clergy were, in fact, not practicing celibacy. His response on TV: "I have no reason to doubt the accuracy of those figures." Already in 1970 at a Synod of Rome where the question of mandated versus optional celibacy for priests was being discussed, Cardinal Franjo Seper of Zagreb made the statement, "I am not at all confident that celibacy is in fact being observed."

It is a source of amazement that with the still huge 'coterie' of Catholic clergy—let alone the long tradition of the requirement—living under to moniker 'celibate' there are so few explorations of the actual practice of religious celibacy. Myth should help explain reality, as Greeley has so eloquently expounds, not serve obfuscation and crime.

Considering the miasma of celibacy, that is its potential harmful, poisonous, and criminal effects, brings us back full circle to the first chapter of this book on the foundation of the current so named "crisis" in the Catholic church in the United States.[26.] It is a crisis of celibacy—misunderstood celibacy, unobserved celibacy, mythical celibacy that proposes that clergy are sexually safe—that has potential to do great harm and wreck havoc on lives under the guise of religion and virtue.

The search for understanding celibacy, in and out of religious traditions, will continue because it is a recurring and persistent drive within the spectrum of sexual adjustments and sustains attraction from impulses to control, to create, and to serve. Celibacy can be a reality in response to the human striving for meaning beyond oneself. Celibacy is part of human experience and spiritual striving. Many people beyond committed religious men and women have garnered knowledge of the value of sexual restraint. It is of nature.

NOTES

SERIES FOREWORD

1. L. Aden and J. H. Ellens, *Turning Points in Pastoral Care: The Legacy of Anton Boisen and Seward Hiltner* (Grand Rapids, MI: Baker, 1990).

PREFACE

1. Cf. A. W. Richard Sipe, *Celibacy in Crisis: A Secret World Revisited* (New York: Brunner-Routledge), 32; and *The Oxford Companion to Christian Thought*, (2000)104–5.

INTRODUCTION

1. Nathaniel Hawthorne, "The Minister's Black Veil," in *Hawthorne's Short Stories*, ed. Newton Arvin (New York: Vintage, 1946), 9–23.

2. Edwin O'Connor, *The Edge of Sadness* (Boston: Little, Brown, 1961).

3. Victor Hugo, "Bishop's Candlesticks," *Les Misérables*, trans. Lee Fhanestock and Norman MacAfee, based on the C. E. Wilbour trans. (New York: New American Library, 1987), 52–113.

4. Leon Bloy, *The Woman Who Was Poor*, trans. I. J. Collins (New York: Sheed and Ward, 1947; originally published 1896).

5. Georges Bernanos's *Diary of a Country Priest* is an account in which a physically ill, saintly, but psychosexually immature man discovers profound inner strength in the solitude of his celibate vocation. Dying in the company of a fallen priest, the protagonist expresses a tolerance and universality beyond that of any particular doctrine. "Tout est grace." We have analyzed this book, but we have not included it in this series. Robert Bresson, who made the book into a movie, recounts, "through the

pages of a diary, the daily life of a young priest, his self-doubts, and the problems of his small parish at Ambricourt in the province of Pas-de-Calais. He is upset that no one comes to Mass. The villagers wrongly suspect that he is greedy and an alcoholic. However, in his own despair he is able to bring spiritual peace to a dying countess, who has long rejected God. He ultimately dies alone, painfully of stomach cancer, murmuring, 'All is Grace.' The dying words of St. Theresa of Lisieux were the same but are often translated 'Grace is everywhere'" (http://www.kirjasto.sci.fi/bernanos. htm). Georges Bernanos, *Under the Sun of Satan*, trans. J. C. Whitehouse (Lincoln: University of Nebraska Press, 2001); Georges Bernanos, *The Imposter*, trans. J. C. Whitehouse (Lincoln: University of Nebraska Press, 1999).

6. François Mauriac, *Vipers' Tangle*, trans. Warre B. Wells (New York: Sheed and Ward, 1953). Mauriac's novels were condemned by the Catholic right when he first wrote them. He deals with the mystery of sin and redemption.

7. Paul Claudel, "The Tidings Brought to Mary," in *Two Dramas*, trans. Wallace Fowlie (Chicago: Regnery, 1960), 161–295; Paul Claudel, *Lord, Teach Us to Pray*, trans. Ruth Bethell (New York: Longmans, Green, 1948).

8. Canon 277 states: "§1. Clerics are obliged to observe perfect and perpetual continence for the sake of the kingdom of heaven and therefore are obliged to observe celibacy, which is a special gift of God, by which sacred ministers can adhere more easily to Christ with an undivided heart and can more freely dedicate themselves to the service of God and humankind. §2. Clerics are to conduct themselves with due prudence in associating themselves with persons whose company could endanger their obligation to observe continence or could cause scandal for the faithful. §3. The diocesan bishop has the competence to issue more specific norms concerning this matter and to pass judgment in particular cases concerning the observance of this obligation"; *Code of Canon Law*, Latin-English ed. (Washington, DC: Canon Law Society of America, 1983).

9. William James, *The Varieties of Religious Experience*, ed. Martin E. Marty (New York: Penguin Books, 1985).

10. Investigative Staff of *The Boston Globe, Betrayal: The Crisis in the Catholic Church* (Boston: Little, Brown, 2002).

11. A. W. Richard Sipe, *A Secret World: Sexuality and the Search for Celibacy* (New York: Brunner/Mazel, 1990).

12. Nathaniel Hawthorne, *The Scarlet Letter* (New York: Modern Library, 2000). The Rev. Mr. Dimmesdale is presumed to be celibate by the entire community, much like the public figure of Father Coughlin.

13. W. Somerset Maugham, "Rain," *Complete Short Stories of W. Somerset Maugham*, 2 vols. (Garden City, NY: Doubleday, 1932). "Sadie Thompson" was Maugham's most famous story, which became the short story and play "Rain" and was made into several movies. A missionary and a prostitute who were among his fellow passengers on a trip to Pago Pago inspired the story. The minister, who demeans and shames Sadie into repentance and conversion, is the archetypical hypocritical clergyman, and Sadie becomes the prototypical good prostitute when the minister tries to rape her on the beach.

14. Ethel Voynich was a fascinating Irish woman and a genuine revolutionary. Her novel *Gadfly* sold 600,000 copies in the United States, 700,000 in China, and

more than 2.5 million in Russia, where she became an icon. She died at 96 years of age in New York in 1960. Pamela Blevins draws a fascinating profile of her in "Ivor Gurney's Friends."

15. Norman Sherry, *The Life of Graham Greene*, 3 vols. (New York: Viking Penguin, 1995–2004).

16. J. F. Powers, *Wheat That Springeth Green* (New York: Knopf, 1988); J. F. Powers, *Prince of Darkness, and Other Stories* (London: Lehmann, 1948); J. F. Powers, *Lions, Harts, Leaping Does, and Other Stories* (New York: Time, 1963). Many of Powers's short stories deal with priests. His observations about his characters never invade the privacy of what cannot be seen by the average parishioner. The sexual/celibate lives of the priests are implied behind the personalities of his characters.

17. Timothy Radcliff, *What Is the Point of Being a Christian?* (London: Burns and Oates, 2006).

18. Sinclair Lewis, *Elmer Gantry* (New York: Harcourt, Brace, 1927).

19. Willa Cather, *Death Comes for the Archbishop* (New York: Knopf, 1927).

20. Graham Green, *Monsignor Quixote* (London: Bodley Head, 1982).

CHAPTER 1

1. Thomas Doyle et al., *Sex, Priests, and Secret Codes: The Catholic Church's 2000-Year Paper Trail of Sexual Abuse* (Los Angeles: Volt Press, 2006).

2. H.O.P. Kramer and J.O.P. Sprenger, *Malleus Malificarum* (New York: Dover, 1971).

3. Rainer Nagele, *Reading after Freud* (New York: Columbia University Press, 1987).

4. Giovanni Boccaccio, *The Decameron*, trans. Guido Waldman (New York: Oxford University Press, 1998).

5. See A. W. Richard Sipe, *Celibacy in Crisis: A Secret World Revisited* (New York: Brunner-Routledge), 297.

6. See *A Report on the Crisis in the Catholic Church in the United States* (Washington, DC: United States Conference of Catholic Bishops, 2004). This report contains a statement from the National Review Board for the Protection of Children and Young People and the results of the survey by the John Jay College of Criminal Justice. At the time of the report, they concluded that 4,394 priests had been reported for sexually abusing a minor between 1950 and 2002. In the year after the report, however, another 750 priests were credibly accused of abuse during that time period. It is safe to say that not more than half of the priests who have abused minors in the United States over the past fifty years have yet been recorded or identified. Their ranks are estimated at 10,000. The casualties from clergy abuse are safely estimated at 120,000; no more than 10 percent of the victims have spoken up in public. See also Richard Sipe, "Why Victims Need to Tell Their Story," March 7, 2006, http://www.richardsipe.com/Click_&_Learn/2006-04-07.html.

7. The paternal uncle of the Marquis de Sade was a Benedictine abbot who kept a stable of mistresses, including a mother and daughter, and a vast library of pornography, from classical works to current pamphlets. Later in life, he participated in orgies staged by Sade at one of Sade's castles. (One group of villains in the novel *Justine* consists of Benedictines.) Sade's absent father, who was the French ambassador to

Bavaria and whom Sade adored, enjoyed picking up young men in the park and wrote a couple of poems celebrating homosexuality. Cf. Maurice Lever, *Sade: A Biography*, trans. Arthur Goldhammer (New York: Farrar, Strauss and Giroux, 1993).

8. Cf. Ethel Voynich, *The Gadfly*, in which the consequences of Arthur learning that he is the illegitimate son of Father Montanelli are life changing; likewise Graham Greene's priest in *The Power and the Glory* recognizes the result of his sin in the sadness of his daughter.

9. Cf. Shanta R. Dube et al., "Long-Term Consequences of Childhood Sexual Abuse by Gender of Victim," *American Journal of Preventative Medicine* (2005): 430–38; D. Finkelhor, *A Source Book on Child Sexual Abuse* (Newbury Park, CA: Sage, 1986).

10. Lever, *Sade*, 117. "A letter (dated June 1783) from Donatien to Renee-Pelagie makes it clear that the couple regularly practiced anal intercourse: 'Here's to a good screw up the ass, and may the devil take me if I don't give myself a hand job in honor of your buttocks! Don't tell la Presidente, though, because she's a good Jansenist and doesn't like for women to be molinized.'" The allusion is to Luis Molina, the sixteenth-century Spanish Jesuit whose doctrine of grace the Jansenists opposed. "She pretends that M. Cordier never discharged anywhere but in the vessel of propagation and that whosoever distances himself from the vessel must boil in hell. But I, who was raised by the Jesuits, who was taught by Father Sanchez not to swim in a vacuum any more than was necessary, because, as Descartes tells us, nature abhors a vacuum—I cannot agree with Mama Cordier." The phrase *nager dans le vide*—to swim in a vacuum—comes from Voltaire's *Dictionnaire Philosophique*. It refers to Epicurus's theory of atoms. There was a sixteenth-century philosopher, Francis Sanchez, who wrote *Quod nihil scitur* in 1580. He was a skeptic and held that a human being can know nothing except through observation and sensation. It seems that Sade was using Voltaire wryly to refer to what his teacher really taught him. Donatien is Sade's Christian name, Renee-Pelagee is his wife, la Presidente is Renee-Pelagee's mother, and Cordier was Renee-Pelagee's maiden name. Sade was at the Jesuit school from age 12 to 15, before he joined the army. The College Louis-le-grand still exists on the Rue St. Jacques in the Latin Quarter. It was nationalized in the French Revolution, and its name was changed to Lycee Louis-le-grand. There is a clear implication that Sade was sexually involved with at least one of his Jesuit teachers who taught him about sex and from whom he learned the connection between pain and sexual pleasure.

11. Cf. J. M. Masson, *The Assault on Truth* (New York: Ballantine, 2003). See also Sigmund Freud, "The Aetiology of Hysteria," in *The Standard Edition of the Complete Psychological Works of Sigmund Freud*, ed. and trans. J. Strachey, vol. 3 (London: Hogarth, 1961; originally published 1923).

12. Sigmund Freud, "The Mechanism of Hysterical Phenomena," in *The Standard Edition of the Complete Psychological Works of Sigmund Freud*, ed. and trans. J. Strachey (London: Hogarth, 1961; originally published 1923), 3: 38.

13. See E. Hollander, *Obsessive-Compulsive-Related Disorders* (Arlington, VA: American Psychiatric Publishing, 1993). See also L. Salzman, *The Obsessive Personality* (Lanham, MD: Aronson, 1973).

14. D. Finkelhor, "What's Wrong with Sex between Adults and Children? Ethics and the Problem of Sexual Abuse," *American Journal of Orthopsychiatry* 49 (1979): 692–97.

15. Kathleen Kendall-Tackett, *Treating the Lifetime Health Effects of Childhood Victimization* (Kingston, NJ: Civic Research Institute, 2003).

16. Scenes in James Joyce's *Portrait of an Artist as a Young Man* indicate this dynamic, particularly when the Jesuit headmaster banters with Stephen about the brown "skirts" that some order priests wear, implying effeminacy or homosexuality. Stephen gives up his resolve to purity and immediately returns to a prostitute. Father Flynn in "The Sisters" and the man in the park from "An Encounter" imply abuse of children. Certainly, Joyce persisted in a lifelong distrust of the church.

17. Jennifer Freyd, *Betrayal Trauma: The Logic of Forgetting Childhood Abuse* (Cambridge, MA: Harvard University Press, 1996).

18. Jennifer Freyd et al., "The Science of Child Sexual Abuse," *Science* 4 (2005): 22.

19. Shirley Jülich, "Stockholm Syndrome and Child Sexual Abuse," *Journal of Child Sexual Abuse* 14, no. 3 (2005): 107–29.

20. Patrick Carnes, *Don't Call It Love: Recovery from Sexual Addiction* (New York: Bantam, 1992).

21. The classic description of this personality is found in Hervey Cleckley, *The Mask of Sanity* (St. Louis, MO: Mosby, 1964). The book is still in print in a fourth edition.

22. In *The Nazi Doctors* (New York: Basic Books, 1986), Robert Jay Lifton describes this psychological dynamic that parallels what many priests employ.

23. See Sipe, *Celibacy in Crisis*; A. W. Richard Sipe, *A Secret World: Sexuality and the Search for Celibacy* (New York: Brunner/Mazel, 1990).

24. National Opinion Research Center, University of Chicago, Rev. Andrew M. Greeley, Director, *The Catholic Priest in the United States: Sociological Investigations* (Washington, DC: United States Catholic Conference, 1972).

25. Cf. *Los Angeles Times* polls in 1993 and 2002 cited by Andrew Greeley in *Priests: A Calling in Crisis* (Chicago: University of Chicago Press, 2004). This is a book that considers some of the research done on celibacy, the priesthood, and the crisis; it is an example of a secular newspaper cooperating with sociological investigation.

CHAPTER 2

1. Mohandas K. Gandhi, *An Autobiography: The Story of My Experiments with Truth*, trans. Mahadev Desai (Boston: Beacon Press, 1963).

2. Fulton J. Sheen, *Treasure in Clay* (Garden City, NY: Doubleday, 1980).

3. Andrew M. Greeley, *Confessions of a Parish Priest: An Autobiography* (New York: Pocket Books, 1987).

4. Gandhi considered Raychandbhai and Gopal Krishna Gokhale to be his teachers. Although married like Gandhi, Raychandbhai practiced celibacy and encouraged Gandhi to do the same.

5. The significance of male-male bonding, master-servant fidelity, and avuncular kinship in the adventure genre, on the one hand, and male celibacy in real spiritual vocation, on the other, can be seen repeatedly in literature, such as Auerbach, Dorfman, and even in the repeated theme of the Grail in Greeley's books. This link deserves further study in relation to the celibate ideal and the resistance to democ-

ratization and feminism both in Western culture overall and within the church in particular.

6. Louis Dumont, *Homo Hierarchicus: The Caste System and Its Implications* (Chicago: University of Chicago Press, 1980). One cannot project contemporary Western values onto Gandhi's apparent indifference to his Hindu culture's class distinctions between master and servant or his describing them with the same enthusiasm usually reserved for friendship between unconstrained individuals. Given the pervasive British colonial influence of Gandhi's India, we should instead note how prominently such relationships are depicted sentimentally in British literature rather than ironically as in Continental literature, such as *Don Quixote* or *Jacques and His Master*.

7. Ariel Dorfman and Armand Mattelart, *How to Read Donald Duck: Imperialist Ideology in the Disney Comic (Para leer al Pato Donald)*, trans. David Kunzle (New York: International General, 1975). This motif is also linked to a world of male-male bonding and the "avuncular genealogies" that Ariel Dorfman detected in the antifeminist and antisex biases of much Anglo-American children's literature and the sexless, misogynist, and avuncular world of the hobbits in J.R.R. Tolkien's *Lord of the Rings*, dominated by the sentimental master-servant relationship of Frodo and Sam.

8. Tolkien, like Gandhi, was educated in South Africa. J.R.R. Tolkien, *The Lord of the Rings*, 3 vols.:

1. *The Fellowship of the Ring: Being the First Part of The Lord of the Rings* (London: George Allen and Unwin, 1954).
2. *The Two Towers: Being the Second Part of The Lord of the Rings* (London: George Allen and Unwin, 1954).
3. *The Return of the King: Being the Third Part of The Lord of the Rings* (London: George Allen and Unwin, 1955).

9. Erich Auerbach, "The Knight Sets Forth," in *Mimesis*, trans. Willard R. Trask (Princeton, NJ: Princeton University Press, 1953), 123–42.

10. George Orwell, "Reflections on Gandhi," in *A Collection of Essays by George Orwell* (Garden City, NY: Doubleday, 1954; originally published 1949), 177–86.

11. Erik Erikson, *Gandhi's Truth* (New York: Norton, 1969).

12. In one conference, Pope John Paul II said that sex between a husband and wife out of lust was not free of sin.

13. Columba Stewart, *Cassian the Monk* (New York: Oxford University Press, 1998).

14. Cf. Italo Calvino, *The Watcher and Other Stories* (New York: Harcourt Brace, 1971). This question of ends is also one of Orwell's concerns in his "For God or Man" credo. Literary reflection offers the best vehicle for reconciliation. Italo Calvino's story "The Watcher," which narrates a Communist Party election observer's day at the polls in a Catholic home for monsters, the ill, and the mad, explores the philosophical limits at which the secular and religious worldviews meet in a contemplation of the mystery of the human condition.

15. In fact, it may be in this area of sexuality that a rapprochement is more possible than in the arena of ultimate ends. Here I am referring to the question of the goals of service; that is, the act of serving versus the eradication of the need. The latter is, of course, the goal of progressive or secular humanism: the curing of disease,

the elimination of poverty, the cessation of war, the promotion of justice and human equality. These also are traditional religious goals and meant to be facilitated by the practice of asceticism, especially celibacy linked with the vow of poverty. There is a connection between charity and economic rights. Both Gandhi and Orwell stood for both. Cf. Georg Simmel, "The Poor," in *On Individuality and Social Forms*, ed. Donald N. Levine, Heritage of Sociology Series (Chicago: University of Chicago Press: 1971), 153–54:

In the cases examined so far, a right and an obligation seemed to be two aspects of an absolute relationship. Completely new forms appear, however, when the point of departure is the obligation of the giver rather than the right of the recipient. In the extreme case, the poor disappear completely as legitimate subjects and central foci of the interests involved. The motive for alms then resides exclusively in the significance of giving for the giver. When Jesus told the wealthy young man, "Give your riches to the poor," what apparently mattered to him were not the poor, but rather the soul of the wealthy man for whose salvation this sacrifice was merely a means or symbol. Later on, Christian alms retained the same character; they represent no more than a form of asceticism, of "good works," which improve the chances of salvation of the giver. The rise of begging in the Middle Ages, the senseless distribution of alms, the demoralization of the proletariat through arbitrary donations which tend to undermine all creative work, all these phenomena constitute the revenge, so to speak, that alms take for the purely subjectivistic motive of their concession—a motive which concerns only the giver but not the recipient.

CHAPTER 4

1. Page Smith, *Redeeming the Time: A People's History of the 1920s and the New Deal* (New York: McGraw-Hill, 1987), 17.

2. Ibid., 26.

3. Ibid., 18.

4. Irving Bernstein, *The Lean Years: A History of the American Worker 1920–1933* (Boston: Houghton-Mifflin, 1960), 2.

5. Frederick Lewis Allen, *Only Yesterday: An Informal History of the 1920s* (New York: Harper and Row, 1959), 261.

6. John Dos Passos, *The Big Money*, U.S.A. trilogy (New York: Modern Library, 1937), 527; James T. Farrell, *Judgment Day*, Studs Lonigan trilogy (New York: Modern Library, 1938), 98–100, 169–70, 174–75.

7. Geoffrey Perrett, *America in the Twenties: A History* (New York: Simon and Schuster, 1982), 440–41.

8. Factual biographical information on Coughlin comes from Allen Brinkley, *Voices of Protest: Huey Long, Father Coughlin, and the Great Depression* (New York: Knopf, 1982), 85; Sheldon Marcus, *Father Coughlin: The Tumultuous Life of the Priest of the Little Flower* (Boston: Little, Brown, 1973).

9. Brinkley, *Voices of Protest*, 91.

10. Frank Sheed.

11. Brinkley, *Voices of Protest*, 96.

12. Marcus as well as Coughlin's other biographers agree that he drew a weekly audience of 40 million listeners. At the time, it was an unprecedented achievement for any religious broadcaster, and it remains a respectable record today.

13. Brinkley, *Voices of Protest*, 98.

14. Page Smith, *Redeeming the Time: A People's History of the 1920s and the New Deal* (New York: McGraw-Hill, 1987), 602–3.

15. Brinkley, *Voices of Protest*, 109.

16. Coughlin's National Union for Social Justice set forth a 16-point plan. Among its demands were freedom of religion, a minimum wage, nationalization of the most basic resources, private ownership of the means of production with government control over the production itself, the abolition of private banking, the protection of unions, a progressive income tax, and the general alleviation of the tax burden. Coughlin recognized that the National Union would attract attacks, but he assured his readers that God would protect them.

17. Marcus, *Father Coughlin*, 156.

18. Ibid. James T. Farrell gives a sickening account of one such beating in *Tommy Gallagher's Crusade* (New York: Vanguard, 1939).

19. James T. Farrell, *To Whom It May Concern: More Stories by James T. Farrell* (New York: Sun Dial Press, 1944), 188.

20. James T. Farrell, *Judgment Day* (New York: Modern Library, 1938), 32.

21. Farrell, *To Whom It May Concern*, 204.

22. Charles Coughlin, *A Series of Lectures on Social Justice* (Royal Oak, MI: Radio League of the Little Flower, 1935), 267.

23. Ibid., 268.

24. Marcus, *Father Coughlin*, 146.

25. Brinkley, *Voices of Protest*, 120.

26. Mary Christine Athans, *The Coughlin-Fahey Connection: Father Charles Coughlin, Father Denis Fahey, C.D. Sp., and Religious Anti-Semitism in the United States, 1938–1954*, American University Studies, Series 7, Theology and Religion (New York: Peter Lang, 1991), 102: 19.

27. Charles J. Tull, *Father Coughlin and the New Deal* (Syracuse, NY: Syracuse University Press, 1965), 246.

28. Marcus, *Father Coughlin*, 222.

29. Ibid., 221.

30. FBI file obtained under the Freedom of Information Act, 62-41602-1.

31. David Grafton, *Red, Hot, and Rich!: An Oral History of Cole Porter* (New York: Stein and Day, 1987), 108.

32. Charles Schwartz, *Cole Porter* (New York: Dial, 1978); Jerry Hughes, "Cole Porter—Larry Hart: Making Beautiful Music," *In Touch for Men* 42 (August 1979): 38–40.

33. FBI file, November 11, 1942, date-stamped November 17, 1942.

34. Ibid.

35. Ibid.

36. Leo H. Bartemeier, personal communications with author, 1979.

37. In April 1934, Treasury Secretary Henry Morgenthau released the information that Coughlin's personal secretary, Amy Collins, held contracts on 500,000

ounces of silver, "purchased for $20,000 on behalf of the Radio League of the Little Flower"; Brinkley, *Voices of Protest*, 125.

38. Marcus, *Father Coughlin*, 135.

39. Ibid., 229.

40. FBI file, November 11, 1942.

41. *The Witness* (Dubuque, IA), June 6, 1940.

42. Marcus, *Father Coughlin*, 228.

43. Ibid., 226.

CHAPTER 5

1. Wilfrid Sheed, *Frank and Maisie: A Memoir with Parents* (New York: Simon and Schuster, 1985), 106.

2. *Newsweek*, October 28, 1957.

3. *Time*, April 14, 1952, 72.

4. John Tracy Ellis, *Catholic Bishops: A Memoir* (Wilmington, DE: Michael Glazier, 1983), 357.

5. Ibid.

6. Fulton J. Sheen, *Treasure in Clay* (Garden City, NY: Doubleday, 1980).

7. Ellis, *Catholic Bishops*, 359.

8. Ibid.

9. *Newsweek*, October 28, 1957.

10. John T. Ellens, personal communication with author.

11. D. P. Noonan, *The Passion of Fulton Sheen* (New York: Dodd, Mead, 1972); reviewed in *Commonweal*, March 31, 1972, 89–92.

12. *Time*, April 14, 1952, 72.

13. Sheed, *Frank and Maisie*, 106.

14. Ibid.

15. Roger A. Burns, *Preacher* (New York: Norton, 1992), 67.

16. Garry Wills, *Saint Augustine* (New York: Viking, 1999), 72.

17. Fulton J. Sheen, *Thinking Life Through* (New York: McGraw-Hill, 1955), 26.

18. Fulton J. Sheen, *Life Is Worth Living* (New York: McGraw-Hill, 1953), 201–10.

19. Ibid., 201–9.

20. Sheen, *Thinking Life Through*, 140–48, 179–89.

21. Sheen, *Life Is Worth Living*, 231–41.

22. Ibid., 234.

23. Sheen, *Thinking Life Through*, 63.

24. Ibid., 129–39.

25. Ibid., 71–80.

26. Ibid., 129–39.

27. Ibid., 221–30.

28. Ibid., 251.

29. Ibid., 117.

30. Sheen claimed, "[T]he reason why chastity is on the decline is that we live in a sensate culture. In the Middle Ages, there was an Age of Faith, then came the Age of Reason in the eighteenth century; now we are living in the Age of Feeling. Dur-

ing the Victorian days, sex was taboo; today it is death that is taboo. Each age has its own taboos. I think one of the reasons for sexual promiscuity today is the absence of purpose in life. When we are driving a car and become lost, we generally drive faster; so when there is an absence of the full meaning of life there is a tendency to compensate for it by speed, drugs and intensity of feeling"; *Thinking Life Through*, 203–4.

31. André Malraux, *Man's Fate*, trans. Haakon M. Chevalier (New York: Modern Library, 1961); André Malraux, *Man's Hope*, trans. Stuart Gilbert and Alastair MacDonald (New York: Modern Library, 1941).

32. Charles Baudelaire, *Flowers of Evil*, trans. James McGowan (Oxford: Oxford University Press, 1998).

33. D. H. Lawrence, *Lady Chatterley's Lover* (New York: Grove Press, 1959).

34. Sheen, *Thinking Life Through*, 54–61.

35. Ibid., 59.

36. Ibid.

37. Ibid., 104.

38. Ibid., 107–8.

39. Sheen, *Life Is Worth Living*, 51–59; Sheen, *Thinking Life Through*, 216–26.

40. Sheen, *Thinking Life Through*, 217.

41. Ibid., 119–28.

42. Ibid., 159–70.

43. Ibid., 171–80.

44. Ibid., 11–18.

45. Ibid., 71.

46. Ibid., 76–79.

47. Ibid., 74.

48. Ibid., 75.

49. "John Rock's Error," *New Yorker*, March 13, 2000, 52.

50. Andrew M. Greeley, *The Confessions of a Parish Priest: An Autobiography* (New York: Pocket Books, 1987), 356.

51. Ibid., 362.

CHAPTER 6

1. Fulton J. Sheen, *Treasure in Clay* (Garden City, NY: Doubleday, 1980), 202.

2. Cf. Sheen, *Treasure in Clay*, 201–13.

3. Even his most significant insight—that his antisexual form of celibacy is best supported by an earlier conception of human sexuality and a premodern life cycle, in which death is more omnipresent than the duration of human desire and relationships—lacks the pathos and insight that would explain how such a new paradigm arose and how the celibate practice can creatively adapt to it:

> During the Victorian days, sex was taboo; today it is death that is taboo. Each age has its own taboos. I think one of the reasons for sexual promiscuity today is the absence of purpose in life. When we are driving a car and become lost, we generally drive faster; so when there is an absence of the full meaning of life there is a

tendency to compensate for it by speed, drugs and intensity of feeling. (Sheen, *Treasure in Clay*, 203–4)

Compare his version with that of a secular thinker. In 1920, the German sociologist Max Weber wrote:

[Does] "progress"…have any meanings that go beyond the purely practical and technical? You will find this question raised in the most principled form in the works of Leo Tolstoy. He came to raise the question in a peculiar way. All his broodings increasingly revolved around the problem of whether or not death is a meaningful phenomenon. And his answer was: for civilized man, placed into an infinite "progress," according to its own imminent meaning should never come to an end; for there is always a further step ahead of one who stands upon the peak which lies in infinity. Abraham, or some peasant of the past, died "old and satiated with life" because he stood in the organic cycle of life; because his life…had given him what life had to offer…and therefore he could have had "enough" of life. Whereas civilized man, placed in the midst of the continuous enrichment of culture by ideas, knowledge, and problems, may become "tired of life" but not "satiated with life."…What he seizes is always something provisional and not definitive, and therefore death for him is a meaningless occurrence. And because death is meaningless, civilized life as such is meaningless; by its very "progressiveness" it gives death the imprint of meaninglessness. (Max Weber, *Essays in Sociology*, ed. H. H. Gerth and C. Wright Mills [New York: Oxford University Press, 1946], 139–40.)

Why does Weber's analysis of this historical process, by which life and death, sexuality and meaning, shift their significance, suggest the continuing need and value of religious questions so much more profoundly than Sheen? Sheen leaves these troubling elements unintegrated, as if we could will away our history or our sexuality. Ironically, he seems to take the institution of religion, the Catholic Church, and its increasing irrelevance for granted.

4. Fulton J. Sheen, *Thinking Life Through* (New York: McGraw-Hill, 1955), 104–11. Sheen often contrasts and compares celibacy with the vocation of marriage.

5. Sheen, *Treasure in Clay*, 212.

6. Ibid., 210–11; Genesis 32:24–32.

7. Sheen, *Treasure in Clay*, 211.

8. Ibid., 213.

9. Ibid., 210.

10. Ibid., 208.

11. Ibid., 109.

12. Ibid., 201–2.

13. Jung, and Freud as well, had grown up and studied under the influence of this economistic rhetoric of "harboring" and "squandering," the accountant's calculation of "sums" (cf. Paul Robinson, *The Modernization of Sex* [New York: Harper, 1977], 59–62), the psychosexual analogue of what Karl Marx called "the Abstinence Theory of Capital Accumulation" (Karl Marx, *Capital* [New York: International, 1967], 591–98).

14. Sheen, *Treasure in Clay*, 210.

CHAPTER 7

1. Julien Offray de La Mettrie, *Man a Machine* (Chicago: Open Court, 1912; originally published 1748).

2. Marie Jean Antoine Nicolas Caritat marquis de Condorcet (1743–94); his most important work was on probability and the philosophy of mathematics: *Essay on the Application of Analysis to the Probability of Majority Decisions* (1785), which contains Condorcet's paradox.

3. Denis Diderot, *Jacques le fataliste et son maître* and *Le Neveu de Rameau*. The French text is in the online edition. The online English translation of *Le Neveu de Rameau*, the 1762 novel by Diderot, is by Ian Johnston and includes links to the French text, http://www.mala.bc.ca/~Johnstoi/diderot/rameau_E.htm.

4. Immanuel Kant, "The Antinomy of Pure Reason," in *The Critique of Pure Reason (Kritik der reinen Vernunft)*, trans. Norman Kemp Smith (New York: St. Martin's Press, 1929), 396–484.

5. H. Frankfort and H. A. Frankfort, *Before Philosophy: The Intellectual Adventure of Ancient Man: An Essay on Speculative Thought in the Ancient Near East* (Harmondsworth, U.K.: Penguin, 1972), 53.

6. Ibid., 15.

7. E. O. Wilson, *Consilience* (New York: Knopf, 1998), 257.

8. *Time*, January 10, 1969.

9. Andrew M. Greeley, *Uncertain Trumpet: The Priest in Modern America* (New York: Sheed and Ward, 1968), 138.

10. Ibid., 158.

11. Andrew M. Greeley, *Letters to Nancy* (New York: Sheed and Ward, 1963), 53–54.

12. Andrew M. Greeley, *Confessions* (New York: Pocket Books, 1987), 248.

13. Ibid., 247.

14. David Tracy, "Theology and the Symbolic Imagination: A Tribute to Andrew Greeley," in *Andrew Greeley's World: An Anthology of Critical Essays: 1986–1988*, ed. Ingrid Shafer (New York: Warner Books, 1989), 47. "In contemporary sociology, the nomothetic-ideographic debate takes the form of experimental statistical methodology as opposed to participant-observer or clinical methods...[the experimental approach's] basic objective is to identify variables that behave in law-like regularities and then to codify these regularities into general theories"; Robert H. Brown, *A Poetic for Sociology* (New York: Cambridge University Press, 1977), 11.

15. Ingrid Shafer, "The Virgin and the Grail: Archetypes in Andrew Greeley's Fiction," in *Andrew Greeley's World: An Anthology of Critical Essays: 1986–1988*, ed. Ingrid Shafer (New York: Warner Books, 1989), 63–76.

16. Andrew M. Greeley, *The Cardinal Sins* (New York: Warner, 1981), 1.

17. Ibid., 38.

18. Ibid., 82.

19. Ibid., 113; emphasis added.

20. Ibid., 480–84.

21. Ibid., 483.

22. Greeley, *Uncertain Trumpet*, 42.

23. Ibid., 51–62.

24. Ibid., 79–90.

25. Michael T. Marsden, "The Feminine Divine: A Search for Unity in Father Andrew Greeley's Passover Trilogy," in *Andrew Greeley's World: An Anthology of Critical Essays: 1986–1988*, ed. Ingrid Shafer (New York: Warner Books, 1989), 175.

26. Greeley, *Confessions*, 490.

27. Andrew M. Greeley, *Love Song* (New York: Warner Books, 1989), 35.

28. Greeley, *Confessions*, 498.

29. G. K. Chesterton, *The Eye of Apollo: The Penguin Complete Father Brown* (New York: Penguin, 1981), 130. Note that Greeley identifies Father Brown with Father Blackie four times in *Happy Are Those Who Thirst for Justice* (New York: The Mysterious Press, 1987), 65, 79, 101, and 265; twice in *Happy Are the Meek* (New York: Warner Books, 1985), 2 and 4; and once in *Happy Are the Clean of Heart* (New York: Warner Books, 1986), 8. He also makes the comparison explicitly in his autobiography, *Confessions*, 496.

30. Chesterton, *The Eye of Apollo*, 255.

31. Georg Lukács, *The Theory of the Novel* (Boston: MIT Press, 1971), 88.

32. Greeley, *Confessions*, 484.

33. Ibid., 496.

34. Ibid., 482–83.

35. Andrew M. Greeley, *The Catholic Myth: The Behavior and Beliefs of American Catholics* (New York: Scribner's, 1990), 183.

36. Greeley, *Confessions*, 496.

37. Ibid., 43.

38. Ibid., 86.

39. James Joyce, *A Portrait of the Artist as a Young Man* (Harmondsworth, U.K.: Penguin, 1964), 158.

40. Andrew M. Greeley, *Crisis in the Church: A Study of Religion in America* (Chicago: Thomas More, 1979), 157.

41. Andrew M. Greeley, *Ascent into Hell* (New York: Warner Books, 1983), 492.

42. Greeley, *Confessions*, 108; emphasis added.

43. Greeley, *Ascent into Hell*, 492.

44. Abraham Maslow, *The Farther Reaches of Human Nature* (Harmondsworth, U.K.: Penguin, 1973).

45. John N. Kotre, *The Best of Times, The Worst of Times: Andrew Greeley and American Catholicism 1950–1975* (Chicago: Nelson-Hall, 1978), 79.

46. Ibid., 80.

47. *Publishers Weekly*, April 10, 1987.

48. *Publishers Weekly*, October 17, 1994.

49. Greeley, *Confessions*, 496–97.

50. Ibid., 505.

CHAPTER 8

1. Andrew M. Greeley, *Confessions of a Parish Priest* (New York: Pocket Books, 1987), 127.

2. Undoubtedly, in his ever-present sensitivity to popular culture, Greeley is referring to a figure that is accessible to his readership via the 1964 musical *My Fair Lady* or the 1912 George Bernard Shaw play *Pygmalion*. The poet Ovid (born 43 B.C.E.) memorialized the original myth in *Metamorphoses*, in which the sculptor had to

remain single because he was so critical of the faults and imperfections inherent in women's nature. He could only be satisfied with his own creation. In Virgil's *Aeneid* (circa 102 B.C.E.), Pygmalion is not represented as a loving sculptor but as the greedy brother of Dido, who kills her husband, Sychaeus, to get his gold.

3. Greeley, *Confessions of a Parish Priest*, 131.

4. The accounts of all three of our celibate protagonists can be contrasted with the autobiography of Abbé Pierre, (2006) the famous priest ragpicker of Paris who frankly admits of his sexual sins early in his priestly life. Of course, he is most similar to Gandhi, who speaks of his falls before he took his vow.

5. Greeley, *Confessions of a Parish Priest*, 107–8.

6. Ibid., 125.

7. Ibid., 126.

8. Hermann Hesse, *Siddhartha*, trans. Hilda Rosner (New York: New Directions, 1957).

9. Hermann Hesse, *Steppenwolf* (New York: Holt, Rinehart, Winston, 1967).

10. Greeley, *Confessions of a Parish Priest*, 108.

11. Greeley's pronoun game gets almost self-incriminating at times: *He* can talk about falling in love with *your* spouse? In addition his repeated reassurance from his own experience has no basis in either research or broad pastoral experience. In fact, repeatedly the history of sexual abuse of minors reflects a close, trusting, and confiding relationship between the mother or both parents of a child who is ultimately abused.

12. Again, we are confronted with a slip in Greeley's syntax. Technically, the sentence means that no married man would dare say anything about the risks that the priest takes. Is this how Greeley keeps potential informants mum?

13. Greeley, *Confessions of a Parish Priest*, 128.

14. Ibid., 121.

15. Ibid., 109.

16. The subtly patronizing use of gender-neutral pronouns when clearly speaking of males is one of the most revealing of Greeley's gestures toward the feminism he simultaneously attacks and appropriates.

17. Greeley, *Confessions of a Parish Priest*, 126.

18. Greeley's emphasis on physical attraction in human bonding ignores two other key aspects of human love (Eros) that one would think a priest would find more significant: the bonding of personalities as the dominant pair-bonding aspect of humans, a sublimation not unlike that of the celibate, and the context of collective cooperation—of the kinship network, the clan, the tribe, the village—in which human sexual relations have always been thoroughly enmeshed. These are the real supports of human attachments over time, something secondary to Greeley's nods-and-winks sexuality.

19. Greeley, *Confessions of a Parish Priest*, 121.

20. Sinclair Lewis, *Elmer Gantry* (New York: Harcourt, Brace, 1927).

21. Greeley, *Confessions of a Parish Priest*.

22. Ibid.

23. Ibid.

CHAPTER 9

1. James T. Farrell, *Studs Lonigan* (a trilogy containing *Young Lonigan*, 1932; *The Young Manhood of Studs Lonigan*, 1934; and *Judgment Day*, 1935) (New York:

Modern Library, 1938); hereafter cited as *YL*, *YMSL*, and *JD*, respectively, from this edition.

2. Alan Friedman, Afterword, *Studs Lonigan* (New York: Signet, 1965), 821.

3. Ibid., 824.

4. Margaret Zassenhaus, personal communication with author, 1990; Margaret Zassenhaus, *Walls: Resisting the Third Reich, One Woman's Story* (Boston: Beacon, 1976).

5. Andrew M. Greeley, *Confessions of a Parish Priest: An Autobiography* (New York: Pocket Books, 1987), 18.

6. Ibid., 5.

7. Ibid.

8. Farrell, *YMSL*, 213.

9. Farrell, *JD*, 427–48.

10. Andrew M. Greeley, *That Most Distressful Nation: The Taming of the American Irish* (Chicago: Quadrangle, 1972), 246.

11. John N. Kotre, *The Best of Times, The Worst of Times: Andrew Greeley and American Catholicism, 1950–1975* (Chicago: Nelson-Hall, 1978), 172, quoting from "Review of Real Lace," *The Critic* (March–April 1974), 59–60.

12. Kotre, *The Best of Times, The Worst of Times*, 174, quoting from "Confessions of a Loud-Mouthed Irish Priest," *Social Policy* (May–June 1974), 11.

13. Greeley, *That Most Distressful Nation*, 250–51.

14. Ibid., 249.

15. Farrell, *JD*, 456.

16. Jimmy Breslin, *World without End, Amen* (New York: Viking, 1973), 97.

17. Georg Lukács, *The Theory of the Novel* (Cambridge, MA: MIT Press, 1971), 85.

18. Farrell, *YL*, 27.

19. Farrell, *JD*, 465.

20. Greeley, *Confessions of a Parish Priest*, 484.

21. Farrell, *YL*, 27

22. Ibid., 33–34.

23. Ibid., 33–34.

24. Farrell, *YMSL*, 299–308.

25. Farrell, *JD*, 130–58.

26. Farrell, *YMSL*, 343–68.

27. Greeley, *Confessions of a Parish Priest*, 45.

28. Farrell, *JD*, 14–15.

29. Farrell, *YL*, 168–69.

30. Farrell, *YMSL*, 116–17.

31. Ibid., 293–94.

32. Ibid., 292.

33. Ibid., 293–94.

34. Farrell, *JD*, 196.

35. Farrell, *YL*, 72–75.

36. Tim Unsworth, *The Last Priests in America: Conversations with Remarkable Men* (New York: Crossroad, 1991), 119.

37. Farrell, *YMSL*, 408–10.

38. Andrew M. Greeley, *Virgin and Martyr* (New York: Warner, 1985), 463.

39. Andrew M. Greeley, *Lord of the Dance* (New York: Warner, 1985), 26–34.

40. Greeley, *Confessions of a Parish Priest*, 108.

41. James T. Farrell, *A World I Never Made* (New York: Vanguard, 1934), 44–48.

42. Andrew M. Greeley, *The Search for Maggie Ward* (New York: Warner, 1991), 359.

43. Kotre, *Best of Times*, 208.

44. Greeley, *Confessions of a Parish Priest*, 487–88.

45. Farrell, Introduction, *Studs Lonigan* (New York: Signet, 1958), vii.

46. Greeley, *Confessions of a Parish Priest*, 486.

47. Ibid., 496.

48. Ibid., 497.

49. Farrell, *YMSL*, 56–58.

50. Greeley, *That Most Distressful Nation*, 249.

51. Ibid., 246.

52. Ibid., 252.

53. Ibid., 248.

54. Lukács, *Theory of the Novel*, 85.

55. Farrell, Introduction, *Studs Lonigan*, xv.

56. Ibid., xv.

57. Ibid., xii.

CHAPTER 10

1. Cf. A.W.R. Sipe, "Clergy Abuse in Ireland," in *Wolves within the Fold: Religious Leadership and Abuses of Power*, ed. Anson Shupe (Rutgers, NJ: Rutgers University Press, 1998).

2. Associated Press, March 9, 2006.

3. Of course, Western authorities were concerned to suppress sexually explicit content, whereas Soviet censors were watching for politically subversive as well as sexually explicit material. Recent scholarship, however, has questioned the distinction.

4. Richard Ellmann, *James Joyce* (New York: Oxford University Press, 1959), 171.

5. Ibid., 228–31.

6. A.W.R. Sipe, *Sex, Priests, and Power: The Anatomy of a Crisis* (New York: Bruner/Mazel, 1995), 10, lists citations from the *Didache*, from the Council of Elvira, Saint John Cassian, the Council of Trent, and the *Confessions* of Jean-Jacques Rousseau as well as clinical and statistical evidence gathered in the United States in support of the position that priestly pedophilia is a systemic problem in the Catholic Church.

7. John Wyse Jackson and Bernard McGinley, *James Joyce's Dubliners: An Annotated Edition* (London: Reed Consumer, 1993), 2.

8. Ibid.

9. Ibid., 3.

10. Ibid.

11. Ibid.

12. Ibid., 6.

13. Ibid., 8

14. Ibid., 8 n.

15. Ibid., 17.

16. Ibid., 9.

17. Ibid.

18. We are indebted to Philip Herring for the simile. See Philip Herring, "Structure and Meaning in Joyce's 'The Sisters,'" in *James Joyce's Dubliners*, ed. Harold Bloom (New York: Chelsea House, 1988), 39–50.

19. Jackson and McGinley, *James Joyce's Dubliners*, 9.

20. Ibid., 15.

21. "They" still usually say it was the boy's—or girl's—fault.

22. Jackson and McGinley, *James Joyce's Dubliners*, 16.

23. Ibid.

24. Ibid., 5.

25. Ibid., 16.

26. Ibid., 17.

27. Ibid.

28. Ibid.

29. Ibid., 5.

30. Ibid., 18.

31. In 1909, George Roberts of the firm of Maunsel and Co., which had expressed an interest in *Dubliners*, apparently conflated *simony* and *sodomy:* "He asked me very narrowly was there sodomy also in 'The Sisters' and what was 'simony' and if the priest was suspended only for the breaking of the chalice"; "Letters, II," in Florence L. Walzl, "Joyce's 'The Sisters': A Development," *James Joyce Quarterly* 10, no. 4 (1973): 305–6.

32. Lucia Boldrini, "'The Sisters' and the *Inferno:* An Intertextual Network," *Style* 25, no. 3 (1991): 453.

33. Dante, *Inferno*, 3: 10–12, in ibid., 454.

34. Ibid., 457.

35. Jackson and McGinley, *James Joyce's Dubliners*, 3.

36. Ibid., 18.

37. Ibid., 16.

38. Ibid., 17.

39. Ibid.

40. Ibid., 18.

41. Ellman, *James Joyce*, 216.

42. Ibid., 169.

CHAPTER 11

1. This issue is discussed in chapter 11, A. W. Richard Sipe, *A Secret World: Sexuality and the Search for Celibacy* (New York: Brunner/Mazel), 222–33, mainly from the point of view of the children and women left behind. This is because of the statistical tendency of the clinical data: "The most common reported is that the pregnancy destroys the relationship, each party usually going his or her own way. The child is most commonly given up for adoption" (224). Both the novels in question here focus on the effects of an ongoing relationship or later reunion between the priest and his child.

2. "Et in Arcadia" is Nicolas Poussin's elegiac meditation on a Latin phrase which translates literally as "Even in Arcady, there I am" or, more accurately in this context, "Death is even in Arcady."

3. Page numbers are cited from E. L. Voynich, *The Gadfly*, 15 (New York: Pyramid Books, 1961).

4. For a description of this type of relationship, see Sipe, *A Secret World*, 76–79, 81–83.

5. Ibid., 62–65.

6. Page references correspond to Graham Greene, *The Power and the Glory* (Harmondsworth, U.K.: Penguin, 1962; originally published 1940).

7. We may wish to explore the extent to which Greene was influenced by the similar portrayal of lost innocence in Georges Bernanos's *Diary of a Country Priest* and what role the repetition of such an image might play in the literary representation of the priesthood. The country priest encounters this girl-woman in the figure of Seraphita, one of his catechism students:

[T]he poor child—probably egged on by the others—pursues me now with surreptitious oglings, grimacing, apeing a grown-up woman in a way that is very hard to bear. She has a trick of deliberately lifting up her skirt to fasten the shoelace which serves as her garter.

But her playacting is the sign of something more profound, more disturbing, and quite difficult to explain:

Met Seraphita yesterday with M. Dumouchel. That child's face seems to alter day by day: her quick-changing mobile expression has now become fixed with a hardness far beyond her years. Whilst I was talking to her she kept watching me with such embarrassing attention that I couldn't help blushing. Perhaps I ought to warn her parents....Only of what?

Georges Bernanos, *The Diary of a Country Priest*, trans. Pamela Morris (Garden City, NY: Image Books, 1954; originally published 1937), 22–24.

CHAPTER 12

1. All unidentified page references are to J. F. Powers, *Morte D'Urban* (New York: Washington Square Press, 1990).

2. Quotations from Luke are taken from the King James Version (Chicago: Gideons International, 1958).

3. Jacques Lacan, *Ecrits* (New York: Norton, 1977), 7.

4. Urban is a model of the tolerant and pragmatic business liberal:

Father Urban believed that there was a great deal to be said for the conservative position, but he also believed...that Mr. Zimmerman and his sort weren't the ones to say it. (213)

5. "The Pharisee and the shopkeeper interest us only because of their common essence, the source of the difficulties that both have with speech, particularly when it comes to 'talking shop'"; Lacan, *Ecrits*, 38.

6. At first he sees none and asks boastfully of the angel escorting him, "have friars such a grace that none of them shall come into this place?" But the angel disabuses him:

"Nay," said the angel "millions here are thrown!"
And unto Sathanas' he led him down.
"And now has Sathanas," said he, "a tail
Broader than of a galleon is the sail.
Hold up thy tail, thou Sathanas!" Said he.
"Show forth thine arse and let the friar see
Where is the nest of friars in this place!"
And ere one might go half a furlong's space,
Just as the bees come swarming from a hive,
Out of the devil's arse-hole there did drive
Full twenty thousand friars in a rout,
And through all Hell they swarmed and ran about,
And came again, as fast as they could run,
And in his arse they crept back, every one.

Geoffrey Chaucer, *Canterbury Tales*, rendered into modern English by J. U. Nicolson (Garden City, NY: Doubleday, 1934), 356; Geoffrey Chaucer, *Canterbury Tales*, *1683–1698* (New York: Dutton, 1975), 203.

7. Lacan, *Ecrits*, 38.

8. Powers must have heard many such partisan political readings of biblical passages in the milieu of the Catholic Worker. Urban, of course, works the other side of the fence in his sermons, and his exegetical tendencies are neatly parodied in his proposed revision of the Robin Hood story:

Now in the case of Robin Hood, Mr. Thwaites plans to move the story up in time, to set it in the so-called Reformation period, keeping it in England, of course. It's all legends, you know, and so you have a pretty free hand. Robin Hood will still steal from the rich and give to the poor—you can't very well get around that—but he'll only steal from the rich who've stolen from the Church. So it really isn't stealing. (191)

9. Studley again repeats the lines of the old script reserved for the devil whenever he hears mention of a "Pharisee"; *From Chaucer to Bunyan.*

10. Carol Iannone, "The Second Coming of J. F. Powers," *Commentary* 87, no. 1 (1989): 63.

11. Compare this theologicohistorical explanation of our apocalyptic century with Mr. Studley's version of "why we fought two major wars."

12. This comment finds a parallel in Greeley's "Don't fuck with God."

13. Iannone, "The Second Coming of J. F. Powers," 62–64. I use "universality" here in the qualified sense of a work's reception within cultures that see the novel as a major form of narrative. Georg Lukács points out:

[T]he danger [is] a subjectivity which is not exemplary, which has not become a symbol, and which is bound to destroy the epic form. The hero and his destiny then have no more than personal interest and the work as a whole becomes a private memoir of how a certain person succeeded in coming to terms with his world. The social world must therefore be shown as a world of convention, which is partially open to penetration by living meaning.

Georg Lukács, *The Theory of the Novel*, trans. Ana Bostock (Cambridge, MA: MIT Press, 1971), 137.

14. See Terry Teachout's formulation of Urban's social context in "Father Babbitt's Flock," *The New Criterion* 7, no. 5 (1989): 72.

15. Ibid., 71.

16. A similar dynamic may motivate Andrew Greeley's desire to combine the "success" ethic and charismatic mystery. Could an Urban have had Greeley's success in the 1950s? If it had been possible, we probably would not have any novel called *Morte D'Urban*, for Fulton Sheen, the successful public priest of Urban's time (whom Urban both disdains and envies), lacks the sophistication of Greeley's double appeal to a modernized sexuality and druidic mystery through the person of the priest, a recipe Urban may have found compelling. If the novel does have less than universal appeal, it may have more to do with datedness than with its denominational specificity.

17. The social novel, whose first great muse was the quasi-religious cause of socialism, focused not on the irrevocable structures of a disenchanted bureaucratic-administrative society but on the highly dramatic and suggestively meaningful moments of class struggle. The idea shared by Marxian and utopian socialists that the proletariat was a class inherently oriented to transcendence (i.e., "with nothing to lose but its chains") gave even the most gloomy naturalist works (Zola's *Germinal*, Hauptmann's *The Weavers*) a romantic and transcendent drive. The stabilizing growth of the middle class (especially in the United States) alongside a more systems-oriented academic sociology had a sobering effect on the U.S. social novel. Sinclair Lewis (Powers's "first serious writer"; Teachout, "Father Babbitt's Flock," 70), the consummate novelist of the Babbitt class, displaced Frank Norris (who also receives a cameo reference in *Morte D'Urban* through Urban's fantasy of the death of the wheat broker, 293) as the U.S. social novelist par excellence.

18. Don Quixote's favorite author of the books of chivalry that are blamed for generating his illusions.

19. Max Weber, "Science as a Vocation," in *Essays in Sociology*, ed. H. H. Gerth and C. Wright Mills (New York: Oxford University Press, 1946), 134.

20. Ibid., 291.

21. Ibid., 303.

22. Ibid., 305.

23. Ibid., 306.

24. "Exceptional" often implies homosexual orientation among the Clementine novices (why else join the order?). Brother Harold "looked quite intelligent," Urban thinks. "Intelligent, yes...but perhaps a bit feminine" (38).

25. Weber, "Science as a Vocation," 96.

26. This is an experience from Powers's childhood, too. For a detailed analysis of this social group, and one fairly contemporary with the writing of *Morte D'Urban*, see C. Wright Mills, *White Collar* (New York: Oxford University Press, 1956).

27. Saint Tarcisius was a 12-year-old altar boy who was martyred in a third-century Roman persecution for defending a consecrated host. Very little is actually

known about him, although devotion grew up around history in the sixth century. In recent years, he has been venerated as a symbol of purity, a boy who overcame "the tortures of his passion." There is a skeleton, preserved in a reliquary in Saint John's Abbey in Collegeville, Minnesota, of a saint, Peregrin, with a similar hagiography. This shrine was well known to Powers.

28. Weber, "Science as a Vocation," 321–22.

29. This ideal fits neither the monks nor the petty entrepreneurs, but rather that of "the salaried employee…in the capitalistic enterprise [who is] separated from the material means of production" (Weber, "Science as a Vocation," 81). In a gesture right out of Marx's *Eighteenth Brumaire of Louis Bonaparte*, in which the "gladiators" of bourgeois society fight their battles in "Roman costume," Urban dreams of making the Clementines into an efficient "outfit" (second only to Standard Oil?), who could come to serve as the bishop's "Praetorian Guard" (173).

30. The gap in this logic emerges in Urban's celibacy, a discipline necessary to maintaining his charismatic position at the margins even as it precludes a life of no regrets.

31. Weber, "Science as a Vocation," 132.

32. Ibid., 148–49.

33. Ibid., 153.

34. Erich Auerbach, "The Knight Sets Forth," in *Mimesis*, trans. Willard R. Trask (Princeton, NJ: Princeton University Press, 1953), 136–37.

35. Weber, "Science as a Vocation," 155.

36. Ibid., 128.

37. Jack's fate is much like that of the Hill's salvaged pickup truck: "Billy and Paul stared at the thing…it seemed to tremble under their gaze" (255).

38. "[T]here was no other word for it. He tooled toward the outskirts of town. The little snub-nosed Barracuda was five months old. Had wire wheels, leather upholstery…and it certainly made a man feel good to drive it. At a stoplight, though, when a girl in a white MG paused alongside him, a girl wearing sunglasses and nothing else—so it appeared from where he was sitting—and with a crisp blue dog beside her, Father Urban experienced a heavy moment, a moment of regret and longing…. When he hit open country, he threw away his cigar and gave the little thoroughbred its head" (207–8).

39. Iannone, "The Second Coming of J. F. Powers," 63.

40. A. W. Richard Sipe, *A Secret World: Sexuality and the Search for Celibacy* (New York: Brunner/Mazel, 1990), 35–40.

41. Weber, "Science as a Vocation," 297.

42. Sipe, *A Secret World*, 42–45.

43. As I pointed out in the introduction, this has been precisely the focus of my ongoing research into religious celibacy. It has received a great deal of opposition from churchmen who fear the destruction of the charism of celibacy (its inexplicability) or the denigration (exposure) of those who profess it.

44. Erving Goffman, *The Presentation of Self in Everyday Life* (Garden City, NY: Doubleday, 1959), 68.

45. A. W. Richard Sipe, *Celibacy in Crisis: A Secret World Revisited* (New York: Brunner-Routledge, 2003), 81–116.

46. The ironic medievalism of the golf "joust" implies a similar layering: Troubadours may have credited the valor of the champions to love, but historians would be more inclined to ask what socioeconomic and political interests were backing each man.

47. Women, here, are equated with alcoholism, insanity, and decay. Although this may have some relevance to preserving one's celibacy, it is also ominously misogynistic.

48. Sipe, *Celibacy in Crisis*, 304–16.

49. In the aftermath of the revelation in the 2004 John Jay Report that 81 percent of the minors sexually abused by priests or bishops in the United States since 1950 were male, homosexuals have become the objects of blame. This clear confusion among sexual orientation, desire, and behavior is another example of the church's inadequate understanding of sexuality.

50. Iannone, "The Second Coming of J. F. Powers," 64. When irony is directed solely at the protagonist, the genre is usually satire, the aim of which is criticism or mockery of a particular social group (whether the cause is good or bad being a matter of the reader's partisanship) rather than the promotion of a more universal understanding of the human condition.

51. I found this naïveté a fairly common factor in affairs between married women and priests: "It seems surprising that few of the husbands appear to be conscious of the sexual dimension of their wives' friendships with the priests"; Sipe, *A Secret World*, 79.

52. It is worth noting a comparison of this wish fulfillment with Urban's earlier lighthearted satire on married life, in which he imagines that he and Wilf are "a couple of average guys…married to a couple of average gals who, at that very moment, on another channel, were washing their husbands' dirty work clothes with the right brand of detergent" (115–16). Urban can only fantasize about working-class life—the world of Father Wilfrid—as a parody (of TV culture), whereas he grants his personal dream, albeit a cliché of affluence, as much dignity as possible. He is thwarted at times only by the ironic perspective of the narrative itself.

53. Dr. Margaret Miles pointed out that Geoffrey Galt Harpham in *The Ascetic Imperative* (1994) presents the thesis that the fourth-century celibate ascetics required temptation, imagined if not actual, in order to develop religious/ascetic self by practicing the dialectic of temptation and resistance; Margaret Miles, personal communication with author.

54. The vividly rendered yet symbolic figures in paintings from Bosch to Dalí on the theme of Saint Anthony's temptation in the desert provide an example. They represent the visualization of the saint's confrontation with his inner conflicts in an empty wasteland. See also Sipe, *Celibacy in Crisis*, 306–7.

55. Compare this with Dante's relatively forgiving attitude toward Francesca, the "lustful," compared with Judas, the "treacherous."

56. "Now, this process of disenchantment, which has continued to exist in Occidental culture for millennia, and, in general, this 'progress,'…do they have any meanings that go beyond the purely practical and technical? You will find this question raised in the most principled form in the works of Leo Tolstoi. He came to raise the question in a peculiar way. All his broodings increasingly revolved around the

problem of whether or not death is a meaningful phenomenon. And his answer was: for civilized man death has no meaning. It has none because the individual life of civilized man, placed into an infinite 'progress,' according to its own imminent meaning should never come to an end; for there is always a further step ahead of one who stands in the march of progress. And no man who comes to die stands upon the peak which lies in infinity. Abraham, or some peasant of the past, died 'old and satiated with life' because he stood in the organic cycle of life; because his life, in terms of its meaning and on the eve of his days, had given to him what life had to offer; because for him there remained no puzzles he might wish to solve; and therefore he could have had 'enough' of life. Whereas civilized man, placed in the midst of the continuous enrichment of culture by ideas, knowledge, and problems, may become 'tired of life' but not 'satiated with life' "; Weber, "Science as a Vocation," 139–40.

57. Cf. the reading of Quixote's death by Rene Girard, *Deceit, Desire, and the Novel* (Baltimore: Johns Hopkins University Press, 1976), 291–92. Graham Greene's re-writing of the Quixote story *(Monsignor Quixote* [London: Bodley Head, 1982]) is also consistent with Girard's understanding of its significance.

58. Iannone, "The Second Coming of J. F. Powers," 63. Her assertion here for the obviousness of Powers's didactic intent would go further to support her argument that the novel is lacking in "universality" than Powers's choice of subject matter or protagonist.

59. Johann Wolfgang von Goethe, *Wilhelm Meister's Apprenticeship*, trans. Thomas Carlyle (New York: Collier, 1962), 446.

60. The contrast between Powers's use of the Cervantean register and that of Graham Greene in *Monsignor Quixote* could not be more striking. Greene's reference to Quixote is romantically optimistic, whereas Powers unleashes the most acid satire of the so-called first novel.

61. Lukács, *The Theory of the Novel*, 137.

62. Ibid., 141–42.

63. Ibid.

64. Ibid., 139–40.

65. "When men reach the age of forty or fifty they tend to observe a curious change. They discover that most of the individuals with whom they grew up and maintained contact now behave in a disturbed manner. One may stop working so that his business fails; another may break his marriage; and yet another may embezzle money. Even those individuals who show no such striking behavioral changes still show signs of degeneration. Conversation with them becomes shallow, threadbare, and boastful. Previously the aging individual found mental stimulus in others but now he feels that he is almost the only one to present objective interest.... Men of the world are not excluded from this general rule. It is as though people who betray the hopes of their youth and come to terms with the world, suffer the penalty of premature decay"; Theodor Adorno and Max Horkheimer, *The Dialectic of Enlightenment*, trans. John Cumming (New York: Herder & Herder, 1972; originally published in 1944), 240–41.

66. Iannone, "The Second Coming of J. F. Powers," 63.

67. Garry Wills, *The New York Times*, April 9, 2006. See also Garry Wills, *What Jesus Meant* (New York: Viking, 2006).

68. The tone is reminiscent of Leon Bloy's *The Woman Who Was Poor*, trans. I. J. Collins (New York: Sheed and Ward, 1947; originally published 1896). "[T]here is but one sadness, and that is not to be a saint."

CHAPTER 13

1. The status, the meaning, of death is, after all, the critical juncture at which a society attempts to cement its relationship to the individual through an exchange of meanings, the point at which personal sacrifice (duty) and social remembrance (reward) are supposed to resolve the rupture of death through the suture of a just and equal exchange. Yet it is precisely at this point of irremediable rupture between social and personal meaning that the spiritual per se (rather than the simply institutional and ritualized codifications of religion) emerges, the great mystery giving rise to consciousness of the mysteriousness of existence.

2. The Berrigans' *Trial of the Catonsville Nine* comes to mind. The *Trial of the Catonsville Nine* was a 1971 movie based on a play written by Father Daniel Berrigan about the October 5, 1968 trial of nine war protestors who burned draft records in Cantonsville, Maryland. I would not disparage such works (especially because the above mentioned movie is appropriately cast in the genre of the docudrama), the novel as a literary form is more concerned with the unique life possible within the social rule. Although conformity to Fascism may have appeared to be that social rule to most Italians during the 1930s, we cannot as readers accept that premise from our own context. Such a conclusion would not be justified beyond the sociological level—after all, we must be suspicious of our reflexive rejection of literature from cultures very different from our own—if it were not corroborated by the fact that Fascism could not produce such a novel internally. The closest attempt may be Alberto Moravia's *The Conformist: A Novel* (first published in 1951 by Farrar, Straus and Company), but this was the work of an anti-Fascist.

3. See Sipe, *A Secret World: Sexuality and the Search for Celibacy* (New York: Brunner/Mazel, 1990), 22. This is also the period the British writer Hanif Kureishi called "the Golden Age of Fucking."

4. Hereafter, all unidentified page references are to Ignazio Silone, *Bread and Wine* (New York: Harper and Brothers, 1937). Page references to the second version will be preceded by the notation "2nd ed." and are to Ignazio Silone, *Bread and Wine* (New York: Signet, 1986).

5. It is worth noting for the problem of gender in questions of spiritual vocation that one cannot refer to Cristina simply by her family name, but one does so automatically for Spina. This problem of naming reflects not only specific aspects of gender in prewar Italy but also ongoing differences in the ways in which men and women are expected to relate to the institutions of family and church. Silone, however, went a long way toward overcoming such thinking within himself, and although he was still limited by social norms of naming in his effort to write a novel capable of a socially broad reception, he called Spina by his Christian name in the second version, thereby putting his male and female characters on the same level.

6. For the importance of beauty in the achievement of celibacy, see Sipe, *Celibacy in Crisis: A Secret World Revisited* (New York: Brunner-Routledge, 2003), 315–16. Kant used the category of the beautiful as a major bridge in his own rationalist defense of

the ethical imperative: In our appreciation of beauty in the objective world, we perceive a metaphor connecting the visible forms of nature with our yearning for the invisible forms of the ethical and the transcendent. The enjoyment of beauty then becomes the link between the truth of the observable world and the good of our spiritual aspirations. Kant left it an open question whether any of these realms existed beyond our perception of them. Because we use the same perceptual apparatus (our senses) to measure the objective world that we use to appreciate beauty, both could just as well be projections of our desire for the good, the spiritual, as proofs of the latter.

7. This melodramatic event occurs only in the first version. Silone seems to have become more accepting of a peaceful spiritual vocation and the validity of withdrawal under even dictatorship. This tolerance appears to be connected with a mellowing of his anger and disappointment with the institution of the church, an issue explored in the section "Hopeful Revisions."

8. "Don Paolo" is Spina's alias in his cover as a priest. The narrator uses the false name or simply refers to Spina as "the priest" whenever he is being perceived to actually be one by the other characters present in a scene. The use of these interchangeable signifiers for the protagonist would make a fascinating study in itself.

9. This glimpse inside the monastery bears a remarkable resemblance to the world of Father Urban and the Order of Saint Clement.

10. The chapters on Gandhi, Sheen, and Greeley contain similar implications.

11. It is so fashionable in the contemporary United States to wear a cross that it has become part of costume as well as religious custom. It is so ubiquitous that its meaning has lost significance.

12. Much has been written on this scene, and an interesting debate has arisen between those who see Spina's lesson as a solid defense of the humanist value system—democratic consensus building, freedom, labor as the source of wealth and meaning—and those who see it as a defense of the radical relativism of meaning in language itself. The latter has been argued convincingly for the scene when viewed only in relation to Spina's disillusionment with Stalinism. Cf. Gregory L. Lucente, "Signs and History in Silone's *Vino e pane:* The Dilemma of Social Change," in *Beautiful Fables: Self-Consciousness in Italian Narrative from Manzoni to Calvino* (Baltimore: Johns Hopkins University Press, 1986), 177–93. Reading it as the positive assertion of a value system, however, is more in keeping with Silone's efforts to construct an ethical practice that is ultimately independent from institutions; that is, an existential vocation.

13. Georg Lukács, *The Theory of the Novel*, trans. Anna Bostock (Cambridge, MA: MIT Press, 1971), 92.

14. Much has been written on the role changing of Spina/Spada, but what is most striking about Silone's narrative strategy is the continuity, the unity of purpose expressed in both roles. In Spina's person, Catholic and Communist combine more smoothly than the roles of man and priest often do. The most noticeable difference is a reversal of expectations. As a layman, Spina is much more constrained and serious than he is as Don Paolo. Like those priests who vacation in mufti (see Sipe, *A Secret World*, 97–98), Spina is freed from his real priestly role, as priest of the party, when he is disguised as Don Paolo.

15. Red and black are used here in their purely institutional senses. Of course, the difference remains that the story could not be told from the black perspective un-

less it is understood to extend to the sincere Christian as well (e.g., Don Benedetto, Cristina). Here the reference to Luke 16 is a focus for vocational struggle just as it is in Powers's *Morte D'Urban*.

16. Cf. the concluding chapter of Georges Bernanos, *The Diary of a Country Priest* (Garden City, NY: Image Books, 1954), 215–21.

17. The symbol of his implicit celibacy (at the stage of "Like Me/Not Like Me"; cf. Sipe, *Celibacy in Crisis*, 293–95).

18. Jürgen Habermas, *Knowledge and Human Interests* (Boston: Beacon, 1971), 314.

19. See Sipe, *A Secret World*, 40–51, 190–93.

20. In this way, Stalinism combined elements from the Orthodox church's mores and Western rationalism to create a sort of perverse parody of Spina's own synthesis of Christianity and Marxism (especially aspects of Henry Fordist ideology such as work, discipline, productionism, and the spermatic economy notion; note Spina's reference to "energies").

21. This physical fact, which should be quite apparent to everyone who meets Spina (we need only think of Philip's clubfoot, a much less noticeable trait, in W. Somerset Maugham's novel *Of Human Bondage*), is never mentioned by the women with whom Spina becomes intimate, a strange oversight on Silone's part, one that suggests its purely symbolic function in the text.

22. Sipe, *A Secret World*, 278.

23. See Giuliana Minghelli, *In the Shadow of the Mammoth: Italo Svevo and the Emergence of Modernism* (Toronto: University of Toronto Press, 2003). The author writes about the irony of men playing the pedagogue with women and its perpetuation of the Pygmalion myth. Andrew Greeley embraces the same stance toward women, freely accepting his resemblance to Pygmalion; cf. Andrew Greeley, *Confessions of a Parish Priest: An Autobiography* (New York: Pocket Books, 1987), 127.

24. Heterogeneous elements are those that escape the aesthetic form of literary classicism or the systems of philosophers. Their presence as an excluded remainder or, in some art and philosophies, their absorption is one of the most troubling questions in the history of ideas. When accused of leaving such elements, such facts, out of his system, German philosopher Johann Gottlieb Fichte responded, "If the facts do not conform to my ideas, so much the worse for the facts!"

25. Encarta World English Dictionary.

26. Miasma is an apt word for culture of secrecy and dominance that has been imposed on religion in the name of purity and sexual deprivation. The system of clerical celibacy has perpetuated a sense of self-superiority and sinfulness of all sex. This culture is a distortion of sexual human nature and has created an unwholesome atmosphere.

INDEX

About the Author

A. W. RICHARD SIPE is a Certified Clinical Mental Health Counselor who earlier spent 18 years as a Benedictine monk and priest. He was trained specifically to deal with the mental health problems of Roman Catholic Priests. In the process of training and therapy, he conducted a 25-year ethnographic study of the celibate/sexual behavior of that population. His study, published in 1990, in now considered a classic. Sipe is known internationally and has participated in 12 documentaries on celibacy and priest sexual abuse aired by HBO, BBC, and other networks in the United States, United Kingdom, and France. He has been widely interviewed by media including CNN, ABC, NBC, CNBC, *The New York Times*, the *Los Angeles Times*, *People* magazine, *Newsweek* and *USA Today*.